THE

ATLAS

OF

AUSTRALIAN
FISHING

DAVID LOCKWOOD

THE
ATLAS
OF
AUSTRALIAN
FISHING

with
contributions from
Warren Steptoe • Laurie McEnally • Bill Classon • Shane Mensforth
Ashley Hallam • Phil Stanley • Hal Harvey • Col Roberts

ANGUS
& ROBERTSON
PUBLISHERS

ANGUS & ROBERTSON PUBLISHERS

Unit 4, Eden Park, 31 Waterloo Road,
North Ryde, NSW, Australia 2113, and
16 Golden Square, London WIR 4BN,
United Kingdom

First published in Australia by Angus &
Robertson Publishers.
Published by arrangement with Mitchell
Publishers Pty. Limited, 6th Floor, 8 Help
Street, Chatswood, NSW
Copyright © 1989 Mitchell Publishers

National Library of Australia
Cataloguing-in-publication data

Lockwood, David.
  Atlas of Australian Fishing.
  ISBN 0 207 16388 X

  1. Fishing - Australia - Guide-books.
  2. Australia- Description and travel -
     1976 - Guide-books.
  I. Title.
  799.1'0994

Produced by Mandarin Offset
Printed in Hong Kong

Contents

Introduction

No country in the world boasts such a diversity of fishing environments as Australia and very few world waterways remain as productive.

Our oceans attract commercial fishing fleets from Russia, Japan, Taiwan, Indonesia and America. Yet aside from Cairns in north Queensland, regarded as the big black marlin capital of the world, very few of our fresh or saltwater fisheries receive the attention they deserve. Only in recent years has there been the beginning of a change in attitude. Fishing charter services, professional fishing guides and organised fishing packages are becoming popular, answering the call of both overseas and local fishermen for sportfishing. But these organised trips don't come cheaply.

Of the more than four million Australian anglers the majority prefer to conserve money and incorporate fishing as an integral part of their annual holidays, or organise specific fishing trips to new destinations for themselves.

But the "travelling angler" often lacks the local knowledge necessary for success.

The Atlas of Australian Fishing provides much of this invaluable, local fishing knowledge on the country's leading fishing spots as is possible in a book. With the help of a group of professional contributors from across the country, each acknowledged as the best in the area, we've pinpointed the most productive fresh and saltwater fishing spots, how to access them, where to launch the boat, what species of fish are available and what techniques to use.

However, we haven't given you all the answers. Fishing is unpredictable and an indefinite pastime. For every rule there is an exception, and it is the exceptions that will sustain your enthusiasm for the sport. While the fishing spots outlined in this book produce good fishing, it is the reasons they do that are the real key to successful angling.

Rock fishing is one of the most popular angling pursuits is Australia.

Fish Habitat Zones

Although many of the world's fish live in fresh water, far more are found in our oceans. There are, of course, a number of species that live in both environments, tolerating the brackish upper estuarine waters, and others that periodically migrate from the sea to breed in freshwater rivers or vice versa. Learning about the varied environments of fish is the first step toward becoming a more sucessful angler.

There are at least 21,000 known species of fish worldwide, and the figure continues to grow as methods of marine research improve and as fishermen search for new and more productive fishing grounds. However, for most recreational fresh and saltwater anglers, the variety of catch is limitied to the more common species that can be caught by line.

However, there's a lot more to Australian angling than merely dangling a line. Fish found in coastal saltwater zones are quite different from those found in the mid-water regions of the open sea, and differ again from those living in the deepest depths. Even in the most accessible fishing spots, where waters run shallow and clear, finding fish is rarely simple. Knowledge of the types of seabeds, affects of currents and varying water temperatures, and the seasonal availability of food is essential if you want to improve the size of your catch.

Despite the many differences between fish habitats and behaviour, there are also similarities. Around any prominent underwater obstacle, such as an offshore reef, schools of fish congregate on the upcurrent side, close to the most pronounced peak. In the reef's gutters, other more sedentary fish may be found, while on the featureless plateaus fish life is likely to be sparse.

We are fortunate to have a remarkable variety of fisheries in Australia. From outback, alpine and tropical freshwaters, through temperate and tropical estuaries, rock and beach fishing fronts, inshore grounds, offshore islands, coral reefs and bluewater fishing frontiers, there are hundreds of variables that must be considered. Versatility is the key to success.

It's hard to imagine a more beautiful scene; fisherman and canoe in the wilds of a tropical rainforest river.

Fresh Water

Despite being the driest continent on earth, freshwater fishing is one of the most popular sports in Australia. Freshwater fisheries in the Northern Territory and North Queensland are among the most productive and avidly fished in the country. It is in these steamy tropical waters that the high-flying barramundi can be encountered, along with a host of other less glamorous but nonetheless great sportfishing performers.

Along the New South Wales coastline, north to southern Queensland and as far south as the Gippsland region in Victoria, the freshwater tableland rivers are the home of the Australian bass. Although spirited fighters, the bass population is dangerously at risk as thoughtless land developers and insignificant protective measures only serve to ensure the destruction of their habitat. But for the environmentalist and the willing bushwalker, bass can still be enjoyed in many of the more inaccessible reaches of coastal rivers.

In the Aussie outback, a different collection of native fish species take over, including the yellowbelly or golden perch, the fickle Macquarie perch, silver perch or 'black bream', the eel-tailed catfish, and the king of them all - the mighty Murray Cod. Again, because of poor waterways management, environmental degradation due to farming, and the ignorance of the breeding requirements of these fish, Australia's outback natives are nowhere near as prolific as they were in years gone by. Nevertheless, the fish are still there for the taking, and with the implementation of State Fisheries' protective measures, there's every chance angling trophies, such as the huge Murray cod often seen gracing outback pub walls, will return with a vengeance to their native river systems.

Heading up into the high-country rivers, creeks and impoundments, where the waters run crisp and clear, the brown and rainbow trout attracts a great deal of attention. In New South Wales alone, in excess of 100,000 people enjoy fishing for trout every year, and there are several breeding and stocking stations established to replenish the trout population. Since their successful introduction into the country's alpine waterways, trout have become very much a part of the Australian freshwater fishing scene.

Unfortunately, not all imported angling species have had a beneficial effect. Freshwater fish, such as the European carp and redfin or English perch, introduced into our freshwater rivers, have become noxious pests, spreading like wildfire into every imaginable pocket of our limited fresh water. Carp, especially, breed like rats and now threaten the very existence of many of our native 'sweetwater' fish. For this reason, State Fisheries have prohibited the release of carp and redfin into our waterways.

Although an introduced species, trout proliferates in Australia's highland freshwater rivers, creeks and impoundments.

Right: A fly fisherman waves his wand on a highland lake in the morning mists of picturesque Tasmania. Trout is the target.

Saltwater

Australia's expansive coastal waters are the major attraction for anglers. The popular saltwater fishing environments are the southern or temperate estuary system, the northern or tropical estuary, rock and beach fishing shores, inshore boat fishing grounds, offshore islands, the coral reefs, and the bluewater game and sportfishing grounds.

Right: Ocean rocks are among the most popular Australian saltwater fishing environments.
Below: A boat is essential if you wish to enjoy some of the most untouched and bountiful fishing locations.

Temperate Estuaries

From Fraser Island in southern Queensland southwards to Shark Bay in Western Australia, southern or temperate-climate estuaries are probably the single most popular fishing grounds in this country.

The area encompasses not only large and well-established bays and harbours such as Port Jackson or Sydney Harbour, Port Phillip Bay, Hobart Harbour and Port Adelaide, but many of the lesser-known inlets, tidal lakes and lagoons, large coastal rivers and the saltwater reaches of their feeder creeks. As most temperate-climate estuary systems are protected bodies of water, they make ideal grounds for youngsters to discover the wonders of fishing. However, estuaries are very much more than mere playgrounds for fish and fishermen, they provide safe feeding stations and breeding bays, act as valuable nursery grounds, and as such are vitally important to the future of fishing wherever they are located.

For the aspiring fisherman, Australia's southern estuaries are in a relatively healthy state - despite pollution problems. Sydney Harbour, Melbourne and Port Phillip Bay, Whyalla and Adelaide are Australia's most popular fishing grounds and still yield plenty of fish, but it is the temperate estuary near quiet, coastal towns nestled in secluded areas that is the leading attraction for fishermen.

Clear, fast-flowing tidal waters, mangrove-shrouded bays, ribbon-weed beds, oyster leases running like picket fences, friendly pelicans, old wooden wharves and row boats - this is all part of the charm of fishing southern estuaries. As mentioned earlier, estuaries are feeding, breeding and nursery grounds, and a great range of fish inhabit them. Bream, whiting, flathead, luderick, mullet and garfish are some of the most avidly pursued fish species. Specialised anglers may pride themselves on landing huge flathead resembling more a surfboard than what you would see in a fish shop window. Yet others take a liking to the art of luderick fishing, or light-tackle breaming, catching beer-bottle size whiting on worms, collecting their own bait, or crabbing for the succulent blue swimmer or mud crab - it's all there in the temperate estuary system.

But that's far from where it ends. True heavyweights, like the mulloway or jewfish, often inhabit southern estuaries, as do snapper in the bays of Victoria and South Australia, and kingfish, cobia and even big sharks frequent other deepwater estuaries along the southern coast. School and king prawns can be caught in impressive numbers throughout most Australian estuaries during summer. Mud or mangrove crabs, blue swimmers and other closely related sandcrabs, are another sweet-fleshed inhabitant of the estuary environment.

Prawn cocktail, oysters au natural, barbecued black bream, followed by broiled mud crab claws and a suitable bottle of Chardonnay, the southern estuary can be an enjoyable shopping place for just about the lot. Follow-up the temptation in the following location guides, you'll find the southern or temperate-climate estuary features prominently on our list of favoured fishing environments.

Despite adverse publicity, Sydney harbour remains a beautiful and productive estuary system. Here, a boatload of hopefuls try their hands near inner North Head.

Tropical Estuaries

Tropical estuaries are extremely fertile fishing grounds, but you'll need to contend with crocodiles, mosquitoes, sandflies, fruitbats, thick mud, extreme tides and sticky, sultry weather. However, with big barramundi, aggressive mangrove jacks, performing threadfin salmon and bucket-mouthed estuary cod as the rewards, it all becomes tolerable.

The tropics can be an uncomfortable place, especially for southerners more accustomed to chilly southerly winds howling off the Tasman, though there are few more productive fishing spots. Everything remotely connected with angling in Australia's tropical north is somehow tied in with the area's myriad of estuaries. Even many of the north's most brilliant marlin fisheries are situated where large estuary systems empty a seemingly never-ending supply of nutrients and baitfish to waiting offshore predators.

Tropical estuaries range north from approximately Fraser Island in southern Queensland, running right across the top half of the continent, to Shark Bay in north west Western Australia. This huge area comprises an interconnected maze of inlets, creeks, rivers and lowlands - an enormous number of potential fishing locations.

Extensive mangrove stands are the most important feature of tropical estuaries. Shrouding the shorelines, they often make it difficult to distinguish between individual estuaries, but the mangroves also provide cover for fish and an ideal protective environment for them to breed. In fact, mangroves provide the very lifeblood of the marine food chain by depositing vital nutrients in the water. The area around the root buttresses of mangroves is an ideal region for presenting both baits and lures.

In the quest for locating fish, there are other signs in this tropical habitat zone also worth bearing in mind, namely where snags are situated, and importantly, where tidal lines occur. Tropical tides vary enormously, emptying almost as fast a couple of kids can devour a tub of ice-cream, and flooding back in with equal enthusiasm. This active waterflow forms the basis of many fish's feeding cycles and, generally speaking, the first few hours either side of the low tide period are the pick, though the beginning of the run-out can be productive around the mouths of estuaries.

Because of the difficult terrain of the tropics - thick vegetation, slippery mud and mangroves - a small, outboard-powered, aluminium cartopper around 3 to 4 metres in length can be a great asset for getting into real 'tiger country'. A necessity if you're planning a serious trip up this way.

However, there are other tropical estuaries for which a boat isn't absolutely necessary. Bay locations with breakwalls, towns or harbours that have wharves, piers or marinas, rocky points or shorelines, and sandy beaches are all worth using as fishing platforms. These areas are often linked more closely to the open ocean than mangrov

Top: A jungle of intertwining mangrove roots is typical of tropical estuaries.
Above: The coral-sand flats of an offshore tropical estuary are excellent fishing territory.

creeks, and as a result fish such as the different species of mackerels, big trevally and various other oceanic reef-dwellers can be expected.

So to the fishing. Most species in tropical estuaries are fierce predators. Artificial baits or lures are favoured for this reason, though live baits often attract a bigger run of fish. Your tackle needs to be tough, strong hooks and other terminal fittings are par for the course, while fishing outfits need to be light-tipped for casting lures, yet have strength for heaving the fish away from the sanctuary of mangrove roots or oyster-covered rocks. Six to 10 kilogram line is adequate, but under certain fishing conditions, a heavier line may be better. Expect barramundi, threadfin salmon, mangrove jacks, tarpon, flathead, pikey bream, trevally, barracuda, catfish and a host of other worthwhile species.

As a final note, the tropical estuary fishing zone is tough territory. The crocodile problem warrants obvious attention, but so do those sandflies, mosquitoes, the searing sun, and the fact that much of this country is well off the beaten track. Be careful of the Wet season. Not only does it rain, but it rains to the extent that trickling creeks become raging torrents that can carry a two-tonne, four-wheel vehicle off the ground into the fork of a tree.

Take heed of the warnings, plan and research your trips well.

A great wall of mangrove trees dwarfs a fishing punt and its occupants in Jacky Jacky Creek, Cape York, Queensland.

Rock and Beach

In the southern half of this continent, rock and beach fishing fronts are two of our most popular angling playgrounds. A wide range of trophy fish inhabit these coastal environments, and are usually convenient, comfortable regions from which to fish. However, the potential dangers of fishing the ocean rocks can't be understated as many lives have been tragically lost.

Our coastal rock and beach fishing areas attracts a colourful kaleidoscope of fish life, most of which is of interest to anglers. From the beaches, it is possible to catch tailor, salmon, bream, whiting, flathead and mulloway or jewfish. Along the rocks, anything from the primarily surface-feeding predators such as tailor, tuna and salmon in southern areas, and with Spanish mackerel also available in more northern latitudes, to the bottom-dwellers such as snapper, groper, black drummer or rock blackfish, bream and mulloway or jewfish are reasonably common. But as with any fishing region, knowing where the fish are located within these two coastal habitat zones, and why, will increase your catch.

Close to the shallow, sudsy, wave-washed regions along the rocks and beaches you will find a different range of fish to those that occur further out in the deepwater regions - the forage feeders such as luderick, black drummer, and bream along the rocks, and whiting and bream in the surf zone along beaches. The larger migratory predators such as tuna, kingfish, mulloway and mackerel tend to prefer deeper waters, though this is only a rough rule of thumb. So in the shallow, washy regions it's often best to use readily available baits such as cunjevoi or crabs and present these offerings with as little weight as possible. When fishing off deepwater headlands and rock platforms, use whole live or dead fish baits floated out to tempt larger predators travelling in passing currents.

One of the advantages of rock and beach fishing is that overly expensive or elaborate tackle isn't necessary. A 3 to 4 metre rod coupled with a sidecast reel and loaded with 6 to 12 kilogram line will suffice in most locations for catching most species of fish. You only need to expand on this basic outfit if you plan to fish in a specific area, or target one specific fish species. Yet another great benefit for the beach, and rockfishing enthusiast especially, is that bait is nearly always there for the picking. Cunje, crabs, certain marine weeds, octopus and other shellfish can all be gathered off the rocks, while pipis, beachworms, and cockles are available off the beaches.

Rock fishing is very popular along the temperate east coast of Australia Wales. Here the location is Woody Head in northern New South

Inshore Grounds

Most organised angling clubs are made-up of avid boaties who venture offshore to fish the reefs and gravel patches wherever they may be. Many club members also specialise in sport and game fishing, and concentrate most of their effort using highly refined techniques to work the wide grounds or fish the bluewater.

The trailerboat fishing grounds are situated between the coastline and the Continental Shelf. These inshore grounds are where most sea fishing is conducted. The techniques used to fish this region apply mostly to temperate waters from the Capricorn Coast in central Queensland, around the bottom half of the continent, to as far north as Shark Bay in Western Australia.

Fishing the inshore grounds can be divided into two areas: the offshore reefs, sand patches and gravel beds (known as the bottom fishing zone) and the coastal bommies and washes. The bottom zone is likely to reward you with prime-eating table fish such as snapper, morwong or deep sea bream, nannygai or redfish, and trevally from off the hard reef areas. You should be able to find sand and tiger flathead, snapper and morwong when fishing over sand or gravel patches.

A seaworthy boat is needed to fish these deep grounds, which are between two and 15 nautical miles offshore. There is a number of chartering services available if you don't have a suitable boat. This style of angling hasn't much finesse, with tackle of either a deck winch, or short boat rod mated to a large centrepin reel, loaded with a suitably long length of line, and a terminal rig with a large enough sinker to take it down to the bottom. However, despite these encumbrances, the pay-off is often a succulent haul of snapper or morwong for the table.

Another method of fishing the offshore grounds is to target larger predatory fish such as jewfish or mulloway, mackerel, kingfish and large tuna, using whole live or dead fish as bait. You can drift and feed a steady trail of minced fish berley over the side to attract these predators or, alternatively, find a prominent underwater reef and apply the techniques while anchored near it's highest pinnacle. Both techniques attract fish, although drift fishing is best carried out in depths greater than 60 metres. Trolling with lures around the offshore reefs can yield surface fish such as tuna, wahoo, mackerel and even marlin.

Further inshore, offshore bomboras, coastal reefs, prominent headlands and other relatively shallow inshore grounds are suitable boat-fishing areas. Trolling with lures or rigged baits, casting these same offerings from a drifting boat, or anchoring in and around the shallow reefs and setting live baits in a berley trail, are the best fishing techniques. Anything from tailor, Australian salmon, Spanish mackerel, cobia and kingfish, to big snapper, mulloway or jewfish, bream, and trevally can be expected.

Top: Unloading the day's catch from an inshore reef on the New South Wales Central Coast.
Above: Mulloway are a keenly sought species on the inshore reefs.

The Islands

From the stormy waters of Bass Strait to turbid Torres Strait, an amazing variety of islands can be found within safe reach of mainland Australia. The reef complexes of larger islands play host to game, sport and bottom fishing, their coastlines are often suitable beach and rockhopping grounds, while the rivers may constitute estuary or, in the upper reaches, freshwater fisheries.

For the most part, islands are the exposed tips of underwater mountains that have been forced upwards by seismic pressures deep within the earth. Nesting birds, sediment, flotsam and erosion all contribute to making suitably rich soils that can then support vegetation, and thus a fertile island is formed. Fish can be found around islands because they have large underwater reef complexes, or exaggerated sand cays, that create a diversion to current flow, support varying forms of marine life, and therefore provide the basic requirements of food and shelter.

As islands include at least a couple of the different fishing environments discussed in this section of the book, the methods for fishing them hardly require repeating. Suffice to say that sport and game fishing, targetting fish such as mackerel, marlin, tuna, kingfish and cobia, will be best on the upcurrent side of islands. Trolling and bait fishing will account for these species, although trolling with lures is often favoured as it allows you to cover more territory than stationary bait fishing. As a rough rule of thumb, areas around islands that are influenced by currents will always support most marine life as it is here that nutrients are first deposited. However, flats fishing and reef fishing can often prove rewarding even on the lee sides of islands, which usually are the safest anchorages anyway.

In short, islands provide the benefits of both wonderful scenery and super fishing, as well as being valuable sanctuaries in an otherwise watery world. For adventurous boaties, they are undoubtedly one of the last great bastions to escape the detrimental effects of mainland living, and experience a standard of angling probably once common around the entirety of mainland Australia.

Above: Islands are fantastic fishing grounds. They have all the necessary marine life- food and shelter.

Left: A small, trailable boat may provide the link to an otherwise inaccessible offshore island.
Above: Spanish mackerel are just one species common to tropical islands.

Coral Reefs

Amongst the branching, inter-twining coral reefs, bomboras and adjoining sand cays, fish life of almost every conceivable dimension, colour and character abound. The coral reefs harbour some of our most aggressive predatory sportfish. Toothy-jawed coral trout, big bucket-mouthed cod, coral-crunching parrot fish and scarlet-coloured emperor are just a handful of the reef-dwelling species. Add to those the fish that commonly patrol the surface layers, such as the big, blunt-headed trevally, marauding packs of ravenous Spanish mackerel, fanged barracuda and acrobatic queenfish, and the viscious nature of coral reef fishing becomes apparent.

Bottom fishing with baits is the most practiced method of coral reef fishing, producing everything from the deliciously sweet-fleshed coral trout to red emperor and host of other species. Occasionally, heavy jigs tainted with squid or a piece of fish flesh on the rear hooks are used, having the added advantage of covering a greater range of depths. The other major technique is trolling or casting lures and baits.

For the mid-water to surface-roaming species such as mackerel, trevally, barracuda and queenfish, lures are a far more efficient than bait. And as sharks are often such a problem in the tropics, there's sometimes no other alternative. When they aren't on the bite however, garfish, pilchards, herring and mullet are some of the better whole baitfish for tempting surface fish, especially school, spotted and Spanish mackerel. Where waters reach six to eight metres over fringing coral reefs and shoal areas, lures often attract coral trout and cod from their hides and up to the surface to strike aggressively. This style of angling is undoubtedly one of the most exciting experiences, yielding not only good numbers of fish, but also often resulting in snapped lines, broken tackle and numerous lure losses as large, determined fish frequently win the struggle back to the sanctuary of their reef hideaways.

Australia's coral reef fishing is a constant source of enjoyment for those anglers fortunate enough to be living in the tropics. From Bundaberg in southern Queensland, across the top, to Exmouth in the west, coral country predominates in the saltwater. For the rest of our angling nation, the lure of fishing this environment must be relegated to annual holidays and organised trips away.

The beautiful barramundi cod is held in high esteem as an eating fish. They inhabit tropical coral reefs and are caught by fishing the bottom.

Top: An estuary cod, common on coral reefs, from the Whitsundays. Above: Coral trout are the ultimate prize on the coral reefs.

Blue Water

Bluewater fishermen either own their own boats, or crew on large game fishing vessels owned by the rich, but either way the idea is the same - to catch the glamour fish of the sea. Black marlin, blue marlin, striped marlin, sailfish, yellowfin tuna, big-eye tuna, dog-tooth tuna, longtail or northern bluefin tuna, wahoo, dolphin fish or mahi mahi, Spanish mackerel, yellowtail kingfish, cobia - the list is extensive, though all the fish are characterised by being oceanic drifters or pelagics, and determined fighters.

Sport and game fishing places emphasis upon the thrill of the catch, rather than the kill. Fish are fought on light tackle to provide the best sport possible, but once led to the boat they are often released to fight another day. This form of conservation ensures the future of the sport, unlike many other types of fishing. In order to fish particular line classes to the maximum potential, high-tech reels and rods are employed, which usually require some bank balance to purchase.

Charter operations offering sport and game fishing, while being expensive, are usually of a very high standard and you can be guaranteed of impressive fishing action, particularly when they travel to remote fishing locations that have seen very little fishing pressure.

Recognising the enjoyment in catching fish and the skill required to land them when pitted against suitable tackle is what sport and game fishing is all about.

Bluewater sport and game fishing can be experienced right round the Australian coastline, and information readily gleaned from the various clubs.

Speedster of the bluewater, the wahoo, is a ferocious predator. This one fancied a trolled minnow lure.

Billfish are the glamour catch of the bluewater. Here, a sailfish spears skyward in an endeavour to break free. But once close enough for tagging, it will be released.

Travelling Tips

Before starting on an angling trip prepare carefully.

1. Study the location. Know which species of fish are available, where to catch them and the required techniques.

2. Make a checklist of everything needed for the trip from food to fishing tackle. Cross checking is recommended before packing. Too often fishing excursions are 'organised' haphazardly, and in the mad panic of trying to get away early, something is left behind.

3. Maps are helpful if they detail access routes and land formations, and water depths. Admiralty maps also show shoals.

4. Approach the local "salts" for local knowledge about a new area, and any special fishing spots.

Weather Watch

Fishing like all outdoor activities, is at the mercy of the weather.

It decides if there will be a fishing trip and if it will be enjoyable, uncomfortable or dangerous. The Department of Meteorology issues boating forecasts detailing wind strengths, wave heights and sea conditions. The Telecom dial-it-information line carries this information and also issues weather warnings.

Of all the weather conditions, the direction and strength of the wind has the most influence on fishing conditions. Strong winds not only generate swell, but also determine the water-surface conditions, and comfort. Onshore winds usually dictate a swell, while offshore breezes tend to flatten the water surface. Wind strength and its effects upon sea, is gauged by the Beaufort Scale.

It is also wise to check the weather map published in the daily papers or the television before taking to the water. It doesn't require much study to understand synoptic charts. As a rule of thumb, low pressure cells generate bad weather, while high pressure cells good weather. The closeness of the isobars or the rings surrounding these systems reflects the strength of the winds.

Winds flow in an anti-clockwise direction around high pressure cells, and clockwise around low pressure cells.

Cloud is a visible indication of incoming weather. Cumulus clouds (puffy and white) indicates fine weather, while the wispy, torn patterns of cirrus clouds indicates rain is on the way. The cirrus clouds are followed by the grey, dense and low Stratus or rain clouds. Nimbus clouds generally always brings poor weather, rain, thunderstorms, wind changes, squalls and even hail. They are dark, gloomy and obvious. Finally, the rippled or wavy cirrocumulus clouds, which also often herald an approaching storm.

Approaching fronts are also sign-posted by a change in air pressure. Fishermen should have a barometer if at sea to note any air pressure variation.

Look to the heavens for clues to weather patterns. Although not a threat in this tranquil New South Wales estuary, offshore that weather change must be regarded potentially dangerous.

Finding Fish

Locating fish can be difficult. It is important to know what the signs are that say, "fish here"; this is the spot, use this bait and you should catch this species.

It is important to understand fish behaviour and to know their feeding habits so they can be pinpointed. If you can gauge what the fish are feeding on, and how to present your "offering", then a significant part of fishing technique has been mastered. Remember fish feed mainly during the low-light or twilight periods, and respond best to naturally occurring foods or baits.

Fish locate around 'structures', underwater which provide food, shelter and something tangible with which to identify. Islands for example, attract fish in otherwise 'featureless' surroundings.

Fish holding structures can be found in any fishing environment. In a river, a stream or a creek, it may be a sunken log, a rocky outcrop, a deep escarpment in the riverbed or any underwater position that alters water flow and determines where the food is carried that attracts fish. Along a beach, the gutters, holes and channels are the key features, while offshore it is the reef complexes and the areas where the current deflects around the reefs that fish locate.

The pelagic or migratory fish because they depend upon small fish for food, are found where baitfish are schooling. Seabirds, scavenging on pilchards or whitebait forced to the surface by predators are a good indicator as to where to find the predators.

Depth sounders are a popular device for locating fish. Chart or LCD display sounders also provide invaluable underwater information removing all the guess work. Different types of seabed, such as hard reef, soft sand and water depth can easily be determined with a sounder. Water temperature gauges are another useful modern-day device for finding fish, especially gamefish in the saltwater, and trout in the freshwater.

Consistently locating fish, in any environment, is a skill that can only be acquired over time. It's a skill that sets top anglers apart from the average and is the reason fishing guides are important when tackling a new territory.

Polariod sunglasses, a brimmed hat and a 'spotter's eye' have contributed to locating a trout that this fly fisherman is about to catch.

Fishing Safety

Fishing safety is largely a matter of common sense, obeying the laws or regulations, carrying the mandatory gear on board boats, and having the necesssary experience.

The old fishing axiom "no life is worth the risk" is true. Fishermen, especially rock fisherman, too often take unnecessary risks in order to land that particular "whopper". Boat-based anglers are also often guilty of heading out to sea in ill-equipped vessels that are without the necessary safety equipment on board, including flares, radio, and a lifejacket for every crew member. Informing authorities and relations where you are heading and your estimated time of return is always essential.

Never fish alone. Accidents can be prevented if a companion is present or if someone has some first aid training. The St John's Ambulance runs several first aid courses and it would be wise for any regular fisherman to take a course. A first aid kit should always be included in every angler's tackle box.

Crocodiles, sharks, stinging seawasps, poisonous fish and bad weather are all encountered in popular angling regions. Pay particular attention to signposted dangers, take heed of any warnings, and don't exercise some courageous display of bravado in order to catch fish and impress your peers.

Above: Fishing can be made even safer by ensuring youngsters wear life jackets

Queensland

Introduction

Queensland is the undisputed black marlin capital of the world. There can be no argument that Cairns has more big black marlin than any other place on earth.

But to think that great billfish the size of a small motor vehicle is all there is to fishing in Queensland is to ignore an incredible diversity of fishing. Queensland is a big state with a climate ranging from warm temperate to tropical.

Queensland fishing is made up of a mosaic of experiences.

There's the crispness of a Fraser Island winter's dawn whilst waiting for the tailor to move in. The total mayhem of queenfish boiling all around the boat as lures fly in all directions. Or,there's nothing like a multiple hookup on Cape Bowling Green or Cape Moreton's marlin and sailfish.

On the other hand, there's the quietude of a grandparent aiding and abetting junior to land his or her first winter whiting, or the pristine magic of a rainforest stream with hordes of aggressive sooty grunter.

Then there's the crunching strike of a mangrove jack; or that heart-in-mouth feeling as a bucket-jawed barramundi inhales a lure at your feet on the mangrove creek.

From the bream run at the Jumpinpin, to the gentle take as a yellowbelly gulps down a live crayfish on a turbid outback river...Queensland has it all...and more!

A juvenile black marlin takes to the air. Black marlin are one of Queensland's glamour catches and a major attraction for visiting anglers.

Gulf Country

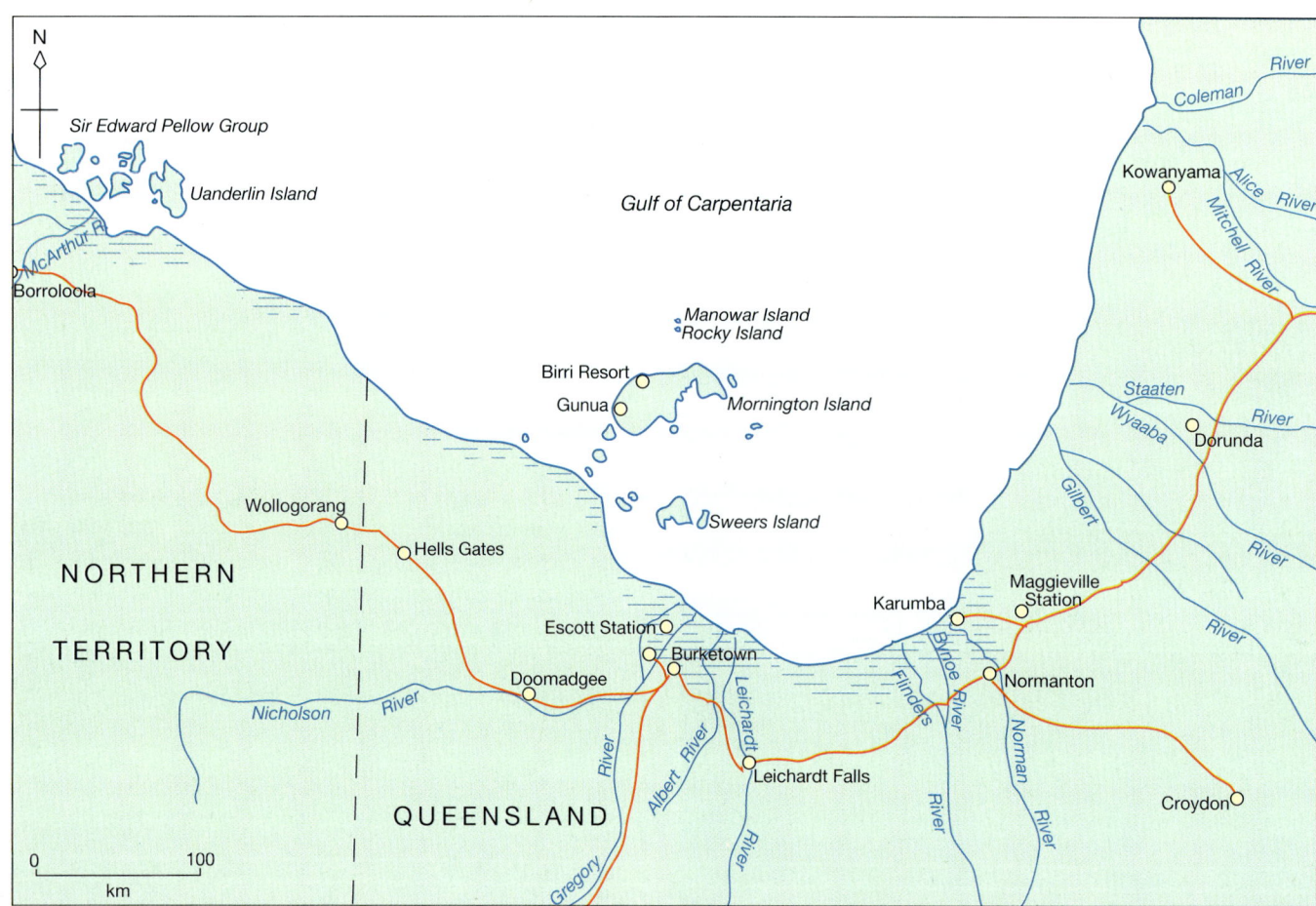

The Gulf Country is the most inhospitable land in Australia but it provides some of the best fishing in the country. The vast region has only four settlements large enough to qualify as towns; Borroloola, Normanton, Karumba and Burketown.

The coastline of extensive mangrove wetlands backed by saline mud flats stretching inland for several kilometres only has one tide a day. The water inshore however, is quite turbid due to infall from many large river systems such as the Nicholson, the Gregory, the Gilbert, the Flinders, the Leichhardt, the mighty Mitchell and the Staaten/Wyaaba system.

Offshore around the scattered islands, the Wellesley Islands including Mornington (an acknowledged hotspot) and the Sir Edward Pellew Group near Borroloola, the water is clear and 'crystalline', except when onshore winds stir sand and sediment left on the bottom by the Gulf's sluggish tidal movement.

Average tidal variation in the Gulf region is 3 to 3.5 metres, with the neaps every 13 to 14 days, causing what most would term a 'normal' tide of two highs and two

lows in each 24 hours. The neaps don't have much movement, usually 0.2 or 0.3 metres. To those accustomed to tidal cycles elsewhere, those in the Gulf take a little getting used to.

The Gulf of Carpentaria sportfishing remains a stronghold of barramundi and numerous other saltwater species, including mangrove jacks, queenfish, threadfin, grunter (javelin fish), fingermark, the so-called black jewfish (a northern mulloway species), several trevally species and estuary cod. There is excellent fishing for bream (the northern pikey bream), whiting and flathead but most visitors prefer to pursue the more exotic species.

In recent years, the roads from Julia Creek and Cloncurry to Normanton and Karumba, have been sealed but elsewhere in the Gulf, long stretches of unsealed 'road' often require a four-wheel drive. Numerous tracks, not marked on any map, lead to the fishing spots. They change year by year at the whim of the first local going in after the wet season.

Travel in the Gulf is governed by the big 'Wet'. Rain clouds gather around the end of November and travelling after Christmas is a game of chance. At the end of the Wet, there's something of a race to be the first into the 'spots'. This too is a game of chance since the mud flats are still wet and boggy from the rains. Even when they dry, a late heavy shower can bog vehicles for days.

The 'king' of Gulf fishing is barramundi. Excluding the annual migration down to salt water to breed and the return upstream as the rivers fall, barramundi are most active when water levels rise and fall. Barramundi rules from the freshwater of the Gregory River, to the turbid, sluggish estuaries where many large rivers wind their way across the flat coastal plain stretching from Borroloola to the Mitchell River.

Borroloola is sited on the McArthur River some 35 kilometres upstream from the mouth. Between the township and the coast, the McArthur spreads into a huge delta with one channel, the Carrington Channel, carrying as much water as the river itself. Junctions of tidal inlets, and freshwater creeks further upstream, such as Crooked Creek and Batten Creek, are the places to look for barramundi. Boats can be launched at Borroloola, Batten Point and at Blackjack Landing.

An all-bitumen road leads to Borroloola from Daly Waters on the Stuart Highway, with an alternative all-bitumen route from the Barkly Highway west of Camooweal.

The Sir Edward Pellew group of islands, offshore from the McArthur River mouth, yield a variety of prize reef fishes; estuarine species such as mangrove jack, queenfish and estuary cod are also available in the region.

Between Borroloola and Burketown travelling is very difficult. An infamous four-wheel drive track leads west from Burketown to Borroloola. Facilities are few and far between and bush camping is the only accommodation available. Hell's Gate Roadhouse and Wollogorang (50 kilometres east and 8 kilometres west of the Northern Territory border) are the only food and fuel stops between Doomadgee and Borroloola.

West of Burketown, Escott Lodge, a tourist development, near Escott Station, lies across the Gregory and the Nicholson Rivers and Gin Arm Creek. Fishing is but one of the activities offered here, albeit at a price.

A boat ramp in Burketown and innumerable four-wheel drive tracks in the area open the door to the mouth of the Albert and the Leichhardt Rivers. Always get local advice regarding the state of tracks. From Burketown an unsealed road leads east to meet with bitumen just south of Normanton. There's a very nice overnight camp 160 kilometres from Normanton at Leichhardt Falls where the road crosses the Leichhardt River.

Normanton and Karumba are both on the Norman River, Karumba down near the mouth and Normanton upstream. Karumba is used as base port by the Gulf's prawning fleet during the season. As a result, it is the only town in the Gulf looking to the future, rather than trying to attract tourism by preserving its past.

Karumba is also the only place where a road leads to the Gulf coast and, as such, is of vital interest to any travelling angler. The port is serviced with all the expected facilities, including a pilot station and a decent boat ramp. This, and the usual web of four-wheel drive tracks across the saline coastal flats, make the Karumba area one of the more accessible regions in the Gulf of Carpentaria.

East of Karumba a road (unpaved) leading to Croydon and points east quickly leads away from the coast into a particularly parched hinterland of little fishing interest.

The west coast of lower Cape York provides worthwhile fishing. Again, this is four-wheel drive country. Well defined, if rough, roads lead north east into Cape York from a turn-off near Maggieville Station, 29 kilometres north of Normanton. Station tracks and the few public roads in this area leads to rivers such as the Staaten, Wyaaba, the Gilbert and the Mitchell.

An Aboriginal community at Kowanyama (Mitchell River) controls access to several waterways. Always check if permission is required (whether from a station or an Aboriginal community) before setting out.

The Burke Development Road leads from Maggieville Station north to Dunbar Station, then south east to Chillagoe and the Atherton Tableland and Cairns. A turn-off leads to Dorunda Station 150 kilometres from Normanton. Dorunda, runs a tourist lodge and has some beautiful water on the Staaten and Wyaaba Rivers with hire boats available on some larger waterholes.

Offshore in the Gulf are two more tourist developments offering fishing remarkable even by the Gulf's standards. Sweers Island and Mornington Island are only accessible to visiting anglers by aircraft and, in both cases, only guests using the facilities offered by the respective operators are allowed on to the islands.

Apart from prawning, there is no commercial fishing nearby, so both reef fishing and light-tackle sportfishing are productive. Red emperor, coral trout and sweetlip are available in abundance from the reefs surrounding the islands. Light-tackle sportfishing there is superlative. Queenfish, threadfin, mangrove jacks, the trevally family, barracuda and even a few barramundi are all available.

Around Sweers and Mornington Island, pelagic Spanish and spotted mackerel can be added to the list of fishing targets. Billfish are in the area, but so far no one has really tried to catch them. Mornington Island and its fishing lodge, Birri, are renowned as THE hotspot for giant herring, a fish destined for international stardom, and the action here could quite easily compete with light-tackle bonefish and tarpon fisheries on the Atlantic coast of America, and in the Caribbean.

Cape York

Gaining access to Cape York's fishing requires a high degree of resourcefulness. Distances are long enough to make logistics (such as carrying enough fuel), a constant concern, and the area is so remote it is definitely not for the inexperienced or ill-equipped. Self sufficiency, careful planning and allowing enough travelling time to take the pressure off are all vital ingredients to ensuring an enjoyable and successful fishing trip to Cape York.

A four-wheel drive vehicle is virtually essential for travelling. The better fishing spots are only accessible by four-wheel drive and to get the best out of the fishing a small boat, seaworthy enough to cope with at least estuarine wind chop, and with enough power to plane easily when heavily laden, is a necessity.

Further north on the west coast of Cape York some pretty rough four-wheel drive tracks lead into the vicinity of the Mitchell, Coleman and Edward Rivers. From there, it's back to the Telegraph Track up the Cape for overland access further north. Both Weipa and Arukun are reached off the Weipa road - Weipa by what few people would call a road, and Arukun by an unformed track.

Arukun is an Aboriginal community and, in common with most of these sites on Cape York, Europeans must gain permission before entering.

Weipa is a bauxite mining town with all modern facilities, including a radio station, a boat ramp and a pub. It also has excellent fishing and is one of a few places on the whole of Cape York where non boat-based or shore angling is productive. Everything from queenfish to black jew and barramundi may be caught from the old ship-loading wharf (now used by trawlers) at Evans Landing, where Albatross Bay is the confluence of the Embley, the Hay and the Mission Rivers. All of these fish well as does the Bay itself and its extremities, Duyfken Point and Pera Head. Be warned: Albatross Bay is a wide expanse of water and unsafe for small 'cartoppers' or 'tinnies'.

Mapoon north from Weipa, is reached by tracks that also lead to a rock bar on the Wenlock River, which is the upper limit of tidal influence. Rock bars where the tides stop their push upstream in the river are good spots for barramundi. Mapoon is the home of mega-threadfin.

The Jardine River is the next worthwhile 'fishing' stop on the way north. The Jardine is an incredible waterway running clean and hard over a sandy bottom nearly all the way across Cape York. Two ferries transport four-wheel drives across it. Boats can be launched at the ferry crossings to travel either upstream (accessible distance

Cape York is incredibly diverse. Fishing on the west coast is similar to the Gulf of Carpentaria except that the coastal mangroves backed by saline mud flats, so typical of the bottom of the Gulf, give way to sandy beaches, rocky headlands and extensive coastal swamps as you travel.

Close to the tip of Cape York the tides become very confused due to a convergence between tides in the Gulf on the west and those of the reef waters on the east coast. Torres Strait has a well deserved reputation for tidal races and overfalls as the two separate bodies of water sort themselves out amongst the rock outcrops and islands.

The east coast of Cape York is different. Some areas such as the controversial Shellburne Bay have sand dune coasts fronted by sandy beaches. In the Portland Roads/Iron Range area, precipitous rainforested slopes run from the mountainous spine of Cape York down to the coast. The largest mangrove wetland on the east coast of Australia lies near the top of the Cape around the Kennedy Inlet and its feeders (Jacky Jacky Creek and the Escape River). Further south, Princess Charlotte Bay is backed by the massive wetlands and floodplains of Lakefield National Park, a tremendous variation in habitat.

depending on how late in the dry you visit and the current river height), or downstream as far as the mouth. Further downstream is reached by a track which leads to Bamaga's water supply pump.

The Jardine runs fresh almost to its mouth and, indeed, past the mouth and out to sea during the wet. The biggest barramundi and some even larger 'swamp geckos' (crocodiles), are found down towards the entrance where tides back up the water.

Right at the mouth, a rising tide brings in giant and golden trevally, queenfish and threadfin salmon. On a calm day, the stumps of an old burnt-out jetty at Mutee Head, north of the Jardine mouth, can be reached by small boats. All the tropical sportfish are found at times around these pylons, while on the bottom, black jew and cod, which can usually only be tackled with heavy handlines, rule supreme. It's no place for sporting tackle.

Red Island Wharf, at Bamaga, is a hot fishing spot where a boat is not required. Locals always seem to know when the wharf will fire, and the chances of success may be judged by the concentration of fishermen there. Huge giant trevally live under the jetty, along with the bottom-dwelling 'ooglies', cod and black jew of such size that despite being regularly hooked, they're rarely decked. The whole spectrum of tropical sportfish, including some very respectable barramundi, are taken off Red Island wharf.

Two resorts have been sited close to the northernmost tip of Cape York:

The very tip of Australia encompasses one of the country's most brilliant fishing regions.

Punsand Bay, some 15 kilometres south-west of the tip, has tent accommodation for guests.

Cape York Wilderness Lodge is only 400 metres from the very tip of the Cape. Everyone making it 'to the top' has to follow a special path laid out by the lodge away from their guest accommodation.

The small lodge set in neatly laid-out gardens. The internationally renowned fishing guide, Gary Wright, operates exclusively from the lodge.

The Tip of Cape York and the rocks surrounding the coastline, don't fish all that well during the cooler parts of the Dry season but early and late in the Dry big queenfish and Spanish mackerel can be live baited off the rocks. Fish species such as coral trout and sweetlip, normally thought to be a boat proposition, can also be taken off any rocky promontory in this part of Cape York.

As is so often the case, a small boat will improve the odds. Trolling between the tip and York and Eborac Islands, some 400 metres, produces good catches of giant and golden trevally, Spanish mackerel and queenfish.

Torres Strait Islands are among the last unexplored recreational fisheries in Australia. A charter boat is available from Thursday Island. It concentrates on reef fishing and heavy tackle trolling for trevally and mackerel. More specialised sportfishing techniques are rarely seen.

Albany Island and the famous Fly Point are just a little way down the east coast from the tip of Cape York. Even small marlin have been taken off the rocks here. There's a camping area at Somerset in the Albany Passage (sheltered by Albany Island). Cape York Wilderness Lodge also runs a camping area for four-wheel drive visitors and the Bamaga community has one at Seisia. The Wilderness Lodge and Bamaga camps have facilities, the one at Somerset is strictly a bush camp.

Kennedy Inlet is accessible via a gravel road leading off near Bamaga airport. A gravel ramp will launch cartopper boats. Kennedy Inlet is a maze of mangrove channels and extreme caution is needed to avoid getting lost. The area is dominated by fingermark rather than barramundi - not such a bad thing. Several rubble bottom 'reefs' in open areas of the inlet also house the fingermark in addition to reef dwellers like sweetlip and coral trout.

Few areas of Cape York's east coast south of Kennedy Inlet are accessible by four-wheel drive, but you can take the turn-off to Lockhart River Aboriginal community, Iron Range National Park and the tiny settlement of Portland Roads.

Portland Roads, in the lee of Cape Weymouth, has the remains of a jetty. Several reefs within a reasonable distance which produce comparable fishing for the region.

Coen, during its gold rush heyday, was serviced by Port Stewart at the mouth of the Stewart River. A four-wheel drive track leads into this area south of the town.

Lakefield National Park is famous for the barramundi fishing in the many lily lagoons on the floodplains of the Kennedy, Hann and Normanby Rivers.

Princess Charlotte Bay, part of the Lakefield National Park, is equally renowned as a barramundi hotspot as is nearby Bathurst Bay. Access to the coast overland is very difficult. The best way to fish the area is from small boats serviced by a mother ship anchored offshore. Operators run trips into Princess Charlotte Bay from Cairns each Dry season.

Rough tracks lead to several fishing spots along the coast between Cape Melville and Cooktown.

A great alternative is to travel the eastern coast of Cape York by boat, fishing en route. Naturally, this requires a large craft such as a cruising yacht, but it does open the door to virtually the whole eastern extremity of the Cape. In addition to the mother ship, a smaller dinghy is essential to penetrate coastal waterways from the many anchorages. Amongst the myriad of coral reefs offshore, the fishing is virtually untouched.

Lizard Island, 95 kilometres north-east of Cooktown, is recognised as Australia's giant black marlin hotspot. A few have ventured out in large trailerboats but it is not recommend.

The reefs surrounding the island also offer superb light-tackle sportfishing, and bottom fishing.

Top: Unloading the camping gear at ideallic Albany Passage.
Above: The remains of old Mutee Head jetty marks a great black jewfish spot.

Cooktown to Cairns

Cooktown was once Queensland's second largest town, boasting some 65 'places dispensing liquor' (hotel is not an appropriate word to describe some of the canvas, corrugated iron and bark slab establishments!).

Cooktown boasts some fine fishing. The Endeavour River flows right through town. The Annan River is a little way to the south.

Cooktown Jetty, fronting the Endeavour River, is the usual starting place for visitors. It's also fished by locals, a sure sign that the jetty produces the goods. A species of herring, known locally as 'sardines' or just plain 'sards', packs in along the foreshore in tremendous schools early in the Dry season. One throw with a cast net usually scores enough bait for a solid session, and then you're in business (bait jigs work well, too). Off the jetty, everything from barramundi, queenfish, the various trevallies to mackerel are caught on the 'sards'.

The Endeavour River upstream produces quite a few barramundi. Fingermark are found on the bottom of deep holes and good-sized grunter (javelin fish) on the flats at night. Both the Endeavour, and the Annan, hold large tarpon weighing 2 to 3 kilograms. They can be identified by their habit of rolling at the surface to gulp air. They're found well up into brackish and even fresh water, as are mangrove jacks. Several trevally species including queenfish frequent both estuaries. The ever-present and often despised but tasty estuary cod is found in the saltwater regions right down this stretch of coast, and are almost as bad as mangrove jacks for 'souveniring' lures and 'hanging' them on the nearest snag.

Archer Point lies 15 kilometres 'as the crow flies' south of Cooktown. An old grain-loading jetty is the prominent feature here. The decking is gone, so don't expect to walk around on it, but the pylons are a magnet for a variety of fish. Archer Point itself is quite a large headland, or rather a collection of headlands, and is a great place to spin off the rocks. Huge giant trevally lurk amongst the jumble of oysters, coral and rock. Queenfish and mackerel are also taken regularly here.

You can get to Cooktown by road from Cairns; the longer inland route is often badly corrugated, the rough coastal route requires a four-wheel drive. At the tiny town of Ayton the coastal route detours inland to cross the Bloomfield River, otherwise it stays close to the coastline.

The Bloomfield River has been described as the prettiest waterway in north Queensland. It can be fished from a small boat all the way from the mouth up into sooty

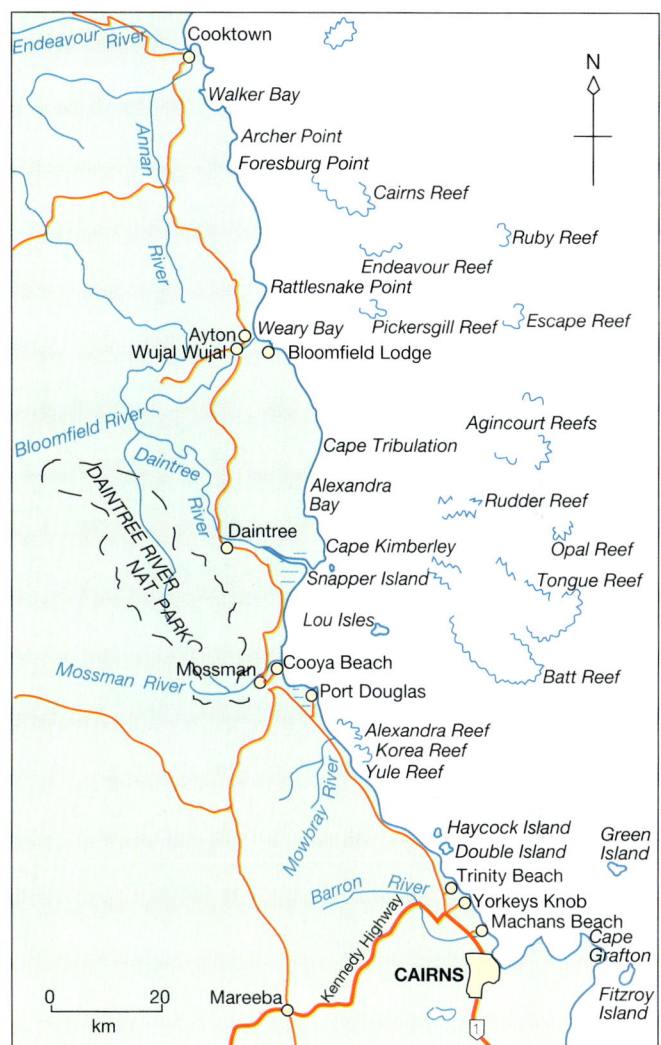

grunter territory in freshwater. Just around the corner to the south of the river mouth Bloomfield Lodge operates fishing trips to the reef.

Another option for anyone equipped with a six-metre-plus boat could be to travel by water from Port Douglas and use the Bloomfield River as a safe haven from which to fish the offshore reefs. Pickersgill, Endeavour, Escape and Ruby Reef are all within range of the Bloomfield River for larger outboard-powered trailerboats. There's a camping area at Ayton and the store can supply food, fuel, and other provisions. Bring enough outboard oil just in case though, supplies can be erratic this far north.

Making a coastal passage from Port Douglas or Cairns to Cooktown is possible in a big seaworthy trailer boat. It's approximately 60 kilometres by sea from Cairns to Port Douglas, a further 60 kilometres to the Bloomfield River, and 60 kilometres again to Cooktown. Secure anchorages and facilities are available at each port of call. Short of hiring charter boats, this is probably the only way to tap the fabulous fishing on some of the least exploited sections of the Great Barrier Reef.

Cape Tribulation marks the beginning (end if heading north) of a road as such. 'No Fishing' signs are the first thing you notice on the beach at Cape Trib'. In this section of the Great Barrier Reef Marine Park from Cape Tribulation to the Bloomfield River, the only fishing allowed is trolling for pelagics such as mackerel.

There's a camping area south of Noah Head on Noah Creek and another at Thornton Beach with a boat ramp of sorts. A track from the turn-off near Tea House leads to the coast at Cow Bay. The coast near Cape Kimberly is also accessible and boats can be launched over the beach here with the aid of a four-wheel drive.

Snapper Island, is just off Cape Kimberley. The Cape and reefs are all good trolling and bottom fishing grounds.

The Daintree River has become a tourist area. Fortunately, it hasn't affected the fishing. The Daintree is not a wilderness river any more, yet astute fishing will still produce results. There are two boat ramps in the Daintree River, one at the ferry crossing (turn off to the right at the Cape Tribulation sign) and the other in the small township of Daintree itself.

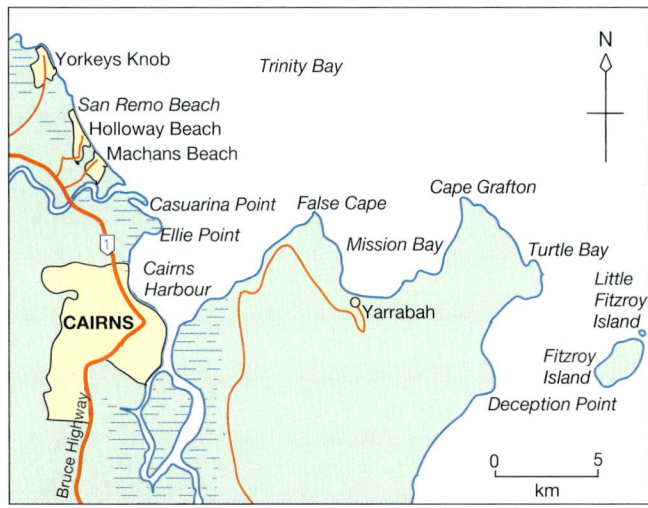

Although becoming increasingly hard to find south of here, good barramundi can be caught in the Daintree. Snags hold mangrove jacks and estuary cod. Grunter, queenfish, the usual trevallies, threadfin and fingermark are available down near the mouth. Upstream there are sooty grunter. The river and its tributary, Stewart's Creek, soon lead into wild country, accessible only to adventurous souls with a canoe and a good pair of walking boots.

Right: A hefty red bass taken on a surface popper lure. They are great fighters, but unfortunately poisonous to eat.

Between the Daintree and Cairns, there are numerous boat ramps. The Mowbray and the Mossman Rivers both fish well. Offshore there are many reefs and a few islands. Close in, reefs off Rocky Point, near Cooya Beach, the Alexandra, Egmont, Yule and Korea reefs south of Port Douglas, and the reefs around Double and Haycock Islands are all worth a look. Even further offshore are the Low Islets and Satellite Reef, the only stops before the reef proper is reached.

The 'Marlin Coast', or the beaches north from Cairns, have seen extensive development in recent years. This has diminished the chances of a encountering barramundi, however, 'in the know' local anglers still take big ones around the creek mouths and rocky headlands. Yorky's Knob in particular is famous for big barramundi. There may be many hours of fruitless lure casting and live baiting but few would argue that a trophy barramundi is worth all the effort. The traditional 'feed' of bream, whiting and flathead is never hard to find anywhere in this area.

Cairns to Tully

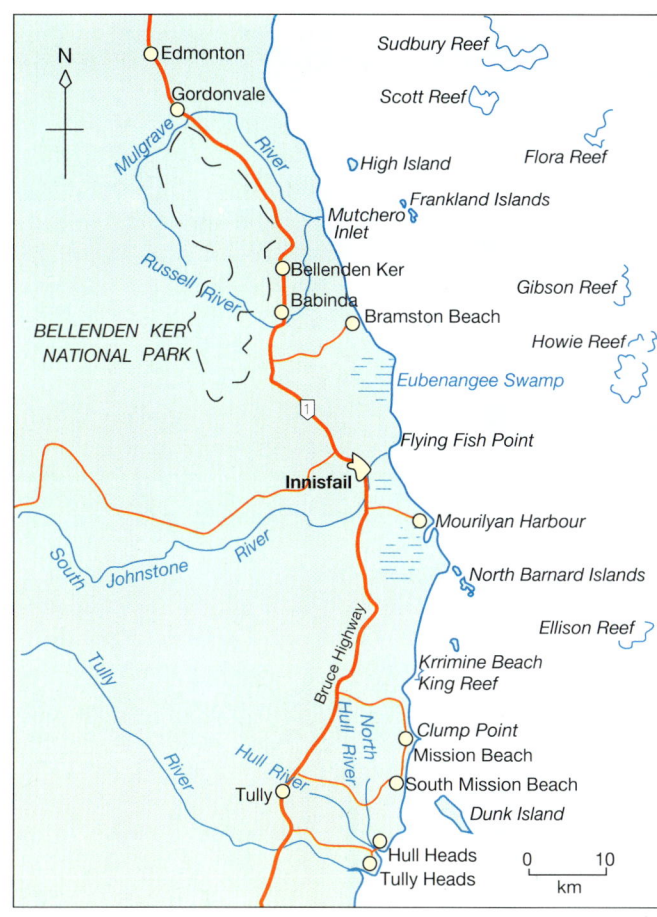

Immediately south of Cairns, overland access to the coast is blocked by the Yarrabah Aboriginal Reserve. However, accessible fishing can be found not too far away.

A turn off to Deeral Landing leads to a boat ramp on the Mulgrave River. Further south another turn-off at Bellenden Ker follows the Russell River Road to a boat ramp on the Russell River. These two have been mentioned together because downstream of the ramps, the Russell and Mulgrave Rivers converge, entering the sea through Mutchero Inlet at a place called Russell Heads.

Russell Heads is renowned in the north. Two of the larger rivers in the Cairns vicinity enter the sea here. There are no roads to Russell Heads, the only access is by boat. A council-run camping area is set amongst trees and has freshwater showers and toilets. It's a great place to camp for a couple of days. Russell Heads is a fishing spot in its own right and a base for exploration of reefs and islands offshore. Mutchero Inlet is quite protected by Constantine Point to the south and east, so it comes as a surprise to learn that mackerel and reef fish, such as coral trout, are far from uncommon inside the inlet.

Further upstream amongst a maze of rainforest-backed mangroves is some of the best estuary fishing in the north. All the usual 'crew', threadfin, fingermark, mangrove jacks, grunter and queenfish are available, as is 'lord barra' himself, for those astute enough to read the water correctly around creek junctions and other likely areas. Further upstream barramundi, mangrove jack and tarpon are joined by freshwater species, as the water first turns brackish and then pure fresh, as it pours off the drainage 'roof' of Queensland. Queensland's highest peaks, Bellenden Ker and Bartle Frere, contribute to the catchment of waters meeting the sea at Russell Heads.

Offshore from Russell Heads, the Frankland Islands, High, Normanby, Mabel, Round and Russell Islands are all within a half-hour boat trip in good weather. The Franklands have been described as a mackerel fishing paradise. Spanish and their smaller cousins, the spotted mackerel, crowd around the Islands. Good reef fishing is available too, although perhaps not of the size and quantity on the reefs found further offshore. Flora, Maori, Scott, Stevens and the southern side of Sudbury Reef are all accessible from Russell Heads. Jackson Patches is a productive submerged reef, and the Staff Patches are about equidistant from Russell Heads and Cairns.

Bramston Beach has a resort and camping area on the site of Australia's oldest coconut plantation and is the only road access to the coast all the way south of Cairns to

Prime freshwater fishing country in the headwaters of a Cairns region river.

Flying Fish Point near Innisfail. A single-lane boat ramp allows launching into Joyce Creek here. Be warned, low water precludes exit (and entry) from the creek to the sea.

Top: Golden trevally are common around Cairns offshore reefs. This one took a deep diving minnow lure.
Above: The profile of a longtail tuna. Another bluewater regular.

Flying Fish Point, on the north bank of the mouth of the Johnstone River, has a much better ramp, although it can be affected by waves in a south-easterly blow. Pearl, Feather and Howie Reefs are all in reach offshore from Flying Fishing Point. Arthur Patches is equidistant from here and Bramston Beach.

Eubenangee Swamp between Flying Fish Point and Bramston Beach, is a major maturation area for barramundi. Access to the swamp is difficult.

Mourilyan Harbour is a sugar-loading facility at the mouth of the Moresby River. The Moresby Range runs right along the coast and the steep slopes plunging to the water ensure deepish water inshore. The Moresby River runs back into an extensive mangrove wetland. Big barramundi come into the harbour but the chances of the average visitor tangling with one are lessened by the efforts of commercial fishing. All the tropical estuarine species inhabit the Moresby, and reef fishing is available offshore. The boat ramp at Mourilyan is excellent but can be swamped by waves driven by south-easterly winds.

Mourilyan to Mission Beach the water inshore is shallow. At Kurrimine Beach, a ramp allows launching into sheltered water between Murdering Point and King Reef. This ramp gives access to the mackerel grounds and reef fishing around the Barnard Islands and reefs further offshore, but not at low tide.

A road south of Tully, near a little place called Silky Oak Creek, leads through Little Tully to Hull Heads at the mouth of the North Hull and Hull Rivers, and to Tully Heads at the mouth of the Tully River.

Hull Heads is the best jumping off point for Dunk and the Family Islands. The ramp here drops off sharply into deep water, so don't try to walk around behind the boat! Some difficulty will be experienced getting a boat in and out of the Hull River at the lower stages of the tide.

Tully Heads and Hull Heads have good estuary fishing although interest is usually directed further afield. Bream, whiting and flathead fishing are often ignored in the north, and in the Tully and Hull Heads regions. A yabby pump will supply quantities of fresh bait; the northern yabby is smaller than its southern counterparts, but nonetheless effective.

Islands in the Sun

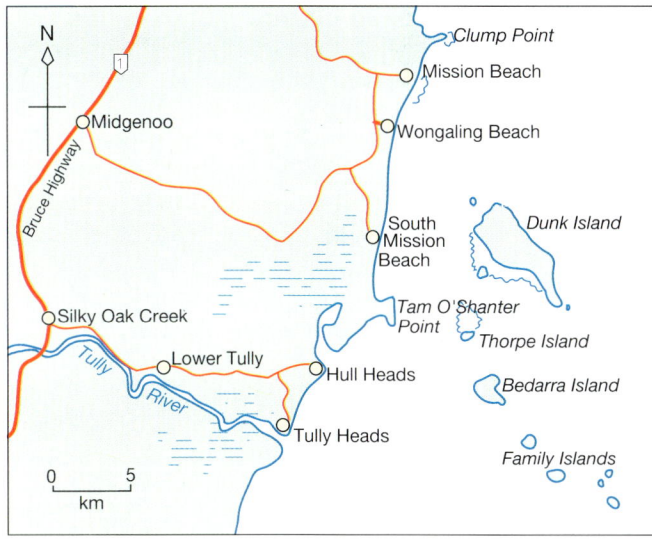

Hinchinbrook Island with crystalline water, clean warm sand and a backdrop of towering rainforested peaks and a massive complex of mangroves on the landward side along the Hinchinbrook Passage is the highest island in Australia.

You can take a boat right through the length of the Hinchinbrook Passage and experience something unique in this country.

Along the coast between Dunk Island and Lucinda at the southern end of Hinchinbrook every type of fishing is available. Light tackle billfishing is found on Dunk Island and the full spectrum of mangrove and creek fishing in the mangrove mazes of the Hinchinbrook Channel.

Apart from some excellent fishing off the old jetty at Lucinda Point, a boat is needed for the whole area covered in this chapter. Inside the Hinchinbrook Channel itself, the open nature of some reaches requires a boat which, if not exactly in the seaworthy class, is certainly in the upper weight-range of cartoppers. A 3.6 metre vee-bottomed dinghy is an absolute minimum.

Offshore, the islands are within reach of any boat with sea-going capabilities. Strong winds can create a dangerous chop, but much of the magic of the islands is there for the taking in any seafaring vessel over about 4.5 metres in length.

Lightweight camping gear will allow stays of several days on Dunk and Hinchinbrook Islands; a true tropical island paradise experience.

Dunk Island has a small National Park camping are tucked away amongst shady trees on the northern tip.

Right: Queensland islands, such as Dunk Island, are not only popular tourist destinations but also attract fish and fishermen.

Dunk is within easy reach of Mission Beach, South Mission Beach or Hull Heads. The boat will be quite secure at anchor behind the sandspit at the south-west tip of the island, and there is a modern amenities block, provided by the resort, behind their Jetty Bar.

Out near Beaver Cay, to the east, marlin and sails are found. They move through the area during the weeks southern anglers know as 'early spring'.

The eastern side of Dunk, closer inshore, is the place to look for smaller sportfish, like queenfish and giant trevally. Some big Spaniards lurk around here, too. Bottom fishing for coral trout and sweetlip is good on reefs along the weather-side of Dunk.

The rest of The Family Group, Bedarra, Tinana, Wheeler, Hudson, Bowden, Smith and Coombe islands are all within a day trip of Hull Heads.

Anchorages off Bedarra and Tinana could be considered for an overnight stay in good weather, but none of the islands are suitable for overnight camping.

Excellent trolling for pelagics is found around the whole Family Group, particularly where the current streams round seaward projections of land. Lure casting is productive in the same areas, especially if there is some form of fish-holding 'structure'. These spots often harbour very large trevally.

Queenfish, Spanish and spotted mackerel are perhaps the most common catches. They too patrol the current lines, and may also be found in deep water close inshore anywhere around the islands ('Spotties' do not mind water a little shallower than their barred cousins, the Spaniards).

Goold and the Brook Islands are best reached from Meunga Creek, a few kilometres north of Cardwell on the mainland. It has a small camping area and a boat ramp. However at low tide the mouth of the creek is unnavigable.

Another ramp at Cardwell has similar problems at low water and may also be affected by wave action.

Goold and the reef-connected Brook Islands, and the northern part of Hinchinbrook Island, are worth a few days exploration in a seaworthy trailerboat. Distances are considerable, so make sure fuel consumption is calculated with the aid of a marine chart, and allow a healthy reserve.

The trolling around Goold and the Brooks is possibly even better than around the Family Group. Reef fishing is best at the Brooks further offshore. A shoal area on the south-western corner of the northern Island produces well at night. An anchorage on the southern or western side of Goold Island may be useful for an overnight stay.

Hinchinbrook Island has two camping areas on the northern side of the island.

Macushla Beach camping area near Macushla Point has a good anchorage, toilets and barbecues. The other camp is directly opposite Cardwell at Scraggy Point. Both are run by the National Parks and Wildlife Service. Sandflies can be a problem so do not forget supplies of repellent. A small resort, popular with folk intent on really getting away from it all, is located a couple of kilometres further north on Cape Richards, the northernmost extremity of Hinchinbrook.

Missionary Bay is a huge mangrove complex on the island's north coast. Nine major creeks form the complex. They are known by numbers. Coral Creek is the only exception. The creeks all pose problems of entry over shallow flats on lower stages of the tide, however once 'in', there is not such a shortage of depth.

Three happy anglers haul a Dunk Island sailfish aboard for a quick photograph before releasing it.

The creek fishing is pretty good. Fingermark are generally called 'red choppers' in the Hinchinbrook area, and here there is a better-than-average chance of tangling with these tasty, larger cousins of the mangrove jack.

The creeks run right across the top of Hinchinbrook Island and end at the line of dunes backing the coast on the opposite side. It is possible to walk across to the beach in Ramsay Bay from the two creeks closest to Kirkland Hills (the southern end of Cape Richards).

It is wise to use the stable weather during the build-up to the Wet season, or immediately following the rains before the south-east trades, if you travel seaward off Hinchinbrook.

Cape Sandwich, the easternmost projection of Hinchinbrook, is a focus of attention for anglers seeking pelagics. Channel Rock and Eva Island east of Cape Sandwich provide more of the same, monster giant trevally and big Spaniards frequent Eva.

Apart from a 'good weather only' anchorage behind a small headland to the north of tiny Agnes Island, the only secure place to overnight on the eastern side of Hinchinbrook is in Zoe Bay. Two creeks at each end of the bay may be entered when the tide height is more than your boat draught.

On an island noted for its beauty, on a part of the coast noted for its beauty, Zoe Bay is the centrepiece. The sandflies, however, are bad, so if sleeping aboard ensure copies supplies of repellent are at hand. The creeks are worth prospecting for estuarine fish as a change from the offshore action available along the rest of the east coast of Hinchinbrook.

To complete the circumnavigation of Hinchinbrook Island, and to reach Zoe Bay and surrounds cross the southern opening of Hinchinbrook Channel near the sugar-loading facility at Lucinda and, in good weather, simply follow the channel marked on the chart. In anything less than good weather, it may be a different matter. A combination of the extensive shallows created by the Herbert River mouth, the tidal movement interacting between the Channel and open water off the coast, and onshore winds, can and does produce hazardous sea conditions. The worst occurs when a stiff sou'easter butts into a falling tide.

At Dungeness a boat ramp gives access to the southern end of Hinchinbrook Channel. Again, there may be hassles getting into the channel proper towards the bottom of the tide. Take local advice.

The old jetty in Lucinda is a good spot for squid, especially at night.

Gentle Annie Creek and Herbert River are fishable from boat or shore but you will need a boat to explore and fish the mangrove-lined vastness of Hinchinbrook's myriad of islands, creeks and inlets.

Barramundi are a distinct possibility but fingermark are more readily available due to commercial fishing of the barramundi. Use live baits in deep water at creek junctions and along steep rocky shores for fingermark. Trolling deep-running lures over the bottom, and along deep structures (located with an echo sounder), will also produce 'red choppers'.

Small baitfish are not hard to come by, using either a cast net or bait net worked over the flats and you will find herrings without much trouble. Bait jigs work very well on herrings and may be a better alternative during the box jellyfish season.

Fingermark are also found around Haycock Island and the Bluff down towards the Lucinda end of the Channel, and Deluge Inlet, Mendel Creek, Paluma Creek and Gayunda Creek.

Grunter, the sometimes maligned estuary cod, threadfin, and the northern black jewfish are all readily available.

Yabbies, the small northern variety, are prolific on the sandflats. They are prime bait for grunter and for bream, whiting and flathead. The flats near the mouth of Deluge Inlet is a place where a yabbie pump, which is familiar to most anglers, can be used to good effect.

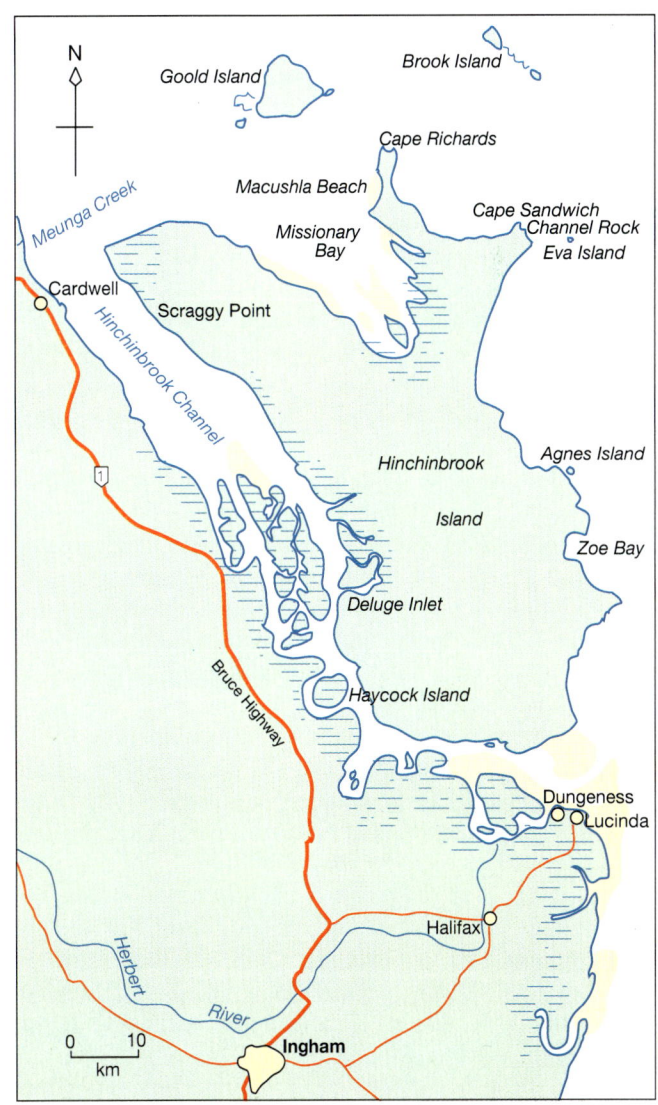

Townsville

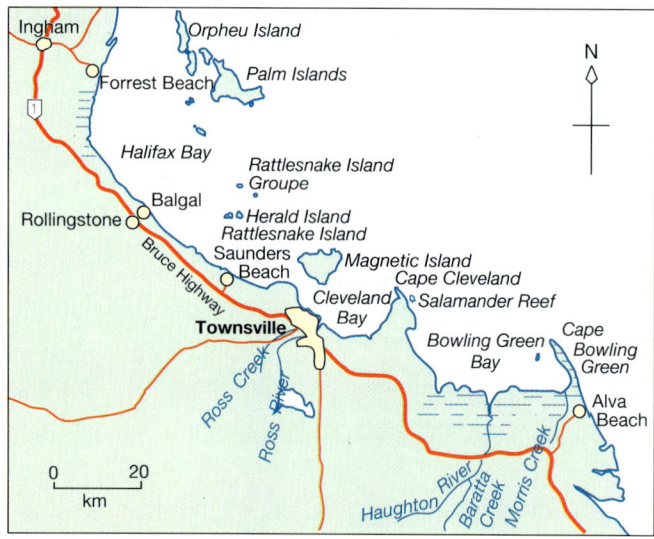

Townsville always suffered by comparison with Cairns, but travelling anglers and locals alike are becoming increasingly aware of the fine angling there.

It may not have a concentration of mega black marlin, but the area around Mymidan Reef has the potential to produce a few, and there is fabulous fishing within striking distance. Townsville has more and better 'tropical island paradises' within reach of the average trailered fishing boat than Cairns and also what is probably Australia's hottest light-tackle billfish ground at Cape Bowling Green.

Not too far down the coast from mighty Hinchinbrook, and just north from Townsville, is the Palm Island group, yet another paradise. There are two settlements in the Palms, Orpheus Island resort and the Aboriginal settlement on Great Palm. Scattered amongst the islands are several idyllic camp sites. Most are bush camps except for Orpheus, which has a National Park camp ground.

All of the islands are under the control of either the National Parks or the Aboriginal community, and permission to camp must be obtained prior to departure from the mainland.

Jumping off points for the Palms are Taylor's Beach, Forrest Beach and Balgal. All suffer the usual north Queensland problem of lack of water at low tide, The turnoff to Taylor's Beach is from the Halifax to Ingham road. Forrest Beach, also known as Allingham Ram, is past Allingham in She-Oak Street. Balgal turn off is near Rollingstone some 50 kilometres north of Townsville. Balgal's ramp is the popular one for Townsville folk, even though a rock bar across the mouth of the creek makes it vital to ensure the tide's height exceeds your boat draught before attempting to enter.

One cautionary note regarding the nature of the coastline, in the entire Townsville area. The mountain ranges are well back from the coast, leaving the actual coastline itself flat and featureless. so, when returning from the offshore islands, it is quite difficult to sight creek mouths. Locals always depart the creek on a compass bearing to a fixed point (a prominent feature on one of the islands, for example). On return, it's then a matter of locating that reference point and steering a back bearing to the creek entrance. Visitors are advised to seek local guidance before proceeding offshore, and this is especially important around Townsville. Then you can enjoy your taste of paradise without hassle.

The Palm Island group offers the full spectrum of fishing options. The islands are coral-fringed, providing residence for all the reef species. Pelagics are more common on the outer side of the islands. Small boats fish there if sea conditions allow.

Points and headlands with a passing current are always worth investigation. Lure casting around 'bommies', coral outcrops and isolated rocks can provide spectacular action with queenfish and other members of the trevally family. Don't be surprised if a 'reefie' like a coral trout nails your popper when worked around the shallows.

The Rattlesnake Islands are closer to Townsville, close enough, in fact, for some locals with larger boats to prefer launching at the all tide ramp in Townsville Harbour, then running the 20 odd nautical miles to the Rattlesnakes by water. The ramp at Saunders Beach has the usual low tide dramas caused by sandbars at the mouth of the creek. Mackerel of all species, Spaniards, 'spotties' and greys or broadbars, are the popular target around the Rattlesnake Islands. Good reef fishing is also to be found here, and night fishing is productive if the weather is good enough.

Herald Island has a beautiful sandspit where you can stretch your legs is quite protected and makes a shelter when waiting for the tide to allow return to the ramp.

Townsville's northern beaches all produce good catches of bream, whiting and flathead through the Dry season, especially around creek mouths, when the onshore winds ease.

Ross Creek is perhaps more recognisable as Townsville's harbour. It has the best boat ramp in the district, able to handle any trailerboat with ease. Fishing from the man-made stone walls is quite productive. Fish don't leap onto your hook - astute thinking and a little hard work are necessary, but nonetheless good catches come from the harbour, including some boasting-size barramundi.

Ross River, in contrast, retains its natural sandbanks and extensive mangroves. Big tides move strong currents through the mouth of the Ross, so stages of the tidal cycle with smaller variations make for better fishing. All the estuarine fishes can be caught at the mouth of the river and upstream. Live baiting at night is the most successful method. A good ramp services Ross River from Drey Street in South Townsville. Big tides move a strong current past this ramp and, as a result, the end of the ramp drops sharply into deep water.

Cleveland Bay, south of the mouth of the Ross River, is a significant area of untouched mangrove. There are many creeks in the Bay and a couple of large ones over in the 'corner' opposite the Ross River mouth are well worth the crossing. Due to the shallow water a nasty chop must be treated with respect. Prawns are prolific in the Bay and its feeder creeks and fishing is good.

Cape Cleveland is within reach of the Townsville Harbour ramp. Isolated rocky outcrops off Cape Cleveland have claimed their share of boats over the years as in calm weather they are almost invisible. The rocks known as 2ft Rock, 20ft Rock, 4ft Rock and (the larger one) Salamander Reef and two rocky islets to the south, Bray and Bare Islands, have produced several world record catches. Big trevally, queenfish and several species of mackerel frequent Cape Cleveland and its rocky outcrops.

Trolling and drifting baits are the most common local methods. The stout of heart may try lure casting around the rocks.

Magnetic Island is the offshore suburb of Townsville. The outside coast of Magnetic is productive when weather allows and there is bottom fishing in some of the sheltered bays. Mackerel and queenfish roam the points. Watch the shallow reef between the island and the mainland on your way over.

The Haughton River/Baratta Creek system, situated between the Cape Cleveland and Cape Bowling Green, is yet another extensive area of pristine mangrove wetlands surrounded by a tidal creeks. Ramps give access to Bowling Green Bay. Travelling south from Townsville the first is the Haughton River ramp. The turn off to this one is approximately 70 kilometres south of Townsville, just south of the tiny town of Giru. The second is on Baratta Creek, turn off to Lockinvar. The third is on Morris Creek turn off (often called Morrisey's Creek) just past the Haughton River bridge on the main road heading south.

Bowling Green Bay has excellent estuary fishing. Mangrove jacks are the most common catch in Bowling Green Bay. A few barramundi are about too, along with the usual threadfin, queenfish, grunter and trevallies.

Morris (or Morrisey's) Creek provides an alternate means of getting to Cape Bowling Green. Take a good look at the mouth as you exit, and take a compass bearing on which to return.

Larger boats prefer to run down from Townsville to Bowling Green, a distance of almost 70 kilometres. The trip down can be a long slog. The south-east trades prevail during the Dry season when billfishing is at its best at Bowling Green, Trailerboats can fish Bowling Green, but the run down by water is out of the question in all but calm weather. Morris Creek is a far safer proposition despite hassles getting in and out of the creek.

The spit at Bowling Green offers an overnight anchorage. It would be possible to camp there with a small boat if permission could be obtained from the National Parks and Wildlife Service.

Billfish off Cape Bowling Green are found anywhere from in close, to the deep side of the spit, to over 20 kilometres out. Look for birds holding or feeding over bait schools, or find the bait schools themselves with an echo sounder. The locally developed deep-drifting of live baits is effective at Bowling Green.

A young angler poses beside his pending Australian Junior Game Fishing Record. The black marlin was caught from Cape Bowling Green, 70 kilometres south from Townsville, which is one of Queensland's best billfish grounds.

Burdekin to Bowen

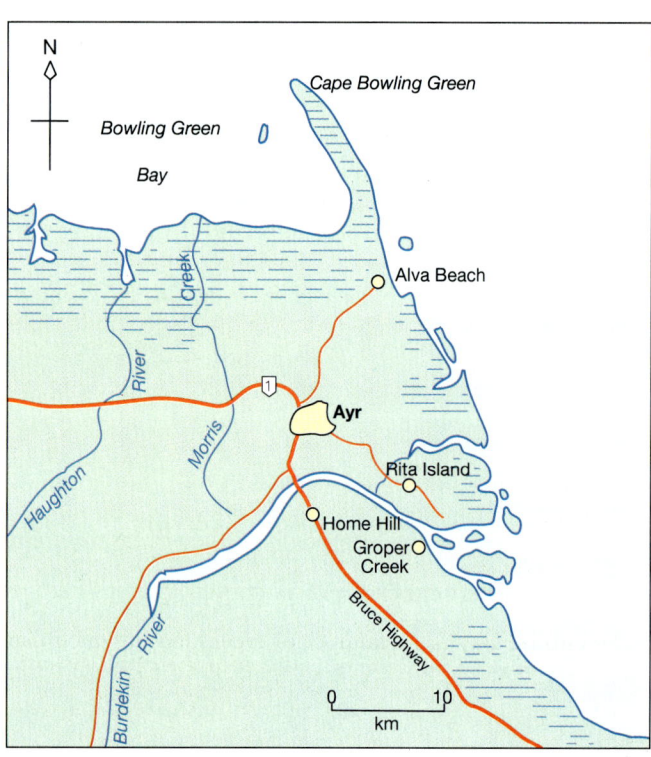

All through this book we've been advocating seeking local advice. For the area covered in this chapter, local advice is doubly important. Virtually all of the area, apart from projections like Cape Upstart, is saline mudflats.

On these flats around the mouth of the Burdekin, and the creeks around Bowen, access to launch sites is almost always by secondary gravel or formed earth 'roads', and a heavy shower can have conventional-drive vehicles slithering around on 'sludge'. Landholders may not allow access to much of the creek fishing around Bowen.

Ask for information. Locals will always guard their secret spots, but are usually pleased to help a visitornot get into trouble if approached in a friendly manner. Try the tackle and bait shops and the service stations selling fishing aids.

The mouth of the Burdekin is serviced by several ramps. Where the Burdekin meets the sea it shifts into a maze of channels. There is always the peril of getting stuck on a mudbank at the lower stages of the tide and in many sections of the delta, movement by boat at low tide is impossible. Nonetheless there is quite good fishing for tropical estuarine fishes if you get some local knowledge.

There are boat ramps at Wallace Landing on Peake Road in Yellow Gin Creek. and two at the little settlement of Groper Creek. Groper Creek, has all facilities, fuel, bait and food. Plantation Creek ramp and Ocean Creek ramp

are both reached via Airdmillan; Plantation Creek has lights and a picnic area, Ocean Creek has no facilities at all. Low water is a problem at both. Another ramp is on Hodder Road at Rita Island at Hell Hole Landing.

Cape Upstart is roughly halfway between Bowen and Ayr. It offers creek fishing, 'pot' fishing on the flats of Upstart Bay and some fast-paced action on pelagics off the Cape itself. In a word, Upstart is one heck of a fishing spot. Jumping off point for Cape Upstart is the Malongle Creek Boat Club on the Creek which flows into Upstart Bay. The ramp belongs to the club, but is available for public use. Creeks in the Bay are worth prospecting for barramundi and are reliable producers of mangrove jacks, estuary cod and other creek fish.

Locals have built weekend shacks along the sheltered western coast of Upstart Bay. Beaches here are idyllic, although the tide retreats a fair way. Cruising yachts and large trailer boats use Cape Upstart's lee as an anchorage.

Cape Upstart is rocky with a rugged, weathered face on east and north. You can get a shock at how strong the winds are when you poke your nose out from behind the sheltering Cape. Fishing for pelagics off the exposed parts of Cape Upstart can be mind-blowing stuff. A large rock called the 'Bun' rises from the sea a couple of hundred metres from the point of Cape Upstart. Between the Bun and the Cape, water movement creates rips and current lines where Spanish mackerel, queenfish and several tuna species feed.

Tossing lures around rocks close to a point or 'bommie' is likely to produce queenfish, giant trevally or even a mackerel if the point has deep water with current working across it. Bait drifting along current lines offshore, and trolling with rigged baits or lures, are all successful techniques at Upstart.

Cape Upstart and Bowen have some of the better, if least 'famous', fishing along the whole Queensland coast.

The salt flats at Bowen bake in the warm months, but the fishing is equally hot.

Abbot Point, between Cape Upstart and Bowen, has a 2.6 kilometre-long ship-loading jetty. Fishing isn't allowed from the jetty itself. A boat brought up by water from Bowen opens the door to fishing here.

Abbot Point jetty in deepish water attracts numbers of pelagics. Cobia can be added to the list of the expected trevallies, queenies and mackerels and good fish around the jetty if you can get them out from the jetty pylons.

Euri Creeks' network, further south towards Bowen and some 10 kilometres from the nearest ramp at Grey's Bay, is a little unusual. You can get into the creek on the lower parts of the tide. Euri Creek has mangrove jacks, fingermark, grunter, some nice pikey bream and mud crabs. Barramundi are scarce. It also has several yabby banks for bait pumping.

Live yabbies or small live herring, mullet or whiting caught in a cast net are top baits around Bowen. Big 2 to 3 kilogram tarpon are a bonus for sportfishers fishing such baits down near the bottom of the holes. Sicklefish are yet another tasty 'oddity' found here.

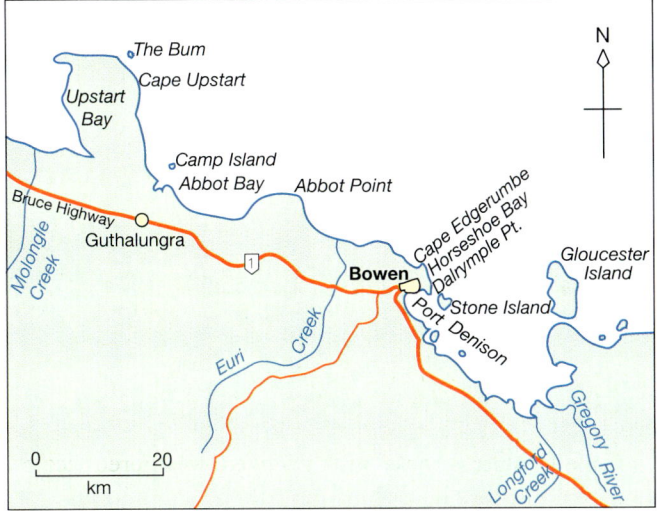

The Mackerel Patches, north of Euri Creek, is a local mackerel hotspot aptly named. All the mackerels, Spanish, spotted, Queensland school and the 'grey' or broadbar, move through this area at times.

You can launch straight into open water at Grey's Beach ramp. It issheltered from the prevailing south-easterlies by Cape Edgecumbe, but is unuseable in a northerly. Low tide causes the usual problem. Launching here is the best way to fish Cape Edgecumbe and Horseshoe Bay.

Massive baitfish schools hold in the Bowen area through what southern anglers know as early summer. Northerners call it the build-up to the Wet, although Bowen doesn't have a Wet of the same magnitude as Cairns.

These baitfish concentrations explain the vast numbers of predatory pelagics present. Bowen is a lure caster's dream. Surface-skipping poppers, in particular, produce memorable fishing.

Cape Edgecumbe and Innaminka Rocks, off the caravan park Horseshoe Bay, are but one place in the Bowen Region where popper tossing can be mind-blowing. Bottom fishing is worthwhile here too.

Bowen's boat harbour, (officially known as Port Denison), has excellent ramps, one on the east and one on the west side of the harbour. They can handle any trailered boat and are useable at all tide heights. Big tarpon frequent the boat harbour and a few jacks and

bream can be found along the man-made rock walls. An old slipway at Dalrymple Point and rocks nearby are a good landbased location with opportunities of tangling with mackerel, queenfish and occasionally giant trevally. Lure casting with poppers or live baiting under a float are popular with local people fishing from Dalrymple Point.

Bowen town jetty always seems to have a few locals trying their luck. The odd big mackerel is taken from here. Squid move in at night. Some people use these for bait, most are eaten. Bait ('sards' or 'herring') may also be jigged or cast netted off the jetty.

Stone, Thongs and Pool Islands are relatively close inshore and within easy reach of Bowen boat harbour. Stone is more or less straight out from the harbour, Thongs and Poole Islands are a little further south. All of these hold baitfish, mackerel, tuna, queenfish, and trevally. Look for current lines for trolling, and work poppers around points and 'bommies'. Bait fishing is good. Shoalwater Bay, on the northern side of Stone Island, has a number of giant trevally and queenfish haunted bommies. North Head Island between Stone Island and the mainland can also be productive and the underwater reefs around the islands holds reef species.

Edgecumbe Bay has a number of creeks, all of which fish well. Getting in and out is strictly a high tide proposition, but once 'in' some have deep holes which can be fished at the lower stages of the tide. Overland access to creeks in Edgecumbe Bay has been stopped by the landholder. Live baits such as yabbies and small fish are best here. Competent lure fishers will score well off the snags.

Gregory River and Longford Creek, in the 'corner' of Edgecumbe Bay, are both quite large waterways with extensive flats at the mouth blocking low water access. These are possibly the best bet for a barramundi in the Bowen region.

Offshore from Bowen the fishing gets even better. Nare's Rock and Middle Islands are en route from Port Denison to Gloucester Island. Distance from the ramps eases fishing pressure and the fish are correspondingly bigger and more plentiful. Queensland National Parks and Wildlife Service maintain a camping area on Gloucester Island (permits available in Bowen). On the opposite side of Gloucester Island is Rattray Island with 30 fathoms of blue water as close in as Nare's Rock. Nare's Rock to Rattray Island is a fishing paradise. All you need is a good boat to get there.

Whitsunday Islands

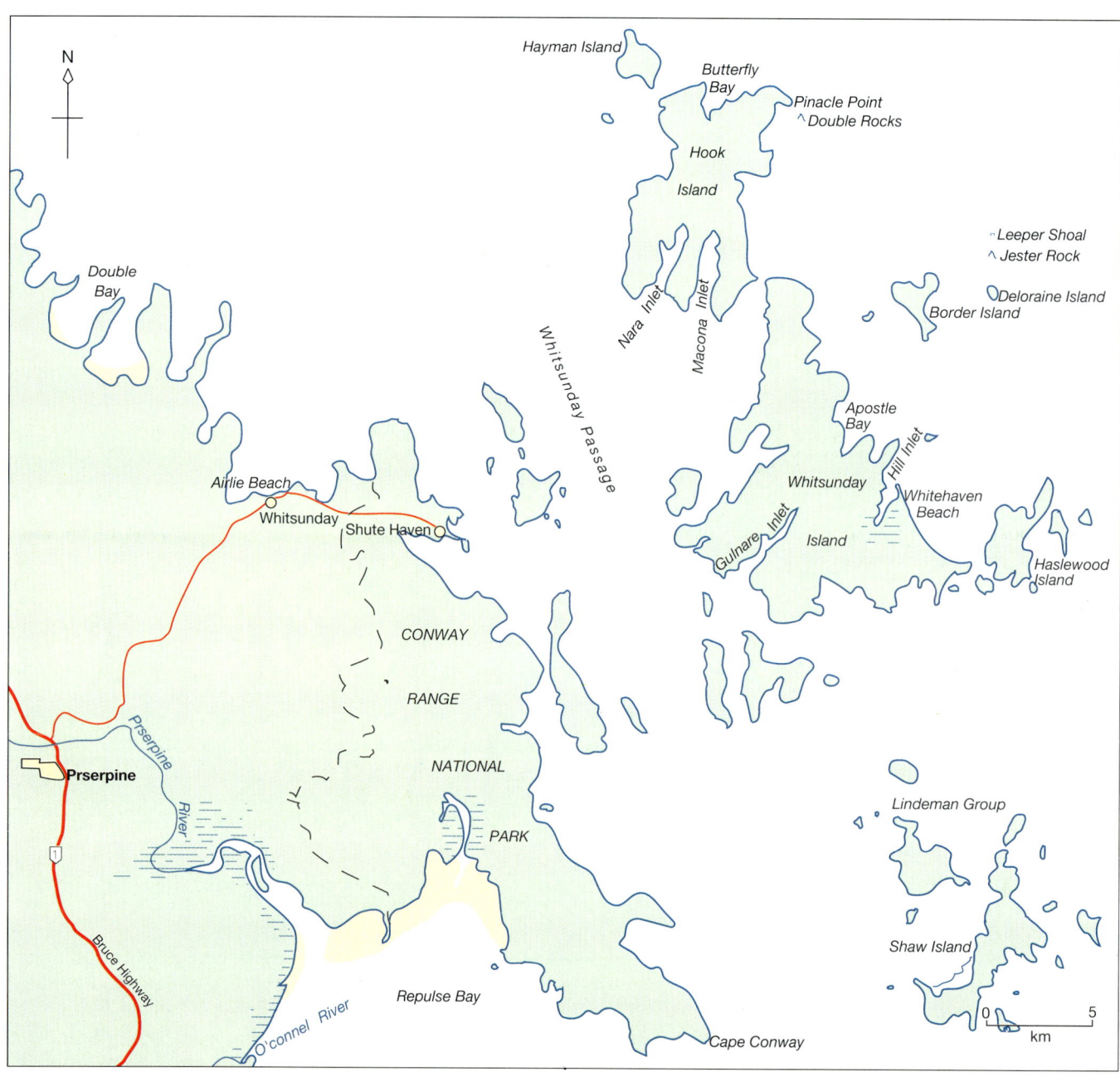

For a place known as one of the world's great cruising grounds it is surprising that fishing around the Whitsundays is largely untouched.

No one person could hope to know the Whitsunday's fishing well, since the area encompasses such a huge amount of fish habitat. Trying to cover the region, and do justice to it, in a few pages is impossible, but we can look at a few areas where the fishing is reliable and leave the rest for readers to discover for themselves.

A boat is a prerequisite You could fish from the island's shores - if you could get there. Or you could take a water taxi from Shute Harbour to Hook Island, set-up camp, and walk overland to the prominent rocky points to fish bream to billfish, but this has never been done.

There are two proven options to fishing the Whitsundays. The first is to trailer a boat there, launch it from Airlie Beach or Shute Harbour, and explore the islands. Anchorages abound. If the boat couldn't be comfortably lived aboard, a lightweight camp set-up in Nara Inlet, or one of the other National Parks and

Wildlife Service's approved camp sites, would make a good home base. The second alternative is to bareboat charter a large vessel from operators at Shute Harbour, and use it either as a fishing boat or a mothership for smaller trailerboats.

A third alternative could be to stay at one of the many resorts. Many of these run 'fishing' trips, but they are designed to cater for the casual angler.

Inside the Whitsundays the water is reasonably sheltered, and a small boat would be satisfactory in many areas. A larger 5.5 to 6 metre-plus boat becomes necessary in crossing the Whitsunday Passage between the islands and the mainland; around the passages between the islands where opposing wind and tides can build nasty seas; and along the eastern 'outside' of the islands, which is exposed to north Queensland's persistent onshore winds.

Boat ramps are situated at Canonvale, as you approach Airlie Beach on the road from Proserpine, in Airlie Beach itself, and at Shute Harbour. Of these three, the Shute Harbour ramp is the only all-weather, all-wind ramp, tucked away as it is inside the harbour. The others are exposed to one wind direction or another, and even the ramp at Shute can suffer from surge in strong winds. At the time of writing, there are several developments underway along the Whitsunday coast which may have added to boating facilities ashore. When completed these may offer better launching than those listed.

Airlie Beach/Shute Harbour, the stepping of points for the Whitsundays, have reasonable fishing along the shorelines. The wharves and jetties in Shute Harbour fish particularly well; the masses of baitfish cluster under them. If boats aren't using the jetties, live baiting or lure fishing is worth a go. Big giant trevally and queenfish are thick, and bottom species such as black jew, cods and emperors are there. Longtail (northern bluefin) tuna are another line-stretching inhabitant of Shute Harbour. You might even line-bait a barramundi from the jetty.

Fishing around the Whitsunday Islands has two faces. The inlets and anchorages of the islands mainly have small fish, trevallies, particularly the giant, big eye, golden and diamond, and their relatives queenfish and dart; the little stripie, sometimes called Spanish flag, provides fun fishing on a single-handed threadline 'flick stik'.

On the Eastern side of the islands big mackerel, giant trevally, big queenfish, barracuda and even small black marlin and sailfish live. Prime billfish water is on the established ground to the north and east of Hayman Island. This has been fished for many years and is a known quantity. The east Australian current is obstructed by Hayman Island, forms eddies holding classic baitfish pools so beloved of billfish and other big pelagics.

Between Hayman and Hook Islands runs a deep channel noted for racing tides. The point at the western edge of the popular anchorage in Butterfly Bay is a focus

The Whitsunday Islands lend themselves to bareboat or skipper-yourself chartering. The fishing can be quite spectacular.

'point' where current streams off, holding baitfish and predators. Huge giant trevally frequent such points in the Whitsundays late in the year. Spanish mackerel, some of which come in XOS-sizes, prefer the cooler months. No fishing is allowed inside Butterfly Bay by the Great Barrier Reef Marine Park Authority.

Pinnacle Point, the easternmost projection of Hook Island, is a rocky promontory weathered by both wind and tide. Two rocks, known as Double Rocks, south-east of Pinnacle Point denote one of the Whitsundays better pelagic grounds. Weather can be a problem though.

Between Hook and Whitsunday Island Hook Passage is subject to fast tidal currents. No fishing is allowed in the immediate vicinity of Hook Island Observatory, however the fishing in the passage region can be of a good enough standard to rival fishing in any coral reef area.

East of this passage lie Border and Deloraine Islands. Fishing is prohibited around Border Island, a Marine National Park 'B' zone.

Deloraine Island has a coral-covered rocky extension of the strata forming the island extending visibly for some distance away from a nice little beach. Deep water separates this coral fringe from Jester Rock, a couple of hundred metres north where the rock breaks water at low tide. Leeper Shoal, a further extension of the rocky spine, is a kilometer or so away does not but is readily distinguishable by the upwellings and current lines it causes.

Minstrel Rocks mark the edge of the coral fringe on the island proper. Pelagics are always to be found in the deep water. Casting lures, especially big, noisy poppers, up onto the shallows and working them back over the edge into deep water will take anything from Spaniards to queenfish and giant trevally known locally as 'kitchen tables'.

Good bottom fishing for reef fish, including the prized coral trout and red emperor, is also available here. Apostle Bay on the eastern side of Hook Island is the closest anchorage to Deloraine Island Hill Inlet.

Hill Inlet is more a protected anchorage than Apostle Bay, but dries at the mouth. Yachts and larger boats take the bottom further up the inlet at low tide, but more than enough water can be found to float an outboard or sterndrive able to, tilt its leg up out of the water. Light-tackle fishing is the forte of Hill Inlet, with rocky outcrops just inside the mouth and mangroves, rock bars and snags further up the inlet producing the full spectrum of tropical estuary sportfish. Reliable reports of bonefish being caught here are on record. Whitehaven Beach stretches south of Hill Inlet to the gap between Whitsunday Island and Haslewood Island, otherwise known as Solway Pass.

Haslewood Island is a top area for pelagics, but sections are closed to fishing by the Marine Parks Authority.

The 'inside' or western coast of the Whitsunday group is, as already stated, largely light-tackle fishing for smaller fish. Points sticking-out into tidal flow and gutters draining flats over a coral ledge are two of the better places to toss a lure or bait for the myriad of small trevally and queenfish. Fishing deeper inlets such as Nara, Macona and Gulnare is much the same as fishing a river or tidal estuary with the coral edges as a bonus. Reefs on the 'inside' of the Whitsundays that appear barren in broad daylight can be productive at night.

Repulse Bay tucks in behind Conway National Park, with the mouth of the Proserpine River entering in the top north-western corner. The O'Connell River also flows into Repulse Bay. Two ramps give access to Repulse Bay, both with no water at low tide. One is in the Proserpine River, off the road to Conway at Wilson's Beach. The other is further south (if to the north of the O'Connel's mouth) at New Beach; turn off the highway to Lethebrook.

All the estuary fishes, including the mighty and much sought-after barramundi, are resident in the rivers and creeks of Repulse Bay which, being open to the south-east trade winds, gets very rough at times. When the weather is good and the tide high enough to launch a boat to open water from the ramps, a trip across to Cape Conway will find good fishing.

Cape Conway and the offshore rocks, Ripple Rocks and Cape Rock, really fire on pelagics.

The Lindeman group, and Lindeman Island, are 12 kilometres past Cape Conway. Queensland National Parks and Wildlife Service maintain camping areas on islands throughout the southern Whitsunday and Lindeman Island groups. A few of these have small boat anchorages. Check with Queensland National Parks and Wildlife Service when arranging your camping permit if intent on taking your own boat out to the islands.

Above: Spinning the flats in Hill Inlet, on the eastern side of Whitsunday Island.
Left: Fishing for Spanish mackerel off Whitsunday Island.

Mackay

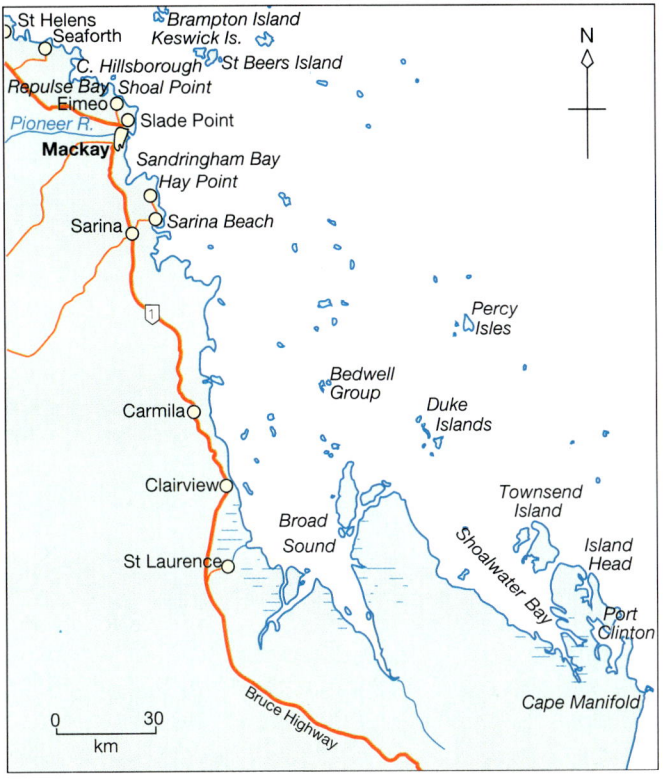

This is an area of big tides of five to six metres. Broadsound and Shoalwater Bay at the lower or southern end of this section regularly experience 8.5 metre tides.

This takes coming to terms with. A fishing spot with 3 metres of water at high tide near Mackay, may (and often does) have 3 metre high dry sandbanks at low tide! Down in the turbid expanses of Broadsound and Shoalwater Bay, creeks can have roaring tidal bores. Tidal currents in some places have to be seen to be believed.

For most of the Queensland coast there is the problem of no water at ramps at low tide, and creek mouths. These hassles take on a whole new meaning in Mackay.

Despite this local folk speak more confidently of catching barramundi here than in other better known parts of north Queensland.

One of the more accessible areas of the Queensland coast between St. Helens and Sarina are tiny coastal towns are tucked away on every decent piece of land. People go straight past with sights fixed elsewhere. They should pause and take a good look around.

St Helens, the northernmost of Mackay's 'satellite' coastal towns, is reached from a turn off between Calen and Kolijo. St. Helen's ramp is at Carpetsnake Point. From here we'll take it as read that all ramps lead to dry sand at low tide. Off St Helens are a number of small islets

frequented by mackerel and tuna, and there is some bottom fishing. A mangrove complex to the south has estuary fishing and mud crabs. Seaforth and the nearby Halliday Bay and Ball Bay is one area where a boat is unnecessary as there's good beach, rock and creek fishing. Some beaches are even steep enough to have water (and fishing) at low tide.

Rocky McBrides Point, is near the resort of Halliday Bay. Take care when walking around on the exposed oysters at low tide. Higher tides make for easier fishing Tossing lures (poppers especially) or using floating baits (live or dead) off the two rocky points each side of Halliday Bay produces queenfish and trevally. Other pelagics may also be found.

Off Seaforth are quite a few islands. Rabbit Island is the largest and there's also Newry, Acacia, Outer Newry, Mausoleum, Rocky and the Fisherman's Reef, and Croaker Rocks. Mackerel and reef fish are found around the outside of the islands, estuary species such as bream, whiting, flathead and grunter inside and in the creeks. These creeks also produce mud crabs.

The ramp at Seaforth in Victor Creek is the closest departure point for Brampton and other islands in the Cumberland Group. The distances involved require a 6 metres-plus boat, and many local people prefer to launch at the all-tide ramp in Mackay Harbour.

The Cumberland Islands, (including Brampton), offer excellent fishing for pelagics, small billfish. Reef fishing is particularly good at night. Queensland National Parks maintains camping areas at Carlisle Island and Goldsmith Island, further north in the Sir James Smith Group.

Cape Hillsborough is reached from access roads leading to Seaforth/Halliday Bay. Two roads lead here, one turning off at Mt Ossa for those travelling south, and the better road 21 kilometres north of Mackay at Yakapari. Cape Hillsborough has a small National Park, a camp ground and a resort; a lovely place, a favourite with locals and visitors alike. At low tide a spit of land between the Cape and Wedge Island dries making it possible to walk across to the island and fish the high tide.

Fishing off the rocks on Cape Hillsborough is a good way to take pelagics or reef fish, but a boat is better. With a boat some excellent fishing a little way offshore is within reach, both pelagic and reef species abound. The bay south of Cape Hillsborough, Sand Bay, produces all the northern estuary fish and both barramundi and threadfin are a reasonable proposition.

43

There's reliable barramundi fishing around Mackay, so long as you are prepared to hike upriver to find holes like this one.

Shoal Point, Eimeo and Slade Point closer to Mackay have rocky points where spinning or bait fishing for queenfish, giant trevally and other pelagics is worthwhile. Offshore, queenfish and travelling schools of tuna and mackerel attract predatory birds.

Mackay Harbour has the best boat ramp in the district for large trailerboats headed wide to the reefs and islands, it shouldn't be overlooked by landbased anglers.

The harbour walls are popular fishing spots with local residents seeking everything from bream to Spanish mackerel. Jewfish, queenfish, grunter, barracuda, tarpon, mangrove jacks, trevally, tuna and reef fish.

Flat Top and Round Top Islands are only a couple of kilometres from the Harbour and the excellent ramp in the Pioneer River in Mackay itself. Huge schools of tunas and mackerel of several species move through this area and come well within reach of a vee-bottom boat of 4 metres or more. Boats of this size are commonly used by people living in Mackay because they can cope with some wind chop and can be used close inshore for pursuing pelagics and aren't too big to be 'walked' through the shallows. The Pioneer River almost drains at low tide but a channel from the boat ramp to the mouth may be navigable to small boats. Local guidance is needed. Hossack's Tackle Shop in Mackay publishes an excellent fishing guide booklet which visitors will find invaluable.

A fish often encountered but rarely landed around Mackay is the oyster cracker or snub-nosed dart. A pugnacious and speedy fish, oyster crackers average around 2 to 3 kilogrammes, and are usually hooked accidentally by people fishing beaches for whiting using yabbies for bait. They are similar to the Atlantic permit made famous by U.S. angling publications.

Offshore from Mackay St Bees is 30 only kilometres away. Within 50 kilometres are Goldsmith, Linne, Tinsmith, Brampton and Carlisle (almost joined at low tide), Cockermouth, Wigton, Keswick, and Scawfell Islands, and a number of smaller islets and submerged reef shoals. That's a lot of good reef and pelagic fishing country. Scattered amongst the islands are secure anchorages where a boat can moor overnight. A large seaworthy boat is needed to fish these wider reefs and islands requires. The distances involved make a two day trip attractive, and allow night fishing while out there.

A reef fish southern anglers might be surprised to find here is the snapper. The reefs and islands just described, are the northern limit of their range.

Sandringham Bay, south of Mackay, is only accessible by boat from the big harbour at Mackay at Half Tide, or a small ramp at Dunrock (turn off left at Chelora 14 kilometres south of Mackay). Sandringham Bay is another reasonable proposition for threadfin, barramundi and estuary fish.

Hay Point has two huge coal loading facilities, which are closed to public access. Boats can be launched in the tug harbour three kilometres away at Half Tide. Hay Reef lies between the ship loaders. Jew and reef fish.are consistent.

Salonika, Grasstree and the Sarina Beaches, east of Sarina, are the last of the small coastal resort towns south of Mackay. All offer beach, rock and mangrove creek fishing. There may be some barramundi.

Cape Palmerston has a small national park with two National Park and Wildlife Services camp sites. A four-wheel drive is necessary for access. One track runs along the beach and the other overland. The beach route is the easier. Mangroves on the western side of the Cape provide the estuary fishing. Temple Island close inshore, and the rocky headland of the Cape itself, have good bottom fishing, trolling for pelagic, and lure casting and bait fishing around points and protruding bommies.

Broadsound. Fishing here is not recommended without first seeking local advice.

Boat ramps at Carmila, Clairview Beach and St Lawrence give access to the Port of St Lawrence, a number of islands offshore, including the Percy Islands 80 kilometres away, the Duke Group and the Bedwells and, of course, the vast expanses of mangrove wetlands in the twin bays.

Shoalwater Bay is part of a military training area and closed to public access.

Capricornia

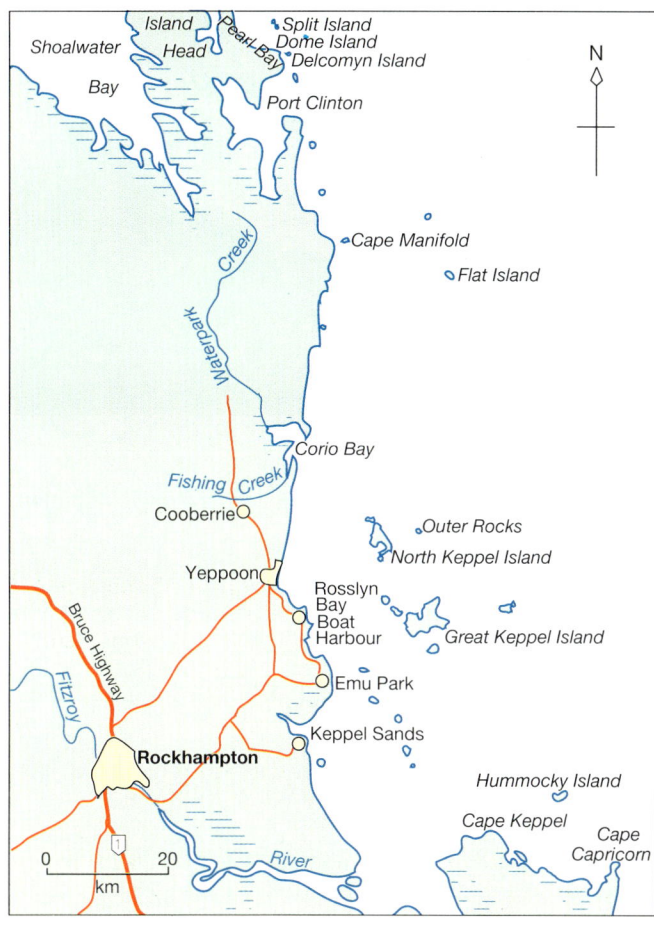

fishing. Red emperor, coral trout, the sweetlip and emperors, big Spanish mackerel, giant trevally, snapper and even an odd stray yellowtail kingfish are the usual fare. This is about as far north as yellowtail kings range. A parasite infests yellowtail kings north of Coffs Harbour, and makes them unpalatable. Cobia are one of the better table fish, and are commoner here than most other places. They move through Capricornia in summer.

The first place accessible by road south of the military area is Corio Bay, reached off the Byfield Road to Corbett's Landing. There are two launch sites, the upstream one, being mud, is only suitable for small boats.

Corio Bay has two large creeks, Fishing Creek and Waterpark Creek. Both are shallow and sandy towards the open waters of the Bay. A prominent rock stands in the open water after Waterpark Creek enters the bay. A rock bar also guards the entrance to Fishing Creek. The channel can wander so care is necessary.

Corio Head shelters the northern side of Corio Bay. Rocky fringes flank the headland with deep water beside the rocks where the tidal currents move in and out of the bay. Several rock 'bommies' off the point at the exit, and several more to the north past Little Corio Bay on Waterpark Point, are worth tossing a popper around for queenfish and giant trevally. Trolling offshore and in the mouth of Corio Bay will find mackerel, tuna, and trevally closer to the rocks.

Fishing Creek and Waterpark Creek hold large stocks of whiting, bream and flathead. More exotic fish, threadfin, grunter, tarpon, mangrove jacks, queenfish, several trevally species and the much sought after barramundi can also be expected in the creeks. Corio Bay has many yabby banks where bait can be pumped, and the same shallows provide live baits for a cast or bait net. Schools of herring, when located, will respond to bait jigs.

Anglers with a four-wheel drive may wish to continue on up the Byfield Road, where a turn off to the right at the end of the pine plantations leads back to the coast at Stockyard Point and Five Rocks. The immediate surrounds of Yeppoon itself, where some local trawlers are based, produces an odd barramundi on lures or live bait at the mouth at night.

Double Head and the rock walls at Rosslyn Bay boat harbour have bottom fish, including black jew and estuary cod, pelagics such as Queensland school or, as they're known here, 'doggie' mackerel, and some excellent bream.
The Causeway Lake, south of Rosslyn Bay, is renowned

The Shoalwater Bay Military Training Area stretches into Capricornia. Access is prohibited overland.

Boats able to make the coastal passage from Rosslyn Bay boat harbour near Yeppoon can fish the area. Sheltered anchorages in Island Head Creek, Port Clinton and in Pearl Bay are used by cruising yachts. The Army allows boats to enter anchorages but may ask them to move on if 'war games' are planned.

From Rosslyn Bay to Island Head Creek, is about 100 kilometres so this is no place for small trailerboats. A larger vessel, however, opens the way to a rarely fished area. A smaller dinghy is essential to prospect the tidal arms and creeks of Island Head Creek and Port Clinton.

Split Dome and Delcomyn Islands, off Pearl Bay, and the Clara Group closer to Island Head Creek, have fishing the way it used to be for both reef fish and pelagics.

Perforated and Flat Islands, east of Cape Manifold and approximately 55 kilometres from Rosslyn Bay, are about as far as trailerboats should venture. Both offer superlative

for good catches of bream, whiting and flathead. Barramundi are also taken here.

Off Rosslyn Bay are a number of islands reachable by seaworthy trailerboats over 4.5 metres in length. Rosslyn Bay has a wide concrete ramp suitable for trailer boats of any size. A lock-up car park operates nearby, where vehicles and trailers may be left safely while over at the islands for a few days.

Great Keppel's resort advertising has made it a household word. Nearby, Wapparaburra Haven has cabin-style accommodation and a camping area. Small boats anchored here are secure unless a thunderstorm or strong westerly winds push waves into the anchorage.

North Keppel Island has holiday cabins and National Parks have a camping area on beautiful Considine Beach where anchorage is like that at Great Keppel, except that a tidal creek may be entered at high tide with outboard tilted up, and once in there the boat is quite safe (high and dry except at the very top of the tide but safe nonetheless).

Around the Keppels are numerous rocks and islets. Inside the Keppels the water is fairly shallow, and subject to an infamous wind chop. 'Doggie' or Queensland school mackerel, and spotted mackerel, move through Keppel Bay in huge schools through winter. Longtail tuna are often mixed in with them.

On the outside of the Keppels the water is oceanic and blue. This is where the Spaniards, and cobia are to be found. Bommies are always worth tossing a lure at, and around the Keppels it's a guessing game whether a big nasty giant trevally, a cobia or a Spanish will get to it first.

Conical Rocks, to the north of North Keppel, is a top trolling and bait-drifting spot. Outer Rock, east of North Keppel, is worth trolling, lure casting along the shore, bait fishing or bottom fishing. Similarly, Man and Wife Rocks north of Great Keppel, Barren and Child Islands east of Great Keppel, Bald Rock closer to Great Keppel to the east, and Egg Rock a little south of Barren and Child, are all top pelagic and bottom fishing locations. Except for Barren and Child Islands, which are about 30 kilometres from Rosslyn Bay, all of these are within 25 kilometres of the boat harbour.

A couple of days camped on either Great or North Keppel is an ideal way to experience Capricornia at its best, and the only way to fish these many locations effectively. The Coast Guard station at Rosslyn Bay operates a log for boats out around the islands, and there is a seven-day-a-week radio watch maintained in the Keppels region by a combination of volunteer base stations and the Coast Guard.

Cooroooman Creek, south of Emu Park and south of Yeppoon, is accessible by road on either side of the

A solid kawakawa or mackerel tuna taken from the Keppel Islands. A red-fleshed fish, they make excellent bait.

estuary. A road leading south from Emu Park leads to a public boat ramp on the north branch of Cooroooman Creek.

From Emu Park take the road direct back to Rockhampton (not via Yeppoon) to a turnoff to the left to Keppel Sands on the south bank of the Cooroooman Creek estuary. It has two ramps; a small boat-only launch site in Cooroooman Creek, and one suited to larger craft, but with low tide hassles, in Pumpkin Creek.

The Cooroooman Creek system comprises Emu Park Creek, Cooroooman Creek, Cawarral Creek, Spring Creek, Miles Creek and Deep Creek. Using camping areas at either Emu Park or Keppel Sands as a base, Cooroooman Creek will keep you occupied for a few days. Bream, whiting and flathead are common, as are the yabbies to catch them. Grunter, threadfin and barramundi are there too, and although they may take a little effort, good specimens are regularly taken.

After a long journey down the Queensland coast, we're just about to cross the Tropic of Capricorn, but just before we leave the Tropics, the mighty Fitzroy River, fed by the Dawson and the McKenzie, to name just two larger tributaries, must be mentioned.

The Fitzroy is a turbid river, so it doesn't look 'nice'. A barrage at Rockhampton blocks passage of barramundi upstream into vast areas of water, which are now fishless except for forktail catfish. Yellowbelly country is reached further up in the Dawson and McKenzie country. Below the barrage, the Fitzroy still holds a copious population of the ubiquitous catfish, however, both barramundi and the species of threadfin known as king salmon, aren't too hard to find. No fishing is permitted in the vicinity of the barrage to prevent slaughter of fish congregated there by the obstruction to upstream migration.

Gladstone to Bundaberg

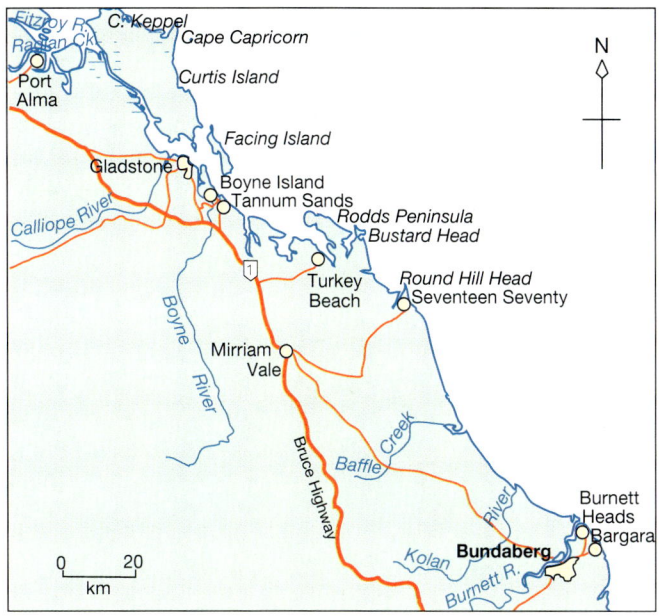

Between Gladstone and Rockhampton is a narrow passage known as The Narrows, running between Curtis Island and the mainland. The mouth of the Fitzroy is a huge delta, with the Calliope River, the Boyne River and countless tidal creeks running into The Narrows from both Curtis Island and the mainland making a huge mangrove maze that stretched almost unbroken for over 125 kilometres from Cattle Point on the north of the Fitzroy mouth south to the tiny town of Seventeen Seventy behind Round Hill Head.

Mangroves are the nursery for marine life. This section of coast is also in the cross-over zone between tropical and temperate fish species.

The Narrows is perhaps the last reliable place for finding barramundi, although technically they range to the Mary River. On the offshore reefs, yellowtail kingfish and snapper are becoming more prevalent, albeit mixed with coral trout, red emperor and various sweetlips from the north whenever the east coast current keeps water temperatures up. Jewfish (mulloway) mix with both the black jew of the north and silver jew of the south.

Port Alma, (turn off the Bruce Highway at Bajool), on Raglan Creek which runs into the Fitzroy delta, is the northernmost access point for boats fishing The Narrows. There are two ramps near Ramsay Crossing in the centre area of The Narrows. Both of these have questionable access over formed-earth roads after heavy rain (turn off at Mt Larcom).

Further south, closer to Gladstone, are several ramps, some in Gladstone itself and a couple of minor ramps up in The Narrows suitable for small boats only, which will get you closer to good spots around Kangaroo Island.

Gladstone is an industrial city. Aluminium smelters and loading facilities for ocean going cargo ships are features of the landscape.

A ramp beside the power station launches boats into the Calliope River. With a small 'tinnie', some top fishing for mangrove jacks, bream, threadfin, flathead and, near the hot-water outlet from the power station, barramundi and queenfish is on tap.

Gladstone's wharves and port complex will suit anglers without a boat. The Barney Point wharf and those near the alumina refinery at South Trees are a good proposition for anything up to big jewfish and barramundi, especially with live baits at night.

Curtis and Facing Islands are reached by boat passing through extensive sandbanks to reach the opening between the two islands. There's good whiting and flathead fishing amongst the banks, and yabbies for bait aren't too hard to find. Rocky coastline around North and South End on Curtis Island marks offshore reefs.

Cape Capricorn, back up the eastern coast of Curtis Island has deep water close inshore. Trolling is the most common method with local anglers seeking pelagics. They take some really big Spaniards from this area. Bottom fishing is also popular off Cape Capricorn. Both tropical reef fish, such as coral trout, and temperate fish, like snapper, are caught here.

Water off Cape Keppel isn't as deep as Cape Capricorn, however a deep hole below the lighthouse keeper's houses fishes well for reef fish and black jew.

Hummocky Island, 10 kilometres east-north-east of Cape Keppel, is an excellent hot spot, with all the bluewater pelagics including a few billfish, and excellent bottom fishing to boot. Port Alma, some 40 kilometres away, is the best departure point for Hummocky Island. Two protruding rocks, Ship Rock and Fairway Rock, south of Hummocky Island add to the appeal of this top location.

Boyne Island and Tannum Sands, south of Gladstone, are the better launch sites to fish the shipping lane entering Gladstone's harbour from the south. Quite deep water in the shipping channel and the opening to the sea brings pelagics well into Port Curtis. Good reef fishing can also be found off rocky points on the south-western corner of Facing Island.

South of Tannum Sands are endless hectares of mangrove wetlands. So one would expect to find a proliferation of mud crabs there. Well, the bulk of Queensland's commercial mud crab catch comes from the coast between Rockhampton and Bundaberg. And there are still plenty left for visiting anglers to feast upon.

Turkey Beach is a small collection of weekenders tucked away in Rodd's Harbour. It's debatable whether Turkey Beach or the town of Seventeen Seventy is the best jumping-off point to great fishing off Bustard Head.

Bustard Head is quite within the scope of larger trailerboats from either direction. Pancake Creek, behind Bustard Head, is a secure anchorage for boats of any size, as long as enough repellent is on board to allow sleep. Inner, middle and outer rocks off Bustard Head are obvious magnets for pelagics. When the Spanish mackerel come through in spring and early summer, some monster specimens frequent the environs of the rocks. Tossing lures, especially poppers, into the washes around the rocks will connect with horse yellowtail kingfish or cobia depending on water temperatures, kingfish when it's cool, cobia when it's warmer. The front of Bustard and Round Hill Heads both have opportunities for 'wash' fishing for giant trevally (warm water), kingfish (cool water) and queenfish (autumn and early winter). Huge schools of spotted mackerel also move through on their way south in late spring.

Seventeen Seventy's access road, via either Miriam Vale or the alternate route through Lowmead, is notoriously rough and must be treated with due consideration when trailering a boat. Once at Seventeen Seventy, there's a delightful van park/camping area on Round Hill Creek, and the ramps are quite good. Commercial fishing is not permitted in Round Hill Creek, so results are good.

Eurimbulla Creek and Middle Creek, north of Seventeen Seventy, are both accessible with a four-wheel drive off the road to Seventeen Seventy, turnoff signposted Eurimbulla National Park. A camping permit from the National Parks and Wildlife service is required to camp at Eurimbulla, (bush camp, no facilities).

All the creeks in this area, including Pancake, Jenny Lind on the south side of Bustard Head, Middle and Eurimbulla, fish very well. Rock fishing off Bustard and Round Hill Head is an interesting diversion. Anything from big trevally to surprisingly large queenfish, and both Spanish and spotted mackerel, are to be expected.

Offshore reefs require local advice to locate with your own boat. The Great Barrier Reef is a long way to sea here at it's southern extremity and, as such, is beyond even the largest trailerboat.

A charter industry operates out of Gladstone, with several boats offering packages of several days' reef fishing out on the Capricorn Bunker Group and the fabulous Swain Reefs. Charter boats may also operate out of Seventeen Seventy over peak holiday periods.

Baffle Creek and the Kolan River, between Seventeen Seventy and Burnett Heads at the mouth of the Burnett River, are two local estuaries that have boat ramps and good fishing for bream, whiting and flathead, with threadfin and mangrove jacks for the lure tossers. Miara, on the north bank of the Kolan, has a caravan park/campground. There are two other ramps on the south bank of the Kolan at Booyan on Baillies Road via Welcome Creek.

Burnett Heads offers both estuary fishing in the Burnett River and fishing offshore for reef fish and pelagics which move through seasonally. Inside Fraser Island and it's northern projection Breaksea Spit, ocean swell from the south is lessened, however, the broad expanse of coast at the top end of Hervey Bay allows a nasty wind chop to develop. Estuary fish to be expected at Burnett Heads are threadfin, mangrove jacks, grunter and, of course, bream, whiting and flathead. Reef fish are mainly squire and sweetlip. Big schools of both species of spotty mackerel move in in late spring and early summer, and there are several tuna species mixed amongst them.

Above: Another day in paradise draws to a close as the sun sets over a safe mooring near Seventeen Seventy.
Right: Evidence that the outer banks in Hervey Bay provide good small-boat fishing.

Hervey Bay - Fraser Island

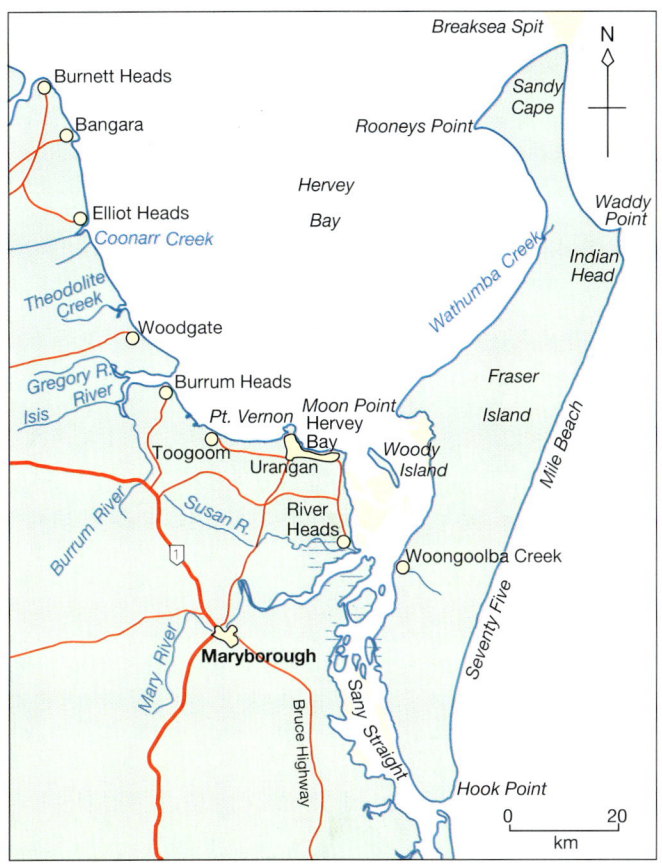

Hervey Bay is a huge expanse of water, measuring some 65 to 70 kilometres wide and the same distance long. That's enough open space to generate a unique set of sea conditions which must never be forgotten when boating.

Virtually all of Queensland needs a boat to find the best fishing, however at Hervey Bay and on Fraser Island at last we've found fishing accessible from both shore and boat.

Urangan's pier is one of the best and most easily accessible. Large shoals of bait hold under the pier attracting predators of all types up to mega trevally, tuna, Spanish mackerel and sharks. Smaller spotty (Queensland school and spotted) mackerel, queenfish and tarpon are also taken.

Whiting are perhaps what Hervey Bay is most famous for. 'I survived the fighting whiting' is a popular bumper sticker for visiting anglers. A commercial fishing ban imposed on beaches around the Hervey Bay, Pialba, Scarness, Torquay and Urangan areas ensure a plentiful supply for recreational fishing. The Urangan pier is a recognised whiting hotspot.

The northern section of the Hervey Bay coastline has many small coastal towns which survive on the good fishing they offer visitors.

Bargara, Bundaberg's 'bayside suburb', south from the mouth of the Burnett, has a beach ramp over sand where a four-wheel drive is needed to launch. A rock known as The Two Mile off Bargara holds quantities of pelagics. Spotty mackerel are the most common catch and there are a few Spaniards, cobia, golden trevally and yellowtail kingfish thrown in for good measure.

Elliott Heads has two ramps. The one just inside the mouth of the Elliott River isn't suited to more than small trailable aluminium boats, and may need a four-wheel drive to launch them except at the top of the tide. By far the better ramp is at Riverview further upstream.

Bream, whiting and flathead frequent the Elliott River. Rocky shores of an island in the mouth turn on big bream in winter, and mangrove jacks along rock shores and snags.

Coonarr and Theodolite Creek are between Elliott Heads and Bargara. Coonarr is reached along four-wheel drive tracks which lead to both sides of the creek near the mouth. Theodolite has a ramp with the access road coming up from Woodgate.

These are small creeks with shallow, virtually dry sand in their lower reaches. Deeper water upstream has plenty of snags holding big bream and mangrove jacks.

Woodgate's caravan park is popular with visitors fishing offshore in Hervey Bay. The ramp there is exposed to wave action and most locals use tractors to launch and retrieve. An artificial reef constructed off Woodgate is a renowned for reef fish including stud snapper at night.

'Reef' in Hervey Bay is more usually a flat rocky bottom than great coral niggerheads. Isolated rock 'reefs' do occur right along this section of coast, although most are small, and are found by looking for clusters of local boats.

Schools of pelagics patrol the coast right along here, often holding for awhile over a patch of reef. Calmer weather after a good blow is favoured by locals to fish the reefs at night.

Burrum Heads is actually an estuarine confluence of the Burrum and Gregory Rivers. Typically of the Hervey Bay area, the estuary has extensive sandflats. There are yabby banks on the south around a cluster of small islands.

The Burrum Heads area has excellent fishing. Bream, whiting and stud flathead are to be found in the complex of sandbanks and channels. Queenfish, threadfin, golden trevally and mangrove jacks keep sportfishers happy, and the Burrum is one of the better spots in Hervey Bay to seek a fish known here as trumpeter or javelin fish, similar to the grunter you can encounter further north.

There are two ramps at Burrum Heads on the south side of the river. One is down near the mouth in the tiny town of Burrum Heads itself, the other further upstream at Buxton. A ramp on the north bank (used by people from Woodgate) is best suited to smaller boats.

Toogoom is the only other ramp before reaching Hervey Bay proper or Point Vernon to Urangan. This area is well serviced with ramps including the magnificent Urangan Boat Harbour, which can handle boats of any size.

On the eastern coast of Big Woody Island, another of Hervey Bay's artificial reefs is situated one measured mile out. Big Woody has copious coral growth and deep water along the eastern aspect. Neap tides are best for reef fishing due to strong currents associated with tidal movement through Sandy Straits. Pelagics including monster Spaniards and giant trevally also frequent Big Woody.

West of Big Woody Island and south of Urangan Boat Harbour is all shallows and sandbank systems with scattered low mangrove islands. In fact, from here south to Tin Can Bay is virtually all shallows with sandbanks and low mangrove islands, although there is a deeper channel.

In the Sandy Straits, deep water yields has plenty of reef, while the shallow reef is also abundant and fishes better at night. Common reef fish from Hervey Bay and Sandy Straits are a real mix of northern and southern species. Coral trout, sweetlip, and red emperor are still prevalent as are snapper, parrot, a morwong known locally as blackall, jewfish (mulloway) and several cod species. One sweetlip very popular as a table fish in Hervey Bay is known as coral bream.

The Mary River enters Hervey Bay through Sandy Straits. River Heads, as the mouth region is known, is serviced by two ramps on North Head in Bingham. One of these leads direct into Sandy Straits and the other into the Mary River itself. The Sandy Straits ramp is affected by strong onshore winds and the Mary River ramp by the

Above: Hookup in Hervey Bay on a northern bluefin of longtail tuna.

Right: A king-size Spanish mackerel from one of Hervey Bay's outer reefs.

Mary's powerful tides. A small ramp near Beaver Rock is the only access to the south bank of the Mary River.

With the huge Mary River to feed it, fishing is good at River Heads. In Sandy Straits, which has the Mary's nutrient input plus its own considerable eco-system it's even better.

At Tin Can Bay, ramps at Maaroom and Boonooroo or to the south give access to the southern section of Sandy Straits. Apart from prolific bream, whiting and flathead fishing, reef fishing and pelagics like spotty mackerel and small tunas, Sandy Straits is notable for three things.

First, it's essential to come prepared for an onslaught by sandflies and mosquitoes, especially at night.

Secondly, Sandy Straits' mud crabs more than compensate for the caked in repellent and the odd itchy bump where you missed a patch of skin.

Thirdly, Sandy Straits hold some really spectacular big threadfin. These are usually taken with live bait as the tide rises around creek mouths. River Heads and the mouth of the Susan River (which joins the Mary) are considered the better places to find king threadfin. They've been taken well over 30 kilograms, enough to delight any angler.

FRASER ISLAND

Fabulous Fraser has been given more exposure in fishing publications than most other fishing spots put together. These days, the huge sand island is in danger of being 'loved to death', and as a result strict management.

Information, camping permits and usage guidelines are available from Queensland National Parks and Wildlife Services offices in Maryborough and Gympie. There is now a fee for landing on the island in addition to barge fees charged by operators transporting four-wheel drives to the island.

The beach is the road on Fraser and a four-wheel drive is essential, as is some knowledge of sand driving techniques and recovery gear; a stout tow rope at least.

Barges taking four-wheel drives across to the island depart from Urangan, River Heads and Inskip Point landing at Urang Creek or Moon Point; Woongoolba Creek and Hook.

Hook Point is right on the southern end of the island and allows a direct run up the ocean beach. Woongoolba and Urang Creek landings lead to tracks across the island to the ocean beach. A landing at Moon Point requires a run up the sometimes treacherous 'inside' beach to Wathumba Creek, where a track leads across the island to the ocean side.

Fraser Island is like a giant sponge and water pours out of creek mouths across the beaches. Never cross a creek without walking across first and selecting the best crossing site. Such is the volume of run-off in some creeks that if a vehicle is stopped in the water, a scouring action takes sand away from around the wheels, literally digging it in faster than you could imagine.

Formal accommodation in units and cabins is available

As an eating fish, it's hard to better a big sand whiting such as this specimen. They are prolific around Fraser Island.

on Fraser Island at Happy Valley, Cathedral Beach, Ewong, and the resort at Orchid Beach. Most visitors to the island prefer the mobility of camping.

Camping areas with facilities are provided at Wathumba Creek, Waddy Point and Dundubara. Bush camping is allowed in most areas, but some may be closed by Queensland National Parks and Wildlife Services after damage from heavy use. Booklets provided by National

"Have trailerboat will travel." A fishing club takes time-out on the sandy foreshores in Hervey Bay.

Parks are very informative about where you can and cannot camp.

The southern section of the ocean beach, all 94 kilometres of it, is best fished by first scouting the beach looking for likely formations. Dart, bream, tarwhine, whiting, flathead and tailor are all prolific along the ocean beach.

Rock fishing is available at Indian Head, Middle Rocks and Waddy Point. Other rocks along the beach, such as Ngala Rocks and Yidney Rocks, are a soft rock which is continually being covered and uncovered by sand. They don't normally provide rock fishing as such.

At Indian Head and Waddy Point, Spanish mackerel can be taken off the rocks in summer and autumn. Boats are launched into the bay behind Waddy Point to fish reefs offshore and the Gardner Bank wider out. Boat trailers must be robust and fitted with oversize wheels and tyres to withstand the rigours of towing on Fraser. Problems getting over Middle Rock's infamous jump up have now been avoided by a corduroyed ramp.

Sandy Cape, at the very northern tip of Fraser Island, is a long haul from anywhere. Breaksea Spit, a vast sandbank system, extends north to the visible horizon. Surf fishing is available on the eastern side of Sandy Cape and some of the best whiting fishing on Fraser on the western side.

The Inside Beach is not as firm as the ocean beach and makes 'hard' going for vehicles. Patches of peat under the sand make conditions treacherous at times, and it's always wise to discuss with the barge operator on the way over to the island whether any of these have been causing problems.

Nonetheless, the whole of the inside beach has top sand whiting fishing. Patches of yabbies are easily found near the mouths of Moon, Coongul, Awinyah, and for many hundreds of metres upstream in Wathumba Creek.

Wathumba holds large populations of bream, whiting and flathead and mangrove and big bream frequent the snags upstream. At lower stages of the tide, Wathumba runs 'Coca-Cola' brown with run-off from inland wetlands and doesn't fish well.

It is not possible to cross Wathumba Creek with a four-wheel drive. To get from one side of the creek to the other you have to drive right across the island, a trip of around 30 kilometres to travel 200 metres.

Wathumba is a secure if shallow anchorage. Boats can be launched here to fish Hervey Bay and Rooney Point areas, which produce brilliant catches of reef fish and pelagics alike. Even small marlin populate this northern area of Hervey Bay.

Severe westerly winds or thunderstorms are a grave concern for boats anchored off Fraser Island's normally serene inside beach. People often come over from Urangan for several days to fish the prolific waters of northern Hervey Bay, however it pays to keep a close eye on the weather, particularly building thunderheads.

The mouth of Wathumba Creek is difficult to enter at low tide and this must be considered if seeking shelter.

The barge service for Fraser Island leaves from Urangan, River Heads and Inskip Point.

Tin Can Bay to Noosa

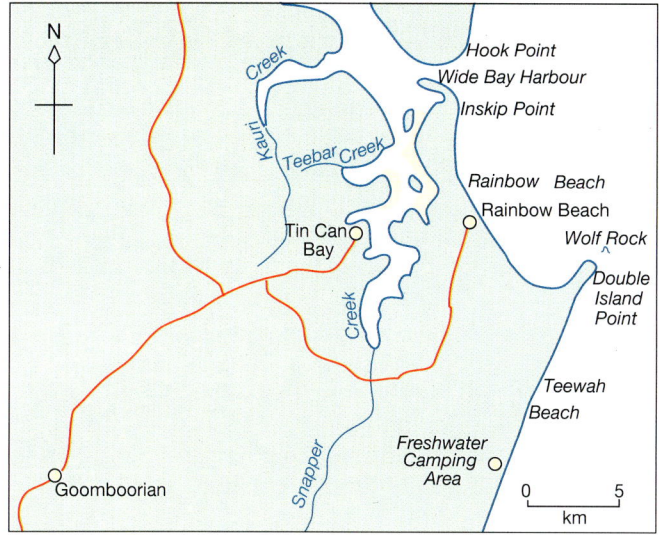

Tin Can Bay is serviced by no less than four ramps, and boats can be launched directly over the beach at Inskip Point. Coming in along the Tin Can Bay road, the first is at Toolaran on the western side of Tin Can inlet. There are two in Tin Can Bay township at Snapper Creek, one in Cod Street on the southern bank, and one at Norman Point at the Snapper Creek entrance. The fourth ramp is at Carlo Point on the eastern side of Tin Can Inlet, reached by turning off at Rainbow Beach.

In Tin Can Bay, bream, whiting and flathead are the mainstays. Deep water behind the Wide Bay Bar has patches of reef or soft coral and sea grass where parrot, blackall (morwong) and cod can be found.

At Inskip Point dart, tailor and an odd jewfish are added to the list. Mackerel work in over the bar and up into Tin Can Inlet and the bottom of Sandy Straits, where they may be caught by drifting baits. Small tuna also move into water between Fraser Island and the mainland providing a ready source of bait for the succulent mud crabs on Tin Can Bay.

Small chopper tailor patrol open water well down into Tin Can Inlet, while mangrove jacks are available in good numbers in Tin Can Bay's Kauri and Teebah Creeks.

Sandy Straits and Tin Can Bay are flat bottomed with extensive shallows. It's very easy to run aground and be left high and dry until the water comes back.

Insect repellent is necessary in the creeks.

Rainbow Beach, from Inskip Point down to Double Island Point, is sheltered by Double Island Point's protruding headland. Gutters along the beach produce good fishing for bream, whiting, flathead and dart.

A ramp at Rainbow Beach gives access for four-wheel drives heading to Fraser Island (via the barge from Inskip Point) or south to Cooloola National Park, Double Island Point and Teewah Beach.

North of Double Island Point, the beach actually orients east/west, facing north behind the lee of the point. Queensland National Parks and Wildlife Service maintain a camping area at Double Island Point.

Due to the northward facing beach tucked away from the predominate southerly winds and swell in southern Queensland, it's often possible to launch boats of up to 5.5 metres over the beach at Double Island Point. Gutters and lagoons form periodically, which can make launching even easier. Although a small swell usually radiates around the corner launching at Double Island Point is much simpler than a true surf launch unless there are northerly winds.

Wolf Rock, a protruding bombora off Double Island Point, and various other pinnacles and bottom structure extending offshore for many kilometres from the rocky headland make this a good bottom fishing and pelagic area.

Access over the Wide Bay Bar isn't viable for small boats due to the volume of water moving over the bar, so a beach launch at Double Island Point is the only way to reach this prolific ground.

The deep reefs and wide grounds off the Noosa Coast harbour provide many trophy fish.

Wolf Rock is renowned for big Spanish mackerel and yellowtail kingfish. Unfortunately sharks are equally as common and can cause problems at times.

Tossing poppers and small metal lures at washes working around Wolf Rock is liable to connect with anything from a small dart to a giant trevally, cobia, Spanish mackerel or yellowtail kingfish.

Bottom fishing produces snapper, sweetlip, parrot, and a smattering of northern fishes when the water in close to the coast is warm.

Double Island Point itself is a top rock fishing spot. With an eye on wave conditions, there are numerous rock fishing possies along the rock facade below the lighthouse. All species expected off the rocks are available here including big Spanish mackerel, yellowtail kingfish, tailor, dart, good bream, drummer, trevally, jew and even sweetlip.

Many of Double Island Point's washes are worth fishing from a boat, as is trolling along the front of the headland.

A sand track over the sand blow behind Double Island Point takes four-wheel drives from Rainbow Beach over to Teewah Beach, stretching 50 kilometres south to the Noosa River.

Along Teewah Beach good gutter formations are always to be found. Queensland National Parks and Wildlife Service have another campground at Freshwater, a few kilometres south of the remains of the Cherry Venture. People fishing Cooloola National Park must camp at either Double Island Point or Freshwater. Bush camping is not allowed.

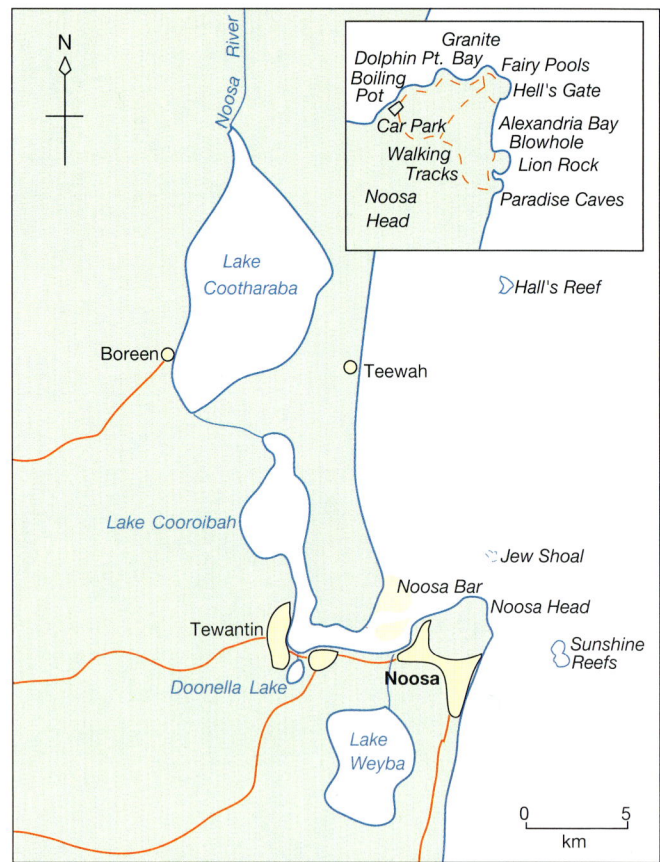

A road leading to Freshwater camping area from the Rainbow Beach road is the only access allowed to Cooloola's beaches apart from via Noosa in the south, and Rainbow Beach in the north. A ferry across the Noosa River puts four-wheel drives onto the southern end of the beach.

People intending to beach launch boats at Double Island Point are advised to travel down from Rainbow Beach. Double Island Point can be impossible to tow a boat across if there hasn't been recent rain.

Noosa: Rampant development has taken over Noosa Heads, spoiling to some extent the once superb fishing estuary. However, despite having its wateflow altered by attempts to deepen the bar entrance, the Noosa estuary is still a reliable producer of bream and whiting, some very nice flathead, mangrove jacks and trevally.

Several large shallow lakes Cootharaba, Weyba, Cooroibah, Cooloolah, Como and Doonella join the Noosa River above the town and canals area. These are very popular with the wind surfing and sailing fraternities. Lakes further downstream, Doonella, Weyba & Cooroibah are salt water, however further upstream is brackish water. Cootharaba is quite brackish, Como is more or less freshwater and Cooloola pure fresh and not connected by a navigable channel.

Left: Bream, such as those in this fine haul, are prolific in Noosa estuary. Locally-pumped yabbies are one of the best baits to use.

Salinity also depends upon rainfall. The lakes are very shallow, too shallow for outboards in many places. Between the lakes the river channel is possibly a better proposition for fishing.

The Noosa River still has good fishing for the southern estuary species and mangrove jacks. There are boat ramps at Elanda Point and Boreen Point, in Lake Cootharaba, in Tewantin and Noosaville. Boats are also launched at the ferry approach.

Noosa's bar is shallow and nasty, despite it facing north and being protected to a degree by Noosa Head. Local advice is essential before attempting to cross the bar.

Offshore Noosa, North Reef is north of the bar off the prominent Cooloola Sand Patch. It's 8 to 10 kilometres offshore in 45 to 55 metres of water. The Jew Shoal and Hall's Reef are closer. Jew Shoal is only about 5 kilometres from the bar and is almost due north of Noosa Head. It comes to within 7 metres of the surface. Hall's Reef is a flat reef on Laguna Bay due north of the bar in 19 metres of water.

East of Noosa Head, the Sunshine Reefs are 2 and 4 kilometres offshore, with 25 to 34 metres over them.

Further east again is the big Chardon's Reef and associated pinnacles in 43 to 52 metres of water.

All of these produce good to great reef fishing for snapper, red emperor, the king of table fish pearl perch, parrot and sweetlip, as well as mackerel and other pelagics.

Noosa Head has some of the best rock fishing in southern Queensland. Walking tracks are the only access to the headland and there are car parks at either end in Noosa and at Sunshine Beach.

Some rocks in Noosa National Park, which encompasses the entire headland, are dangerous in a swell, particularly one pushed by south-easterly winds. Even in the worst conditions, however, it's usually possible to fish somewhere on Noosa Head.

Starting from the Noosa car park, the first spot is the Boiling Pot only 250 metres away. There's deep water along here which holds jew fish in the early morning and at night, and is also renowned for tailor and bream.

Dolphin Point has a similar reputation and may hold trevally in the autumn.

The Fairy Pools, 3 kilometres from the Noosa car park, is one of the safer spots and far enough along the head for Spanish mackerel and yellowtail kingfish.

Hell's Gate has possibly the largest jewfish and best pelagic fishing. It has several fishable ledges, however a big swell closes these out very quickly.

Alexandria Bay forms a gap between Hell's Gate and Oyster Rock on the southern protruberance of the headland. Oyster Rock and Lian Rock produce bream. Schools of mullet present in this area often attract predators, including trevally, jewfish and tailor.

Paradise Caves and Barton Rock are the southernmost rocky point of Noosa National Park. Good bream and tailor are available, plus there's a chance of a jewfish.

Anywhere in the National Park where washes are working along the rocks, dart are always a possiblity. Luderick are another prevalent resident. Snapper and reef fish are often taken while fishing the bottom in Noosa National Park.

The Noosa River is an excellent flathead spot.

A 'gold bar' or large sand whiting.

The Sunshine Coast

Queensland's Sunshine Coast, like the Gold Coast to the south of Brisbane, is a holiday playground. The rivers are far from their natural state, being characterised by canal subdivisions. Fishing in the rivers of the Sunshine Coast has suffered as a result, though there's still good fish to be caught if you're prepared to work for them.

Beach/rock and offshore fishing are more productive, and the Sunshine Coast has much to offer in this regard.

South of Noosa, Peregian Beach stretches to Point Arkwright, the next rocky headland. Some smaller rocks on the beach at Coolum are always worth a try for bream.

The rest of Peregian, or Sunshine, Marcus and Coolum, is quite accessible at a number of points along the small holiday settlements and good fishing formations can always be found.

Hancock Shoal is 2 kilometres offshore between the townships of Peregian and Coolum. This is a large area of reef rising to within 12 metres of the surface. Best fishing is at night.

Point Arkwright is a reliable producer of tailor and bream. The Arkwright Shoal is an extension of Point Arkwright's rock strata extending 2.5 kilometres offshore. It fishes better at night when good catches of reef fish are made. During daylight, the Arkwright Shoal may reward patient trolling with an odd Spaniard or the more numerous spotty mackerel. Schools of small yellowtail kingfish are often found on the surface.

Mudjimba or Old Woman Island is a small rocky islet a few hundred metres offshore between Point Arkwright and the mouth of the Maroochy River. Along the eastern face of Old Woman the water is quite deep. Night fishing the shallow reef along the mainland side of Old Woman is the most productive, and good catches are taken, including a few big snapper.

Small yellowtail kingfish get to be a problem at times all around the island. Summer brings mackerel and it's not unusual to catch four species in one session here; Queensland school, spotted, Spanish and broadbar.

Depending upon swell direction and sea conditions, washes form along the seaward face and on the north-east or south-east corners. Small kingfish abound, but if they're not a problem, the washes can turn on great fishing.

Tossing lures or unweighted pilchards is liable to connect with anything from a stud tailor to a decent Spanish mackerel. Spotty mackerel, trevally, dart and snapper are all common catches at Mudjimba. Some really big bream are also available around the rocks.

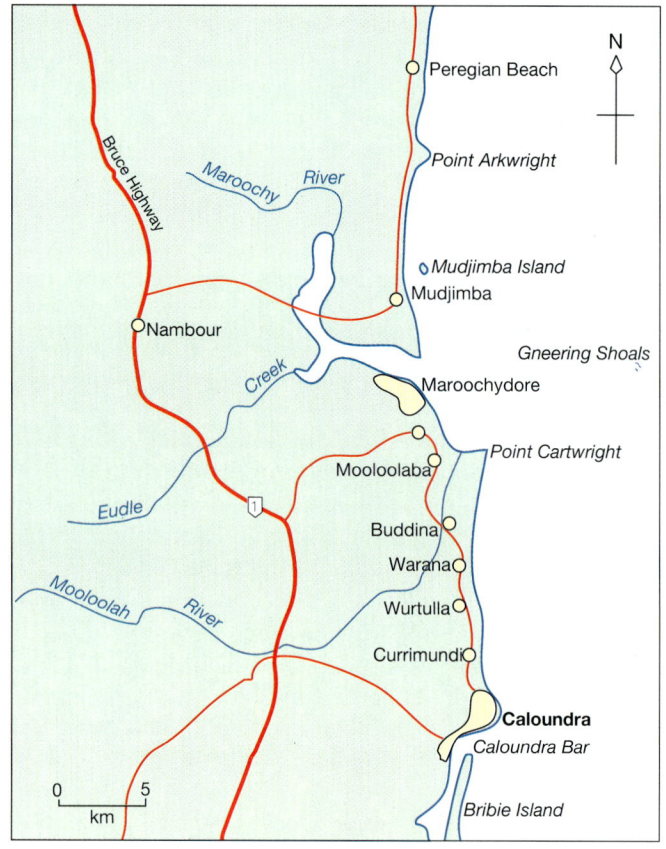

The Maroochy River is a shallow estuary not used as an exit to the sea. Three islands down towards the mouth - Pincushion, Goat and Channel - have very interesting formations and sandbank systems. Tailor are found around Pincushion Island bar in winter.

Bream, whiting and flathead are the most common catch around.

the Maroochy mouth. Good catches of luderick are taken in winter.

Upstream the junction of Bli-Bli, Eudlo and Petrie Creeks is an interesting and productive area.

Three ramps service the Maroochy, two on the south bank and one on the north.

The Mooloolah River is the best and safest exit to the sea in southern Queensland. Facing north and tucked in behind Point Cartwright, the Mooloolah has a deep entrance without a bar.

It's obviously popular as the packed marinas and trawler berths inside the river attest. Good ramps in several locations inside the river complete the attraction of the Mooloolah. They're well sign-posted and on both sides of the river.

Off Mooloolaba, there's no shortage of productive bottom fishing. The Inner Gneering Shoals are only a few kilometres outside the river. The Blinker is an anchored buoy marking the very beginning of Brisbane Port's shipping channel located about 6 kilometres north-east of Point Cartwright. It's plagued with yellowtail kingfish of all sizes, and mackerel.

The Outer Gneering Shoals are east of the Blinker. They're extensive, and pinnacles and humps are to be found for another 5 kilometres out to sea. Good reef fish hold on the Outer Gneerings and can be found with astute use of a sounder. Trolling for Spanish mackerel, cobia, wahoo, yellowtail kingfish, small yellowfin tuna is popular.

Murphy's Reef is south of the Outer Gneering area and almost due east of Point Cartwright. Being a little harder to find it doesn't receive quite as much attention as the Gneerings and produces better results.

Between the Blinker and the mainland, extending north to Coolum and south to Caloundra, is a strip of water known as the Alley. This is frequented by mackerel and longtail tuna.

Barwon Banks run from Noosa to Mooloolaba, around 35 kilometres offshore, and are not for smaller boats travelling alone but are well worth the trip for bigger boats travelling in company.

An echo sounder is essential to locate the Barwons. Coming out from shore, they rise from 60 metres to 30 and then drop-off suddenly to 80 and 100 metres on the seaward side.

Trawlers sometimes anchor on the shallower sections of the bank during the day. Top reef fishing and trolling or drift fishing for enormous Spanish mackerel and wahoo is just a taste of what's available.

Point Cartwright isn't a bad rock fishing spot. Tailor work through in big schools in winter and an odd big mulloway is taken by local specialists. There's good bream fishing in the right sea conditions.

Similarly the breakwalls at the mouth of the Mooloolah are always worth a try. They have a large bream population, and spotty mackerel can be taken from the walls when they're working inshore.

From Point Cartwright to Caloundra, good formations will be found along the beach after heavy weather, but to fish anywhere along this section of coast requires an early start and finish before the beaches become overrun with surfers.

Offshore, Currimundi Reef (off Currimundi) is within easy reach of Mooloolaba or Caloundra. Night fishing is the more productive.

Off Caloundra, the Fairway Buoy and Bray's Rock are popular for yellowtail kingfish, a few cobia and spotted mackerel.

Caloundra's bar entrance is a natural one without training walls or other encumberances. It's one of the better bars, but is dangerous nonetheless. Seek local advice before attempting to cross it.

Above: Success in the form of a Maroochydore Spanish mackerel.
Left: A fine longtail or northern bluefin tuna waiting to be released.

Moreton Bay North

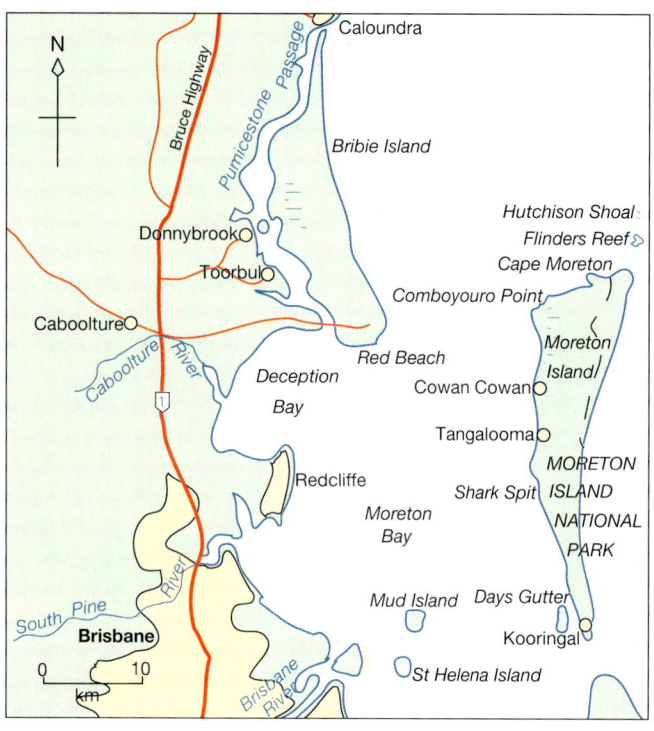

Brisbane is fortunate in that of all the state capitals, it has the best fishing. From the billfish grounds off Moreton Island to winter whiting off the bayside suburbs, Brisbane's fishing isn't just good it's great.

Moreton Bay extends from Caloundra to Southport. Where it begins and ends depends more upon where an opinion resides than on any loose fitting official definition. Various sections of the Bay go by names such as Pumicestone Passage, Jumpinpin, The Broadwater and even 'The Bay' to describe the open water section from Bribie Island to Peel Island. To avoid confusion with the all-encompassing Moreton Bay, the section from Bribie to Peel wil be referred to as Moreton Bay and the other areas by their own names.

From Caloundra in the north there's a choice of travelling down either the western or eastern shore of Bribie Island. In either case a boat is required. There are few roads accessing the shores anywhere in Moreton Bay due to the characteristic mangrove shoreline.

Bribie Island's ocean beach is traversable by four-wheel drive, however a beach permit from the controlling Caboolture Shire Council is necessary. There's no way of crossing the northern end of Pumicestone Passage from Bribie Island to Caloundra by vehicle.

Pumicestone Passage between Bribie Island and the mainland has a marked channel navigable by any trailerboat. Any of the several ramps along Golden Beach in Caloundra give access to the full length of the Passage, as do ramps at Toorbul in the centre of the Passage, and on Bribie at the southern end. Smaller 3 to 4 metre aluminium boats are fine in most areas of Pumicestone Passage if due care is taken in the more open water at the northern and southern ends.

Pumicestone Passage is largely undeveloped and holds good fish stocks. Bream, whiting, flathead and mud crabs are standard fare. The northern end of the Passage near Caloundra produces some big flathead each spring.

Creeks running into the Passage hold more of the same with mangrove jacks and big bream on the snags, and bass further upstream.

The Bribie Bridge at the bottom of Pumicestone Passage is built in deep water. Deep holes near the piles are known mulloway hotspots. A few cod are taken and there are quality tarpon under the bridge at night.

Red Beach, Bald and Skirmish Points on the southern shore of Bribie Island produce copious amounts of sand whiting every summer. Skirmish Point is one of few places inside Moreton Bay where tailor, mostly smaller choppers, are caught regularly.

Along the ocean side of Bribie Island, the shipping channel for the Port of Brisbane is marked with a chain of navigation markers. Beacon fising is a local 'contact sport' when yellowtail kingfish are present, which is most of the time. Deep jigging and baitfishing will also find Spanlsh, Queensland school and spotted mackerel, amberjacks in summer/autumn, and cobia.

Further east, access to the open sea is prevented by sandbanks stretching north from Moreton Island. To get to sea from ramps at Caloundra or Bongaree (over the bridge and turn left or right) on Bribie, it's necessary to go either due east from Caloundra or across Moreton Bay to Comboyouro Point on Moreton Island.

Here there's a choice between sneaking past the point itself, which gets very hazardous when wind opposes a strong tidal run, or running north a few kilometres to a gap in the banks known as the north-east channel. Once out to sea it's plain sailing.

Cape Moreton, the rocky headland on the north-eastern extremity of Moreton Island, runs in a ridge rising to within 3 metres of the surface at Smith's Rock then on to Flinder's Reef where it is always visible protruding above the surface, and Hutchison Shoal where it rises to within 6 metres of the surface.

This same line of rock extends south of Cape Moreton as Brennan Shoal, Roberts Shoal, Shallow Tempest and

Henderson Rock. Further south again it's known as the northern and southern Twenty-Nines (referring to the depth in fathoms).

East of Henderson Rock by 10 kilometres is an extensive reef known as Deep Tempest. It rises from 90 metres to 75 metres and is best located with an echo sounder.

All these reefs fish well for bottom fish such as snapper, sweetlip, teraglin and, in deeper water, pearl perch. Spanish mackerel move through the area in summer. Wahoo, dolphin fish, amberjacks, various tunas and small black marlin are found in summer through into autumn.

North of Moreton Island are the famous sailfish grounds. These concentrate along the 40 metre line running east from the sandbanks to Hutchison Shoal, and south past Cape Moreton. Sailfish are best in autumn.

From Bribie to Mud Island, the open water is a happy hunting ground for spotty mackerel, longtail and mackerel tuna, along with smaller species like Australian and Watson's leaping bonito. Tuna are found all year round. The spotty mackerels move in in early summer and stay to gorge on masses of baitfish until late autumn.

Two artificial reefs have been constructed in Moreton Bay. One of these is located only a few hundred metres off Moreton Island's insidebeach near Cowan Cowan. The other is near the Rous Channel mouth east of Brisbane's bayside suburb of Wynnum.

Moreton Island's beaches are traversible by four-wheel drive, except for rocks around Cape Moreton and an area south of Tangalooma. Barges transport over to Moreton from Scarborough in the north and Manly or Cleveland in the south.

The outside or surf beach always has good formations holding bream, whiting, flathead, dart or tailor. The inside or western beach is a reliable for whiting and flathead.

A permit from Queensland National Parks and Wildlife Service is necessary to camp on Moreton Island. There's a resort at Tangalooma on the western side of the island and holiday cabins may be rented at Bulwer and Kooringal.

Boat ramps servicing northern Moreton Bay are in the bayside suburb of Scarborough on Redcliffe Peninsular. This is a boat harbour with all facilities able to handle any size boats. Smaller ramps are situated in the Brisbane River and in Cabbage Tree Creek at Sandgate. These are reasonable for the average trailerboat, and sometimes preferred by local anglers due to more direct access to their planned fishing location. However, the channel to and from the ramp at Cabbage Tree Creek may require care at lower stages of the tide.

The Brisbane River is a renowned bream hotspot. Down towards the mouth, the Pinkenba Wall, Luggage Point, Bishop Island and the wall at Fisherman Island fire in late summer through into early autumn. A boat is a virtual necessity to fish for bream in the river. The ramp at Pinkenba is the closest launch point.

Further up the Brisbane River towards the city fishing results taper off accordingly where water quality deteriorates. Surprisingly, the bridges in town can really fire for large jewfish when they are feeding on mullet attracted by the lights at night. Like mulloway anywhere, catching them is time intensive, but even one decent fish can be ample reward.

Top: *Trolling the wrecks on the inside of Moreton Island, near Tangalooma.*
Above: *The billfish grounds off Cape Moreton yield sailfish and marlin.*

Moreton Bay South

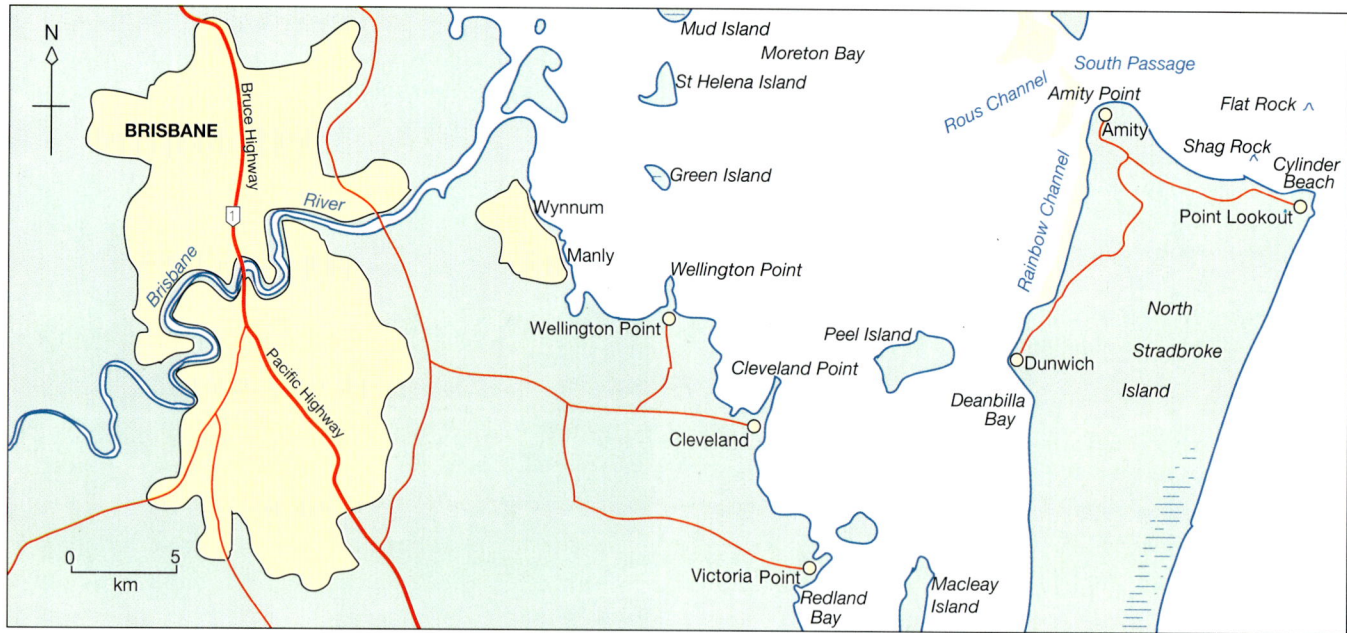

The southern part of northern Moreton Bay has some great whiting fishing and sand crabbing. Sand crabs are caught in any month containing an 'R' in its name around Wynnum/Manly at Mud, St Helena and Green Islands, and along banks running south from the prominent sandhills visible on the bottom end of Moreton to Peel Island, known as the Moreton and Amity Banks.

Larger sand and smaller diver whiting are known respectively as summer and winter whiting, in line with their seasonal runs. Some of the best whiting fishing in the bay is to be found in the same areas as the sand crabs.

A notable feature of the southern end of the open water section of Moreton Bay is fringing coral reefs around Mud, St Helena, Green and Peel Islands.

The eastern side of Mud, St Helena and Green Islands are the more productive, and similarly the northern side of Peel Island. Sweetlip, parrot fish and small squire are the usual catch on these reefs. Large bream respond to a berley trail. Better snapper are taken at night off Mud and Peel on floating baits.

South Passage Bar fills the gap between Moreton and North Stradbroke Islands. It's an infamous piece of water with a well-deserved bad reputation. There are normally two exits, a northern one found by running along behind a group of sand islands, and a southern one in the vicinity of the wreck of the Rufus King (visible at low tide).

It's strongly recommended that only experienced people attempt to cross South Passage Bar, and even those should seek local advice from the Coast Guard or

Moreton Bay Trailer Boat Club at Manly's Boat Harbour.

Day's Gutter, just inside the south western tip of Moreton Island, is one of the most secure anchorages in the open water section of Moreton Bay. Entry to Day's Gutter is found by running through a channel until deep water is reached, before turning left to Moreton Island then following the beach west into Day's Gutter.

Many local people fishing the many reefs and bommies off the northern end of North Stradbroke Island, anchor overnight to sleep in Day's Gutter before crossing South Passage Bar at first light the next morning.

Ramp access to the South Passage, St Helena, Mud, Green and Peel Island areas is from the full facility boat harbour at Manly, or from smaller ramps at Cleveland, Wellington Point, Wynnum or the Brisbane River. Manly Boat Harbour is the pick of ramps, with a public ramp at both southern and northern ends.

The bottom end of Moreton and Stradbroke Island accommodate beach fishing. Tailor are often present at Reeder's Point on Moreton and Amity Points on Stradbroke. Sand whiting form the bulk of the catch in summer, with a few bream over the cooler months.

There are boat ramps at Amity and Dunwich on North Stradbroke. An alternative to crossing South Passage Bar is to launch over the beach with a four-wheel drive at Cylinder Beach in the lee of Point Lookout. Boats on trailers must be ferried across to North Stradbroke from the ferry terminals at Cleveland or Redland Bay.

Point Lookout offers superlative rock fishing. Snapper, mackerel and some big jewfish join catches of common rock-dwelling species such as bream and tailor. Whale Rock, a separated outcrop is difficult to reach and can also be a dangerous place in a big southerly swell, as can many other places on Point Lookout.

Point Lookout's rock strata has spawned a number of protruding rocks and bommies. Shag Rock is north of Cylinder Beach. Boat Rock and the northernmost Flat Rock are north of Point Lookout itself. These rocks have reef around them frequented by squire and sweetlip. Flat Rock, in the deepest water, is the better place to look for pelagics, although when they're about in good numbers Boat and Shag Rocks are also liable to hold them.

The most sought-after pelagic around Point Lookout's rocks is Spanish mackerel. These are present in summer through autumn; when water is cooler, yellowtail kingfish plague all three. In spring, these three little rocks are one of Queensland's most reliable producers of cobia.

North of Flat Rock and east of South Passage is an extensive reef known locally as the 35s (referring to 35 fathoms). It rises 10 to 15 metres to 60-64 metres.

South-east of Flat Rock is yet another big reef known as the One Mile. It's about 3.5 kilometres from Flat Rock. A good sounder is needed to find the One Mile, it being a flat reef rising only 5 metres or so from 57 metres.

These deeper reefs hold quality snapper, teraglin and the much sought-after pearl perch, along with a host of smaller reef species.

The Cathedrals is 9.5 to 10 kilometres south-east of Point Lookout, and flat reef along a drop-off from 50 to 70 metres. Here good reef fish are joined by amberjacks.

The wave-height recorder buoy is the last point of interest inshore from Point Lookout. It's 5 kilometres past the One Mile Reef. When warm currents move inshore, it's a magnet for dolphin fish, cobia and mackerel.

North Stradbroke's ocean beach is accessible to four-wheel drives all the way south to Jumpinpin Bar at the opening between North and South Stradbroke. Good formations for bream, whiting, dart and tailor and gutters for flathead are found along the beach.

Development has degraded fish habitat around Brisbane's bayside suburbs from the mouth of the Brisbane River to Victoria Point. In between development, the shoreline is basically shallow flats and mangroves.

Jetties at Cleveland Point and Wellington Point aren't bad for casual fishing, and can produce good catches of squid at night.

Shallow coral reefs off these bayside suburbs still produce a few mulloway and snapper for local specialists.

The Rainbow Channel, near Peel Island, have schools of spotty mackerel chopping into bait in summer. Big schools of yellowtail kingfish patrol the channel in spring.

Deanbilla Bay, south of Dunwich, is another holding area for spotty mackerel.

South of Peel Island, Moreton Bay is a maze of sandbanks, mudbanks, mangroves and channels, with a few larger islands. The area is well-serviced by ramps at Cleveland, Victoria Point, Redland Bay and in the Logan River.

The sheltered waters from Peel Island to Jumpinpin are a boating paradise, and the fishing for the family fish, bream, whiting and flathead, isn't bad either.

School and spotted mackerel proliferate throughout Moreton Bay. Succulent sand or blue swimmer crabs are also common in the bay.

Jumpinpin to the Broadwater

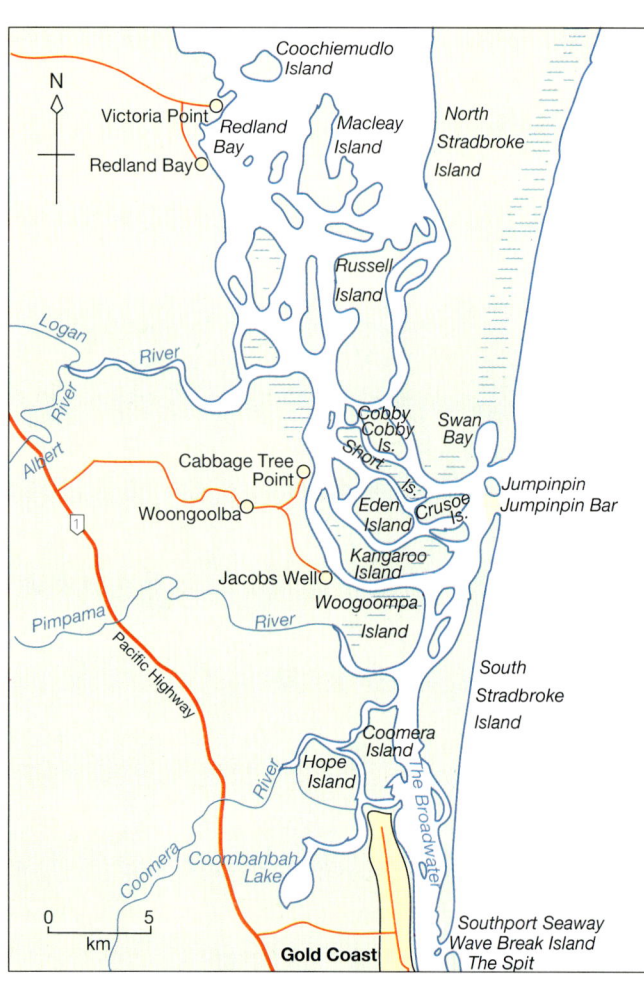

Tropical fish such as giant trevally reside in the Broadwater estuary.

Jumpinpin and the Southport Broadwater provide the reason that south-eastern Queensland has one of the highest per-capita boat ownerships in Australia. Both areas are bar openings where the waters or rivers entering southern Moreton Bay - the Logan, Nerang, Coomera, Albert and Pimpama - have forced their way through weak spots in the sand barrier islands to meet the sea.

They are areas of open, yet fairly protected water, where families are able to enjoy an outing with little regard to wind strengths below 35 kilometres per hour. The amount of tidal movement ensures silt doesn't settle, leaving clean sandy beaches.

Away from the brunt of tidal energy, silt does settle and along with it nutrients from the river systems. This, of course, promotes lush mangrove growth. And mangroves being the cradle of marine life, estuarine fishes like bream, whiting, flathead and jewfish (mulloway) are present in large numbers.

A word of warning, however. The Jumpinpin and the Broadwater are ideal for small boats, but tides here move

with vigour and more than one ill-prepared craft has been literally sucked into the bar when a motor failed or an anchor didn't hold. Adequate sand anchors with ample chain and rope must be carried at all times. Remember, anchoring properly is often the first line of defence for a boat in trouble, and done properly it is more often than not the salvation.

Jumpinpin is well serviced by ramps although there is no road access to the area. Travelling south from Brisbane, turn off left to Woongoolba at Yatala. This road leads to several ramps near Cabbage Tree Point and further south at Jacob's Well.

The public ramp at Cabbage Tree Point is excellent unless strong winds are expected, when it's open aspect makes it subject to an awkward wave action. Private ramps at Walker's, Steiglitz and Rudy Maas further south behind Tabby Tabby and Kangaroo Islands are more protected and offer the advantage of security for vehicle and trailer if staying down at the Jumpinpin overnight or for several days (the owners charge for use of ramps and vehicle security, of course). Further south again is a well-protected public ramp at Jacob's Well. From any of these it's a 10 to 15 minutes run down to the Jumpinpin.

Ensure an up-to-date chart is aboard. Channels at the Jumpinpin are constantly on the move and can change literally week by week. Until some degree of familiarity with the area is achieved, try to avoid travelling to and from the ramp to the Jumpinpin at low tide. Once down at the bar area it's not such a problem, but it's possible to run aground at speed even in the marked channel.

Jumpinpin is justifiably famous for its bream run. Each winter, spawning bream move into the Jumpinpin in their millions. Various experts extoll the virtues of full moons and new moons, however there's no need to catch a hundred bream for a feed; any more than a dozen or so per angler feeds egos more than stomachs.

Good areas to start looking for bream are the banks in the Canaipa Passage downstream from the sand cliffs, known as the Slipping Sands, along a bank known as the Stockyards in the same area, and along the north shore of Crusoe Island, particularly towards the 'corner', facing the back of the bar, known locally as the Mud Clump

The mouth of Whalley's Gutter and the channel upstream along the south of Eden Island is another popular fishing area.

It must, however, be pointed out that this whole area is so dynamic that fish are where you find them and today's hotspot can be unworthy of wetting a line a month later.

Spring is the best time for flathead at Jumpinpin. Again, they move into spawn, and fish larger than 4 kilograms are far from rare. Kalinga Bank is the famous flathead drift at the Jumpinpin. Yet again, the advice that fish are where you find them holds true with flathead. Lure casting or fishing a small baitfish as a lure around tidal flats and their draining gutters is a positive way of seeking big flathead.

Luderick or blackfish are fished for by a few local specialists working steep banks and timber with the traditional weed bait fished under a float. The eastern tip of Short Island, the southern side of Crusoe, the Stockyards, and the southern side of the Tiger Mullet Channel are all places where luderick are regularly found.

With all that sand and yabby banks, the Jumpinpin is a natural for quality whiting. Best fishing for these is in summer. Good whiting areas are virtually everywhere at Jumpinpin making details pointless, although the area closer to the bar is probably the better place to start. Jumpinpin also produces big jew fish, and large schools of tailor move into the estuary at times. Catching Jewfish is a waiting game the same as anywhere else but remembering that they aren't averse to a feed of bream themselves and, in season, anywhere that numbers of bream are found is liable to be patrolled by these big predators.

Tailor normally hold in eddies and around current lines streaming off points down in the bar area. At times, when baitfish schools are present, they may be found working the open area behind the bar, signposted by birds wheeling overhead.

The ubiquitous yabby is the best bait at the Jumpinpin, and there's certainly no shortage of banks where bait can be pumped at low tide. A little way back into the channels away from the immediate bar area is better for yabbies.

A cast or bait net is all that's necessary to supply small fish bait, live or fresh.

The Coomera River, south from Jumpinpin, enters the crossover area between the Jumpinpin and the Southport Broadwater.

There are two 'mouths' called the north and south branches exiting each side of Coomera Island. Coombabah Creek enters the south branch at 'The Junction' behind Paradise Point.

Development has taken the edge off the once fantastic Coomera. Regardless, it still fishes well.

Take care in crossing the infamous Southport Bar; the gateway to Brisbane's offshore fishing grounds.

Ramps on Hope Island at Boynambil, and Santa Barbara each side of the massive Sanctuary Cove development, and in the boat harbour at Paradise Point, are the best access points to the Coomera mouth area.

Interestingly bream, whiting and flathead aren't all that Coomera offers. Sport fishers may find mangrove jacks around snags and tarpon deep in the big holes.

The Southport Broadwater itself is a very different waterway than left by nature's design. Along the western shore is virtually wall-to-wall suburbia. The Spit is one big tourist attraction, and the old Southport Bar is now the deep-water Southport Seaway. Because of regular flushings of good clean sea water, the Broadwater remains a top fishing spot. Changed it may be, but catches are still impressive.

An interesting aspect of the opening of the Southport Seaway is that oceanic fish now regularly enter the estuary. Yellowtail kingfish, spotty mackerel and several tuna species regularly enter the opening of the seaway, working well inside to the deep water around the new wave break island.

The addition of rock breakwalls has been a real enhancement, and they fish well for big mulloway, tailor, bream, luderick and the odd yellowtail bandit on patrol.

Around the Wavebreak Island, the rock walls attract good bream and luderick with plenty of chopper tailor thrown in when they're about.

The oyster leases around Crab Island still hold plenty of bream. North of Crab, the extensive sandbanks and small mangrove islets are a happy hunting ground for bream, whiting and flathead.

Like Jumpinpin, the Southport Broadwater is a breeding ground. Winter sees bream 'runs' when they move in to spawn. Spring brings flathead and astute fishing around banks and tidal gutters will find some monsters. Whiting are mainly a summer fish which do not appear to have dropped off in quantity or quality since all the changes.

Traditionally, the Broadwater held the biggest whiting in south Queensland, with several fish over a kilogram being taken each season. The best whiting fishing is at night, anchoring across current on the edge of the strong tidal flow and fishing shallower water as the tide rises.

An oddball that turns up each winter is the hairtail. These 'chrome-plated' enigmas are caught in deep water every June and July. They're not a prolific fish, but perseverance is often rewarded with reasonable catches.

Yabbies and various worms are top baits in the Broadwater. Yabby banks between Sea World and Loders Creek, off the old Grand Hotel and south towards the Nerang mouth can always be relied on for bait.

Sandbank systems in the southern section of the Broadwater produce good catches of bream, whiting and flathead although as a general rule these tend to be smaller fish than north of the Seaway.

Ramps leading to the Southport Broadwater are at Paradise Point, Hollywell (in Jasmine Avenue off Centenary Drive), at Labrador near the famous Grand Hotel, in Loders Creek at Labrador, near the Olympic Pool at Southport and beside the Gold Coast Highway bridge at Main Beach.

Top: The Jumpinpin Estuary is a mecca for mega flathead.
Above: Bream are the most common estuary catch.

The Gold Coast

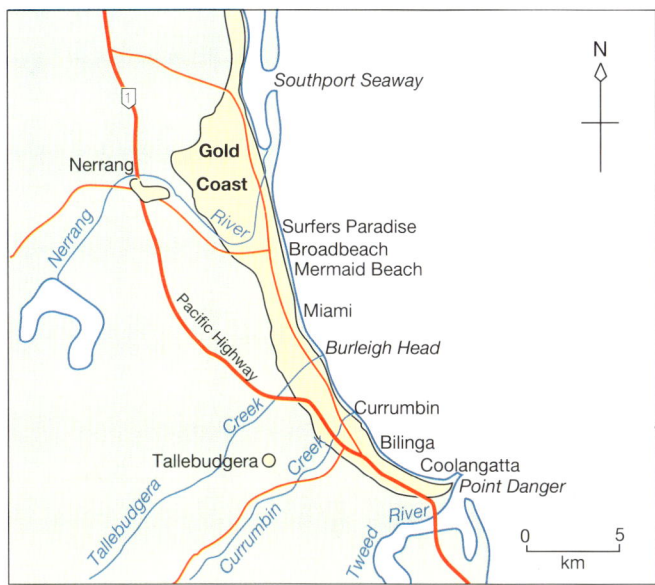

Although there can be no argument that shore-based fishing along the Gold Coast has deteriorated, there's no reason not to take fishing gear on a Gold Coast holdiay.

The canals of the Nerang River, Tallebudgera and Currumbin Creek are almost marine deserts, and are not worthy of too much attention, with the exception of deep water at the entrance to large canal estates, where the mainbody of the river passes.

A few of these are haunted by big jewfish waiting for mullet moving in and out of the canals with the tide. Canals with rock on the bottom may hold bream and mangrove jacks.

Tallebudgera Creek has good estuary fishing away from the canal areas. At the mouth, the rock walls produce tailor and bream. Whiting move over the banks just inside the mouth and upstream past the bridge. Flathead are found in the warmer months.

Yabby banks upstream of two canal entrances on the south bank are reliable bait areas, and are worth fishing while you're bait gathering.

Chopper tailor don't move this far upstream above the Gold Coast Highway Bridge on Tallebudgera Creek.

At Burleigh Heads, the rocks are easily reached along a graded walking track built by the National Parks and Wildlife Service. There are good spots for bream and tailor to be found on Burleigh Heads.

Between Southport and Burleigh is Queensland's most urbanised beach, yet somewhere along it fishable formations can always be found. Fishing in early mornings before and after beach crowds is worthwhile.

Currumbin Creek, like Tallebudgera, has reasonable fishing away from the canals. The mouth is excellent for whiting and bream at night. Tailor are found in numbers on the south breakwater and along Currumbin Rock.

Currumbin Rock and the nearby Elephant Rock are two of the Gold Coast's tailor hotspots, although this depends upon the amount of sand that's affecting the formations.

Upstream, Currumbin Creek has yabby banks where bream, whiting and flathead are caught. The pylons of the Gold Coast Highway Bridge produce nice bream, as does the older bridge further upstream.

Boat ramps in both Tallebudgera and Currimbin Creeks are more than adequate to launch the small boats suited to fishing them. Both creeks do, however, fish almost as well from the bank.

The beaches between Elephant Rock and Kirra, and the beach between Tallebudgera and Currumbin Creeks, doesn't normally have features conducive to top beach fishing. The same applies to Greenmount. Rock walls along these beaches provide bream, tailor and a few whiting by fishing back into the broken water on the beach beside them.

Point Danger is bisected by the Queensland/New South Wales border. Rock fishing off Point Danger is excellent, especially the area known as Snapper Rocks near the old swimming pool.

Snapper Rocks are so named because of the snapper caught there, although these days it's only an odd one. Washes here are reliable tailor spots. Big bream are common, while yellowtail kingfish, spotty mackerel, Spanish mackerel and an odd cobia pass by.

Whiting caught on yabbies, a bait that's prolific on the sandbanks in Tallebudgera Creek.

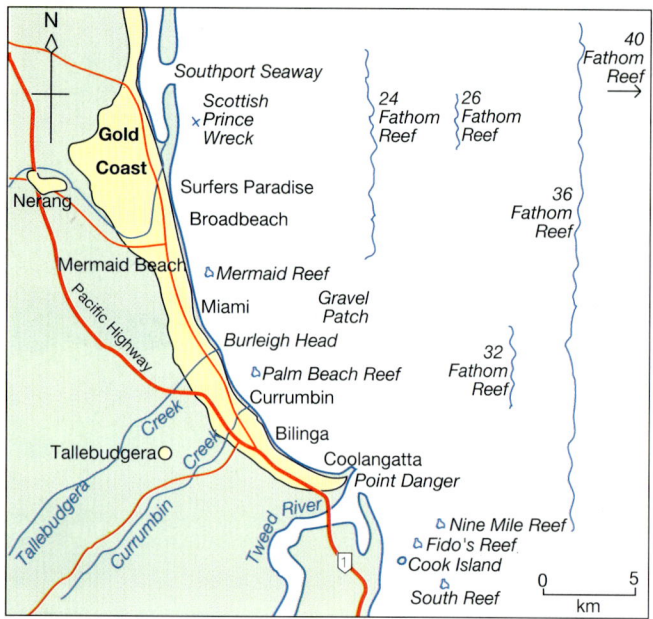

Offshore

Two areas off the Jumpinpin bar should be mentioned. North-east from the bar is the North East Pin Reef. It lies in 60 metres of water with the high points rising to 55 metres, and is about 17 kilometres north-east of the bar.

East-south-east of the 'Pin bar is a collection of pinnacles known as the Cotton Reefs. These are about 10 metres deeper than the North East Pin Reef and are about 16 kilometres out from the bar.

Another reef, known simply as the Pin Reef, also lies about 15 to 16 kilometres due east of the bar and in 60 to 65 metres of water. Being fairly deep reefs, these produce snapper, pearl perch and amberjacks.

Off the Seaway there are a number of major reefs, and of course the little ones who's locations are furtively guarded by locals. All of these are located south of a direct line east of the breakwalls. The closest to shore is the 12 Fathom Reef. It's in about 22 metres of water and lies about 2 kilometres off the beach.

Due east of the 12 Fathom Reef are scatterings of flat reef at 20 Fathom Reef (38 metres of water) and the extensive 24 Fathom Reef which extends north to east of the Seaway with scattered pinnacles all along its 4 kilometre length.

The 26 Fathom Reef is a flat reef with an odd rise another couple of kilometres seaward from the 24 Fathom.

All of these reefs are roughly east of the two in-line beacons that mark the measured nautical mile that runs from these markers to two more on the sand-pumping jetty south of the Seaway exit. These are quite visible from the 12 Fathom Reef, but have faded into obscurity by the time the 20 and 24 Fathom Reefs have been reached.

Snapper, tragalin, parrot fish and sweetlip provide the bulk of the catch from these Southport reefs. Monster

amberjacks, cobia, yellowtail kingfish and Spanish mackerel reward deep-drifted live baits.

An old shipwreck a kilometre south of the southern end of the measured mile is a reliable source of live bait. It's only a couple of hundred metres off the beach in about 10 metres of water. There's usually a local boat there early in the morning on weekends.

Wider out again, some 23 kilometres off the Seaway, is the northern end of the 36 Fathom Reef. The 36 is a narrow reef, mostly 200 metres or less, running north-south for about 15 kilometres to right down past the mouth of the Tweed. Being a deeper reef, the 36 adds pearl perch to the list of potential catches. The 36 is in 60 to 65 metres of water.

Off Mermaid, Miami and Palm Beach, closer to shore and now well south of the Seaway, are three major reefs.

The Mermaid Reef is only 3 kilometres off the beach and, being closer in and 20 metres, holds large schools of spotted mackerel during summer. Big Spaniards and cobia also move through. At other times bottom fishing will produce a mixed bag of reef fish.

The Gravel Patch is perhaps more flat reef than its name suggests, and needs a good sounder to locate due to a lack of prominent features. It's approximately 4 kilometres off the beach running all the way from Miami to Burleigh. This reef sometimes has schools of tailor, which may be caught on floated pilchards. Otherwise, the Gravel Patch has the usual reef species, and good tiger flathead are also taken here at times.

Palm Beach Reef is a large reef extending north from Currumbin Creek towards Tallebudgera Creek. It's only 1.5 kilometres off the beach with copious lumps and bumps in around 40 metres of water. When spotted and Spanish mackerel are about, Palm Beach could use traffic lights! Bottom fishing produces the usual mixed bag. Some very nice cobia come off Palm Beach in early summer, especially on week days when boat traffic is lighter.

Wide of Palm Beach, but inside the 36 Fathom, is the 32 Fathom Reef. It's quite a good piece of country in around 55 metres of water running north-south in a narrow strip no more than 100 metres wide.

Wider again is the 40 Fathom outside the 36.

Getting to all or any of these reefs offers a choice of the safety and longer travelling distances from the Seaway, or running the bar on either Currumbin or Tallebudgera Creeks. The bottom end of the 36, the 32 and the 40 are all a better proposition from the Tweed in the south.

It must be stressed that these bar crossings are not for the inexperienced or faint hearted. Even skippers experienced on bars elsewhere should seek local advice before attempting a crossing.

Currumbin and Tallebudgera bars both require a high degree of local knowledge as both are shallow and almost always have breaking water.

Fresh Water

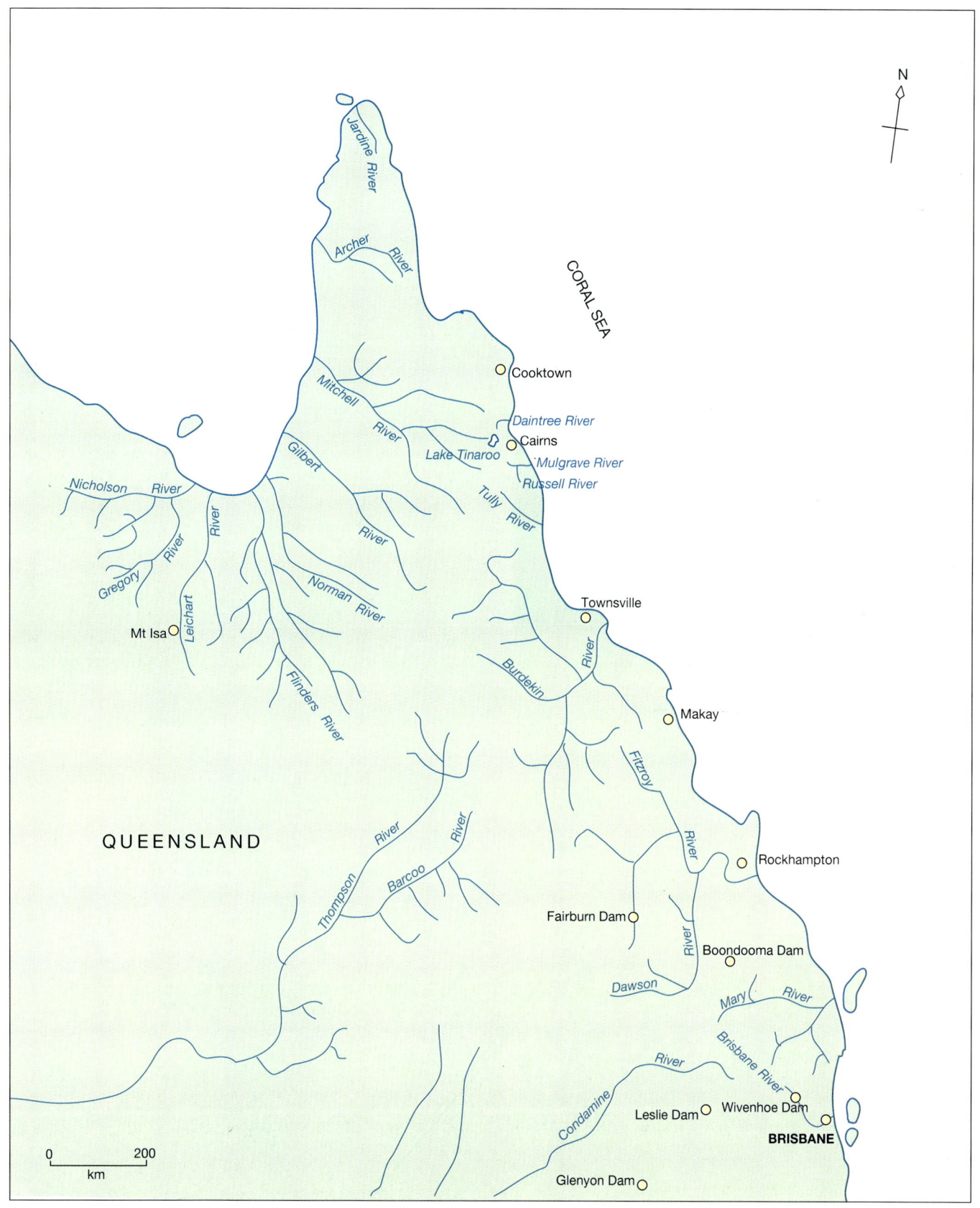

N

CORAL SEA

Jardine River

Archer River

Mitchell River

Gilbert River

Nicholson River

Gregory River

Leichart River

Norman River

Flinders River

Mt Isa

Cooktown

Daintree River

Cairns

Lake Tinaroo

Mulgrave River

Russell River

Tully River

Townsville

Burdekin River

Makay

Fitzroy River

QUEENSLAND

Thompson River

Barcoo River

Rockhampton

Fairburn Dam

Boondooma Dam

Dawson River

Mary River

Condamine River

Brisbane River

Leslie Dam

Wivenhoe Dam

BRISBANE

Glenyon Dam

0   200
km

A Murray Cod worth a thousand smiles. Fish of this size are rare today in Queensland's freshwater rivers.

Freshwater barramundi are different to their saltwater cousins. They are darker in colour, in extreme cases being green/brown and yellow, much thicker set through the body and without tides to govern their feeding habits are an easier fish to locate.

Freshwater barramundi prefer to be near structures, be it snags, lily pads or a rock bar. They're a more sedentary fish than their saltwater brethren, tending to lie deep in cover and feed in the evening or early morning.

Bait fishing with small live fish or live shrimp, lure casting, lure trolling and fly fishing all work on freshwater barramundi. Remember to present your offering close to the cover you suspect holds fish.

Queensland's larger river and freshwater wetland systems are the place to find barramundi. The rivers of the Gulf country and Cape York - the Staaten/Wyaaba, Mitchell, Gregory, Wenlock, Archer, Jardine and so on - and large lagoon/floodplain/wetland areas such as Lakefield National Park are the best bet for freshwater barramundi.

Sooty grunter are the bream of Queensland fresh water and are known as 'black bream' in most country areas. They are pugnacious and aggressive by nature and amenable to all styles of fishing.

Edibility is dependent upon diet. Rainforest fish tend to dine on a lot of vegetative food and aren't so good. Those in clear, sandy bottomed streams in the Gulf and Cape York are delicious.

In virtually every Queensland coastal stream north of Mackay which has a reasonably constant flow in its freshwater reaches, sooty grunter can be found. This includes the massive Burdekin system, the comparatively short rainforest streams like the Tully, Daintree, North and South Johnstone, Russell, and the streams of Cape York and the Gulf.

Saratoga are a poor table fish, but a great sportfish deserving careful release after capture. They feed largely in the top metre or so of water. As they are naturally curious, noisy splashy surface lures and shallow running minnows or fly rod poppers are best for saratoga. Baits work well too. Local people often splash the float, working it in similar fashion to a popper lure to attract the saratoga's attention.

Queensland has two species of saratoga: In the streams and lagoons of the Gulf and Cape York the northern species is found.

The Fitzroy/Dawson system is the only natural habitat for the southern saratoga species, but it has been stocked into many impoundments on the Mary and Brisbane River systems.

Rifle fish, a small fun fish with the fascinating habit of shooting down its prey with droplets of water, also take small lures and flies with gusto. Fished on ultra-light tackle, rifle fish can colour an otherwise dull fishing day.

In all Queensland's tropical freshwater fisheries, rifle or archer fish are likely inhabitants.

The forktail catfish, available in good sizes in all of Queensland's coastal rivers, are sometimes maligned, yet their table qualities often surpass other more favoured fish from the same waters.

All lure and bait techniques work for forktail catfish.

Bass occur in reasonable numbers as far north as Tin Can Bay. Fishing techniques cover the full spectrum, from lure casting to live baiting with shrimps or insects suspended under floats. Bass may be found anywhere from brackish reaches up to the first notable waterfall.

Queensland's better bass streams are those north of Brisbane, including those flowing into the Pumicestone Passage, behind the Sunshine Coast and in Cooloola National Park.

The Noosa River is possibly Queensland's best stream. The fish aren't large on average, but are plentiful.

Spangled perch are a small fish which don't grow to sufficient size to attract much sportfishing attention. However, they're great fun for all the family. Garden worms threaded on a small hook, suspended under a float, is the best way to go for these fish.

Many of Queensland's inland impoundments have a proliferation of spangled perch.

Snub-nosed garfish are the best freshwater table fish in Queensland. They're a surface feeder taking small insects and shrimp baits with gusto. The usual garfish technique is a 30 millimetre long shrimp on a fine wire hook suspended 50 to 300 millimetres under a 'quill' or 'pencil' float lying horizontal on the surface.

Snub-nosed garfish are prevalent in lower freshwater reaches of rivers around weed beds.

Queensland impoundments such as Awoonga and Wivenhoe dams support excellent snub nosed garfish.

The Murray cod lives on in the turbid waters of Queensland's outback rivers. These days the monsters of Australian legends are rare, but there are plenty of small ones of 2 to 5 kilograms.

Live fish, crustacea (yabbies) and the traditional bardi or witchety grubs are the best baits. Murray cod are also partial to lures, trolled or cast into likely hidey holes in timber and rock structure.

The headwaters of the western flowing rivers, where they run off the Great Divide, provide superb lure fishing in the much clearer water than the downstream reaches.

Yellowbelly perch are the bream of the inland. They're caught on the full spectrum of techniques the most successful being that known as 'bobbing' with a small sinker running down to hook baited with shrimp or crayfish. Yellowbelly are similar to bass in that they prefer to lie up in cover.

The table qualities of yellowbelly are consistently high and should never be disregarded, no matter how turbid the water they've come from.

The inland, western-flowing Queensland rivers are the home of yellowbelly, as are many impoundments in the far west of the State.

Silver perch, in the wild, prefer areas of running and/or highly oxygenated water. They're a mid-water species, rarely caught fishing the bottom, with a preference for smaller baits and lures to suit their small mouths.

In impoundments all over Queensland, silver perch have been stocked in large numbers. Their edibility varies.

Eel-tailed catfish are rated by some as the inland's finest table fish. They are easily caught on baits fished on the bottom.

In both impoundments and western rivers, eel-tailed catfish proliferate, and are one of the mainstays of Queensland outback freshwater fishing.

Impoundments or dams well stocked with barramundi, sooty grunter, silver perch, yellowbelly, Murray cod, bass and eastern cod are a prominent feature of Queensland's freshwater fishing.

Impoundment fishing techniques vary, though it is always vital to locate sub-surface structures, which may involve use of sophisticated echo sounders to find fish.

'Bobbing' with live shrimp or crayfish and trolling of deep-running lures are the most successfull techniques.

Highly productive dams are Glenlyon near Texas, Leslie near Warwick, Boondooma near Proston, Tinaroo on the Atherton Tableland, Lake MacDonald near Noosa and Lake Borumba near Gympie.

Many more dams have been stocked and these should evolve into superb fisheries over the ensuing years.

Upstream hiking brought this angler to some prime Queensland freshwater fishing country on the Condamine River.

New South Wales

Introduction

New South Wales is the most developed angling State in Australia. Many of the successful fishing techniques used throughout the country originated in New South Wales.

Encompassing saltwater fishing options ranging from convenient city settings, to remote estuary, rock, beach, and offshore angling destinations, the New South Wales coastline appeals to a broad cross-section of anglers. Throughout the summer, and especially during the holiday periods, bait and tackle businesses flourish, coastal tourist towns that have been lying dormant during winter suddenly spring to life as hopeful anglers adorn wharves, beaches, and rocky headlands in an attempt to catch fish. Local boat ramps attract scores of anglers rushing to launch boats, or happily retrieving their vessels after a successful day's fishing. And for offshore anglers, the warm oceanic currents bring game fish such as marlin, varying species of tuna, Spanish mackerel in more northerly regions, and wahoo within safe boating range.

For the freshwater fishing enthusiast, the Great Dividing Range is the line dividing the east and westward flowing rivers. The Australian bass, a popular angling target frequents the coastal streams, while over the ranges, outback fishing for native species such as the yellowbelly (golden perch), black bream (silver perch) and the mighty Murray cod is available.

In the highland regions of the Great Dividing Range south from the New England Tablelands, rainbow and brown trout proliferate in rivers, streams and impoundments. While the dry fly fisherman eagerly awaits the summer hatches of insects, when trout rise to a well-presented imitation, lure and bait fishermen catch trout year-round at places such as Lake Eucumbene and Jindabyne.

New South Wales contains much of the country's finest salt and freshwater fishing and, with sensible environmental measures to protect our fisheries, will continue to do so for many years.

Oceans rocks are one of the most popular angling environments in New South Wales. Here, a group of 'rock hoppers' are in the midst of a hot luderick bite off Sydney's Curl Curl headland.

The Tweed

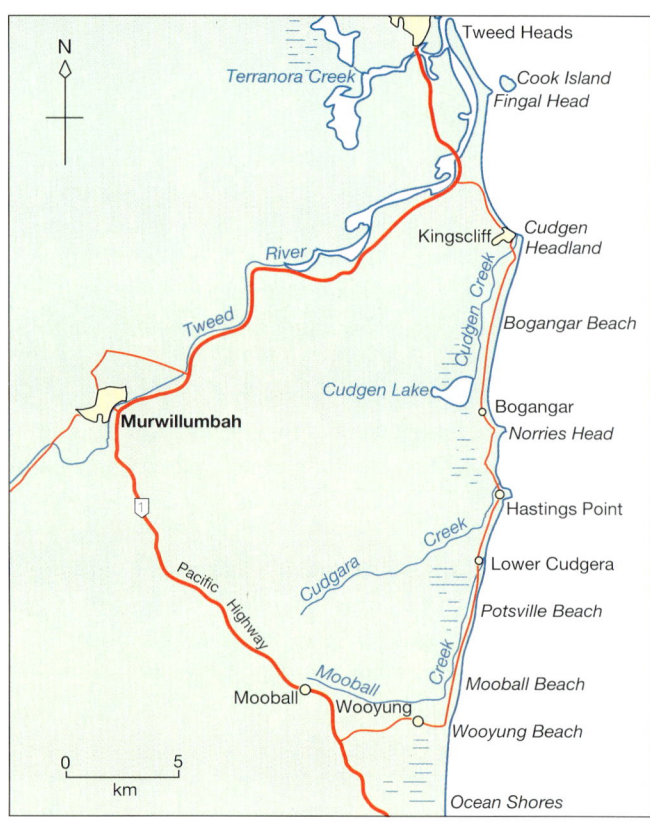

Time to clean the day's catch.

Offshore the Tweed River has much to offer. The Tweed bar is a better prospect for a crossing to get to offshore grounds than the Currumbin or Tallebudgera Creek entrances further north.

Reef fishing due east of the bar concentrates on the southern end of the 36 Fathom Reef which runs along a large portion of the Gold Coast.

Cook Island, Fingal and the complex rock reefs extending eastwards from it has good bottom fishing and a few pelagics.

Washes around the Giant's Causeway contain good tailor fishing and there are also several renowned jew spots. Caution is needed in a swell as some sections are dangerous.

The rocky extension of Fingal Head and the Giant's Causeway is a hotspot. The bottom fishing is some of the best, and pelagics concentrate in an area where the food chain runs thick and strong. Yellowtail king and Spaniard move through in summer.

Washes around the Island also hold big tailor. Depending on the direction of the swell these can be on the north eastern and south eastern corners. Yellowtail kings also frequent Cook Island around Mary's Rock on the north east corner.

Fido's (or Fideaux) Bommie is a kilometer to the east of Cook. It is unpredictable and can be quite dangerous with ugly shaped and breaking waves suddenly rearing up out of nowhere, especially when a south easterly opposes a strong northern current. Nonetheless the reef area has a prodigious supply of squire, snapper and other reef species. Spanish mackerel, cobia, yellowtail kings and other pelagics (even small marlin) also frequent Fido's in numbers.

Nine Mile Reef further to the east is less than 8 kilometers from the Tweed, is an underwater cliff face rising almost vertically on its northern face to within 6 metres of the surface from around 30 metres on the western side and over 40 on the eastern side. The shallow area on the south western corner is jokingly known as "The Ripples" in reference to the huge breakers that form in similar conditions to those described on Fido's.

Dolphin fish come in onto the outer Nine Mile. Wahoo move in in schools in Autumn with trevally, amberjack, mackerel tuna, school yellowfin and other species.

When the southerlies push a stream of warm blue water in from the north onto the reef complex, small marlin can be about in droves.

South Reef, south west of a line between Cook and the Nine Mile also rises to within 6 metres in one place. It too can break and deserves a watchful eye.

The Tweed River is well serviced with good ramps in both arms. Offshore anglers are advised to use the Kennedy Drive ramp beside the Tweed/Coolangatta bypass road off the Pacific Highway.

Inside the river there is good bream, whiting and flathead fishing up as far as Murwillumbah. Rockwalls down near the mouth fish well for bream and blackfish. The walls guarding the Tweed entrance are copious producers of beam and tailor and on jewfish after rains as are other river walls in northern New South Wales.

Cudgen Creek is an alternative crossing to the Tweed Bar. Reefs guard the entrance from the brunt of south easterly swells and it is sometimes possible to exit Cudgen Creek when a swell has closed out the Tweed Bar. Low water can cause serious problems however, when the creek virtually dries in some areas. This is a condition that varies and local advice should be sought.

Upstream from the bridge on Cudgen Creek is an area of shallow sandbank systems which fishes well for flathead and whiting. The south breakwall is the better area and good catches of tailor, bream and a few jewfish are possible.

Rocks to the south of the south breakwater fish well but can be dangerous.

Norries Head is the next feature south after Bogangar Beach. Bogangar always has good gutters and is one of the best beaches in the area. Parts of Norries Head known as Toss Point and Razorback are top spots for tailor and bream.

South Bogangar Beach between Norries and Cudgera Creek is best known for quality whiting. Cudgera Creek and its neighbour Mooball Creek are both small and shallow virtually drying at low tide. Mooball produces whiting and flathead down near the mouth. Both creeks have good yabby pumping banks.

Between the mouths of these two creeks are a number of protruding rocks near the popular holiday village of Hastings Point. These produce anything from tailor to a few snapper off the appropriately named Schnapper Rock.

Hastings Point to Wooyung is the last accessible beach area. Pottsville Beach and the rocks between Pottsville and Wooyung, Mooball Beach and Wooyung Beach all fish well if beach conditions are read and the formations interpreted.

The only access to the Ocean Shores development is between Wooyung and New Brighton on the north side of the Brunswick River as there is no road from Wooyung to New Brighton.

Pottsville is reached by turning off the Pacific Highway at the small town of Mooball or at Wooyung at the turn-off on the Burringbar Range. This leads to a road following the coast all the way to Kingscliff where it connects again with the Pacific Highway.

The New Brighton turn-off is a few kilometres north of Brunswick Heads. The beach here is always worth a look and the shallow north arm of the Brunswick River is very productive of whiting and flathead in the warmer months.

Top: Cook Island washes are a favoured haunt of big tailor.
Above: Even bigger kingfish and cobia can be taken on surface lures.

Brunswick to Byron Bay

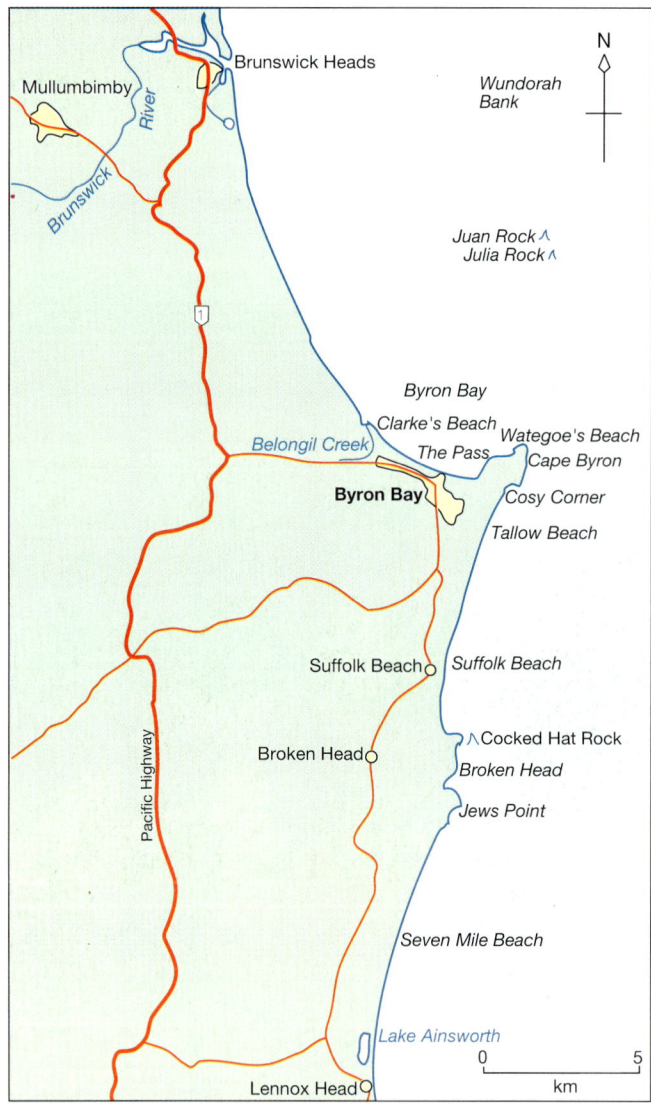

At **New Brighton and north towards Hastings Point** is an inshore reef only a couple of kilometers offshore. In addition to mixed reef fish all year round this reef really fires for spotted mackerel and Spaniards during summer. The cooler months often find it holding tailor schools.

For those with a four-wheel drive, an alternative to braving the Brunswick bar is to beach launch at Byron Bay at the surfing beach called "The Pass". There is a concrete ramp down onto the beach which sometimes has soft sand at the bottom of it but once onto the harder sand a four-wheel drive has few problems. The worst problem of launching at the Pass is returning to the beach later in the day when the surfers are about.

Juan and Julian Rocks are two prominent rocky islets off Byron Bay, popular with divers, but are marine parks and

fishing is restricted to one line per angler within 1 kilometre.

Great care must be taken to avoid divers who tend to be very protective of Julian Rocks, so close checking on the extent of the marine park at Byron Bay dive shops is advisable.

Wundorah Bank, north of Byron Bay, is an extensive raised rocky reef marked on charts and usually referred to locally as The Cod Ground. Wundorah Bank and Juan and Julian Rocks are possibly the best 'undiscovered' game and sportfishing hotspot in New South Wales. Boat access is awkward. Marlin, wahoo, mackerel, several tunas and other surface fish are in plague proportions. The quantity of bottom fish is seemingly never ending.

The Brunswick River is excellent upstream to the township of Mullumbimby. It's shallow in many places which is conducive to fishing for whiting and flathead.

Closer to the mouth, the breakwalls and training walls produce bream, tailor, and mulloway. During winter the Brunswick's breakwalls boast excellent luderick fishing. Yabbies are easy to find in the many shallow areas of the Brunswick and are a top bait in the river.

The Brunswick has a good boat ramp on the south bank of the river between the trawler harbour and the highway bridge. Access to the north wall and New Brighton beach is via New Brighton (with some walking to reach the wall). Access to the south wall is over South Creek bridge towards the surf beach.

Beaches in Byron Shire require the Shire Council permit to travel by a four-wheel drive. The beach between Brunswick and Byron Bay is closed to all traffic and must be accessed on foot. It's around 10 kilometres from Brunswick Heads to Byron Bay with the only road access points being at the Brunswick Heads surf club and Belongil Creek north of Byron Bay. South Beach always has good fishing formations.

The beach in front of the Byron Bay Surf Club is sheltered and doesn't often have gutter formations, but it does produce whiting.

Clarke's Beach often has a large lagoon which may or may not be open to the sea. This is all whiting country, with a few bream and (around the lagoon) flathead.

Wategoe's Beach itself is one of the most popular swimming spots at Byron Bay and not fished much.

Tallow Beach extends into Suffolk Park, a little holiday village south of Byron. There are four-wheel drive tracks into some sections of this beach where good fishing formations are found.

At Cape Byron, rocks along the edge of the Pass and around to Wategoe's Beach are crowded in daylight hours and best fished at night. From Wategoe's around underneath the towering Cape Byron requires negotiating the weathered rocks.

By driving up to the lighthouse, the best fishing water is easily observed, although reaching it is an entirely different matter!

Bream and tailor are the most common catch close into the rocks. In several places deep water harbours pelagics.

Cosy Corner is tucked in beside the southern corner of Cape Byron and is the best place to shelter from northerly winds.

Broken Head is the next rock headland south of Byron Bay. It has an attractive little campground, and walking tracks over the headland to several fishing spots.

Cocked Hat Rocks, just offshore, are out of reach (unless you like to swim), but nonetheless there's plenty of rock fishing territory on Broken Head and on a series of small headlands interspersed with tiny beaches to the south.

A dirt road leads around the back of Broken head to the northern end of Seven Mile Beach which runs unbroken to Lennox Head.

Seven Mile Beach is magnificent, one of the most brilliant beaches in Australia. The only vehicular access point between Broken Head and Lennox Head is reached by a road leading around the back of Lake Ainsworth, a popular swimming spot. This leads down onto the beach but remember to check with Ballina Shire Council for your beach permit.

At Lennox Head boulders are an added fishing attraction on an already great beach. The boulders form the coastline around the foot of Lennox Head and extend north along the tiny township for up to several kilometres, depending on recent weather and whether or not sand has been deposited.

Lennox Head is a tailor mecca, and the rock-studded gutters along the beach also produce big bream. A gap through the bouldered beach at the southern end of town close to the headland is called the Boat Channel. Locals launch small 4 to 4.3 metre boats here to run through the shallow narrow entrance to catch offshore pelagics.

The point at Lennox Head is one of the top tailor spots on the north coast. Surfers are such a problem, however, that the rocks are unfishable.

Reaching the southern aspect of Lennox Head is strictly for the fit and healthy. Two spots known as the Ledge and Shag Rock front deep water and produce pelagics when warm currents are inshore, while snapper predominate as soon as you can get on the rocks after big seas.

Left: The Byron Bay region is Spanish mackerel territory.
Above: Bream do not come much bigger than this Byron specimen.

Skennars Head to Evans Head

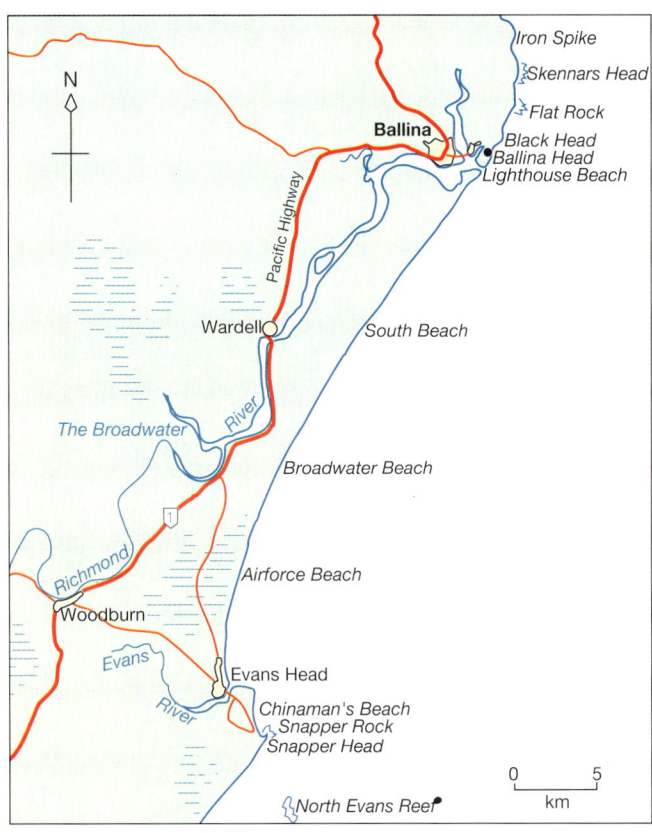

top beach fishing. Gutters along this beach are fished effectively for flathead using fresh prawns suspended under a float.

Black Head is virtually a suburb of Ballina. It was quarried to supply rock for the Richmond River breakwaters, and access to some parts is awkward. Black Head is close enough to the outfall of the river to attract mulloway after heavy rains. The rocks are safe except in rough seas. Tailor and bream frequent Black Head and some nice whiting are caught in the gutters where sand fringes the rocks.

Shelley Beach and Lighthouse Beach, popular surfing beaches, run north and south of Lighthouse Hill or Ballina Head as it's also known. Lighthouse Hill's rocks fish reasonably well for bream and tailor. There's often a strong rip running along the face of the headland.

All the beaches and rocks between Ballina and Lennox Head are accessible from the coast road on to Byron Bay.

The Richmond River's north wall is the least productive of the two but is shorter and an easier walk than the south wall. Both are bream and luderick hotspots with big schools of tailor available on their annual migration in winter and early spring.

Ballina enjoys some of New South Wales' most brilliant beach fishing. Such as Black Rocks at Bundjalung National Park.

Between Lennox Head and Skennars Head is a spot named the Iron Spike after an old iron bar concreted into the rocks. This is a brilliant land-based game fishing location, though it is dangerous and has been the site of several fatalities.

Spanish mackerel, longtail tuna, cobia, yellowtail kingfish, snapper and other rock species are available off the Iron Spike and on nearby rocks. But be warned: for safety's sake it should only be fished in calm conditions.

Skennars Head has always fished well.

Where Skennars Head joins the beach is the last of the boulder coastline that begins at Lennox Head. These boulders are at times covered with sand, however there is a deep gutter formation caused by current sweeping around the rocks. The gutter is a renowned year-round mulloway and tailor spot.

Flat Rock, a tailor hotspot, is a shelf found after following the short beach that runs along the coast. The rock shelves very gradually making it a hard place on tackle, however it is reasonably safe.

The beach either side of Flat Rock, north to Skennars Head and south to Ballina, has good formations and offers

Left: Tailor abound in the washes around Evans Head.
Above: Offshore from Ballina are some bountiful fishing reefs.

Large concrete blocks at the end of the breakwaters make a long gaff a prerequisite to land a mulloway. The best time for them is when the turbid run-off has eased enough after heavy rains for high tide to begin pushing clean water back into the river.

To get to the South Wall from Ballina the quickest way is over the Burns Point Ferry (turn off towards the river from the big straight leading south. The South Wall in summer and autumn is one of the better land-based locations to catch Spanish mackerel.

Inside the Richmond River there is a complex of low walls on the south bank known as the Porpoise Walls. These produce bream and luderick. Further upstream the river is drift fished by local anglers seeking flathead and any area with a rock wall or wharf is worth a try for bream.

There are good boat ramps in Ballina and at Wardell.

South Beach, not to be confused with the South Beach north of Lennox Head, stretches over 20 kilometres from the South Wall to Evans Head. At various places it is known as Broadwater Beach, Patches Beach and Air Force Beach.

There are signs off the old highway between Burns Point Ferry and Wardell to Patches Beach. Broadwater Beach is reached through the sugar milling town of Broadwater, where the road to Evans Head first goes to Broadwater Beach and then runs through the hinterland of Broadwater National Park to Evans Head.

South Beach is negotiable by four-wheel drive all the way from Ballina to Evans Head. A permit from Ballina Shire Council is necessary to drive on the beach. Some caution is advised at Broadwater Beach and at the exit of a lagoon system behind the dunes known as Salty Lakes in Broadwater National Park. Depending upon sand movements, soft sandstone may be exposed at Broadwater Beach. Salty Lakes flood heavily after a lot of rain.

South Beach is a great beach fishing location with productive formations assured somewhere along its length. Beachworms and pipis are readily available on the beach.

The Riordan Reefs, halfway along South Beach, are only about 2 kilometres offshore. These aren't easy to locate, and visitors are advised to seek local advice.

The Ballina bar is a deep-water entrance but can break badly on a falling tide. There are several ramps suitable for smaller boats in Ballina (Riverview Park, Faulkes Park, Burns Point) besides the main ramp on the western side of Fishery Creek bridge beside the Pacific Highway.

The Evans River bar is protected from southerly wind and swell. Evans Head has an excellent boat ramp with cleaning tables and wash down facilities. A low bridge between the ramp and the mouth of the river doesn't normally cause problems, however rods in a high-mounted rack aren't likely to fit underneath.

Evans Head contains many good rock fishing spots, as does Snapper Rock to the south. Access is strictly by foot. All rock species are present along the headland, reached by driving over the bridge to the south side of the river and then taking the turn-off to Snapper Rock and Chinaman's Beach to reach the southern end, or driving up to the lookout on top of the headland overlooking the breakwalls and walking from there to the northern end.

The breakwalls fish well, although they don't extend far offshore. Bream, tailor and mulloway are common. There is one spot on the headland which fronts deep water over a sand bottom where Spanish mackerel and other pelagics are caught.

There are many reefs off Evans Head named by the usual method of depth in fathoms. An exposed bombora to the south-east called Chaos is of interest to sportfishers wishing to tangle with the huge kingfish and Spanish mackerel.

Woody Head to Woolgoola

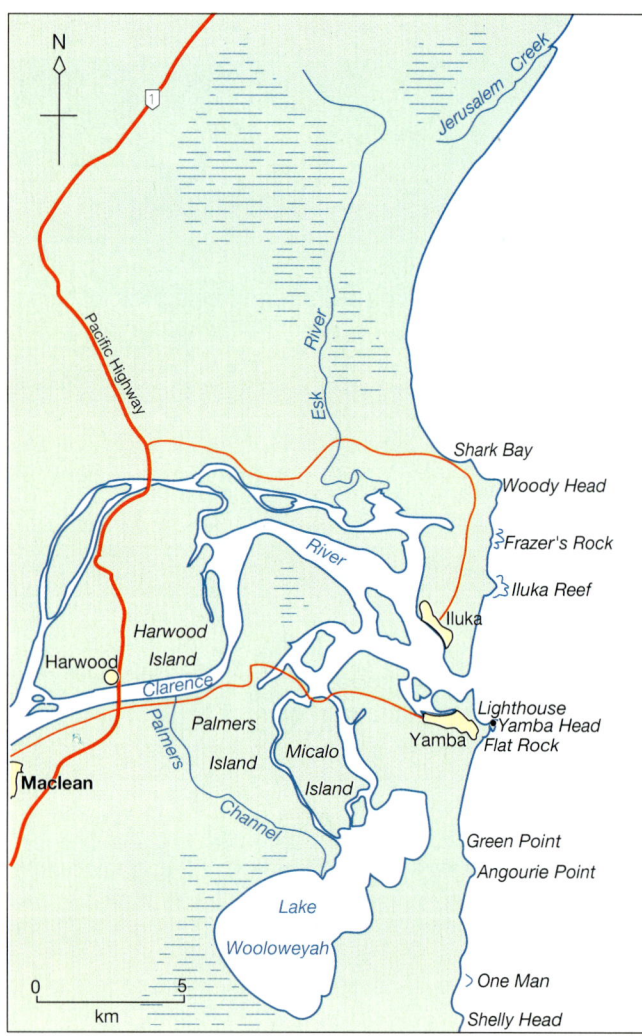

of reef fish and spotted and Spanish mackerel are caught offshore.

Between Woody Head and Iluka are a series of weathered sandstone bluffs. Woody Head itself, the Iluka Bluff, the Little Bluff, Frazer's Reef and the beaches between are all top rock and beach fishing spots rivalling the best anywhere.

This area has a well deserved reputation for quality tailor, mulloway, bream, whiting, blackfish, flathead, dart, tarwhine and several rocks front deep water where Spanish mackerel, other pelagics and snapper are caught.

There's camping at Woody Head and units at Iluka, and anything from a little aluminium dinghy to an offshore boat opens the door to the Clarence estuary or, with a larger boat, the grounds offshore.

Bomboras north of Woody Head are a holding ground for immense schools of spotted mackerel and the reefs offshore still yield as many big snapper.

The Clarence River is the most prolific fish producer in New South Wales. Breakwalls extend well to sea, providing a platform for fishing tailor, mulloway and surface fish. Inside the mouth, bream and luderick frequent the rock walls. Yamba's Middle Wall is one of the most famous bream spots in the country.

Extensive sandflats hold whiting and flathead. Flathead are caught by drift fishing well up river at least to Harwood where the Pacific Highway crosses the river.

Bundjalung National Park is unusual in that a large portion is an RAAF bombing and gunnery range, closed to public access. The RAAF restricted area extends from Snapper Rocks just south of Evans Head to Jerusalem Creek. The Gap Road around 19 kilometres south of Woodburn leads into Jerusalem Creek, which has a small bush campground and 'coffee rock' formations.

Four-wheel drives may be used on the beach from Jerusalem Creek to Shark Bay. There are access ramps at each end.

Woody Head has a pretty National Parks and Wildlife Services campground tucked away in the lee of the headland much used by holiday anglers fishing the beach, rocks and offshore on the north side of the mighty Clarence River.

Trailerboats larger than 5 metres are launched with a four-wheel drive over the beach at Woody Head. The beach is firm and sheltered from the south. Good catches

Luderick are 'on' at Iluka Bluff. At other times, it may be bream, tailor, Spanish mackerel or snapper.

Woody Head, Iluka and the north bank of the Clarence are reached from a well signposted turn-off to Iluka 65 kilometres south of Wodburn. Iluka has several boat ramps. Smaller boats may be launched near the hotel and upstream at an old ferry approach near the big power lines. Trailerboats of any size may be launched from the main ramp at the end of Spenser Street.

Yamba turn-off is just on the southern side of the big bridge over the Clarence at Harwood. It, too, is well signposted. From Yamba there's a choice of fishing the Clarence or the rocks and beaches to the south, which equal those to the north of the river.

There are several boat ramps in Yamba, two of which are quite close to the main road and easy to find.

Yamba and Angourie (a small collection of houses south of Yamba) have rock fishing from Flat Rock, Green Point and Angourie Point.

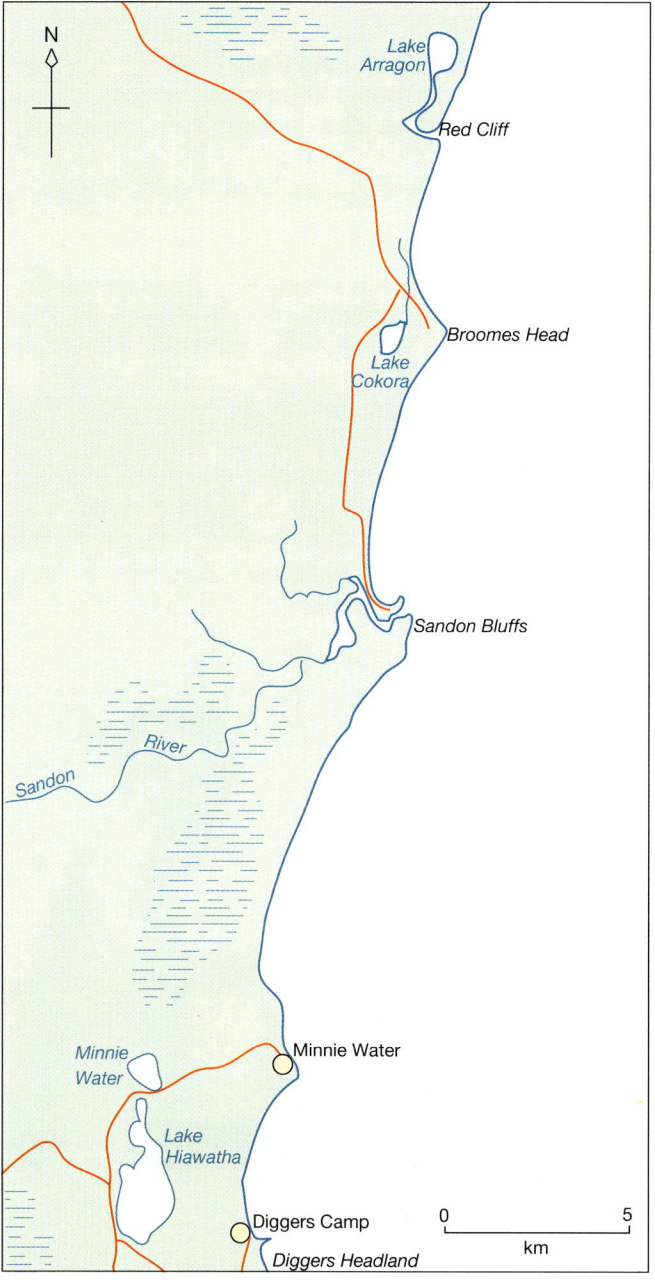

South of Angourie is Yuraygir National Park. A dirt road leading off to the right in Angourie crosses heath country to Angourie Point. From here you walk to a number of prime rock fishing platforms.

These are some of the best around and there are two spots with deep water visible from the walking track where snapper and surface fish are likely. Tailor, bream, mulloway and other rock species are abundant, too. The biggest problem is carrying out a big mulloway or Spanish mackerel!

Rocks fronting the bluff, known locally as One Man, need extra caution as there have been fatalities there.

Shelley Head has a small walk into the National Parks and Wildlife Services' campground. The front of Shelley Head is a top rock spot with all the rock species and occasional surface fish available.

Shelley Head is approximately the halfway mark in the northern section of Yuraygir National Park between Angourie Point and Red Cliff. From either end it's a 5 to 6 kilometre walk in.

Buchanan's Head is the only rock fishing feature to the south of Shelley Head as there is more beach than rock to the north.

The turn-off to Red Cliff is at Maclean on the Pacific Highway. This same road leads to Brooms Head and the Sandon River.

Brooms Head is a small village existing on holiday trade and retired residents. There's a council-run caravan park and a store, and a few cottages and flats are for rent. It is possible to beach launch at Brooms Head as the beach shelters in the lee of the headland. Beach and rock fishing here is good and there is reef fishing offshore. Location of the reefs requires local knowledge.

The business end of a dusky flathead sporting a diving minnow lure. Flathead are common in the Clarence and Sandon Rivers.

Sandon River is further down the road from Brooms Head. It's the end of the road though houses on the opposite bank may be reached from Minnie Water to the south by four-wheel drive.

The Sandon has a lovely little National Parks and Wildlife Services camping area, very crowded at holiday times. The boat ramp there gives access to reefs offshore and to the south of the entrance. The entrance lacks a bar and is quite reasonable in southerly weather. It can, however, become nasty in a northerly. Smaller boats are launched beside the road to the camping area.

The river is quite shallow in many areas and has rock bars upstream, but is a consistent producer of flathead and whiting. Rocks down near the mouth and deeper water upstream are the places to seek bream and luderick. Yabbies are available upstream and gathering beachworms and pipis presents few problems on the beach.

To travel the 10 kilometres as the crow flies from the Sandon to Minnie Water requires a roundabout detour back to the Pacific Highway, then south to Ulmara. Minnie Water, Digger's Camp and Wooli are all off this

same road. Another road connecting with the Minnie Water/Wooli Road comes in from the Pacific Highway south of Grafton.

Wooli is yet another delightful small coastal town dependent on holiday trade with top fishing and offshore access for those experienced enough to tackle the shallow bar entrance. Bear in mind that a commercial fishery does operate out of here so the bar is workable often enough. It is strictly off limits for novices, though . Wooli has quite a good boat ramp, facilities and plentiful accommodation for rent.

The beaches and rocks at Wooli, on the headland near Digger's Camp and at Minnie Water are all of similar high' quality to the rest of this area.

Breakwalls at the mouth of the Wooli River add spinning and live baiting for big mulloway to the list of possibles, especially after heavy rains.

The Wooli River has extensive shallow areas and plentiful whiting and flathead around the sandbanks. There is a channel leading upstream suitable for smaller boats, which deepens once past the caravan park near Rum Island, to continue up to Collet's Crossing. Mud crabs are available in the river.

North Solitary Islands, some 12 to 13 kilometres offshore, can be reached from the closest access point, the Wooli River.

The islands hold large numbers of pelagics, and bottom fishing is excellent.

Red Rock is at the mouth of the shallow Corindi River. It has a caravan park, flats and cottages for rent, and a store.

The river may be waded at low tide to reach beach fishing north of Red Rock, or a dirt road leading through Barcoongere State Forest turns off the highway to a National Park rest area at Station Creek. From here it's only a short walk to the beach.

Kingfish such as this jig-caught specimen are the dominant catch around the Solitary Islands.

Coffs Harbour

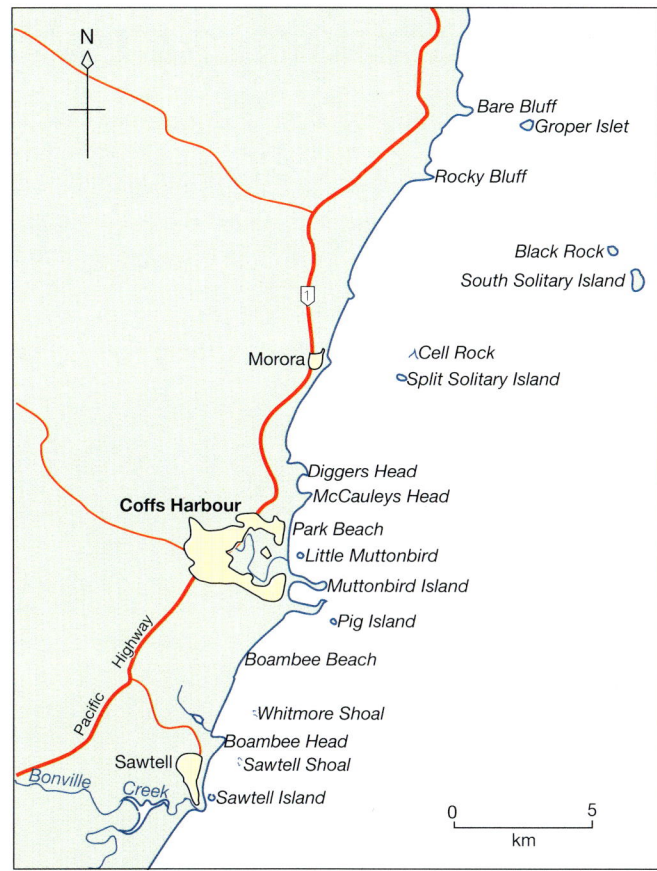

With this number of offshore reefs, it is little wonder Coffs Harbour is renowned as the home of huge amberjacks and kingfish; big Spanish and spotted mackerel; outsize tailor; cobia; billfish, yellowfin, and dolphin fish around floats marking fish traps on many reefs. There are longtail tuna, mackerel tuna and bonito. And that's just the surface fish.

Suitable bottom fishing reefs are in abundance and as happy as any sportfisher will be with the islands, bottom fishers will be every bit as happy with the big snapper, pearl perch, teraglin and other reef fish available.

Coffs Harbour's ramp is excellent with facilities for fish cleaning at the Deep Sea Fishing Club House. However a big swell pushes a surge into Coffs Harbour which rises and falls 0.5 of a metre at times, and has swamped many tow vehicles which backed down the ramp past the high water mark. Watch how far up the ramp the water surges and launch at the appropriate time.

Between Woolgoolga and Sawtell, fishing from the shore is almost as good as offshore. Within the suburbs of Coffs Harbour Diggers Head, McCauleys Head, the harbour walls and Mutton Bird Island are all superlative rock fishing spots with an abundance of all the rock-dwelling fishes. Pelagics and snapper are available off Mutton Bird Island (which is connected to the mainland by the harbour works).

To get to sea north of Coffs there are two beach launching options at Arrawarra and Woolgoolga. Both are sheltered bays behind a protruding point, fine in a southerly but unusable in a northerly. The beaches are hard but very flat which can cause problems for large deep-vee boats.

Off Red Rock is North West Solitary Island and a bombora known as The Wash, the haunt of huge tailor and yellowtail kingfish big enough to eat them whole.

The Wash is a twin-peaked pinnacle that barely breaks the surface at low tide. There is over 30 metres of water quite close to the rocks. Trolling the Wash will yield big Spanish mackerel, cobia, wahoo and other pelagics.

Other Islands offshore include South West Solitary which is to the south off Woolgoolga and just a few kilometres offshore; Groper Island closer inshore; South Solitary, sometimes called the Light because of its lighthouse, about 9 to 10 kilometres from Coffs Harbour ramp; Black Rock; Cell Rock; Split Solitary (so named because of a huge split down the centre of the rock); Muttonbird Island and Pig Island a short distance off Coffs Harbour.

South of Coffs Harbour there isn't the profusion of islands and bomboras there are to the north. Nonetheless, off Sawtell and Boambee the Whitmore Reef, Sawtell Shoal and Sawtell Island close inshore all produce mulloway, snapper and kingfish. Local anglers always use wire here, is an indication of the regular occurence of mackerel.

There are three ramps servicing the area. One in Boambee Creek, one in Bonville Creek at Sawtell and one into the gutter behind Sawtell Island. With the closeness of Coffs Harbour's ramp, visitors are advised to use it for offshore fishing.

Bonville and Boambee Creeks and the little creek at Coffs itself all fish well for estuary species, and even hold a few big mangrove jacks.

Boambee Head has some good gutters which hold bream, tailor and mulloway. Four-wheel drives are allowed on Boambee Beach between Coffs and Boambee.

The front of Sawtell Island contains good spinning ledges and live baiting platforms.

Sawtell to Nambucca Heads

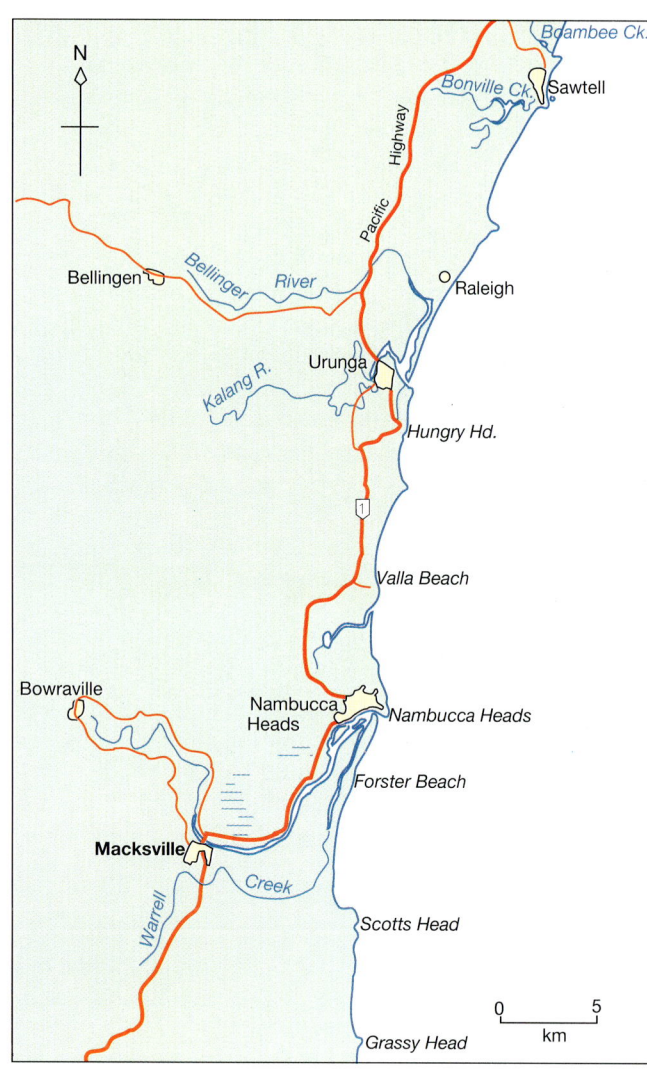

This long expanse of coastline holds a wide variety of fish and fishing locations, although access for boat fishermen to outside waters is difficult.

Sawtell has a small but productive estuary, a number of surrounding creeks and estuary systems worthy of note, and caravan park, flats and a motel available.

Boambee and Bonville Creek hold solid populations of bream, flathead, whiting and blackfish. Both creeks are of interest to sportsfishing lure tossers as they harbour mangrove jacks and tropical trevally. Flathead and bream can also be spun here creeks.

The Bellingen River at Urungan, and the smaller Kalang River system, are noted for good flathead fishing and winter runs of blackfish.

The best fishing is concentrated in the lower reaches between Urunga and Raleigh where mixed estuary catches include mud crabs trapped.

Reasonable beach fishing is available north of Urunga by following the Pacific Highway to the Repton turn-off, for North Beach.

Offshore angling produces good hauls of snapper, and Spanish and spotted mackerel in the warmer months. Most of the mackerel are taken fishing near Hungry, several kilometres south of the river entrance.

Valla Beach, a small coastal town between Urunga and Nambucca Heads, is a good place to launch small aluminium boats for offshore fishing.

Deep creek enters the sea and holds reasonable stocks of flathead and bream and some mangrove jack and tarpon.

Bream, whiting, tailor and mulloway can be fished both north and south of Valla Beach.

Nambucca Heads, one of the major tourist towns on the mid North Coast, is on the very productive Nambucca River estuary.

Excellent catches of flathead are available from the mouth of the river to Macksville, and in Warrell Creek on the southern side. The river also has good numbers of whiting, bream and blackfish. School mulloway are found near the entrance.

Wide off Scotts head during the height of summer is the place and time for dolphin fish. This one's about average size.

Unfortunately, the river mouth at Nambucca Heads is badly silted, shallow, dangerous, and usually covered by breaking surf. Most offshore anglers choose to launch at Shelley Beach just north of the town. For radio cover call Valhalla Base on channel 27880. Local fishermen will give advice on the launching procedure at Shelley Beach. A fishing club tractor is available to assist those without a four-wheel drive.

Offshore angling out of Nambucca is very good. The main reef areas east and north-east of the river mouth and 2 to 7 kilometres offshore yield snapper, trag, mulloway, pearl perch and morwong.

Inshore headlands produce plenty of Spanish and spotted mackerel, (and all areas along this stretch of coast).

Beach and rock fishing in Nambucca is quiet compared to other locations; most anglers head north to the Valla.

Scott's Head, a small town with only a camping ground and flats for accommodation, has no estuary. Boat access to the sea is over the sand in the protected corner of the beach below the town.

Offshore fishing is good, although launching is mostly suited to small craft. Many anglers who fish off Scott's Head run south to Grassy Head. Spanish and spotted mackerel are the major catch, the reefs fish well for mulloway, kingfish, cobia and teraglin.

The whole area between Scott's Head and Grassy Head is dotted with reefs. A depth sounder will be helpful. Start in areas where traps are visible.

For the owner of a four-wheel drive, Forster Beach, which runs for 10 kilometres north of Scott's Head to the mouth of the Nambucca River, and Grassy Head beaches fish very well.

Above: Wahoo roam the warm currents off Grassy and Scotts Head from December to May.
Below: Beach fishing near Grassy Head for Whiting.

Southwest Rocks to Hat Head

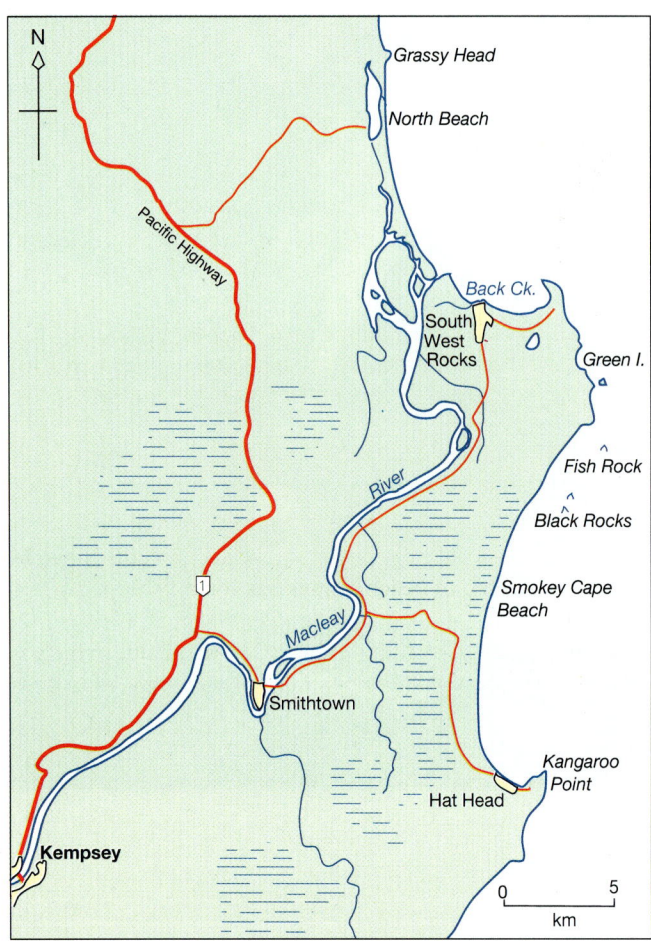

South West Rocks provides access to some of the best all-round fishing in New South Wales; there are tropical and temperate fish species and the closeness of the Continental Shelf ensures excellent game fishing.

South West Rocks is reached by turning off the Pacific Highway at Kempsey. The town is 490 kilometres from Sydney and about the same distance from Brisbane. The Hat Head turn-off runs south off the main road into South West Rocks. On average, both places are about a six to seven hour drive from Sydney or Brisbane.

Motels, caravan parks and flats are found at South West Rocks. Bait, ice, tackle, fuel and outboard service are readily available.

Bait, ice and fuel, a caravan park and rental flats are also available at Hat Head.

At South West Rocks there are three boat ramp sites.

The Macleay River ramp near town is quite good, but there may be a few problems experienced at dead low tide. It is illuminated at night and has a cleaning table with running water. A boatshed at the ramp has self-drive launches for hire and a reasonable supply of bait for sale.

The second is seven kilometres upstream from the river mouth on the northern side of Jerseyville Bridge.

Access offshore is most popular via Back Creek which runs along the northern edge of the town. The ramp is very good with plenty of parking and cleaning tables. Unfortunately, sandflies are exceptionally active at dawn and dusk.

Both the Macleay River and Back Creek offer sea access over a surf bar, but can be dangerous, so local advice should be sought before heading out. Back Creek is shallow at the bottom of the tide.

Hat Head Creek is very badly silted due to flood mitigation works in the surrounding catchment, and is only suitable for boats under five metres. The surf break is generally harmless because of the protection offered by the headland, but care is always necessary.

The South West Rocks/Hat Head offshore area has distinct seasonal runs of fish. The main interest is in the light-tackle game fish that haunt the area for most of the year. Spanish mackerel, spotted mackerel (known locally as snook) and cobia are plentiful. Marlin, tuna, dolphin fish, wahoo, kingfish and sharks, are all common in season. The hot current that touches the Rocks also carries a range of tropical species, and many unexpected visitors turn up each season, including a few sailfish.

Bottom fishing at South West Rocks is still very good, with mulloway, snapper, teraglin, morwong and flathead making up most of the catches. Pearl perch provide one of the sea's tastiest rewards here.

The area is dotted with reefs north and south of South West Rocks, but in front of the town is mostly sand and is trawled heavily for prawns.

Bottom fishing off Hat Head is also very productive with a range of reefs extending out to some very deep grounds that produce excellent captures in the right conditions.

Green Island is close inshore just north of Smokey Cape, and only a short run by sea from South West Rocks. The island holds a wide variety of fish, with tailor, bonito, bream, kingfish, cobia and bluefin tuna most prominent. It is also a good spot for catching live bait.

Black Rock is further south past Smokey Cape, but also close to shore. It yields the same sort of fish as Green Island, though cobia and mulloway are more prolific.

Black Rock is best avoided in big seas as it is a shallow area that breaks at odd angles with any sort of a roll.

Fish Rock is one of the most productive locations along

the coast. It sits on the edge of the bluewater current east of Smokey Cape, and has everything from game fish through to bottom fish. When Fish Rock is firing the captures can be staggering.

The Macleay River estuary is very productive for bream, whiting, flathead, blackfish and mulloway. In the freshwater reaches west of Kempsey, there are also good bass in the river.

One of the highlights of the Macleay River is the run of big mulloway at the river mouth during a flood. As the muddy water of the Macleay meets the cleaner water of the Pacific Ocean, a distinct line is formed where big mulloway prowl in search of hapless prey washed out of the river.

At these times, keen mulloway anglers line the wall and fish with heavy tackle and live baits or lures. The usual combination is a stout beach rod loaded with 24 kilogram breaking strain line. Many locals use 40 kilogram line straight through to the hook. There is little science in the fishing, but the resulting struggles are hard fought.

Floods aside, there is always good fishing throughout the estuary with a range of fish available, especially in the main arm that runs off the river just opposite the boat ramp. This area is known as Kemps Corner and runs up to a 'T' junction where Clybucca Creek runs in from the west and the Stuarts Point arm joins from the north.

Jerseyville Bridge is easy to fish. Like most bridges it attracts bream in big numbers, but also holds plenty of school mulloway, flathead and tailor. The area also fishes well at night, particularly with live nippers, prawns or worms as bait.

Throughout the river system there are plenty of

sandbanks and drop-offs that yield flathead and whiting. The same areas are also good for lure casting to flathead.

The rock fishing at South West Rocks and Hat Head is excellent. It peaks in late autumn and early winter with runs of tailor and drummer. The tailor runs are exceptional at times with large fish common.

Access to many of the spots is good but the ability to walk long distances is needed to reach North Gap, Hat Head and Hungry Head.

Hat Head is a magical rock fishing location. In summer it has runs of solid Spanish mackerel, cobia and longtail tuna. As the season gets colder, tailor show up, along with mackerel tuna.

Hat Head itself has about a dozen spots that all produce good fish. The walk out is long but easy. Walking back with a heap of fish is a whole lot harder.

The beaches of the area also feature exceptional angling for whiting, bream and tailor.

Smoky Cape Beach, which runs south to Hat Head, is open to four-wheel drive vehicles under permit. This 14 kilometer stretch of beach always has some fish available.

Other beaches of note include North Beach, which is reached via Stuarts Point; Gap Beach, an excellent producer in slight seas and yields the largest tailor in the region; and the small beaches south of Hat Head which are also reliable. Hungry Beach, which runs from Hungry Head to Crescent Head is an excellent location.

Hat Head is a sporting mecca. Everything from Spanish mackerel to big tailor and bream are available from the rocks.

Port Macquarie

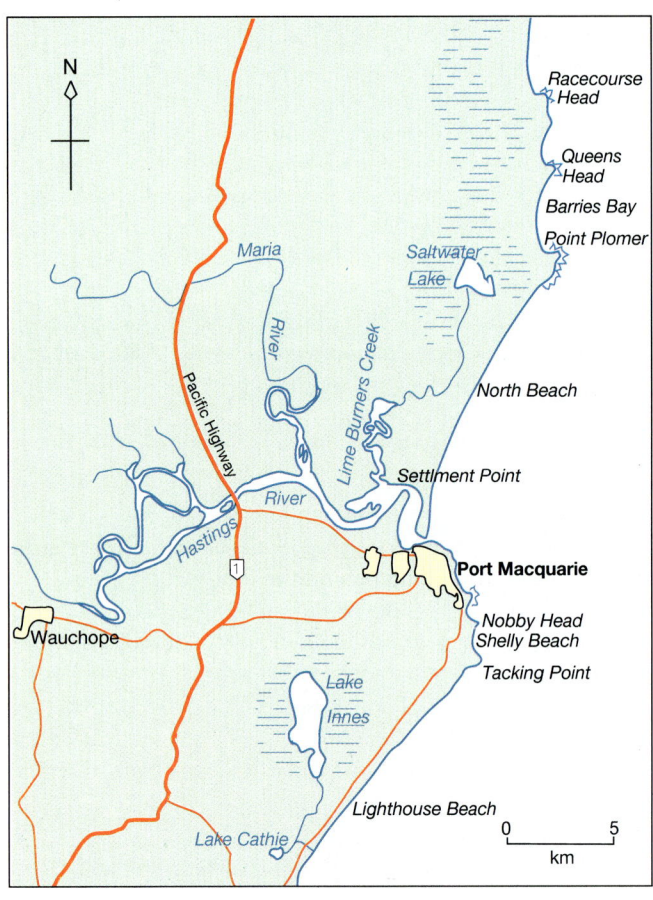

Two of the best eating fish; a snapper (left) and the much sought-after pearl perch. Both inhabit the reefs of Port Macquarie.

Port Macquarie, 435 kilometres north of Sydney, is one of New South Wales' most popular tourist towns. It has been the centre of a great deal of development but despite this, high quality angling is available for most of the year.

Being a popular boating and fishing location, the town offers excellent facilities with good boat ramps, bait, ice and tackle. Marine service and repair is also available.

Accommodation of all standards can be found in Port Macquarie and some waterfront facilities with boat moorings are available.

The only problem at Port Macquarie is the mouth of the Hastings River which can be quite dangerous. It has claimed boats and should be avoided when conditions are bad. Problems usually occur on a run-out tide when strong north-east winds are blowing. Seek local advice before venturing to sea.

Small boats can be launched at Point Plomer and Crescent Head. Access is by way of a short surf break.

Offshore fishing in Port Macquarie is assured of being productive with reefs located north and south harbouring both bottom and surface fish. Angling can be arranged to suit prevailing or expected weather conditions.

The area features top snapper fishing on its shallow, inshore reefs, using lightly weighted baits drifted down a berley slick. The best time is following a big sea.

There is excellent game fishing, both inshore and offshore, at Port Macquarie.

Barries Bay, north of Point Plomer, has excellent Spanish mackerel, longtail tuna and cobia, plus other light-tackle game fish.

The area in front of Point Plomer is dotted with shallow reefs which produce very good bream and tailor, particularly in late autumn.

The washes between Point Plomer and Racecourse Head are all good for big tailor. Just watch the boat handling near the bommies and breakers. The same style of fishing can also be had around the washes going south, with the area around the lighthouse being very productive.

Bluewater game and sportfishing has been growing rapidly in Port Macquarie. In summer, good runs of marlin, wahoo, dolphin fish, medium-sized yellowfin tuna and sharks occur. Late winter and early spring is exceptional for large catches of yellowfin tuna, and plenty of acrobatic mako sharks.

There is a local game and sportfishing club in town, and the members are always keen to provide advice.

The game fishing grounds are in 30 to 100 fathoms east of Port Macquarie, working north and north-east towards Hat Head.

The best of the winter yellowfin and mako sharks are found in the 200 fathom area halfway between Port Macquarie and Point Plomer.

Bottom fishing drift grounds supply generous amounts of flathead, morwong, snapper and other reef fish off Port Macquarie.

Straight in front of the Port and from 5 to 7 kilometres offshore is a very large flathead ground that runs 4 kilometres north to south and 2 kilometres east to west.

A little further south off Shelly Beach from 2 to 6 kilometres offshore and then south to just past Summit Hill is a large area of broken bottom dotted with a couple of large reefs.

The Hastings River estuary is very productive and yields consistent hauls of mulloway, flathead, bream, luderick and whiting. Tailor are also common, although they tend to be small in summer. The larger fish turn up in late autumn and early winter and work the channels close to the mouth and along the walls.

Mulloway are caught throughout the system with most of the larger fish taken off the training walls at the mouth of the river. Heavy gear is needed as the terrain is too rough for sporting tackle.

The standard tackle is a stout beach rod and large Alvey or multiplying reel full of 24 kilogram line. The most popular bait is live black fish or luderick, which are prolific along the wall. Don't be afraid to use a bait as large as half a kilogram.

Drifting the channels is very productive for flathead, whiting and flounder. Anywhere with a drop on the edge of weedbeds will provide a few fish.

Luderick or blackfish are prolific along the deeper banks and around the weedbeds in the river during autumn and winter. The best bait is live nippers from the tidal flats in the estuary. Local weed is also available from the bait shops for those seeking blackfish.

Limeburners Creek is an interesting spot for flathead, particularly if you work lures. The bay has many oyster leases, weedbeds and banks and yields a lot of flathead, while bream can be found at the top end of the bay.

A boat is necessary to get the best out of the estuary and there are plenty of local hire craft available.

From Racecourse Head south to Queen's Head provides an enormous number of productive and safe fishing spots.

The area is reached by taking the vehicular ferry across the Hastings at Settlement Point and heading north. The road is rough and is best suited to a four-wheel drive or other work vehicle, though the average family car can handle the road with a little care.

The best fishing period is in autumn and winter, although some fish will be found all year round.

The tailor on this part of the coast can be large, and fish from 1 to 3 kilograms are common, so make sure that heavy tackle is used.

Drummer are also very common in the area, even close to town at the lighthouse.

The rock areas close to town are very convenient and productive for holiday anglers. Tailor, drummer and bream predominate, with mulloway also available.

North Beach, which runs north from the breakwater, is by far the best beach fishing area. This is reached by crossing on the Settlement Point vehicular ferry and following the road along behind the dunes.

This beach has spectacular whiting fishing during summer using beachworms, and equally good tailor fishing during the winter.

Big tailor gather in the deep gutters along the beach when the winter westerlies blow, and the action is easily located by anglers skipping them up the sand.

Fishing the Hastings River breakwall for bream and luderick. After a flood, big mulloway move in.

Camden Haven

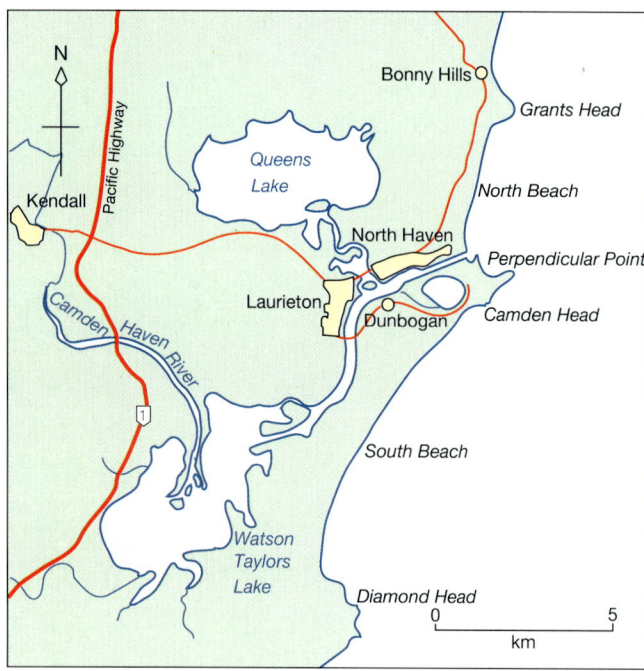

The Camden Haven, Laurieton, Dunbogan area is a complex estuary system linked by channels. The area has suffered badly from erosion and some parts of the system are badly silted. That aside, the river still produces some very good catches.

The area is reached by turning off the Pacific Highway at Kew, about 390 kilometres north of Sydney.

Accommodation is available in good motels, flats and several caravan parks, some conveniently right on the river. Anglers can also hire good quality boats to get on the river. Bait, ice, fuel and mechanical repairs are all available and the area is a good family holiday location.

Launching ramps are available throughout the system and large trailerboats can be handled easily.

For offshore anglers, the bar at the river entrance is very safe by comparison with other north coast rivers.

The Cod Ground is the focus of offshore angling in the area. Located 6 kilometres offshore from the river entrance, it yields average catches of snapper, mulloway and teraglin.

The area in front of the river is mostly sand and good bags of flathead can be taken on the drift.

Telegraph Rock is in front of Perpendicular Point, to the south-east of the river mouth. It is a handy live bait location and a producer of bream and tailor. The washes around Perpendicular Point also produce tailor, particularly on the southern side.

The northern breakwall is always good for a mulloway or two, particularly at night. Sturdy gear is needed and the best bait is small chopper tailor which can be caught along the wall. School mulloway are also caught here, particularly on the rising tide.

The river shallows quickly but there are plenty of spots for flathead and whiting. There are also numerous sandbanks where nippers can be pumped at low tide. The edges of these same banks are also good locations for larger fish.

The North Haven Bridge is always a good spot for big flathead. A great deal of bait gathers here at night, and the big flathead are aware of this.

Luderick and bream are located in the deeper pockets of the system and also along the retaining walls.

As much of the river has roadway close by, anglers who just want to cast a line can find a great many locations to try. There are also ramps and cleaning tables around.

The south side of the river is reached by crossing the Dunbogan Bridge which is not a bad spot itself. The shoreline along the southern side of the river is deep and good bream and flathead are taken here.

The Dunbogan Bridge also gives vehicular access to Point Perpendicular in one direction and Diamond Head in the other.

Watson Taylor Lake and Queen's Lake do hold a lot of fish, but because of minimal tidal movement they are well spread and hard to locate. The lakes are also extensively netted.

The river and the channels that connect them offer far better angling than the lakes.

Point Perpendicular offers good fishing for big fish. The ledge is high off the water and a cliff gaff is needed to land the catch.

This spot yields some very good game fish and has been overlooked by many land-based game fishermen who drive to Hat Head or the southern ledges.

The point yields kingfish, cobia, longtail tuna, Spanish mackerel and mulloway. Almost anything can turn up here. The area also produces bream, drummer and tailor.

On the southern face of Point Perpendicular there are a couple of good spots for bream, tailor, drummer and blackfish. Just watch the sea as these spots are exposed in a southerly roll.

The inside northern corner of Point Perpendicular also fishes well for luderick when there is a big roll wrapping around the headland.

A four-wheel drive can save a long walk when fishing Point Perpendicular.

Diamond Head is south of Camden Haven and a very popular rock fishing spot, especially for tailor.

North Beach at Camden Haven is a good whiting spot running right up to Grant's Head, halfway to Lake Cathie. The beach also produces bream and chopper tailor in winter, but is not as productive as South Beach on the Dunbogan side of Camden Haven.

South Beach is always worth a cast as the long gutters formed along this stretch hold a lot of good fish.

A road runs the entire length of the beach behind the dunes, and is passable in standard vehicles. A number of access roads also run through to the beach from Diamond Head Road.

Right: By drifting offshore boat-based anglers catch flathead by the basket-full . This one is the more unusual marbled species.
Below: Mackerel tuna or kawakawa are common in autumn off Point Perpendicular

The Manning River

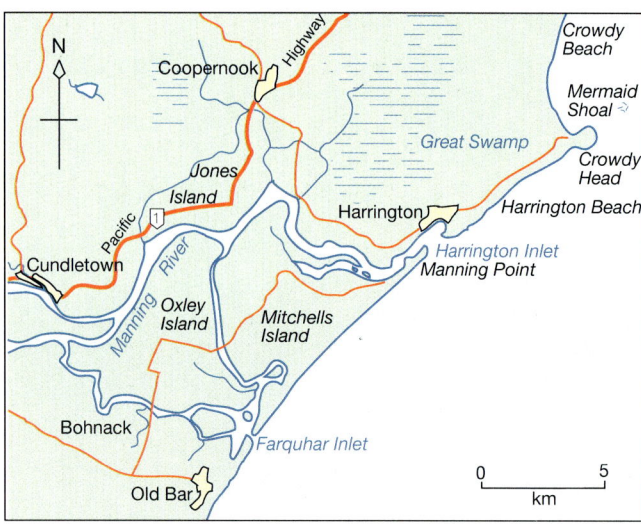

Harrington, at the mouth of the Manning River, provides access to the Manning estuary. The town has a range of accommodation, and bait, ice, fuel and boat maintenance is available. Hire boats are available at Taree at the top end of the estuary.

Most sea-going boats launch 8 kilometres to the north at Crowdy Head because it has a protected anchorage and no bar. Harrington has a shallow and unpredictable river entrance, though there are two good boat ramps.

On the other side of the estuary at Old Bar (reached by turning off just south of Taree) it is possible to launch small aluminium boats off the beach and through a sheltered shore break.

As access is from Camden Haven, the most popular offshore fishing spots are Mermaid Reef and the reef areas east of the Haven itself.

Mermaid Reef is a huge, shallow reef 6 kilometres north east of Crowdy and 2 kilometres offshore. It produces snapper, mulloway, kingfish, bonito, bream and other reef-dwelling fish. Travelling surface fish turn up in summer.

East of Crowdy is a wide range of reef formations from close inshore all the way out to 140 metres deep.

The best snapper fishing is in the 45 to 60 metre depth range, where numerous reefs can be found by locating the professional fishermens' trap floats set around the perimeter of the reefs.

Game fish are also available with marlin, wahoo, dolphin fish and yellowfin tuna prolific in summer.

The Manning River estuary is not as productive as many others along the coast, but it still yields good catches. The area is riddled with channels and sandbars, so care should

be taken navigating the estuary at low tide.

School mulloway are reasonably common in the deeper holes in the river, and are best caught on small live fish or live prawns, while luderick proliferate around the deep tidal areas close to the shore.

Flathead and whiting are common with some very good-sized fish being located in the Old Bar area. There are plenty of weedbeds in this area and good luderick can also be found here.

Other spots of interest include the Bohnock Bridge, the first bridge you come to when you take the Old Bar road and turn off at the Oxley Island sign. This is a top spot for big bream and school mulloway.

Cattai Bridge, on the road from Coopernook to Harrington, is a handy land based location. Bream, flathead and luderick are taken here. Fish the eastern bank of Cattai Creek.

A channel marker pole identifying the eastern channel bank is located between Jones and Mitchells Islands. Just out from this marker is a top spot for bream, flathead and big mulloway.

The sea wall at Harrington is a consistent producer of mulloway, flathead, bream and blackfish. The best spot for mulloway is between the Gantry and the Spur Wall on the rising tide.

The ocean end of the wall produces tailor and bream, and drummer on cunjevoi baits. The ocean wall extends out to sea quite a way and a deep hole located on the northern side produces good tailor and bream.

Crowdy Head has the best rock fishing out of Harrington, with snapper, groper, drummer, tailor and bream available.

Quite a few big bream are caught inside the boat harbour on lightly weighted baits of peeled prawns or strips of tuna or bonito. No sinker is best.

The ledges to the north and south of the headland produce a range of real quality fish. The best fishing, particularly for snapper and groper, follows storms. Big winter tailor provide excellent action in the washes.

Crowdy and Harrington Beaches have good stocks of summer whiting plus a few bream. Tailor also turn up in the gutters on a regular basis.

Forster/Tuncurry

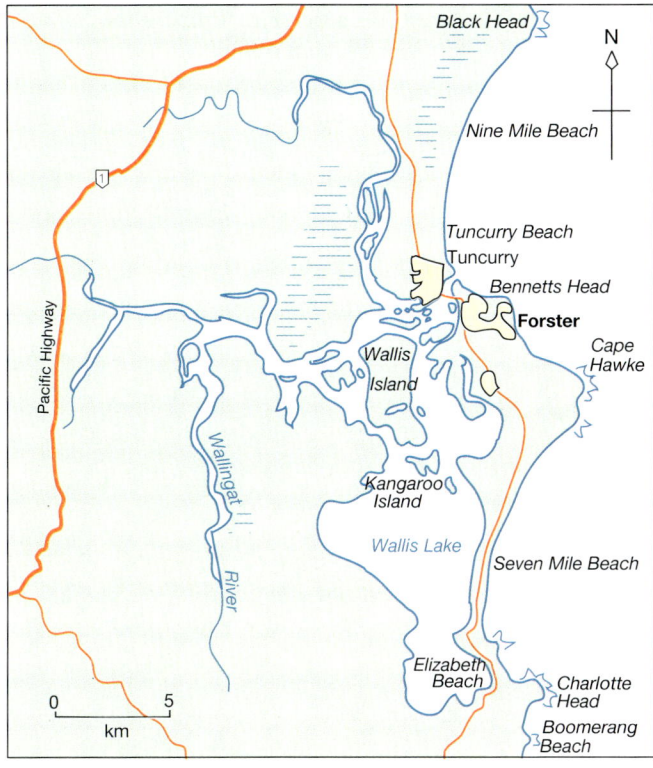

The twin towns of Forster/Tuncurry have grown from sleepy fishing villages to boom towns in under 20 years with Sydneysiders flocking to the area en masse, looking for somewhere to relax.

A full range of accommodation is available. Boating anglers are well catered for with excellent boat ramps, boat harbours, marinas and on-water fuel.

A selection of hire boats grant fishermen access to the best spots on the lake. Bait, ice, good fishing tackle and mechanical repairs are on offer at the many marinas.

For the holiday angler the area has much to offer, particularly in the estuary.

The Wallis Lake estuary contains some of the best flathead country anywhere on the coast. Apart from flathead the lake also has very good luderick fishing. The big luderick show up each year at the end of March and stay until late July, though there are luderick available all year round.

The same sandbanks and weedbeds that provide flathead also have big numbers of whiting on offer. These fish are excellent size and provide fine sport on light tackle.

The Lake yields great runs of prawns and hundreds of boats gather in the channel with each new moon in the summer to net the prawns as they head out to sea on the run-out tide. These prawns are good eating and top bait when fished alive the next day.

Lure anglers will find plenty of willing flathead plus quite a few tailor and long tom in the lake.

The Tuncurry channel and the 'Step' on the eastern side of Wallis Island, are tailor hotspots.

The Step, where the sand at the entrance shelves deeply into the main body of the lake, is also a good spot for big flathead, bream and school mulloway.

On the rising tide, predators move along the deep edge of the Step waiting for small baitfish to be swept to them. Anglers should moor in the shallows and feed their baits into the current and over the drop-off. Live poddy mullet and live prawns work best. Pilchards and whitebait fished on ganged hooks are also effective.

Around the bridge linking the two towns is always worth a throw. The big sandspit on the Tuncurry side is

Wallis Lakes are full of bream. Try night fishing Forster's town jetties using tuna bait.

very productive when worked with lures for flathead. Large flathead are also taken here at night in the lights of the bridge using live bait.

On the Forster side, the flats are shallower compared to the deep Tuncurry Channel and hold a lot of very tasty sea garfish and whiting. By night, big bream move away from the shelter of the bridge pylons and to the sand flats.

Big bream can be located at night around the many oyster leases the estuary. The best baits are hermit crab tails and strips of fish such as slimy mackerel or bonito. The channels and weed beds around the leases also hold many luderick.

The deeper waters of the upper lake have excellent stocks of blue swimmer crabs which can be be trapped with witches hat crab nets.

Offshore fishing off the Forster/Tuncurry coast is keenly pursued by both recreational and professional anglers.

The entrance to Wallis Lake has a bar that demands respect. Do not attempt to traverse it without local advice, and then viewing it from the Forster wall. Avoid the run-out tide where possible.

The most popular fishing outside Forster is for flathead. There is not a great deal of reef until well north or south of the port. However, large hauls of flathead more than make up for the lack of reef fish.

Black Head, 8 kilometres to the north, has excellent snapper reefs both in close and offshore in the 60 metre depth.

South of the entrance there is better bottom fishing water at the Pinnacles, east of Cape Hawke. This ground produces extremely good hauls of mulloway, kingfish, snapper and teraglin.

A number of smaller patches of reef are in this area and drift fishing can yield good hauls of morwong and snapper.

The Cape Hawke area features excellent rock fishing spots for bream, drummer, tailor, mulloway and luderick. Access can be difficult without a four-wheel drive vehicle, but the long haul is rewarded with spectacular catches.

Charlotte Head, a little further to the south near Pacific Palms, produces excellent game fish from the rocks. Longtail tuna, cobia and kingfish are regularly caught, while quality yellowfin tuna have been landed.

Charlotte Head also produces tailor, a few salmon in winter, and drummer in good numbers.

The best ledge on Charlotte Head is right at the northern point; the eastern and southern edges are fairly dangerous.

Small boats can be launched across the hard sand at the southern end of Elizabeth Beach at the headland.

The area has reasonable to good beach fishing with whiting, bream and tailor being the main quarry.

Nine Mile Beach at Tuncurry produces whiting and bream in the summer, and chopper tailor during winter.

Seven Mile Beach, 8 kilometres south of Forster, is the spot for really big tailor. This deeply shelving beach encourages the tailor to push bait fish close to shore, and close to the fishermen! Be prepared to follow the schools of feeding fish as they tend not to hold in any one area.

Seven Mile Beach also yields big bream at times.

Top: A trailerboat fisherman about to land a small tuna.
Above: Sand whiting are common off Seven Mile Beach.

Seal Rocks

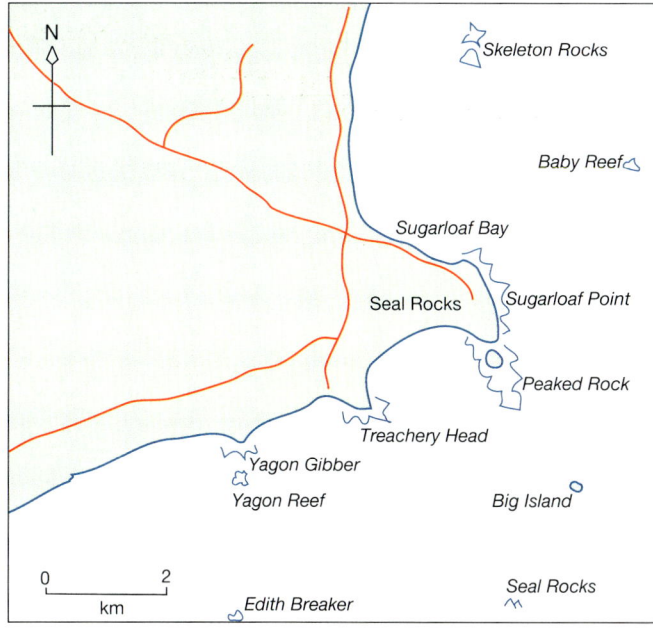

Seal Rocks is one of the few unspoilt fishing villages along the NSW coast. The town is reached by turning-off the Pacific Highway just north of Bulahdelah, and following the Lakes Way until the Seal Rocks turn-off is reached.

The town has fuel, bait and ice, plus a caravan park and a few holiday flats. There is a general store and a club.

Boat-launching facilities at Seal Rocks are nonexistent and all vessels are launched over the beach at Sugarloaf Bay. The sand is very hard and the bay is quite protected. Launching is best effected with a four-wheel drive vehicle, though handling boats over 6 metres may cause problems here. The ideal vessel for the area is a 4 to 5 metre aluminium runabout.

Most of the offshore fishing is concentrated around a variety of shallow and/or exposed reefs to the north and south of Sugarloaf Point.

Black or Skeleton Rocks, rising to the surface from 15 metres of water, is 5 kilometres due north of Sugarloaf Bay off the rocks at the southern end of Sandbar Beach. It is a good spot for kingfish, snapper, bream and mulloway.

Baby Reef, 5 kilometres north-east of the port, is harder to find but very productive. Line up the eastern point of Sugarloaf Bay with the end of the sand on the western edge of the beach. Then line up the rocks at the end of Number One Beach with the centre of the big hill behind it. There is 7 metres of water on top of the reef.

Moving to the south, there is a group of small, rock islands off Sugarloaf Point. This area produces plenty of small to medium-size snapper and bream on the bottom, with kingfish and big tailor on the surface.

Treachery Head is the next headland to the south, and it fishes the same as the islands. Don't get too close in any sort of sea as the waves can rear up around this area.

Yagen's Reef is about one kilometre off the next headland, which is called Yagen Gibber. Line up Bridge Hill with Yagen Gibber. This reef produces small snapper and mulloway. There are a couple of sizeable reefs in the 14 to 16 metre area off Yagen's Head, popular with night anglers seeking mulloway.

Edith Breaker rises to just under the surface, 5 kilometres due south of the lighthouse and 3 kilometres east-south-east of Yagen Gibber. it produces a huge amount bonito and kingfish. A few big tuna, kingfish and cobia also turn up here.

On the bottom, a lot of snapper are found around the edge of this reef, while mulloway patrol the pinnacles.

Seal Rocks are 3 kilometres south-east of the lighthouse, quite visible to the boater. These rocks produce big snapper, particularly after a heavy sea.

Surface fish, including kingfish, bonito, tailor, salmon, mackerel tuna and yellowfin tuna , abound in this region.

The area around the easternmost rock supports a very healthy population of snapper, and drifting floating pilchards or lightly weighted strip baits can yield big catches. Good mulloway also turn up in this area.

Sugarloaf Point is a superb rock fishing area. There are good ledges that produce tailor, bream, drummer, snapper, mulloway and luderick. Spectacular tailor fishing occurs in April and May each year.

Good surface fish are also spun and live baited from Sugarloaf point, with kingfish, bonito, mackerel, yellowfin and longtail tuna being common candidates.

Treachery Head to the south has a number of ledges worth fishing but it is exposed to big seas.

Seal Rocks' beaches provide quality beach fishing, but a four-wheel drive vehicle is required to access them.

A huge expanse of beach stretches from Yagen's Head down to the entrance of Port Stephens, and is intersected by the famous Big Gibber and Mungo Brush.

Really big bream can be located on this beach along with tailor, whiting, flathead and mulloway. There is camping at the Big Gibber.

Port Stephens

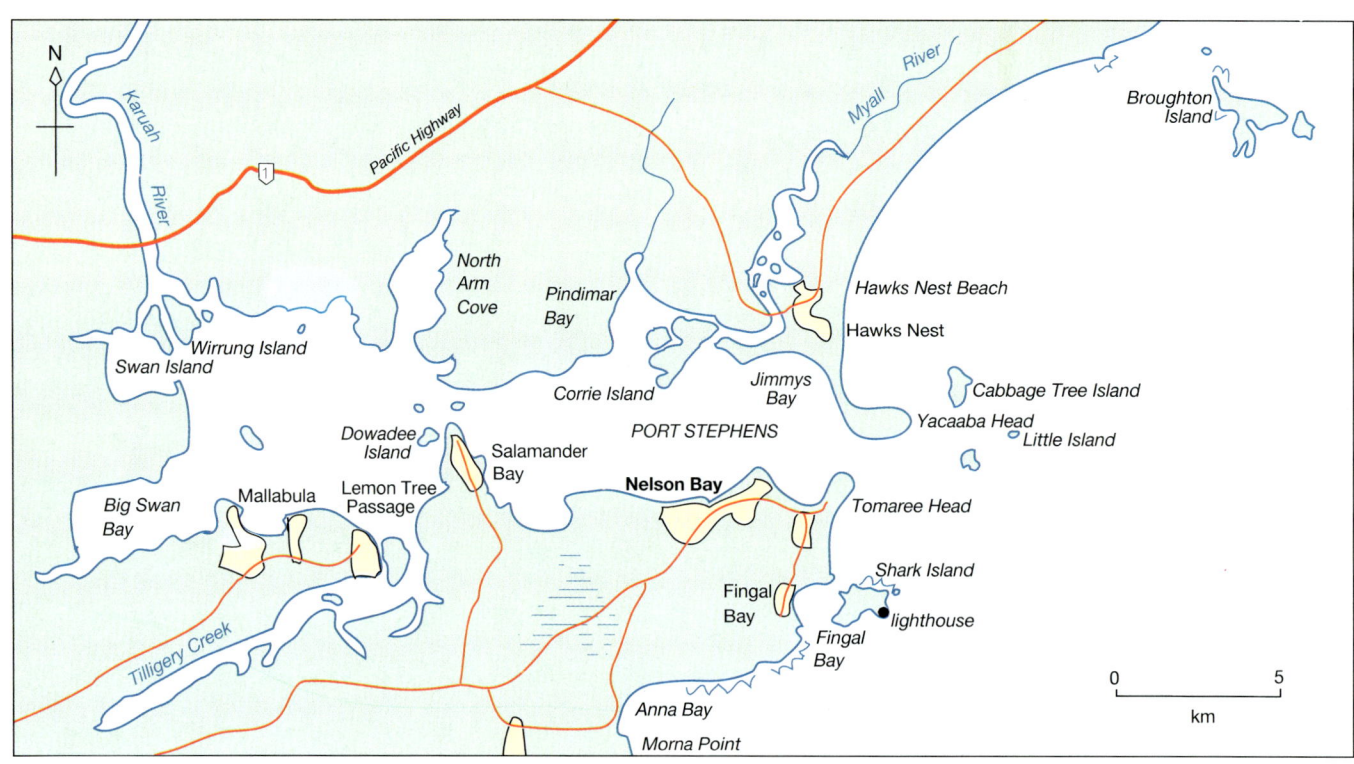

Port Stephens boasts outstanding game fishing. Here, an average size black marlin is being hauled abroad after a long struggle.

Fast becoming Sydney's major holiday playground, Port Stephens is a beautiful area for all types of fishing. The best time to visit is late summer and autumn. The Christmas period is too chaotic to allow a peaceful existence for anglers. Accommodation is available to suit all budgets and there are some very good restaurants.

Despite probable over-development in the coming years, the area has very good water quality in the estuary and offshore which provides top catches of fish for classes of anglers - game fishermen, bottom fishermen, sportfishermen, estuary, rock and beach anglers. Trailerboat anglers are very well catered for with excellent ramps and cleaning tables.

No discussion of Port Stephen would be complete without mentioning the Inter-Club Game Fishing Tournament held each year on the last weekend in February and the first weekend in March.

The competition attracts over 200 boats each year and is taken very seriously. Catches are often outstanding with marlin, tuna, sharks, wahoo and dolphin fish predominant.

The islands offshore from Port Stephens typify the outstanding bluewater or offshore angling that's available. A great many marlin and big tuna are taken around them, while they also hold great amounts of bait. Slimy mackerel, garfish and bonito are on tap. The best spot is

on the western side of Cabbage Tree Island, where some great bream are present.

The game fishing areas are fairly well spread with a lot of activity concentrated on the Continental Shelf, 23 kilometres offshore. However, there are plenty of fish closer in.

For anglers new to the area, a troll with lures from Little Island up to the eastern end of Broughton Island and then east for 4 or 5 kilometres, should produce a few tuna.

Drifting with live slimy mackerel as bait is popular, particularly in the 60 to 100 metre depth east of Port Stephens, or down towards the lighthouse. Marlin and tuna are the common catch. The addition of plenty of berley will usually attract a shark or two while drifting.

For those in small boats, trolling live slimy mackerel on the eastern side of Little Island is the best marlin hotspot close to town. Big yellowfin tuna also turn up here.

Anglers fishing for a feed are very well catered for with many reefs well documented in the area. Mulloway, teraglin, snapper, kingfish, flathead, morwong and other reef fish are prolific, and the local tourism association has had the foresight to employ a local professional fisherman to draft a very clear map of the top spots.

There are good bream, snapper and kingfish around the washes close to the islands in front of Port Stephens, and this area can be fished in almost any weather.

Flathead, flounder and small snapper can be found drifting between the islands.

At Broughton Island to the north there is a feast of hard bottom for snapper anglers. All round the island there are deep drop-offs and a few washes that will yield big snapper on floating baits.

A lot of the reefs have big numbers of trevally on them, particularly during the spring.

Top: Port Stephens hosts Australia's largest game fishing tournament. Above: Rock fishing at Yacaaba is great for big tuna.

95

Live bait trolling is also successful on the eastern side of Broughton Island, with the bluewater current running right into the front of the island and moving off towards the east.

Gunsight Reef, just north of Cabbage Tree Island, is always covered with hungry trevally.

The Port Stephens estuary is in excellent shape, and great catches of fish are made within the system.

One of the highlights is the springtime invasion by mackerel and striped tuna. These hard-fighting fish tear into big schools of whitebait, making for fast and furious action in an otherwise tranquil setting.

Summer whiting are very common in the Port Stephens area, particularly in the upper reaches of the estuary around Lemon Tree Passage. All the sandbars and mudbanks can be counted on for good-sized whiting. Live worms or nippers are the best bait.

Flathead are also very common in the upper reaches. Some very big fish appear in the channels on the northern side the estuary.

Big mulloway haunt the deeper holes of the estuary, especially around Dowardee Island and in the channels leading up towards the Karuah River.

The oyster leases in Port Stephens supply the best and juiciest oysters for human consumption. Plenty of bream get amongst the leases for a feed.

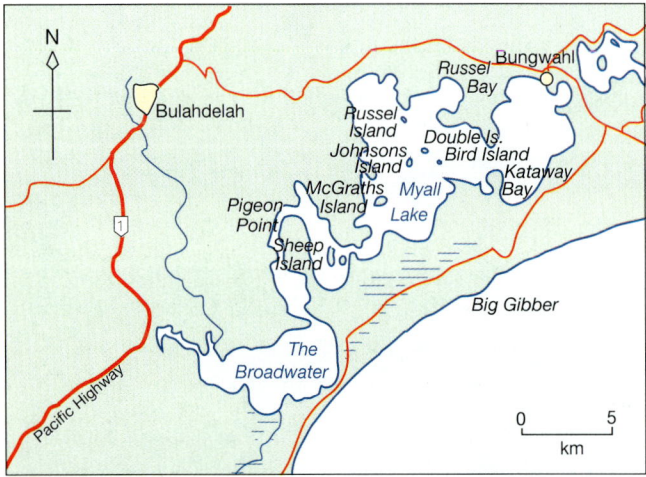

The beautiful Myall Lakes, on the north side of the system, add to the complexity of fishing options. Compared to Port Stephens estuary, fishing in the Myall system is not that great, although there are plenty of flathead, whiting and blackfish in the Myall River before it enters the lakes.

Once in the lakes, bream, mullet and blackfish are the main fare.

Yacaaba Head, on the northern side of Port Stephens, provides a rugged rock fishing spot with good ledges for

A keenly targetted sportfish, mackerel tuna enters Port Stephens estuary during autumn and, as this happy angler can attest, can provide thrills a minute.

catching tailor, bream and drummer. Longtail tuna, kingfish and cobia are a available if using live baits.

Tomaree Head, the southern point at the entrance to Port Stephens, is known as 'heart attack hill' as the walk in is strenuous. It is a well known spot for catching big longtail tuna, mackerel tuna, bonito, tailor and the occasional cobia on locally caught live slimy mackerel. There are nearly always live bait available off the ledge.

Between Anna Bay and Fingal Bay there is a scattering of small ledges, mostly yielding luderick and drummer, but access is difficult.

Morna Point and Cemetery Point, at the top of Newcastle Bight, also have a few little ledges but nothing of any great note.

Hawk's Nest Beach has outstanding fishing, especially at Little Gibber.

The beach is rich in worms and pipis and splendid catches of big bream are made. Tailor and mulloway also feature in anglers' creels.

Best time is late autumn, although bream and whiting are available all year round.

South of Port Stephens there are a lot of little beaches that do not yield much variety, though good whiting are caught with worm baits.

Stockton Beach is where the real beach fishing starts and runs all the way down to Newcastle. This is one of the best tailor beaches along the coast with deep holes and gutters close to shore.

Newcastle

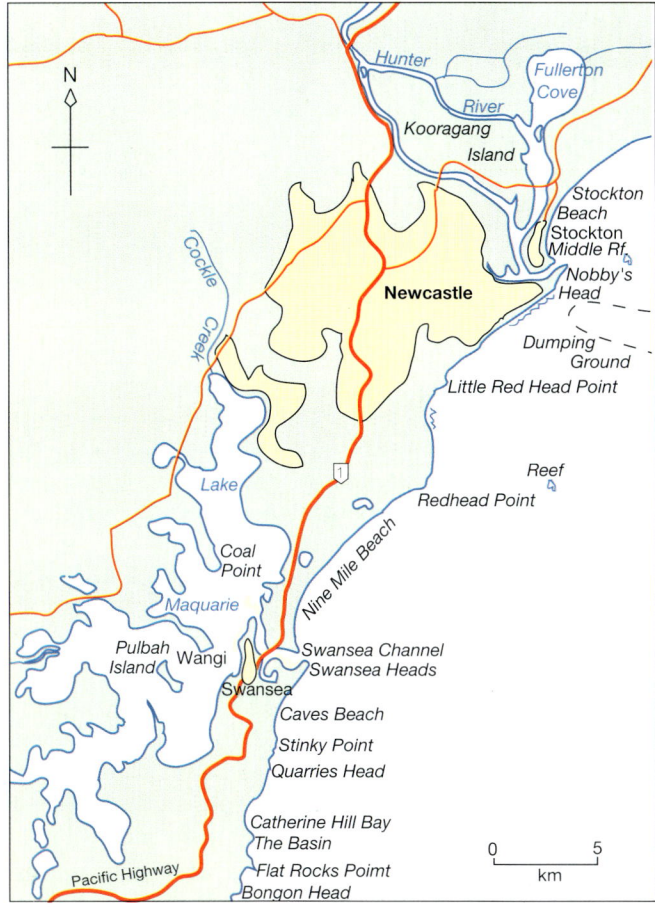

Newcastle City is a busy industrial and port area. With the activity of shipping and the steelworks on the lower part of the harbour, it may surprise many that the fishing in the Hunter River is impressive.

Due to the tidal flushing of the system, most pollutants are dispersed quickly, and the port area has had only a minor impact on the lower part of the river.

The Hunter River produces excellent catches of bream and school mulloway, and the port area has become renown for its massive hairtail catches.

When the hairtail are in the harbour, it looks like fairyland at night, with hundreds of illuminated boats and glowing cyalume light sticks attached to the top of floats. Top bait is blue pilchards and live yellowtail.

Around the edges of the channels is the place where most of the bream and school mulloway are caught in the Harrington River.

Stockton is the port area, and also a good spot for flathead. Bream are caught in the channel that runs along the main road from Sandgate to Hexham.

Hexham Bridge also returns a few good catches of bream and flathead.

A boat is definitely an advantage when fishing the Newcastle estuary.

The Middle Reef, straight off the port, is a very good spot for mulloway, small snapper and bream. Fish with as little lead as possible.

The reefs off Redhead Beach are also good for catching squire and mixed reef fish.

The Dumping Ground is a good spot to catch a feed of fish. Drift across the entrance to the port between 3 to 5 kilometres offshore. This area is covered by the rubble from harbour dredging a few years ago. Good medium snapper and flathead are the main catch.

The Stockton Breakwall offers interesting fishing, with rock fishing on one side and estuary angling on the other.

Big mulloway are taken on the ocean side with live tailor fished under a bobby cork the most popular technique. The tailor are extremely common on both sides of the wall and those on the ocean side can be of good size.

Bream are available, with the estuary side being very consistent. Hairtail also turn up here on occasions.

Nobby's Head fishes well for smaller fish working back towards the river side. A lot of chopper tailor are taken at the front of the headland.

Redhead is the only other rock spot of any significance. Bream, luderick, drummer, tailor and salmon are caught here.

Stockton Beach is one of the best surf beaches along the coast. Everything from whiting, bream and flathead, to tailor, salmon and big mulloway are caught from the deep channels and holes.

The wreck of the Signa is lodged on the beach about halfway along and is reached via Lavis Lane at Williamtown. This is a top spot for mulloway, tailor, bream, salmon and some very big snapper.

Along the beach, whiting, bream and tailor are regulars. The winter run of tailor can be quite spectacular with big specimens working the deep shoreline gutters. Without a four-wheel drive, the easiest access is via Stockton Wall.

Nine Mile Beach, running from Redhead to the mouth of Lake Macquarie, carries a few whiting and chopper tailor, but does not generate the same fish populations as Stockton Beach.

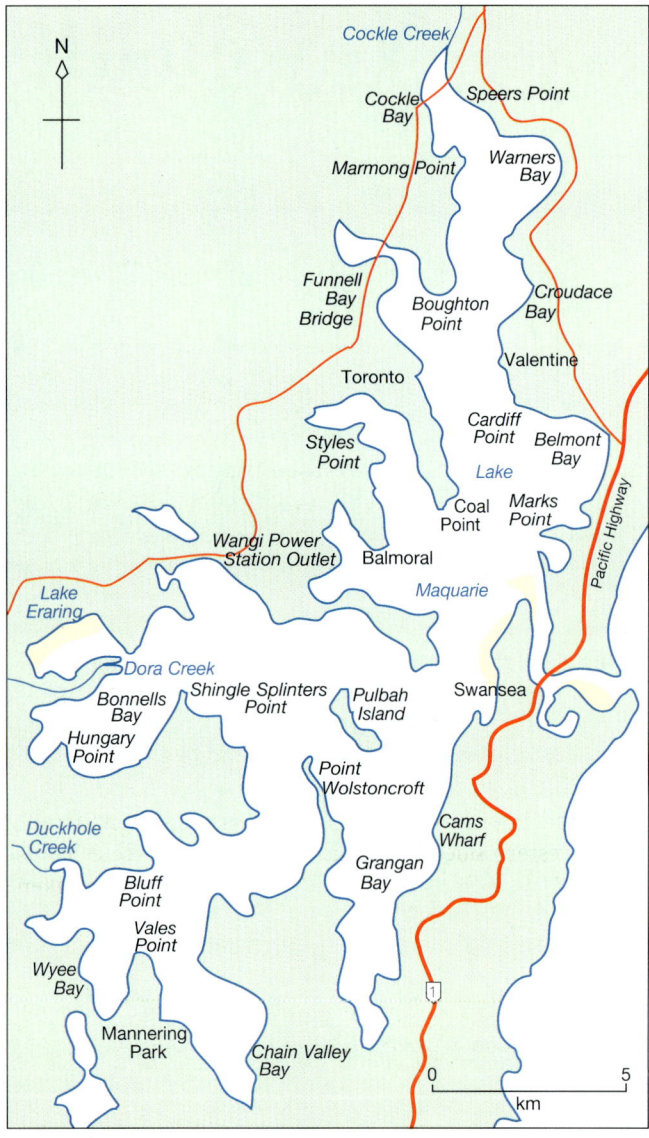

the flats at the western edge. These are best taken on live worms or nippers with the night run of fish usually exceptional.

Bream and luderick also find the deeper sections of Swansea Channel very attractive. The area around the bridge is good and the wall areas are the best for blackfish.

Because of the fast flowing currents in this area a lot of attention must be paid to the tides to find the peak fishing times. Tides with small ranges, say a 1.4 metre high with 0.5 metre low, are ideal. Fishing on really big tides is a waste of time.

At the western end of the channel a big sandbar fans out to a long drop-off not far from Pelican and Spectacle Islands. This drop-off is a top spot on a rising tide as fish wait in the deep water for bait to be swept to them. Mulloway, flathead, bream and tailor are common.

Yellowtail and small tailor can be taken here and used as live bait.

There are five artificial reefs in the system and these are very reliable spots, particularly at night. During the day small bream and tarwhine can be a pest, but leatherjackets can be the saving grace during daylight.

At night, large bream and even a few squire make the fishing more lively.

In the broad body of the lake, finding fish becomes harder as there is not a lot of tide to form good locations.

Trolling for tailor is popular in the area from the sandspit across to Wangi and down to Pulbah Island. Large tailor are often found in the lake and an unweighted pilchard set while the boat drifts along with the other lines fishing the bottom, will often add a few extra fish. Bream, flathead and whiting are well spread around shorelines rather than in the centre of the lake. Pulbah Island also holds a lot of good fish at each end in an east-west direction.

The northern end of the lake has a lot of good bream off rocky shores from Coal Point up to Cockle Creek.

Blue swimmer crabs are available throughout the lake with the judicious use of witch's hat nets.

Prawns are also common in the lake and a bit of work in any of the shallow bays will turn up enough for a feed or for bait. During the night run-out tides of the no-moon period a lot of prawns and crabs are scooped in the channel as they migrate to the sea.

Lake Macquarie has been developed for housing and this urban pressure has badly affected the estuary. However, the fishing remains good.

Boat hire, bait, ice and fuel are all available and there is plenty of accommodation at Swansea. Boat ramps are located along the channel on either side of the bridge. The lake can be divided into two separate fishing areas; the fast flowing channel area and the expanse of the lake with little or no tidal movement in many areas.

Swansea Channel flows very quickly as the tide races to fill and empty the enormous volume of the lake. Silting of the channel is a growing problem.

Flathead fishing is particularly rewarding. Many keen lure tossers spend their time flicking deep divers and Mr Twisters along the banks and drop-offs of the channel. Some of the flathead taken are enormous. Other flathead chasers spend their time with live poddy mullet or pilchards drifting the area.

Whiting and flounder are also in reasonable numbers in the channel, particularly whiting which are at their best on

Central Coast Lakes

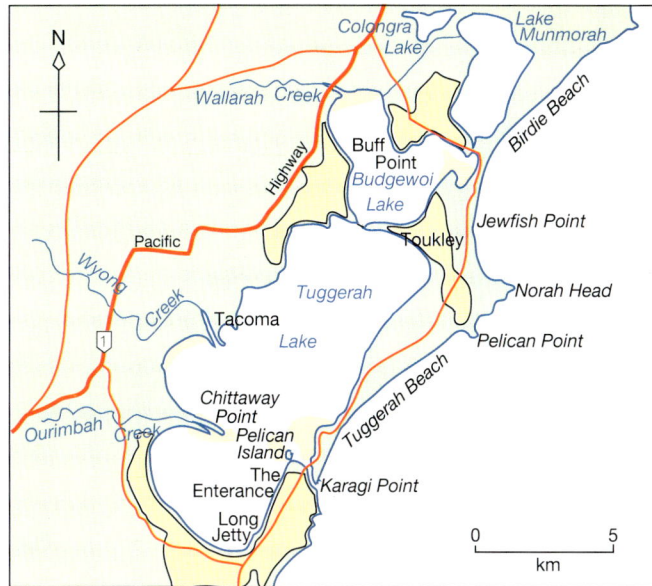

The three lakes that make up the Tuggerah system are Lake Munmorah, Budgewoi Lake and Tuggerah Lake. This area has always been a popular tourist location and with the new section of freeway bypassing Hornsby, it is now an easy day trip from Sydney.

The urban sprawl around the lakes has not helped the ecosystem but the lakes produce fish throughout the year.

Whiting, flathead, flounder, bream, blackfish and tailor are the most common fish in the lakes, and they make up the bulk of anglers' catches.

Apart from the estuary, the area has two long beaches that yield whiting, flathead, mulloway in warmer months, and tailor and bream in autumn and winter.

Rock fishing is also good in the area, particularly around Norah Head and Pelican Point.

Offshore, the waters around Norah Head are famous for their snapper catches plus many other species. Further south off Toowoon Bay there is more good ground.

With its closeness to Sydney, good tourist facilities, and accommodation of all standards from motels through to caravan parks, the Lakes area draws many anglers.

Boating facilities such as ramps and channel markers are well located in the lakes, but offshore access is a problem.

Ocean access is by way of ramps at Norah Head, Toowoon Bay and Terrigal Haven. All these ramps are effected by surge and are best suited to aluminium craft under 6 metres. Terrigal Haven ramp is the safest and easiest use.

The Entrance is the most heavily fished part of the Central Coast lakes, and is the point where the lakes meet the sea via the Entrance channel.

When the Entrance channel is deep and flowing, it yields great catches of whiting, along with flathead and some bream. When sanded up, fishing starts at the sand edge near the bridge.

Above the bridge, flathead, bream and luderick are the main species. The luderick are found along the channel edges and the deeper weeded banks. Bream and flathead are mostly located by drifting the area with quality bait such as live yabbies, bloodworms or prawns.

Upstream from the Entrance bridge are numerous channels and sandbanks and care should be taken with a boat. There are many weedy areas and lightly weighted baits will work best.

Many of these channels can also be reached by wading, and it is safe to wade and fish over quite a large area of the lower part of the lake.

The broad expanse of the lake is best fished by drifting and quite a few good tailor turn up each year on unweighted pilchards.

Bream anglers make very good catches in Wyong Creek on the western side of the lake in autumn. The best bait is chicken gut. A lot of bream and a few bass are also taken with lures in Wyong Creek.

At the top end of the lake is Toukley where a short channel joins the two systems. This channel and areas close by are very popular with anglers and yield flathead, bream and luderick. The bridge is particularly popular with holiday anglers.

Lake Budgewoi has another channel at the top end that joins Lake Munmorah to the system. This is a top luderick spot, with a few good bream also available around the jetties. Night fishing is best to avoid the crowds.

Lake Munmorah is shallow and weedy, and apart from the channel and the power station outlet, where long tom, hundreds of small, pesky bream, the occasional flathead and odd keeper tarwhine or bream are caught, there is not a lot of good territory.

Anglers still manage to catch luderick and bream from the weeded foreshore, but local knowledge prevails.

Prawning on the lakes is probably as popular as fishing with the best locations at Long Jetty, The Entrance channel, Canton Beach, Elizabeth Bay and the many sandy beaches along the eastern shoreline of the lakes.

Offshore from Norah Head, boats do not have to travel very far for fish. A large area of reef known as The Shallows runs from the lighthouse to just south of Pelican Point, and produces snapper, mulloway and kingfish, particularly in the warmer months.

A view of the mouth of Tuggerah Lakes, otherwise known as the Entrance. Excellent fishing also exists along the 9 kilometres of beach stretching northwards.

A large patch of broken reef behind Bird Island can also produce quantities of good snapper and tailor.

For those looking wider there are numerous reefs off Norah Head. The best of these is located by positioning Bird Island just below the crest of the bluff behind it. Looking south to Toowoon Bay, line up the two side-by-side pines in the middle of the two distinct humps in the horizon behind Toowoon Bay.

Two kilometres off Toowoon Bay is a group of shallow bomboras. These break in most sea conditions and the area is famous for its huge hauls of kingfish. At night, this same area also produces good mulloway and snapper.

The major beach fishing location is the 9 kilometres of sand that stretches north of The Entrance. This beach has good access along most of its length via tracks from the main road and through the tip. The northern end of the beach is National Park and has fewer access tracks, but it is still possible to get through to the base of the dunes and then walk on to the beach.

Tailor are often found along this beach in huge numbers, particularly during winter. Mulloway also work along the beach at night and are regularly caught at the mouth of the lake when it pours into the sea. Heavy tackle is needed to land them.

Top: Beach fishing north of the Entrance is excellent for whiting.
Above: The Entrance and Tuggerah Lakes has both character and fish.

Rock fishing ledges at the southern end of Norah Head are famous for their snapper, mulloway and tailor catches. Autumn is the peak period, but some fish will be found here all year round.

Pelican Point, to the south of Norah Head, is a low rock shelf that can be fished on very low tides and in slight seas.

This spot yields bream, drummer, blackfish and tailor. The area is riddled with holes and gutters and provides a great many spots to search for a fish or two. Just watch the sea conditions.

The Entrance to Broken Bay

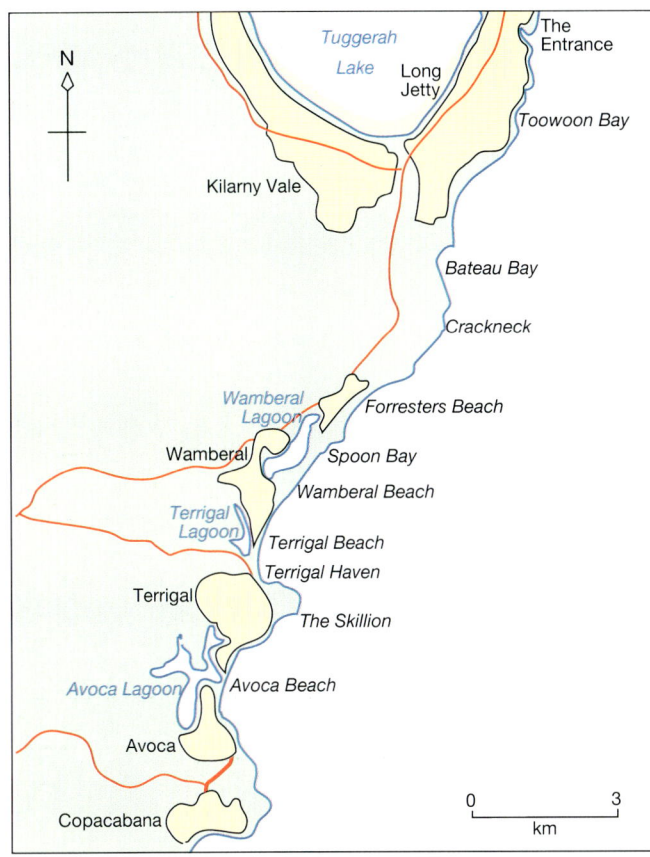

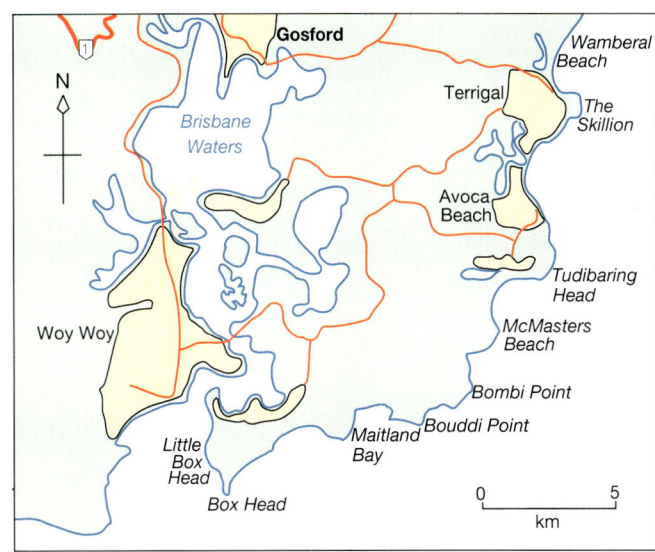

The small, broken headlands and short beaches at the northern end of this sector yield a few bream, whiting and luderick for the persistent.

Access is straightforward, with no long hikes required. As with most of the Central Coast, this area is well serviced by all facilities, ranging from shopping centres to garages, and bait and tackle outlets.

Toowoon Bay's protected waters are a haven for sunbakers, swimmers and families alike, though early morning or late afternoon fishing can be productive. There are some enormous whiting in Toowoon Bay, and they respond keenly to bloodworm baits. The occasional bream and tailor is also a chance.

Forresters and Wamberal Beach carry some excellent tailor during the cooler months, with large whiting in summer. In winter, there is usually only a shore dump to contend with, and as the tailor work very close to the beach, they are easily reached with unweighted pilchard baits on four-hook rigs.

Bream inhabit the surf breaks of both beaches, and respond best in the late afternoon using tuna, pilchard or worm baits.

Terrigal haven offers some very good rock fishing, particularly for surface fish. The protected waters are often invaded by frigate mackerel and anglers gather with lightweight high-speed spinning gear. Fishing is done from the headland, casting back towards the beach. The haven also carries a few good bream at night, particularly in a big sea.

The Skillion at Terrigal is a top tailor and bonito spot. Long casts are needed here, and most fishing is done with lures. The Skillion also produces good numbers of bream, luderick and small drummer. This spot is popular and often crowded at weekends.

Avoca Headland, just south of Terrigal, gets even more crowded with car parking within metres of the rock ledge.

However, Avoca does fish extremely well for surface fish, with excellent catches of kingfish taken. Also caught here in numbers are tuna, tailor and salmon.

Live baiting is practiced along the front ledge and quite a few big tuna and even an odd marlin have been taken here. Spinning is also extremely popular and when the action is hot, fish and enthusiastic fishermen blanket the rocks.

A few big snapper and mulloway are caught along the ledge and are usually on ganged-hook pilchard rigs.

Bream, blackfish and drummer are also in reasonable numbers in the washes along the headland. The top spot for these fish is at either end of the ledge.

Copacabana and McMasters Beach are one of the same, divided by a large lagoon which harbours good bait-size mullet. Both beaches provide whiting and a fair number of good mulloway in summer. Tailor and salmon are the extent of winter fishing.

Little Head to southern Kilcare Beach, in the Bouddi National Park, is a declared marine sanctuary, with no fishing allowed.

Box Head, looking across Broken Bay, is an excellent spot in rough seas, and when floodwaters pour out of the Hawkesbury this spot comes alive with mulloway anglers swinging big gear and lures.

The action gets really hot at times and only those with gear to handle the situation should make the long walk in.

Bream and tailor are caught right along the area from Box Head to Little Box Head.

Rock fishing scene on the north eastern side of Terrigal Skillion. This is generally a safe fishing area where all kinds of rock-dwelling fish can be caught. Tailor are especially prolific during winter.

A hefty luderick such as this one caught from Terrigal Haven rocks is worthy of an ear to ear grin.

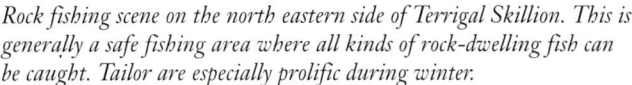

WoyWoy and Brisbane Waters

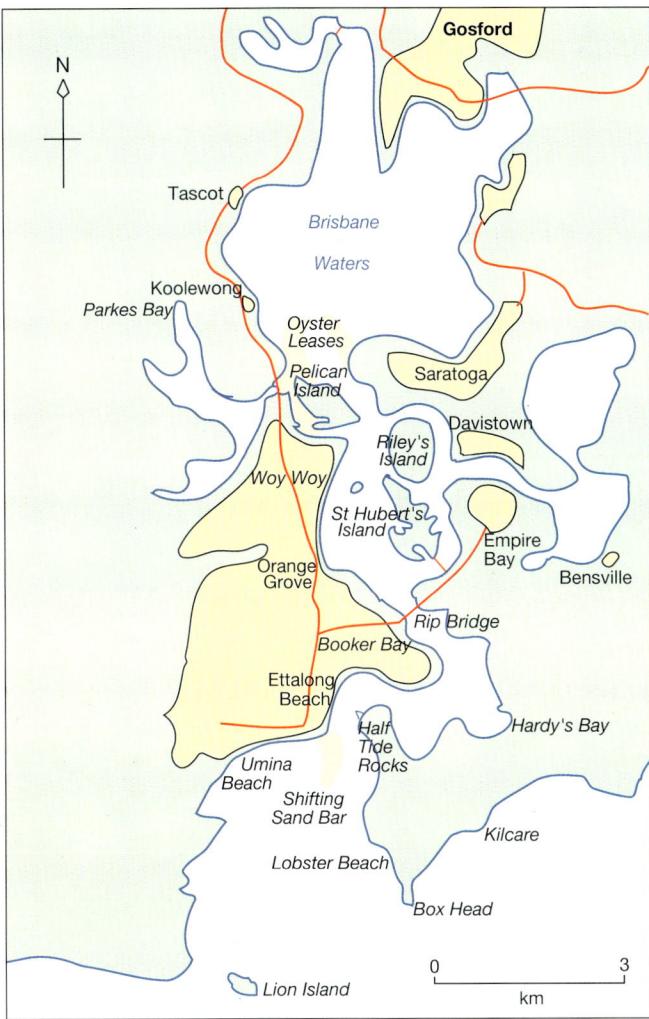

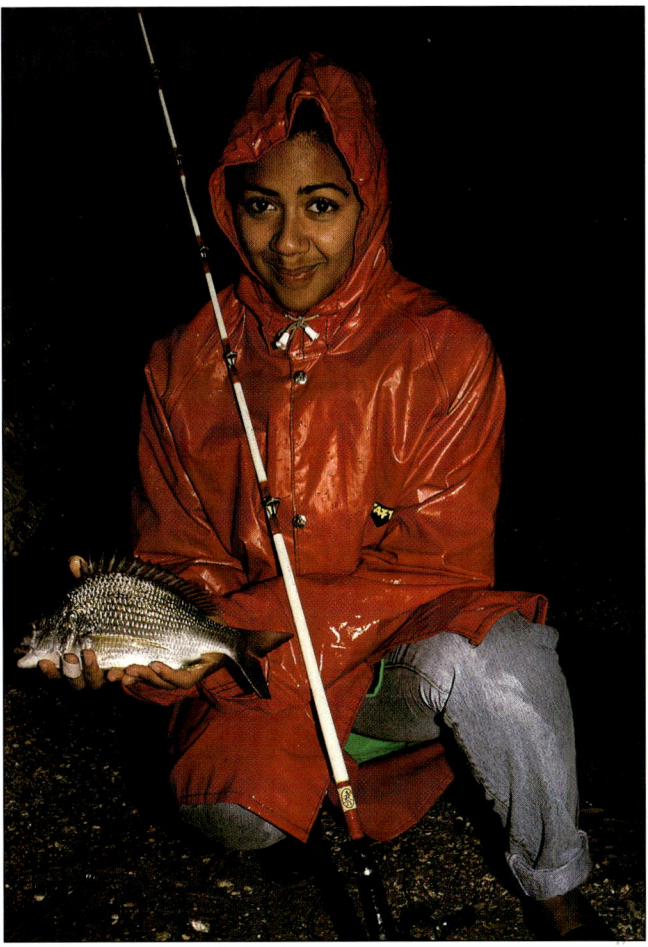

the coast. The tides affect the fishing and are a prime consideration when selecting a likely fishing spot.

The area fishes well year round apart from September when the winter species leave and the summer fish have yet to arrive.

Summer and autumn provide the peak fishing seasons with bream, blackfish, whiting, flathead, flounder, mulloway and tailor. There are some very big flathead and mulloway in the system and live bait fished with heavy tackle will often yield results.

The lower part of the system from Paddy's Channel to Broken Bay yields most of the big mulloway.

The range of fish habitats provides is plenty of diversity in the places to be fished. However, a few general areas can be covered in association with the map.

Suitably dressed for a wet winter's night, this angler has caught a well deserved silver bream from the rocky foreshores around Woy Woy. Bream are the most common inhabitant of this complex and massive estuary system.

Brisbane Waters feeds into the expanse of Broken Bay on its northern side and runs all the way up to Gosford.

The area is fish rich and provides a safe, enclosed estuary for the large Central Coast fishing population plus numerous visiting Sydney anglers. The area is completely closed to all forms of netting, including witch's hat crab snares. No nets means more fish for recreational anglers.

There are very good boat launching facilities and hire boat, bait, ice, tackle and accommodation are all available.

The main access points are at Gosford and Woy Woy, although many anglers launch in Pittwater or the Hawkesbury and run the short distance to Brisbane Waters to avoid driving too far.

This area has a complex arrangement of channels, sandbanks, weedbeds and oyster leases. The channels are signposted, but care should be taken, particularly at night.

It also has swift tidal flow and the aptly name Rip Bridge passes over some of the strongest running water on

103

Half Tide Rocks and Wagstaff Point have fast flowing, deep water and produce very large flathead and quality bream. An echo sounder will yield a very promising bottom structure with plenty of bait fish.

This area is extremely productive when the Hawkesbury River floods.

The Rip Bridge, further upstream, produces a lot of bream, flathead and mulloway. Top or bottom of the tide is best - slack water and live bait is the key to success. Again, a sounder helps as most big fish will be located on the channel edge.

Above Rip Bridge, the system broadens, shallows and the currents become slow. Sandbanks, weedbeds and islands become part of the landscape, along with oyster leases and flash waterfront homes.

The marked channel edges provide good flathead and luderick, with whiting on most of the sandbanks. Deeper waters will yield big bream. Luderick are also found along the weedy edges of channels.

In the Empire Bay/Davistown region, good drifting for flathead, whiting, bream small tailor can be experienced.

On the Woy Woy side, the channels are clearly visible and the tide runs quickly along Riley's Island.

Paddy's Channel, at the top of Riley's Island, is one of the most productive fishing grounds in the system, producing all common estuary fish in both numbers and large sizes.

Opposite the ramp at Woy Woy, about halfway across the channel is a deep hole that produces mulloway and bream. A little further upstream, large oyster leases line both sides of the channel.

The edges of these leases are prolific bream spots by night and yield luderick by day. The key to the bream fishing is to use chicken gut as bait and to fish with as little lead as possible.

Many of the sandbanks exposed at low tide also yield nippers or yabbies. Almost all the available fish in the system will take yabbies.

Small mullet and yellowtail can be caught throughout the area by using berley and a pinch of prawn on a small hook and are the key to catching big flathead and mulloway. If live bait is not available then blue pilchards are best.

Further up the system towards Gosford the bottom becomes rather featureless, but quite a few bream roam the areas close to the shore. Flathead can be located by drifting across the bays.

Narara Creek, which runs into the system just west of Gosford, is a noted flathead producer, and is well worth a throw with either baits or lures.

Above: Back at a Woy Woy ramp, the local pelicans wait for a handout.

Above: Dusky flathead are a regular catch in Brisbane Waters.

The Hawkesbury River System

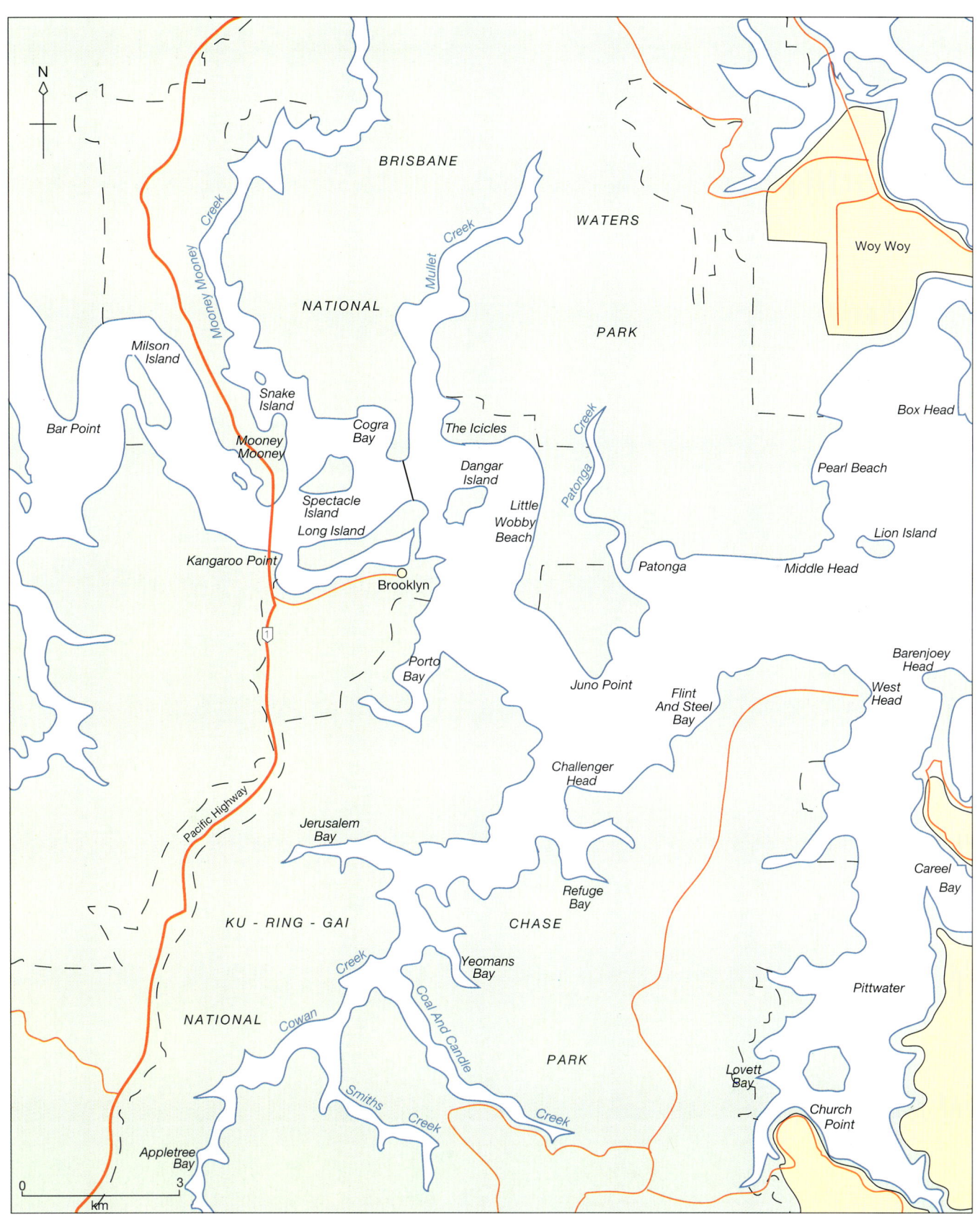

Brisbane

Mooney Mooney Creek

Milson Island

Snake Island

Cogra Bay

Mullet Creek

The Icicles

Dangar Island

National

Park

Waters

Woy Woy

Box Head

Pearl Beach

Lion Island

Bar Point

Mooney Mooney

Little Wobby Beach

Patonga Creek

Spectacle Island

Long Island

Patonga

Middle Head

Kangaroo Point

Brooklyn

Porto Bay

Juno Point

Flint And Steel Bay

West Head

Barenjoey Head

Challenger Head

Careel Bay

Pacific Highway

Jerusalem Bay

KU - RING - GAI

CHASE

Refuge Bay

Pittwater

Cowan Creek

Yeomans Bay

Coal And Candle Creek

PARK

Lovett Bay

NATIONAL

Smiths Creek

Creek

Church Point

Appletree Bay

0   3
km

The Hawkesbury is one of the great river systems in New South Wales. Rising in the Great Dividing Range near Goulbourn, it flows along Sydney's western suburbs as the Nepean River, gaining the Hawkesbury title from Windsor onwards. Eventually it enters the sea at Broken Bay, north of Sydney.

There are many access points and facilities are first class with good boat ramps, ice, bait, fuel, food and a huge range of hire boats available. Some of the hire boats are live-aboard cruisers and houseboats, offering anglers the chance to fish while enjoying all the comforts of home.

The best way of describing the Hawkesbury system's fishing is to divide it into sections, as each area has different characteristics that require different methods.

Pittwater is a shallow, open body of water that forms part of Broken Bay. The eastern shore is settled, but National Park dominates the western side.

The main species in the area are bream, flathead, whiting, luderick and tailor. Blue swimmer crabs are also prolific.

Drifting is the most productive way to fish Pittwater, with nippers or yabbies the best bait. They can be pumped in many of the bays.

Pittwater features calm, clear water, so the best way to ensure good catches is to fish with lightly weighted baits and fine line.

Cowan Creek is a drowned river valley in the Ku-ring-gai Chase National Park, and has an almost totally protected catchment. Magnificent scenery compliments the fishing.

The arms of this system tend to end as sandy bays that yield flathead and whiting, while the rocky shores produce bream, leatherjackets, blackfish and mulloway.

Most of the good fishing is along the shoreline rather than in the very deep middle section of the river.

Hairtail appear in Cowan Creek from late autumn until early spring and are caught in big numbers once located. The most popular bait is a blue pilchard fished on a three-hook rig, but good catches are also taken on live yellowtail. A short wire trace is needed to prevent their razor-sharp teeth from severing the line.

The best spots for hairtail are Waratah Bay, Jerusalem Bay, Yeomans Bay and Akuna Bay, mostly at night, but the fish can be taken in daylight.

The Cowan Creek system yields a lot of John dory and squid during winter, and its sheltering hills make it one of the best waterways to fish in the colder months.

Berowra Waters is very much like Cowan Creek, but is shallower, muddier and, in most cases, yields fewer fish. Nevertheless, it is a visually appealing and productive fishing location. Road access is only available at the Berowra Waters ferry where there is a very good boat ramp, plus food, fuel, ice and hire boats.

Berowra is one of Sydney's few good estuary lure-casting locations. Upstream from the ferry, the river gets shallow and is lined with channels and mangroves, where flathead and bream are the targets. Near the ferry, good catches of bream and school mulloway are taken, particularly at night. The area holds a lot of bait and small yellowtail, tailor and mullet can be caught near the marina.

Further downstream there are many shallow bays, which yield flathead and flounder. Oyster leases in Cob Bay, Marramarra Creek and the mouth of the Berowra River, near Bar Island, hold good stocks of bream.

Beauty Point at the entrance to Cob Bay yields school mulloway in summer with high tide at daybreak or dusk a likely period for fish in the 1 to 5 kilogram class. Best baits are live prawns and small live yellowtail.

The main river downstream from Wisemans Ferry to the mouth is the most successful fishing stretch. The sheer volume of water here makes the river prone to heavy tides, so anglers need to plan with this in mind.

The main river is one of real strongholds for mulloway, and good catches are made in summer, though they are available throughout the year. The best spots for mulloway are at Flint and Steel, Juno Head, Gunyah Point, the rail and road bridges, and at Bar Point.

Live baits and strong tackle are required when fishing for the larger mulloway. Best times are at night around the change of tide.

Small, school mulloway are very common in the Hawkesbury, particularly fish that are just legal size. Called 'soapies', they feed extensively on prawns, which are their favoured bait. Larger school mulloway between 2 to 5 kilograms are always a chance if using small live fish, live prawns or bottle squid as bait.

Bream are also prolific in the river, caught in the deep river channel by day, and close to rocky shorelines at night. Best baits are prawns, worms, mullet gut and chicken gut by night.

Drifting in the system is popular for flathead, flounder, bream and school mulloway.

At the mouth of the Hawkesbury River, from Barrenjoey across to Lion Island and up to Juno Point, large numbers of tailor often congregate to feed on bait fish. These fish are of good size and are regularly accompanied by bonito and salmon.

Great sport can be had by casting or trolling lures around these schools. Just watch for the wheeling flocks of seabirds that follow the action.

Sydney Northern Beaches

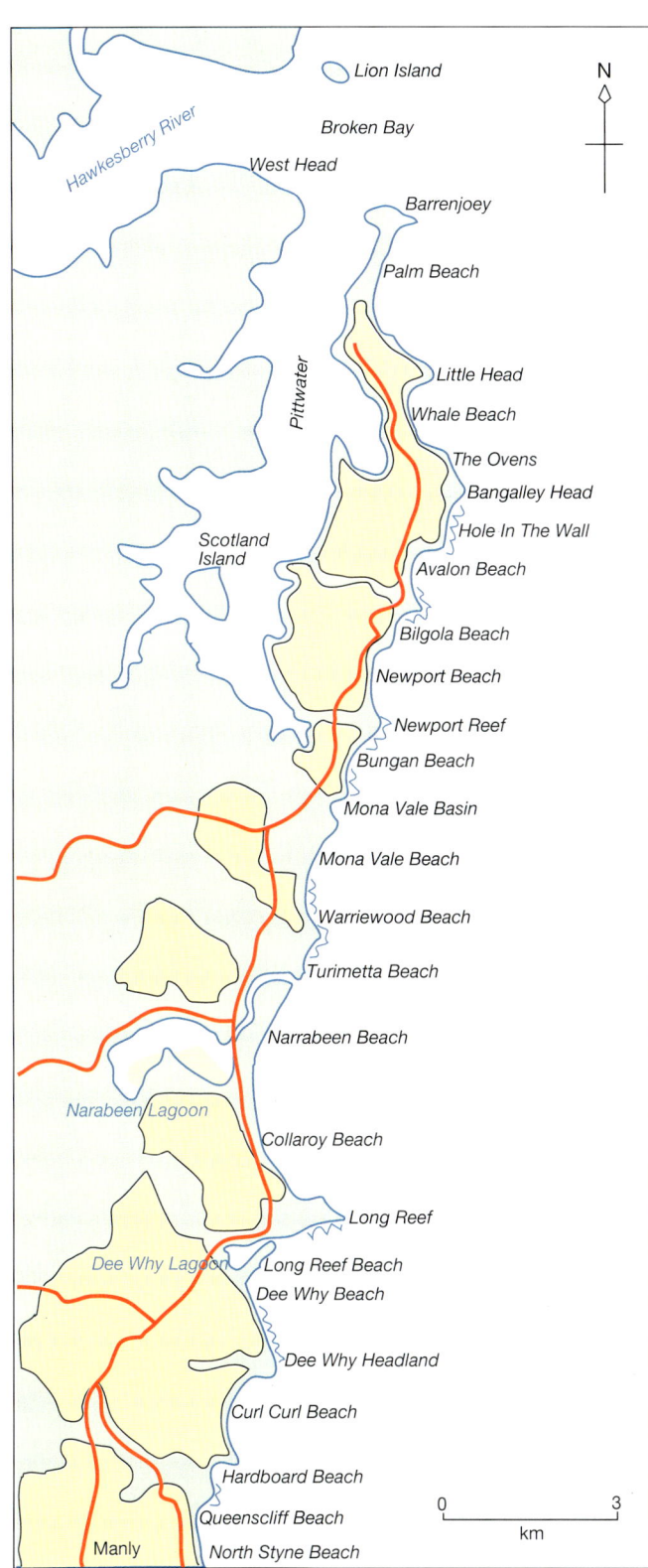

Sydney's Northern Peninsula, with it's long beaches and rocky headlands, offers the full range of angling styles; from land-based live baiting for kingfish and big tuna to light-tackle rockhopping for luderick.

From North Head to Palm Beach, the Peninsula has over 17 beaches and 20 rocky headlands. Depending on where you intend fishing, access is by Barrenjoey, Pittwater or Sydney Road.

The North Head region from Bluefish Point to Manly Beach is a vast rocky headland that encompasses numerous rock fishing spots, though the Bluefish Point sewerage outlet is not recommended as it's extremely dangerous. Access to North Head is by either walking around the rocks from Bluefish Point or by descending the ladders and ropes on North Head.

With access from Bower Street, the stretch between Fairy Bower and Bluefish Point is highly productive. Several rocky gutters and washy rock-studded holes yield good numbers of luderick, drummer and bream.

Manly Beach to Queenscliff is over run by surfers, however, whiting, bream and small tailor can be caught off the beach in the early morning or at dusk. Queenscliff Point and Harbord Point are excellent for tailor in winter. Salmon and various species of tuna and kingfish can be caught by spinning with lures or pilchards off Harbord Point while luderick, bream and drummer abound in the washes. Further along the point towards South Curl Curl are several low-lying platforms where luderick are the mainstay. In a big sea, fish for tailor from the high ledges.

Right: Tailor proliferate in the washes surrounding the northern beaches headlands. This one was caught at Bangalley Head.

Luderick fishermen at South Curl Curl, an easily accessible and often extremely productive fishing ledge.

Curl Curl Beach yields whiting, bream and flathead during summer from the baths at the southern end or in the protected northern corner. Curl Curl Headland, however, is a more reliable location.

From the sea pool to Dee Why there are washes that bream, trevally and tailor inhabit during winter, while luderick and drummer are year-round residents. The prominent rock platform just north from Curl Curl Point itself is a reasonable live baiting and spinning ledge for kingfish, tuna and salmon, though live baits will need to be carried in. Access is limited from the Dee Why Beach side of this headland; better to park at North Curl Curl Surf Club and walk around.

Dee Why and Long Reef Beaches yield big hauls of tailor around the green pole in the middle of the beach, known as No-man's Land, while the vast reef platform at Long Reef itself is an excellent rockhopping location. Fish the incoming tide for drummer, luderick, bream and trevally. Out on Long Reef Point is a snapper spot with a long cast, but like much of the platform, it is cut off from the mainland at high tide. Take care, especially if the seas are predicted to build. Fisherman's Beach, nestled in the northern corner of Long Reef, is a rough-weather retreat for catching bream, especially near the boat ramp.

Collaroy and Narrabeen Beaches are productive for whiting, tailor, bream, flathead, and the occasional mulloway where Narrabeen Lagoon empties out to sea.

The pipe in front of the car park at the southern end of Collaroy Beach marks a tailor ground. Narrabeen Headland is best accessed from the swimming pool car park at North Narrabeen, and a long cast south-east will put you in contention to catch snapper, trevally and bream, while drummer are a chance anywhere along the ledge. Narrabeen Headland is dangerous when there's a sea running.

Little Narrabeen or Turimetta is the next beach north. Great luderick fishing can be encountered in the rocky gutters at the southern end, while bream, tailor and mulloway are a chance off the beach on a rising tide and around dusk. Suicide Head, at the northern end of Little Narrabeen, is aptly named when the sea is running, though in calm conditions drummer, luderick, bream, tailor, salmon and snapper are all possibilities. Further around the Warriewood side, past the effluent outlet, the high ledges are probably Sydney's most productive snapper fishing ground for rockhoppers. Mulloway are also encountered here, while the low ledges below are worth fishing for luderick and drummer using local cabbage weed, but only when it's calm.

Mona Vale Basin is worth a cast for snapper in heavy seas while the low rock platform surrounding the sea pool produces bream and large numbers of luderick when seas permit fishing here. North Mona Vale or South Bungan Headland still produces snapper from off the high rock on the point, while luderick, drummer and bream are common in the washes. Because of it's low-lying and exposed nature, North Mona Vale Headland is only safe to fish in calm weather.

Bungan Beach is a useful beachworming ground, while whiting and bream are caught in summer. Better fishing prospects exist to the north around Newport Reef, where luderick, healthy numbers of bream, and drummer can be caught at the old sea pool. For the adventurous, Newport Reef island can be reached safely in calm seas by surf ski. Everything from tailor to bream and groper are a chance off the island.

Bilgola Beach is a pretty setting; fishermen will find bream and drummer in the gutter next to the sea pool at the southern end. A rising tide and early morning are necessary requirements for landing a catch here. Bilgola Beach yields beachworms, while North Bilgola Headland is a productive ground for bream, trevally, drummer and luderick. Fish over the top of the shallow reef, but expect some gear losses as a consequence.

Hole in the Wall, at the northern end of Avalon Beach, is a great rock fishing region. Luderick and drummer are caught on local cabbage weed baits fished in the gutters below St Michaels Cave; groper and bream will respond to crab baits fished in these same washes, while snapper are taken with a long cast off the boulders down off Avalon Point. Further to the north, Bangalley Head is a top rock fishing region. Bream, trevally, tailor, salmon, bonito, luderick, drummer and big kingfish are all a chance. Early morning fishing on the rising tide is preferable.

South Whale Beach's The Ovens is Sydney's most famous rock fishing spot. It is a big fish producer; kingfish, tuna, salmon, tailor and snapper are taken. Live bait in the form of yellowtail can be caught in the gulf at the outer Ovens, and produce best results when floated out under a balloon or bobby cork from the tip of the point, while luderick, bream and drummer are more common back towards the inner Ovens ledge. Access to both these spots is from a track leading from the end of Rayner Road a rope is recommended for assisting climbing down the point, though it is only a short descent or by walking around from South Whale Beach itself. The Ovens is reasonably protected in southerly seas, and as it is a deep water ledge, isn't as dangerous as many other Peninsula rock fishing spots, though it still demands respect.

North Whale Beach platform is another productive big fish ledge. Live baiting here produces kingfish, bonito, salmon and larger tuna at times, while snapper are a chance if you're patient. Luderick and drummer inhabit the washes around towards Palm Beach, while tailor salmon, bream and trevally are a surety of the point on slow-spun pilchards at dawn during winter. North Whale Beach is exposed to prevailing sea conditions and is dangerous when there's a swell running.

Palm Beach itself is a reliable summer whiting and flathead spot, while bream, tailor and salmon are encountered sporadically throughout the year. The rocks at South Palm Beach are a reasonable bream, trevally and tailor producer, particularly off the rocky outcrop just around from the pool known as Mushroom Rock. Casting baits into the gutter adjacent to Palm Beach Pool is an excellent rough weather solution for catching tailor, bream, flathead and luderick.

At the northern end of Palm Beach, Barrenjoey is a prolific surface fish ground; bonito, kingfish, tailor, salmon and various tunas are practically year-round candidates for lures, pilchards or live baits fished off the point. Bream, trevally, luderick, drummer, and groper are also encountered around the headland, while mulloway and snapper are a good chance off the northern side during a run-out tide when the Hawkesbury River is in flood. In really big seas, rockfishermen will find sanctuary fishing off the western side of Barrenjoey. Bream, tailor, salmon, and mulloway at night, are all possibilities. Access to Barrenjoey Headland is gained by a reasonable walk from the car parking area near the golf course at the northern end of the beach.

Sydney's northern beaches are an angling heaven, but take heed of this notice at South Curl Curl. If fishermen are to be allowed continuing access to this great fishing region respect of the environment is essential.

Sydney Harbour

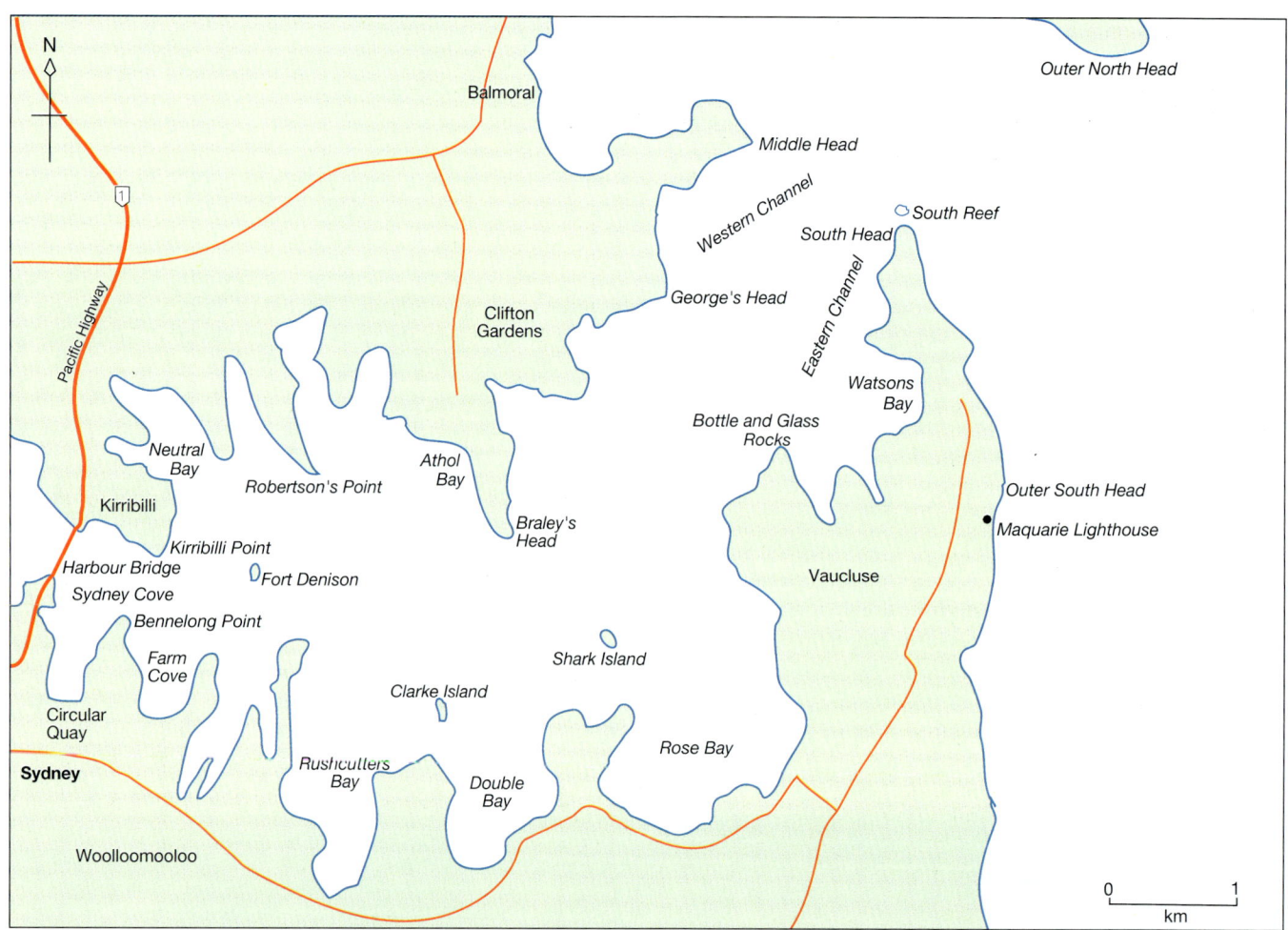

Sydney Harbour is an extensive estuary system, comprising Port Jackson and the Parramatta and Lane Cove River tributaries, North Harbour and Middle Harbour, and the outer harbour. All regions cater for shore-based and boat angling.

More than 50 different fish species have been discovered in Sydney Harbour, but only a handful of these are caught regularly by anglers. Common captures include the east coast black bream, red bream or juvenile snapper, luderick or blackfish, flathead, whiting, mullet, tailor, garfish, John dory, leatherjacket, trevally, mulloway and yellowtail.

Because these fish species have different environmental preferences and the harbour encompasses different estuary environments, it is best to examine these fishing regions separately.

West of the Harbour Bridge, much of the upper harbour shoreline is blanketed by industry, limiting the angler in where he can fish. Nevertheless, wharves, jetties

and recreational parklands with accessible shorelines can be found in most waterfront suburbs, and these locations frequently yield impressive catches of bream, luderick and leatherjacket around reefy areas, while flathead, whiting, mullet and good hauls of crabs and prawns can be encountered over sandy or muddy bottomed regions.

Among some of the recognised land-based locations to fish for bream and luderick are the piers around Walsh Bay, Long Nosed Point and the Dawn Fraser Baths at Balmain, Wolseley Street Wharf at Drummoyne, Riverview Ferry Wharf, the rocky shoreline known as Kellys Bush off Nelson Parade in Woolwich, the retaining wall off Elizabeth Street in Hunters Hill, Greenwich Wharf, Berry Island shores and Blues Point near North Sydney.

Like any city fishing spot, these areas fish best early morning, late afternoon into the night, and during the week as opposed to weekends, using only the freshest bait available. For luderick, Parramatta River weed is widely regarded as the prime offering, and this is available from most good tackle and bait suppliers in Sydney. Berley liberally with a sand and chopped weed mix, and vary the depth at which the bait is set beneath the float until luderick are encountered.

Upper harbour bream can be taken by spinning small diving lures from along the rocky shore, though by far the most successful technique is to use live bloodworms, fresh harbour prawns or pink nippers. Neatly cut cubes of tuna or pilchard can also produce bream if used in conjunction with a similar berley, as can small black crabs found under the rocks at low tide. Peak breaming periods west of the bridge are the last few hours of the rising tide and the first few of the falling tide, especially if these combine with a late afternoon or early morning.

Hen and Chicken Bay, Half Moon Bay and Tarban Creek are all upper harbour fishing spots where good crabbing and prawning can be experienced during summer, while bream, whiting and flathead also often reside around the shallow sandflats in the bays. Similarly, the Lane Cove River supports a healthy population of these fish, as well as crustaceans. Bream are regulars around Greenwich Reserve, Longueville and Bay Street Wharf in the river, while prawns, mud crabs, flathead and whiting are possibles around and above Fig Tree Bridge, especially the sandflats and mangrove areas.

Boat-based anglers will find launching facilities adequate in the upper harbour; the fishing can be excellent. Anchor close to deep, rocky shores and berley heavily using light tackle and lightly weighted baits for bream, but only when boat traffic is minimal. Luderick can be taken around these same areas using green weed baits suspended between 3 and 4 metres beneath floats,

especially along the rocky shore from Pulpit Point in Drummoyne all the way to near Tarban Creek.

Most boaties choose to drift the upper harbour for bream, trevally, whiting, flathead and school mulloway. Bloodworms and fresh prawns are the top offerings with the deep water between Spectacle and Cockatoo Island, the mouth of the Lane Cover River and the main channel upstream of the Gladesville Bridge being productive.

Port Jackson, or the harbour arm stretching from the bridge to South Head, is Sydney's busiest recreational fishing region. Land-based anglers crowd wharves, rocky points and any other accessible shores, mainly in the hope of catching bream, which can be found both in the deep main channel and in close among the rocks. Late afternoon into night and dawn fishing sessions will prove most productive for shallow-water breaming, while long casts to the deep channel using a rig incorporating a large ball sinker and bloodworm or fresh prawn bait is the only answer during daylight. Weekends are usually unproductive as boat traffic churns the water to foam and puts the fish off the bite.

Other predominant species caught by shore fishermen in Port Jackson include tailor, leatherjacket, luderick, flathead, trevally, and whiting over the sandflats in places such as Rose Bay, Double Bay, Camp Cove and Sirius Cove. Again bloodworms are the answer for most, though luderick favour fresh string or cabbage weed depending on which is in season.

Boat-based anglers can fish some real harbour hotspots in Port Jackson which are not accessible to those confined to the shore, namely Sow and Pigs Reef in mid-channel off Obelisk Beach, and the deep shipping lanes and marker

The Author demonstrating that Quakers Hat Bay in Middle Harbour is a productive flathead fishery.

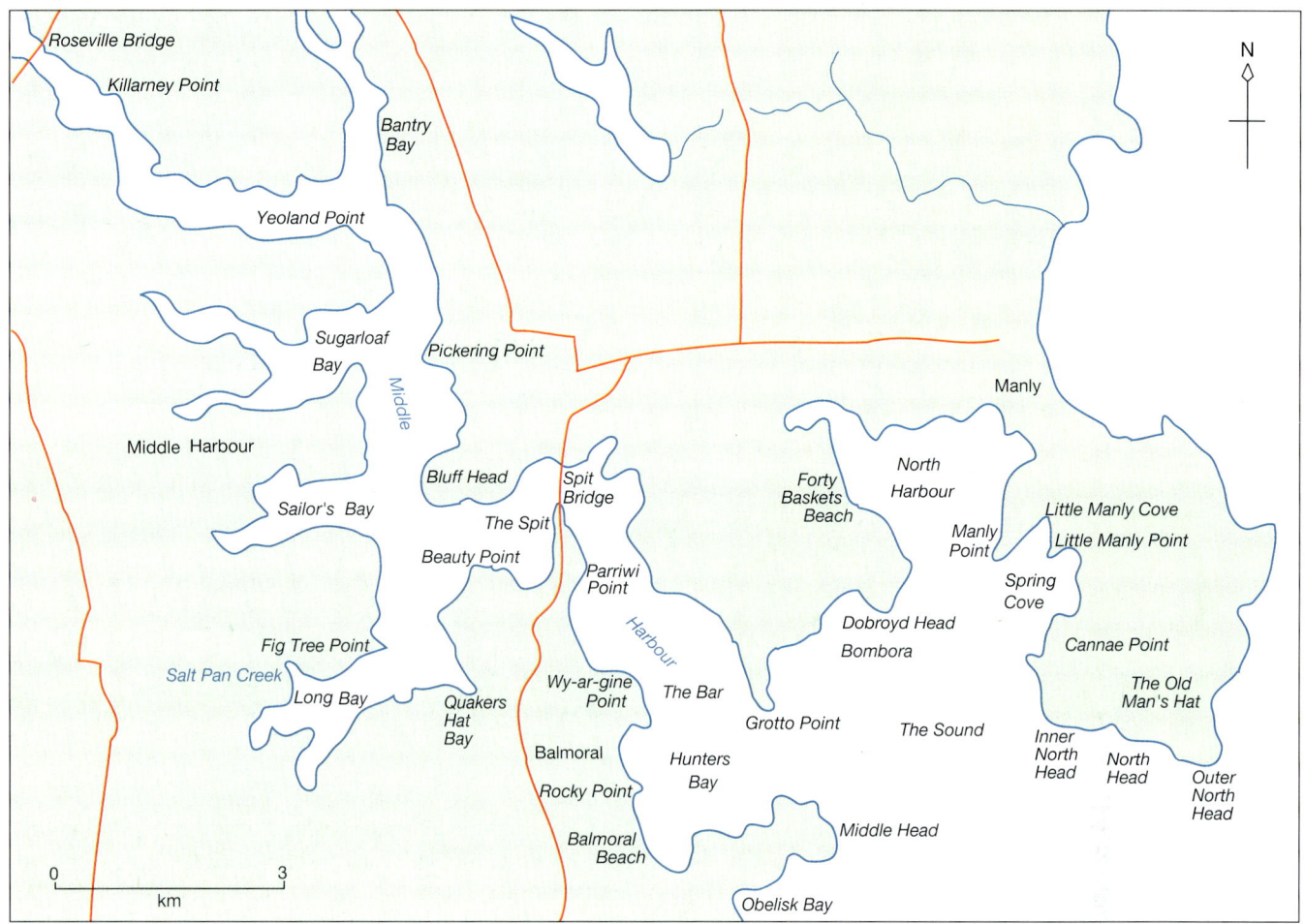

buoys that dot the lower reaches. By anchoring up-tide of Sow and Pigs and floating baits back towards the reef, especially at night on the first of a run-in or run-out, scores of bream, tailor and trevally are possible. Similar results can be achieved around the channel marker buoys, especially the wooden fixtures known as the Wedding Cakes, by presenting baits around the chains that anchor them to the bottom. Kingfish school here in summer, and mulloway can be caught if using live baits.

Rose Bay boat ramp services eastern suburbs anglers, Little Manly the north, while there are ramps in either upper Middle Harbour or west of the bridge.

The outer harbour is flushed regularly by ocean waters, so it is not suprising that ocean species can be caught in the region. During summer, small tuna species, salmon and tailor school on the surface, but only early before boat traffic intensifies. Trolling and casting lures at these fish can be highly productive, either from a boat or from the rocks along inner North Head, Middle Head and South Head. Drifting the bottom or anchoring where the reef drops away along inner North Head, and using pilchard or tuna baits, can produce small snapper, dusky and sand flathead, bream, trevally and mulloway.

The closest boat ramp to the region is at Rose Bay, a crowded twin-lane launching site, but with good parking.

Others exist west of the bridge and in upper Middle Harbour and North Harbour, while small boat beach launching is at Balmoral Beach, The Spit and Clontarf.

Land-based access is limited in the outer harbour area though the rocks along inner North Head at a spot called The Old Man's Hat, plus Middle Head and South Head provide rock fishing. Safety should be emphasised as these spots are exposed to weather and sea conditions.

North Harbour is the official name given to the Quarantine Beach to Dobroyd Point region, which includes Manly Wharf and surrounds. Although not a huge area by harbour standards, the extremely productive Dobroyd Point is a great boat spot for bream, small snapper, trevally and tailor near the bombora markers but only when seas are calm. Rock fishing, again bearing safety in mind, yields good numbers of luderick and bream in this area, while tailor frequent the washes early morning.

Land-based locales in North Harbour include top breaming ground Forty Baskets Beach, Manly Point, Spring Cove and the old Gas Works opposite the Australian Police College. At the latter, leatherjacket, luderick and John dory can be encountered. Manly wharf, although always a hive of activity, is a dependable bait catching ground, while a live yellowtail set off the wharf is bound to find a lurking John dory during winter.

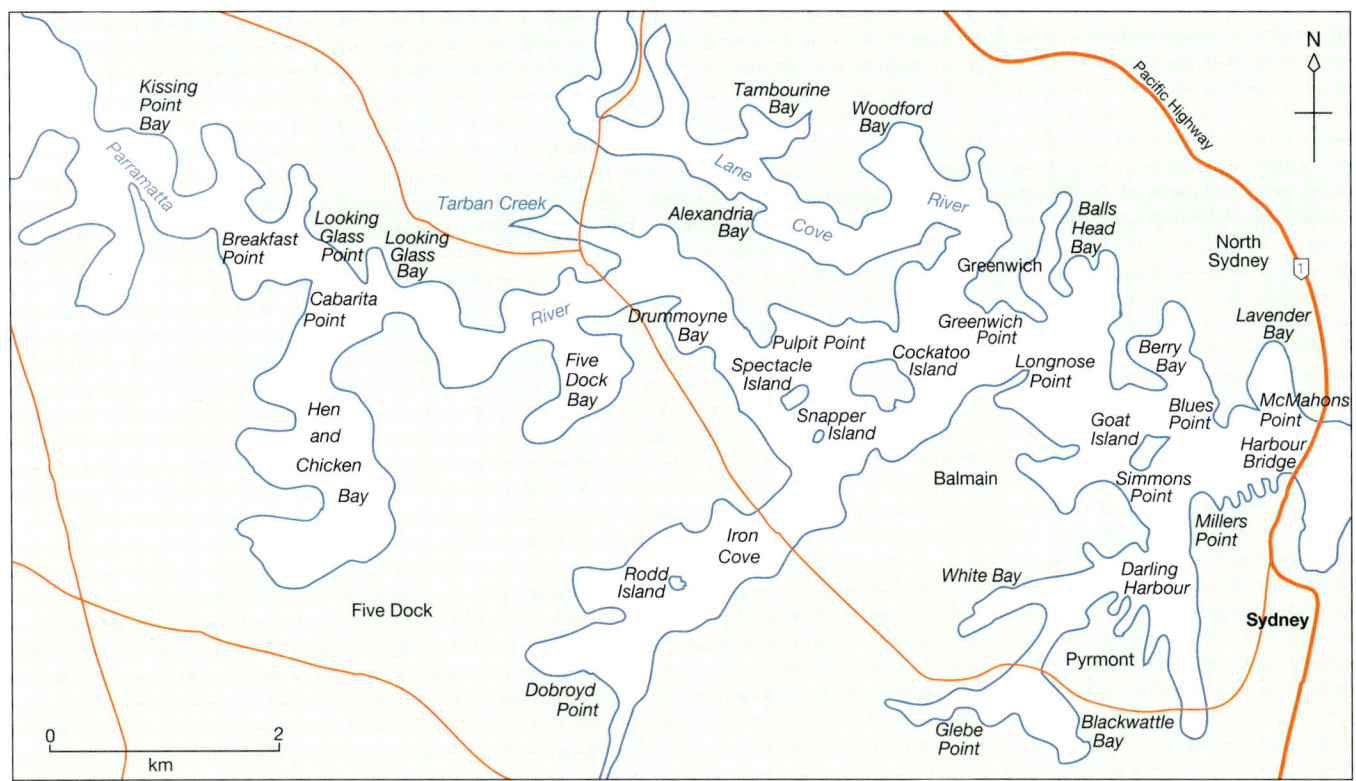

Boat fishermen might try drifting for flathead, flounder, bream and trevally out from Quarantine Beach while tailor can often be found schooling on the surface early morning. There is a boat ramp at Little Manly, though it does get very crowded and parking is a problem.

Middle Harbour stretches upstream from between Middle Head and Dobroyd Point, running as far west as the Roseville Bridge and Davidson Creek. Its is perhaps the cleanest Sydney Harbour arm, and catches reflect this. The region is best known for its often superb land-based bream fishing along the rocky foreshores west of the Spit Bridge, namely at Quakers Hat Point, Fig Tree Point, Sugarloaf Point, Roseville Bridge Reserve, and around Bluff Head. Generous berleying with a sand and pilchard or tuna flesh mix or crushed oysters and chopped crabs is essential for attracting bream and encouraging them to bite freely.

Luderick, flathead, whiting, flounder, tailor, and school mulloway are also encountered from the shores in Middle Harbour. For mulloway, look for deep water rocky points that have good tidal flow, or large bays where there is deep water and good concentrations of baitfish. Yellowtail, small tailor, mullet, slimy mackerel and garfish can be found around most wharves, so these can produce mulloway when using live fish as bait. The Spit area yields mulloway, as well as tailor and kingfish at times.

Boat fishermen will discover good flathead, whiting, and bream drifting grounds in Sugarloaf and Bantry Bays, while the deep holes of Bluff Head, Sugarloaf Point and east of Beauty Point are the best chance for mulloway, as well as the odd big flathead. East of the Spit, excellent flathead drift exist off Balmoral and Chinamans Beaches, while around Middle Head is a good spot to anchor, berley heavily, and catch bream and trevally in the early morning. There are ramps at Northbridge and Roseville Bridge, while small boat beach launching exists at The Spit, Balmoral and Clontarf beaches.

The Wedding Cakes or channel markers at the opening to Port Jackson are a kingfish spot during summer. Here's proof.

Eastern Suburbs Rock Fishing

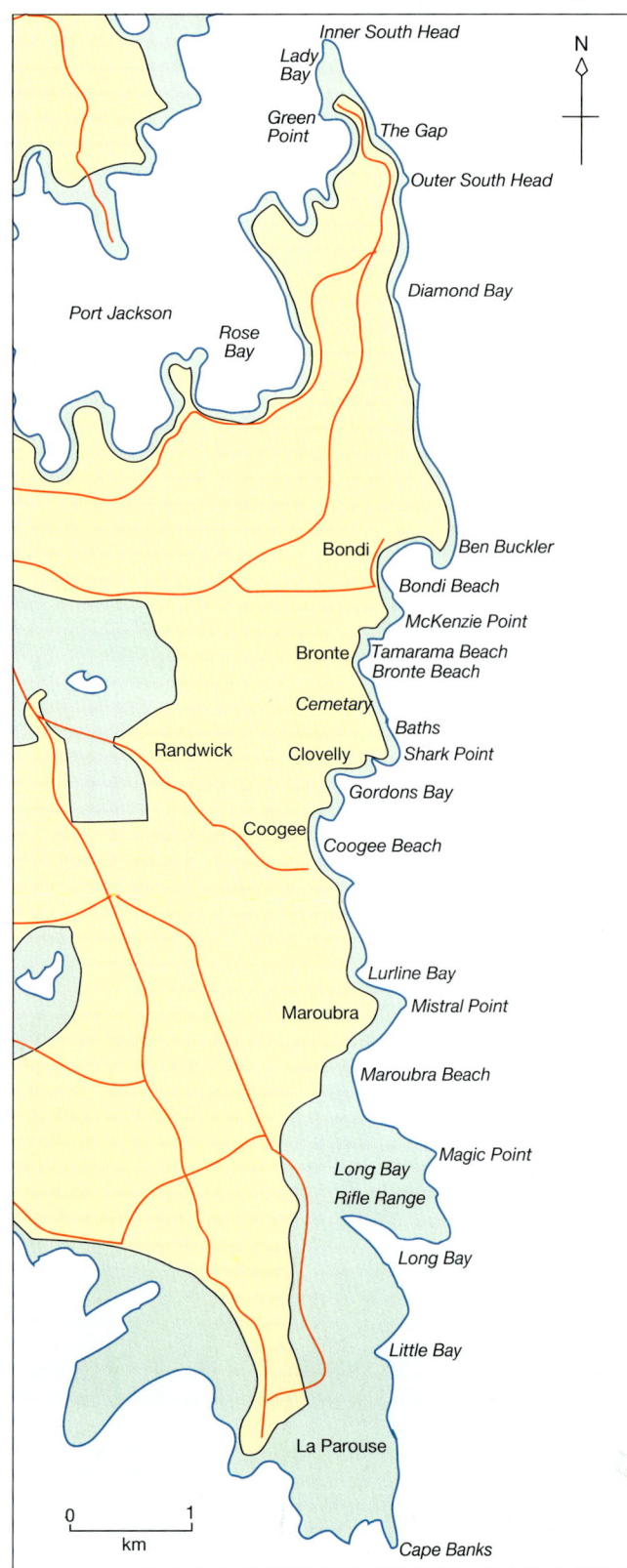

From Sydney's South Head to Botany Bay, the coast is composed of towering sandstone cliffs and wave-washed rocky platforms, making for ideal rock fishing territory for anyone with a sense of adventure. Access to some locations may involve climbing ropes, ladders and using hand toggles, though we strongly advise against fishing these areas unless you are an experienced rock climber. Most rock fishing platforms in this area are easily accessible.

South Head is a recognised rock fishing spot, yielding bream, luderick, drummer and tailor, while during summer bonito can be tempted with lures. Elephant Rock is one of the better vantage points, being surrounded by relatively deep water, but when the seas are rough, move around to the pillbox on the inner side of South Head and try for bream in the evening or early morning.

Rosa Gully to The Gap is all high cliffs, and access to the fishing spots below is very dangerous. To reach Rosa Gully's rock fishing spots it's necessary to climb down a steel ladder at the northern end of the gully, however it is an easy descent. Drummer, luderick, groper, bream and tailor can be caught, but only in calm seas, as the area is very exposed.

Bondi's northern point, known as Ben Buckler, is a reliable producer of luderick, drummer and bream. Tailor and salmon can be caught on pilchards or lures during winter mornings, while various small tunas are a chance when summer's warm currents prevail. At the southern end, McKenzies Point around to Tamarama is bream and drummer country, while winter fishing for tailor and salmon is worthwhile from the high ledges when there is a moderate sea running.

Bronte Point at the southern end of the Bronte Beach, presents limited rock fishing for bream and luderick, though the rocks at the southern end from Suicide Point to Clovelly are more productive. Excellent bream and luderick fishing can be encountered in the washes along the rocks behind Waverley Cemetery, while groper and drummer also reside in the area. Snapper are a chance for those prepared to put the time in.

Shark Point, at the southern end of Clovelly Pool, has long been regarded as a good producer of tailor, salmon, small tuna and the occasional kingfish for lure casting and live baiting enthusiasts. Luderick, drummer, bream, groper and the odd snapper can be taken on the bottom using crab or cunjevoi baits. Just inside Clovelly Pool is a rough weather luderick hotspot, and bream are a chance at night here, and in Thompson's Bay around to the south.

Coogee Beach is well protected from ocean swell by neighbouring Wedding Cake Island, which makes it one of the only rough weather fishing beaches in Sydney. During summer, whiting, bream and flathead are possibilities, though early morning or night fishing is necessary to avoid the many bathers. To the south of Coogee, there are numerous productive luderick, bream and drummer

washes, particularly between Trennery Reserve and Lurline Bay. Cabbage weed and crabs are readily available baits.

The Stakes is a popular rock fishing ledge at the southern end of Maroubra Beach. Luderick and drummer are taken using local cabbage weed fished in the washes at both ends of the platform, while a long cast to the sand patches may produce a bream or two if using fresh tuna or pilchard baits. For those hardy souls who fish through winter here, the pay-off for early morning spinning with whole pilchards is often a mix of tailor, salmon, trevally and bream. Along the rocks at the southern end of Maroubra, there is Little Greeny, Big Greeny and the Blessings, three excellent luderick and drummer fishing ledges adjacent to Mistral Point.

From Long Bay south to Cape Banks at the entrance to Botany is all excellent rock fishing territory, the area could be described as Sydney's luderick fishing mecca, though

Luderick are caught regularly from Sydney's eastern suburbs rocks. They inhabit the wave-washed margins of rocky headlands and ledges and feed almost exclusively on a green sea lettuce. This specimen exhibits lighter colouration than normal due to being caught over a predominately sandy seabed.

bream, salmon and tailor can be caught if using fish bait.
Maroubra south to Cape Banks can be very dangerous, and many of the productive spots have iron stakes driven into the rocks so as to provide a hold in the event of a wave washing over. Over the years, several anglers have been washed to their death fishing this region, so exercise caution and wear rock plates. Some of the better known spots include Donkeys and Julieann just north of Little Beach; The Gutter, Doctors Rocks, the well-known Trap, and the Pinnacle south of Little Beach; Jolong down towards Cape Banks; and Shakey on the Cape itself.

Botany Bay / George's River

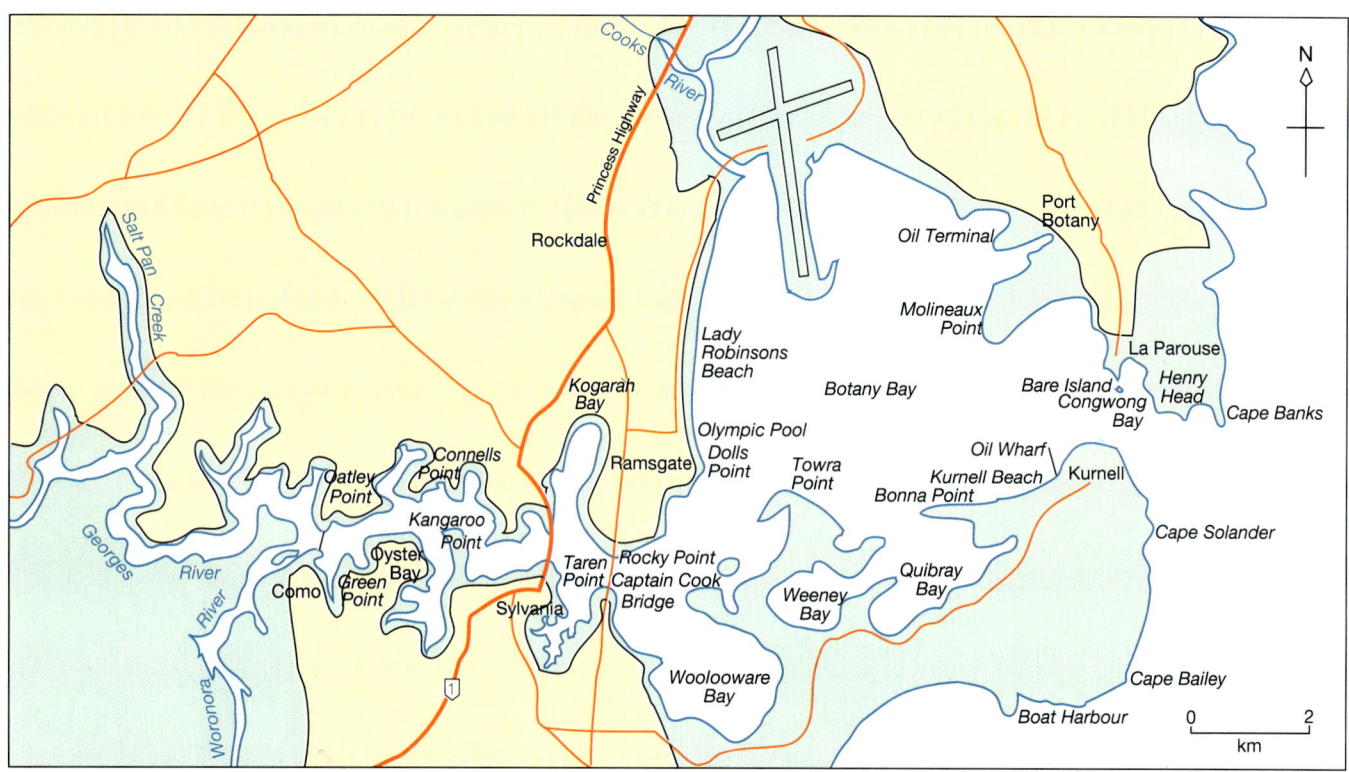

For more than 200 years Botany Bay has provided impressive catches, even despite oil spills, mangrove destruction and heavy professional fishing. Including its major feeder the Georges River, along with its tributary the Woronora River, the Botany Bay system will no doubt continue to fish well for many years to come.

Successful fishing in Botany Bay and adjoining rivers depends on fishing the right tides, using only the freshest bait, and employing light tackle. As different parts of the Bay fish best at different stages of the tide, it is rather difficult to list when to fish every location. Nevertheless, there are guidelines to follow: most places will produce best around the first few hours of the run-in and the start of the run-out tide. Towra and Weeney Bay, and the entrance to the Georges and Woronora River are the exceptions, the run-out is necessary to fish these properly.

Like most Sydney fisheries plagued by boat traffic, Botany Bay and the Georges River are better early morning, late afternoon and night fishing locations than they are during the middle of the day. 'Foul' weather fishing is another way of avoiding the crowds. Throughout the Bay and adjoining waterways, summer will prove the most productive fishing season, though bream, luderick and tailor can be caught year-round.

Without doubt the top bait for tempting bream, whiting, flathead and trevally in this area is bloodworms.

They can be bought from most local bait suppliers, as can fresh harbour prawns, which rate a close second. Nippers are another top offering, being available by pumping the sandflats on the northern shore downstream of the Captain Cook Bridge. Squirt worms available here make a great whiting bait in the Georges River.

One of the most popular means of fishing Botany Bay is to drift for flathead, particularly around Yarra Bay, off the airport extension, Quibray Bay, Weeney Bay, Towra and the entrance to the Georges River. Bream, whiting and trevally may supplement the catch depending on the time of year.

For those anglers without a boat, the runway extension off General Holmes Drive and the training wall in the corner, Cooks River Breakwall, the retaining wall at Port Botany, Bare Island and the Kurnell Groynes all provide good catches of luderick, bream and flathead. Tailor are a common catch during winter from the breakwall locations, while Bare Island requires respect in rough seas, though the western side is an all-weather breaming spot.

Along the western side of the bay, Brighton wharf, Ramsgate Baths, Lady Robinson Bay and Dolls Point are popular with weekend hopefuls who take delight in catching yellowtail, small tailor, the odd bream, flathead and whiting. Kurnell is another popular picnic fishing ground, with bream, flathead and whiting a chance if using bloodworms. The rocks around to the east are good luderick and drummer fishing grounds, particularly near Inscription Point.

Boat anglers have the advantage in Botany Bay as they can fish the shipping buoys, which are a top kingfish attractor during summer. Bare Island bombora, which is dangerous when there's a swell running, and Cape Banks are worthwhile trolling for bonito, tailor and small kingfish. As a night fishing ground, Watts Reef off the Captain Cook Reserve and in line with the Kurnell oil wharf is a superb bream and trevally producer. Fish the rising tide with floating baits, and berley heavily.

Heading west, the ribbon weedbeds and oyster leases in Towra Point, Weeney and Quibray Bay are all top bream, flathead and luderick grounds. Garfish and mullet are also common in these protected bays, while lure fishing can yield dusky flathead during the run-out tide.

The lower reaches of the Georges river to the Captain Cook Bridge is a good flathead drifting region, the bridge itself is popular for bream from either shore, while Shipwrights Point, Baldface, Kangaroo Point, Caravan Head and Oatley Point are popular land-based locations for bream, luderick, and flathead. At Baldface there is a good mulloway hole out about 30 metres from the point during a run-out tide, while 20 metres off Caravan Head and the mussel beds 80 metres off Connells Point are worthwhile boat marks for bream and flathead. Oyster Bay is a good crabbing spot.

Upstream from the Como Bridge on the Georges River is mainly luderick and bream country, though big whiting and flathead are caught during summer on bloodworms. Among some of the better boat marks are Cranbrook Leases, Little and Big Moon Bays and Russel Jones, which is marked by powerlines crossing the river above Soily Bottom. Salt Pan Creek yields mud crabs for those willing to set traps.

In the Woronora River, Thompsons Bay, Audrey Bay oyster leases, Bonnet Bay and drifting the entrance down from Mangrove Island are all productive for bream, flathead and whiting. Big hauls of luderick are taken by anchoring close to the rocky shores and using string weed baits. Berley is essential, as is a run-out tide.

The Cooks River breakwall is a popular fishing location, thanks to easy access and productive bream and luderick fishing.

Kurnell to Port Hacking

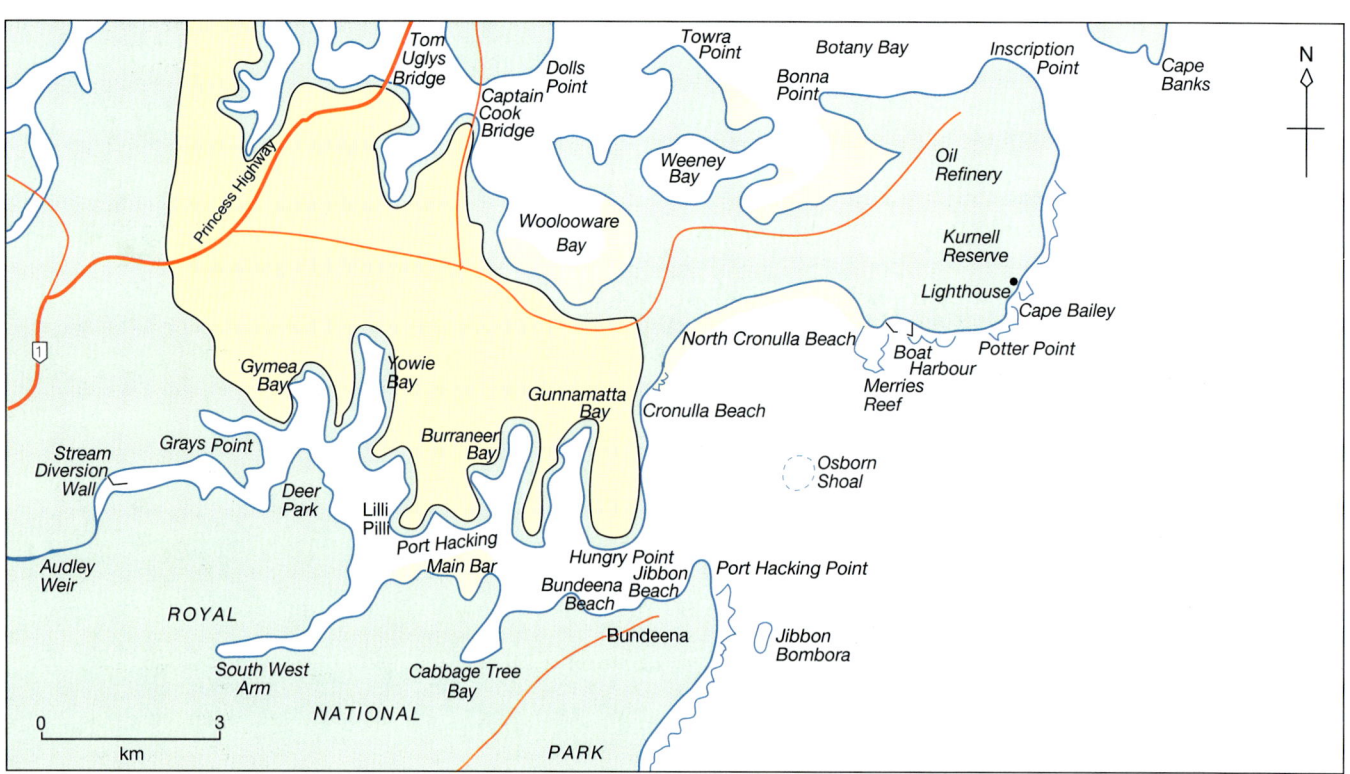

Kurnell Peninsula has been a recognised fishing area since before The Great Depression. Even now, the remains of old stone fishing shacks, where struggling anglers lived on the doorstep to their fishing spots, can still be found.

Access to this area can be gained from either Cape Solander Drive, where the National Park gates open between 7.30am and 7pm in winter and a parking fee is charged, or by following a goat track behind the refineries that leads north from Sir Joseph Banks Drive out to the historic Tabbigai and adjoining fishing spots. The area from Potter Point down to Merries Reef is accessible by another rough 'road' that forks to the south of where Sir Joseph Banks Drive actually ends. Both tracks should be avoided after heavy rain.

By parking along Cape Solander Drive, Inscription Point and surrounding rocks are only a cast away. Pig Rock, Little and Big Yena are all good areas for luderick and drummer. The Poss, KB and the Althouse are rock spots south from the parking at the end of Cape Solander Drive. They are dangerous in even a reasonable sea, though in calm conditions highly productive for luderick, drummer, groper, bream, tailor, salmon and trevally.

Further south is Tabbigai, a series of ledges tucked beneath the cliffs which are great drummer, luderick and bream fishing. From here to Cape Bailey is all high cliffs where numerous perches can be found from which to cast

a bait, though care needs be taken around the fragile, eroding sandstone cliff tops. Tailor, salmon, bream, drummer and snapper are the targets.

At Potter Point is a sewerage outlet, a popular fishing spot for luderick, but very dangerous. Boat Harbour and Pimelwi Rocks in the corner of the beach are more pleasant, and bream, whiting and tailor are possibilities if casting behind the surf zone at Green Hills.

From Green Hills to Port Hacking is a long stretch of very productive beach where tailor, bream, whiting, flathead, salmon and the occasional mulloway and whaler shark is available, particularly in the deeper gutters and holes at night. The rocks around Cronulla to the entrance of Port Hacking aren't heavily fished, though good numbers of bream are taken by locals who use light tackle, berley, and fish the high tide in the evenings.

Port Hacking, on the southern outskirts of Sydney, is the cleanest and most unspoilt city estuary. The fishing is excellent as long as you follow a few vital ground rules.

Port Hacking is comprised of vast sandflats, shallow weedbeds and narrow channels, and as most fish are caught in the same channels that boats use to navigate the estuary, it is vital to fish early morning or late afternoon into the night. Weekdays are also less busy than weekends.

Low tide, especially the last half of the run-out tide when fish retreat from the shallow flats back into the sanctuary of the deeper channel waters, is the prime fishing period in the The Port. During the flooding and full tide , over the sand and weed beds is better fishing.

Bream, whiting, flathead, flounder and mullet all proliferate throughout Port Hacking, though mulloway and kingfish are taken on occasions from the deep holes in the system. Luderick are plentiful around the rocky shores. It is important to note than the use of any type of fish trap, crab or prawn net is prohibited in Port Hacking, though a landing net for fishing is allowed.

Port Hacking is best fished from a boat as many areas aren't accessible to the shore-based fisherman. Launching facilities can be found in Gunnamatta Bay, Burraneer Bay, Gymea bay and near Grays Point. Small boats can be launched at Maianbar and Bundeena on the Royal National Park side.

One blessing for fishermen tackling The Port is that the top baits of pink nippers and squirt worms are readily available by pumping the enormous sandflats at Maianbar at low tide grounds but it is illegal to remove any type of shellfish. For luderick, string weed can be collected at some swimming baths and around wharf pylons, though it isn't a reliable supply. It's better to bring it with you. Live baits such as of yellowtail, small tailor and mullet can be caught near Lilli Pilli, Gunyah Beach and Bundeena Bay.

Some of the hotspots in Port Hacking are Hungry Point where luderick are caught in big numbers on a making tide; Gunnamatta Bay where both shore and boat fishermen can catch flathead, bream, and trevally in winter; Bonnievale Spit for flathead on an outgoing tide in summer; Dolans Bay Wharf for bream, flathead and catching bait; Maianbar for whiting, mullet, garfish,

flathead and bream on a making tide along the edge of the channel; the Ballast Heap for bream at night; South West Arm where mulloway, bream, flathead and the odd kingfish are all possibilities; and Lilli Pilli Baths for bream, luderick, trevally, tailor, kingfish, John dory and school-size mulloway. Further upstream, Grays Point is a top whiting, flathead and bream spot. The stream diversion wall and Audley Weir yield bream, luderick and mullet.

Above: A fine haul of luderick caught from the Potter Point region on Kurnell Peninsula.
Below: Flathead can be caught throughout Port Hacking estuary. This dusky fell for a drifted pilchard bait.

Sydney Offshore

Sydney's offshore or 'outside' anglers still catch good hauls of snapper, kingfish and mulloway anywhere from Broken Bay to south of the Royal National Park.

Offshore from Sydney there are three main fishing regions: the close grounds which run out from the coast to the 30 metre depth, the middle grounds which run from 30 to 100 metres, and the wide grounds which descend from 100 metres to the Continental Shelf and beyond. The seaworthiness of the vessel, the weather, and the species being hunted decide which of these to fish.

Within the close grounds, anywhere from the coastal washes surrounding headlands and offshore islands to bomboras and underwater reefs is productive for snapper, trevally, bream, tailor, mulloway, kingfish and various small tunas. Off beaches and around the mouths of estuary systems are sandy areas that yield flathead on the drift, especially during summer.

Aside from trolling lures around deep water headlands for tailor, salmon, tuna and kingfish, anchoring over underwater reefs and using light tackle and unweighted baits is by far the most popular and productive method for fishing the close grounds. Liberal use of berley and pilchard or tuna strips is a necessary combination, while live yellowtail or slimy mackerel are worthwhile if kingfish and mulloway are the targets. Live baits can be procured at bait grounds, and bite best during the early morning.

East and West Reefs, off the Boudd National Park north of Palm Beach, are two excellent snapper and mulloway grounds, which also yield tuna, tailor and small kingfish on the troll. Watch for breakers around the bomboras off Maitland, particularly when the swell is up. Across the mouth of Broken Bay is a vast flathead drifting region as it is all sand bottom.

The washes surrounding Barrenjoey Headland, North and South Whale Beach, Hole in the Wall to Avalon and Newport Reef are all productive areas for trolling for winter tailor, while bonito and small kingfish are the common summer catch. Newport Reef is a good spot for tailor, anchoring adjacent to the reef and casting pilchards into the washes. Bream and trevally can also be caught here, and at Bangalley Head or Hole in the Wall near Avalon, the front of Long Reef and Dee Why Headland.

North and South Head are worthwhile wash trolling regions, and the Colours Reef off Macquarie Lighthouse is a handy spot to catch yellowtail, kingfish, trevally, small snapper and bream. Further south, Wedding Cake Island off Coogee, Cape Banks and Kurnell flanking the entrance to Botany Bay, Merries Reef and Jibbon Bombora at Port Hacking, and north North Marley and Little Marley Headlands in the Royal National Park are all productive trolling, wash fishing and shallow reef fishing grounds.

One of the many faces of Sydney's offshore fishing - a mako shark making short work of a bonito that almost made it to waiting hands.

Between 3 and 5 kilometres offshore are the middle grounds. Snapper, kingfish, mulloway, morwong, nannygai, pigfish, leatherjacket and other assorted 'table fish' can be located on the reefs and gravel patches in this depth range, while flathead locate over sandy bottomed areas. Sydney's charter boats regularly fish here.

Sydney's middle grounds are also a magnet for pelagic fish as they travel south with warm water currents during summer. Prominent underwater reefs between the 60 and 100 metre mark can yield yellowfin tuna, wahoo, dolphin fish, sharks and even marlin. Trolling skirted pusher-style game lures, skipping baits such as garfish and small tuna, and drifting or anchoring with a berley trail and live baits set astern are the most successful techniques for catching game fish.

The cream of the Northern Peninsula middle ground includes Broken Bay Wide 15 kilometres east of Lion Island, Boultons 3 kilometres off Whale Beach, Esmerelda 8 kilometres east of Bangalley Head, Long Reef Wide 10 kilometres north-east of Dee Why Headland, The Whale 8 kilometres off Dee Why, and The Masons, an extension of the Whale, but located south about 2 kilometres.

Off the eastern and southern suburbs, Rosa Gully Wide is a popular bottom fishing reef located 6 kilometres out from the gully, The Six Mile off Ben Buckler is a charter boat favourite, Coogee Trag Ground off Lurline Bay has a rough bottom where teraglin, mulloway, kingfish and trevally are taken, The Four Mile is south-west off Coogee's Wedding Cake Island and is a great bottom fishing and trolling ground, while Sydney's Peak is synonymous with catching everything from big tuna, kingfish, marlin, and sharks, to bottom fish such as snapper, morwong, and trevally. Anglers either launch in Sydney Harbour and run south, or head-out from Botany Bay, which is an easier run, particularly in summer when north-easterlies prevail.

Port Hacking is serviced by numerous boat ramps which grant access to reefs like Port Hacking Wide 10 kilometres off Port Hacking Point, Osborne Shoals 3 kilometres north-east of Cronulla, and Marley Wreck in 46 metres of water south-west off Wattamolla in the Royal National Park, a ground that attracts aggregations of fish, including snapper, kingfish, mulloway, and trevally.

Sydney's wide grounds are the domain of big boats and the local game and sport fishing fraternity, especially the pulse game fishing region known as the Shelf, which is in fact the Continental Shelf located between 25 and 35 kilometres offshore and in 200 metres of water. Between the middle grounds and the Shelf there exists numerous underwater reefs, including outer Broken Bay Wide, outer Long Reef Wide, wide of The Peak, and wide off Port Hacking. Bottom fishing can be productive on these

grounds, although bad weather and the great water depth can make getting baits to the bottom difficult.

Blue, black and striped marlin, yellowfin tuna to 100 kilograms, albacore, wahoo, and sharks, including tigers, makos, blues and whalers are all encountered off Sydney. The metropolis game fishing season relies upon fish-rich tropical waters flooding south from about early December to late May each year.

Top Right: Sydney's bottom fishing mainstay, the morwong.
Right: Sydney's game fishing is surprisingly good, as this marlin captured off Long Reef demonstrates.

Royal National Park

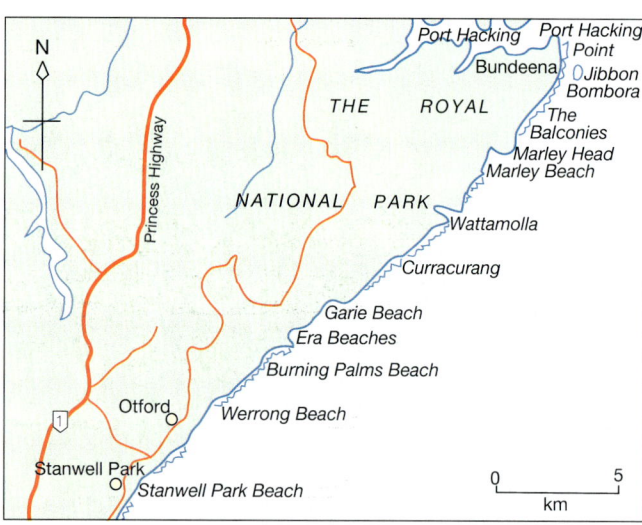

Situated south from Sydney with vehicular access from the Princess Highway near Sutherland and also further south at Waterfall, the Royal National Park is one of Sydney's most extensive flora and fauna reserves. Covering more than 30 kilometres of coastline, city-based anglers revel in the superb rock and beach fishing that exists within the Park.

With Port Hacking estuary marking its northern border, The Royal National Park is safely segregated from the city's suburban sprawl. Aside from settlements at Bundeena on Port Hacking's southern shore, a shop at Wattamolla and a shop and surf club at Garie Beach, The Royal National Park is largely unspoilt. Rugged ocean coastline, native scrubland, sub-tropical rainforest, crystal clear creeks, clean beaches, kangaroos, deer and abundant birdlife combine to make the Park a most interesting fishing destination.

Vehicular access is limited in the Park, so hiking is the usual means of reaching most of the recognised fishing spots. A good pair of sandshoes, set of rockplated fishing shoes, back-pack and ample supplies of food and drink are necessary provisions. The access tracks are usually well-defined, and there are camping grounds throughout the Park, though a permit from the Park Ranger is required to camp. Day trippers will find the Park's fishing brilliant, with crowds less of a problem than many areas situated further away from the city.

Jibbon Beach and the rocks running south to the Waterrun, accessed from Nell Street at Bundeena, aren't a particularly popular fishing area, nevertheless bream, luderick, drummer and tailor can be caught. The Cobblers and The Waterrun are north and south of where the main hiking track from Bundeena to Marley through the

National Park first arrives at the coast.

The Cobble is recognised by the obvious boulder pile behind the bay. Luderick and drummer abound in this region. The Waterrun and The Balconnies are south along the track and consist of a series of high rock ledges where luderick and drummer are taken in the washes. Tailor and salmon are available by floating a pilchard out under a bobby cork, while snapper are also a chance from off the point. A long-handed or cliff gaff may be required to land large fish here.

North Marley Head is a reasonable hike south from Bundeena. Access down to the point is dangerous, but around from the beach there are some good washes to fish for drummer and bream. South Marley ledges run from Marley to Little Marley Beaches and provide drummer, bream and luderick fishing. Both beaches are reasonable bream and whiting grounds, while tailor and salmon are possibilities in winter. From the ledges at the southern end of Little Marley, bream, luderick and drummer can be taken in the washes, while a long cast presents the bait in snapper territory. Spinning and live baiting can result in kingfish, tailor, salmon, and various tunas during summer.

Wattamolla can be driven to and is a rough weather retreat for catching bream and tailor, especially at Floating Rock just inside the southern point. The north point of Curracurang promises luderick, drummer, bream, groper and leatherjackets in the washes, while snapper are a chance with a long cast. Tailor, salmon, kingfish and tuna are also likely if using lures or live baits.

The Gulf on the southern side of Curracurang identifiable by the large gutter running back into the rocks south from Curracurang Bay is famous for producing everything from marlin, tuna and kingfish on live baits which are caught out of the gutter or gulf itself, to tailor, salmon, snapper, bream and trevally if using pilchards slow-spun through the washes. Luderick, leatherjackets, groper and drummer work the washes. There is a separate access track leading from the Wattamolla road.

Garie Beach can be reached by car. Tailor, salmon, bream, and trevally using slow-spun pilchards worked through the washes around dawn can be caught from the point to the north. Seldom Rock, marked by an Iron Stake driven into a single high rock at water level, is also good for snapper with a long cast and squid bait. Southwards, Era beaches are great for whiting, flathead and bream, and Semi-Detached Point for snapper, tailor and salmon.

Wollongong

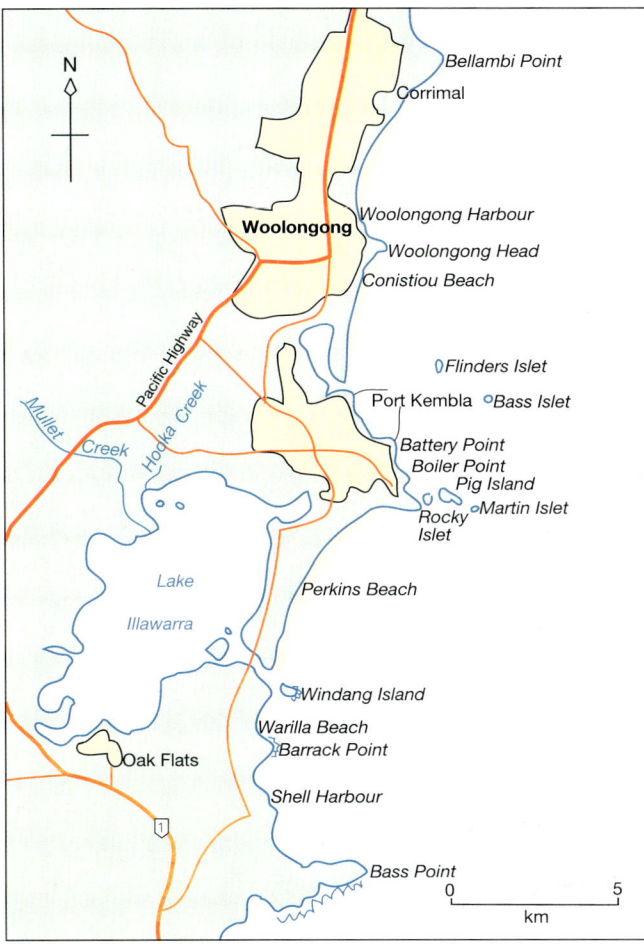

The near south coast offers a wide choice of fishing. Accommodation is available in either caravan parks or motels with a few holiday cottages at Lake Illarwarra, and bait, ice, fuel and tackle are all in good supply.

Lake Illawarra is the estuary fishing centre for the area.

Apart from the fishing, there is excellent prawning in the lake. Each new moon in the warmer months sees hundreds of anglers with scoop and drag nets working the shallow areas. The quality of prawns taken from the lake is outstanding, particularly those that head to sea down the narrow channel at the mouth of the lake.

This area also produces flathead, whiting and bream.

The best fishing in the lake is around the shoreline for blackfish, bream, mullet, flathead and whiting.

The sandbanks in the open part of the lake are prolific whiting producers in summer. Live worms, yabbies or shrimp are essential bait.

Windang Beach on the northern side of the entrance to Lake Illawarra is one of the only reliable spots on either

side of the mouth of the Lake for what is not a spectacular beach fishing area. The beach is consistent for bream, whiting and tailor and mulloway if the lake is running out after heavy rain.

Warilla Beach on the southern side of the lake is very good for summer whiting and bream. Winter tailor fishing is also productive.

Windang Island is a tied island connected by sand and a hot spot for bream, particularly during winter. The best spot is out the front of the island on the southern side.

Coledale, Austinmer, Corrimal and Bellambi Point are among the deep headlands and good fishing ledges throughout the area which have good bream, blackfish and drummer. The entrance to Wollongong Harbour also has consistent rock spots, particularly close to the lighthouses.

Port Kembla, on the walls both sides of the entrance, features quite good fishing for big fish. Snapper, mulloway, groper and drummer are all taken from here plus more standard fish such as bream, blackfish and tailor.

The shipping wharves of the harbour also turn on some excellent fishing with bream around the pylons and John Dory, school mulloway and kingfish taken on live bait out the front.

The rocks to the south of Port Kembla are very good for blackfish and drummer.on the southern point in front of Hill 60 is a very good spot for mulloway and snapper.

Bass Point has top fishing for snapper, drummer, tailor, salmon, kingfish, bream and blackfish.

The point has many ledges but some are low and should be considered before fishing if the swell is rolling.

Right in the middle of the point is Bushrangers Bay which is a marine reserve closed to all fishing.

Offshore Wollongong does not get the run of big game fish that spots to the north and south receive. The big reef off Bellambi is the most consistent for yellowfin tuna and an odd marlin.

Closer in, there are large numbers of small kingfish around the islands offshore from Port Kembla. A few big kingfish also turn up. Around these same islands, the washes produce bream, tailor and salmon and out a little further good snapper and an odd mulloway. These islands must be fished with berley to achieve top results.

Boat launching facilities can be found at Bellambi Point and Wollongong Harbour. The entrance to Lake Illawarra is shallow and dangerous and is best avoided.

Windang to Shoalhaven Heads

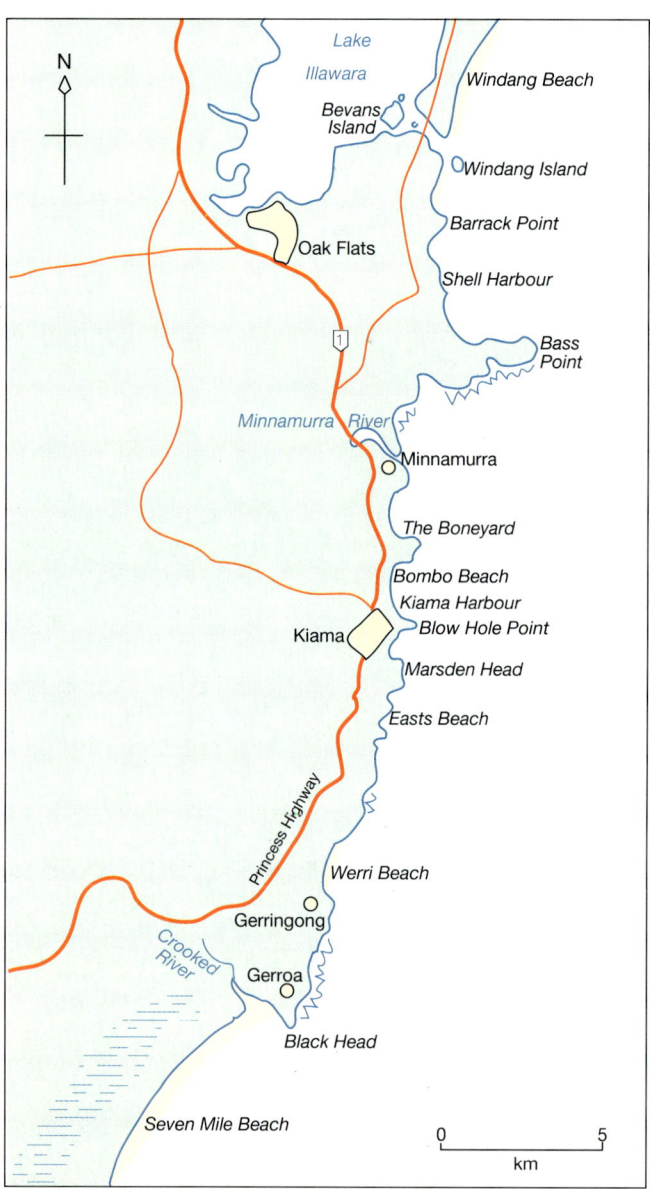

Most New South Wales offshore anglers look for snapper like this.

From Port Kembla to the entrance to the Shoalhaven River near Nowra, the coastline is largely basalt headlands with small beaches nestled in between. For both shore-based and boat anglers, this stretch of south coast is highly productive, yet still within a day trip of Sydney.

Windang Island, a rocky islet that can be easily accessed over a sandspit around low tide is difficult and dangerous to reach around tide, especially when a sea is running is good for bream, tailor, drummer, luderick and groper in the washes, while a long cast locates snapper. Big kingfish and tuna patrol the deep water off the eastern side, and live baiting or spinning is recommended.

At Shellharbour luderick and bream are taken by shore-based anglers fishing off the harbour's rocky retaining walls, especially when the seas are rough. There is a harbour ramp and excellent boat fishing.

Bass Point to the south of Shell Harbour is a good kingfish and tuna trolling ground. Around 500 metres north-east off the point kingfish, mulloway and snapper are found by anchoring on the reef drop-off, berleying heavily, and using live baits or fresh squid. There is a productive flathead drift from the gravel loader inside Bass Point right across to Windang Island. Further south, Stack Island off the Minnamurra River is a great boat ground for mulloway, snapper and tailor.

Rockhoppers will find Bass Point a good area for drummer, luderick, groper and bream in the washes, especially around the north and south fingers on either side of the Bushrangers Bay Marine Sanctuary. Spinning towards the island off the northern tip off Bass Point can yield tailor, salmon and small tuna, however better spinning and live baiting ledges exist south from Bushrangers Bay. Snapper are also on the cards in this region if long casts are made using fresh squid or cuttlefish baits. Due to its eastern prominence, Bass Point is a great surface fish ground during summer when warm currents lick the rocks, but care also needs to be taken in any reasonable sea because it is very exposed.

The Minnamurra River is a small boat waterway where flathead, bream, mullet, whiting and luderick abound. Prawns are netted in summer, while shore anglers favour the road bridge area for catching luderick and bream. There are launching facilities here and further down past the golf course. To the south, Boyds Beach produces whiting and bream during summer, while the pebbly bay known as The Boneyard is a great rough weather luderick, drummer and bream sanctuary using locally collected cunjevoi as bait. Over the headland, Bombo Beach is popular with surfers, though whiting, flathead and bream can be caught on locally collected beachworms.

Kiama Harbour yields bream and luderick after a big southerly sea, while boats can be launched to fish the reefs out wide for snapper, morwong and other assorted reef fish. Productive flathead drifting can be encountered off Bombo Beach. Offshore, yellowfin and striped tuna are trolled up between the 60 to 120 metre depth during summer, while albacore, yellowfin and marlin are regulars out on the Shelf. Live yellowtail are easily caught from around the trawlers in the harbour, and land-based live baiters float them off Kiama Point for kingfish and the chance of a big yellowfin, bluefin or mackerel tuna. Salmon, tailor and small tuna are regularly spun-up on lures from off the point, while snapper are a chance with a long cast. Bream, trevally, drummer, groper and luderick inhabit the washes around the Blowhole. Kiama Point is dangerous when there is a sea running.

Kendalls and Bubbley Beaches are just south from Kiama; the rocks are worth a cast for snapper after big seas, while whiting and bream are taken off the beaches. Marsden Head is a hot spinning ledge for tuna, tailor, salmon and kingfish in summer, while snapper and trevally are a chance on pilchard baits during winter. From Marsden Head to Werri Beach are numerous rocky points where local anglers catch snapper, drummer, luderick and bream. Big kingfish frequent Red Cliff, the northern point of Werri Beach, and live pike are the pulse offering.

At Gerringong, Werri Beach yields salmon, tailor, bream, flathead and whiting at various times of the year, while Walkers Beach is a salmon and tailor ground, with big mulloway a chance during summer. Black Head is a prominent rocky point that produces anything from luderick, drummer, groper and bream in close, to snapper with a long cast. Surface fish such as salmon, tailor, bonito and kingfish are encountered on lures or pilchards cast off the point, while bream, tailor and mulloway are all possibilities where Crooked River empties out to sea. Seven Mile Beach runs all the way to the Shoalhaven River and yields whiting, bream, flathead, tailor and salmon in the gutters.

Boats can be launched at Gerringong boat harbour or small boats can run out from the southern corner of Seven Mile Beach. Healthy quantities of snapper frequent the shallow reefs in this area, while trevally, mulloway and kingfish are caught in close off the southern side of Black Head. Trolling with diving minnow lures around the headland washes can result in bonito, tailor, salmon and small kingfish, while these same species can often be located on the surface during summer where small boaties cast lures to the schools for great results. Offshore in the 60 to 100 metre depth range, there are morwong, snapper and assorted table fish over the reefs while lure trolling can yield yellowfin tuna in this same region. From Gerringong all the way south to the Shoalhaven River is unlimited flathead drifting, with cricket-score catches common during summer.

Bass Point has outstanding fishing with a varied catch available.

Shoalhaven

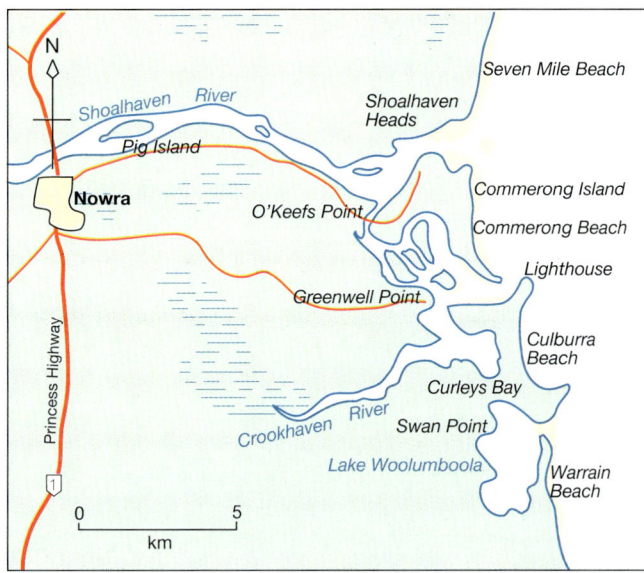

The Shoalhaven is southern New South Wales largest and most significant coastal river. It rises on the high plateau country between Braidwood and Araluen, flowing north, then east, for over 400 kilometers before entering the sea between Shoalhaven Heads and Greenwell Point.

In its headwaters, the Shoalhaven is a fast flowing stream with a reasonable population of brown and rainbow trout, freshwater blackfish and small native forage species. After turning eastward, it plunges through spectacular sandstone gorges, past the site that will one day be inundated by the massive Welcome Reef dam project, until reaching the backed-up waters of Talowa Dam which was built during the late 1970's just downstream of the Shoalhaven's confluence with the Kangaroo River. Fish present in Talowa include Macquarie perch and at least some trout.

Downstream of Talowa, the Shoalhaven emerges from its forges to flow through rolling pastoral land and areas of eucalypt forest, becoming a brackish tidal estuary well before reaching the large regional centres of Nowra and Bombaderry.

The Shoalhaven at Nowra is broad, relatively shallow and dotted with sandbars, mud flats and reefs. Just downstream of the twin highway bridges, it splits around Pig Island before flowing on to Shoalhaven Heads, where it once joined the sea. However, since the construction of a convict-built canal linking the lower Shoalhaven with the Crookhaven River late last century, the natural river mouth at Shoalhaven Heads has often been silted shut for many years at a time. Even when this broad, shallow mouth is open, most of the river's flow enters the sea via 'The Canal' and the Crookhaven estuary beyond.

Once an important shipping route for coastal trade, the lower Shoalhaven is today too heavily silted to be navigable to large vessels. It is, however, still immensely popular with recreational boat owners.

Major sport and commercial fish species in the lower Shoalhaven are bream, luderick (blackfish), flathead, whiting and mullet. Juvenile mulloway may be seasonally abundant, and the occasional larger specimen is still taken. These estuary species are mostly fished for in the stretch between the highway bridges at Nowra and the ocean entrance at Crookhaven Heads. The river also provides important commercial and amateur fisheries for prawns and oysters.

The Shoalhaven was once a famous home of the Australian bass, but today's stocks are a pale reflection of the river's earlier glories. Construction of Talowa Dam dramatically reduced the potential range of these unique fish, while reduced stream flows, siltation, over-harvesting and degradation of remaining habitat compounded the bass' problems. Yet, despite these negative influences, some reasonable summertime bass angling is still to be had upstream of Nowra, between the Bomaderry Gold Course and Talowa Dam, particularly at spots such as Longreach, Burrier, Grady's and Coolendell.

The Shoalhaven River offers bream, flathead, mullet and flounder in a very pleasant environment close to excellent facilities.

Jervis Bay Offshore

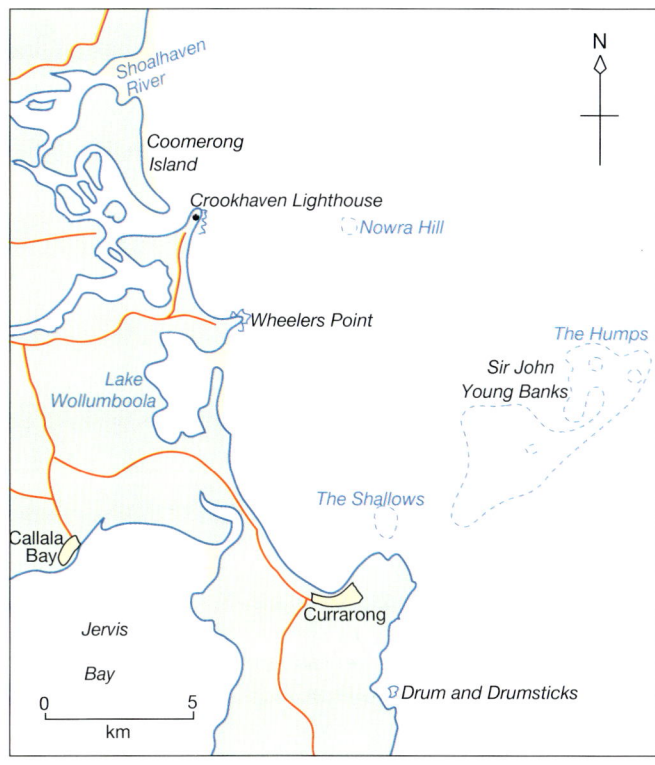

The Sir John Young Banks is one of the great offshore fishing grounds along the Eastern Seaboard. This underwater rock plateau holds game and table fish, attracting the attention of anglers throughout the year.

Access is by way of the Shoalhaven River with ramps at Greenwell Point and Culburra, while Currarong has beach launching in a sheltered but wave-surged cove. Boats also make the trip up from Jervis Bay. Facilities and accommodation are very good.

As most anglers fishing the Banks operate out of the Shoalhaven River via Crookhaven, Heads note should be made that the bar can be dangerous here in big seas. However, it is one of the best bar entrances on the coast and you need to be fairly inept to get into trouble here.

Sir Joseph Young Banks lie 14 kilometres east-south-east of Crookhaven Heads. The marks for the reef are obvious once at sea.

Inshore, line Mount Coolangatta (the cone-shaped hill to the north of the river entrance) with the northern edge of the third group of trees in the saddle of the escarpment on the western horizon. Looking south, put the point where the rocks and sand meet at Currarong's northern edge in line with the centre of the two hills at the south-western horizon. The cluster of boats in the area will show where most of the action is concentrated.

The Banks are shallow and affected by strong currents with an unfavourable wind, big seas and a strong current the Banks can be like fishing in a huge rapid.

The fishing is seasonal, with the premium action from October to May. Big kingfish are found on the Banks around the humps at the northern end of the ground, and are prolific in spring.

Yellowfin tuna and marlin work the eastern drop-off during summer, with the marlin at their peak in January, February and March. The big yellowfin tuna move into the area from March to May.

Anglers will find snapper, morwong, trevally, pigfish and kingfish by drifting the area with baits bouncing over the seabed. The best snapper fishing is found north of the main reef area, and exceptional catches are made in April and May. Many snapper anglers prefer to moor over the shallow reef and fish lightly weighted baits down a berley trail; large snapper are caught using this technique.

Sir Joseph Young Banks, is a most interesting and productive offshore fishing ground, well worth a visit in good weather. During the height of summer, this stretch of New South Wales South Coast is often windswept with gusty north-easterly sea breezes, which make the run back to port long, wet and possibly dangerous.

Apart from the Banks there are plenty of other grounds in the area that also yield very good catches.

Nowra Hill ground, 4 kilometres straight out from the lighthouse at Crookhaven Heads, yields snapper, mulloway, teraglin, morwong and kingfish. It fishes best at night.

The Shallows is a large ground to the north of Currarong, and top spot for small kingfish, snapper and other bottom fish.

The ground is found by lining up Big Beecroft and Little Beecroft headlands and is 4 kilometres up the beach from Currarong.

Good angling can also be found by drifting along the huge cliffs of Beecroft Headland. Live baits produce kingfish and yellowfin, while bottom anglers catch quality snapper throughout the whole area. A sounder is needed to locate the prominent underwater reefs.

Beecroft Peninsula

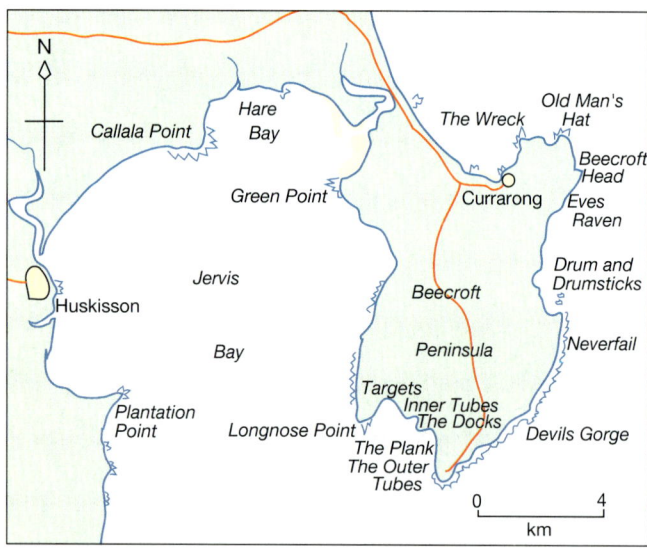

Beecroft Peninsula near Nowra on the New South Wales south coast is a extraordinary rock fishing area. In fact, it is one of the few places where really large game fish can be taken off the shore. Marlin over 100 kilograms and yellowfin to 80 kilograms have been caught off Beecroft, along with big kingfish, middleweight tunas and sharks.

Land-based game fishing aside, the area is acclaimed as the best snapper location for rock fishermen, with bream, tailor, salmon, drummer, blackfish and leatherjackets all quite common around the rocks at Beecroft, too.

Currarong, has a camping/caravan park and flats for rent. There is also food, ice and fuel available in this tranquil coastal town.

Access to Beecroft Peninsula is restricted at times as many of the fishing areas are part of the military bombing range. Some areas have reasonable access although the peninsula's roads are rough and most fishing spots require you to walk in. Almost all the spots demand some hard climbing to get down to the fishing ledges.

The other problem to be considered is walking or climbing out with a haul of fish, or even one big tuna. The popular land-based game fishing spot, The Tubes is a long walk in, and seems a lot longer walking out with a good catch.

The Wreck of the Merrimbula is visible on the rock shelf and it is an easy walk out from the car park at Bosom Beach. Fish for bream, tailor, small snapper and leatherjackets. This spot is protected in a southerly, but needs berley to work well.

The Old Man's Hat is reached from a rough track at the back of town, but is an easy climb in and out. Drummer,

luderick, tailor, salmon and bonito are available, though pike can be a pest at times.

Beecroft Head is one of the best spots on the coast; almost anything can be caught here. Reasonable access, though the climb in requires care.

Eve's Ravine is a hard climb in, with ropes necessary. Good fishing for bonito, tailor, salmon and tuna.

Drum and Drumsticks is a sheltered spot that produces bream, blackfish, drummer, tailor and salmon. Berley is necessary to attract the fish. Garfish, trevally and leatherjackets are also caught here.

Never Fail is dangerous, but does yield good fish. Local knowledge is needed to locate the access track. Most fishing is for surface fish and big snapper. Tailor and salmon proliferate at times.

Devil's Gorge is the site where high-speed spinning was founded, and it still fishes well for surface fish.

Plenty of big snapper are also caught here along with bream, drummer, groper and blackfish in the wash. The ledge is high and fairly safe, though the climb in demands respect as anglers have fallen to their death!

The Outer Tubes are the remnants of old torpedo tubes and mark the sight of some extraordinary big fish captures. Yellowfin and marlin are landed here on live baits, and even though the Tubes is inside Jervis Bay, the current sweeps the oceanic blue water right up to the rocks.

The Plank is a long walk in but good tailor and small kingfish are caught on this inward facing ledge.

The Docks has good fishing for bream, trevally and small snapper, and tailor, salmon and small kingfish on pilchards. Very safe, easy spot to fish.

The Inner Tubes is another safe spot with mixed species, including bream, small snapper, trevally, tailor, salmon and kingfish.

The Targets is a top salmon spot with bream, whiting and flathead from the beach.

Longnose Point has snapper, drummer, trevally and leatherjacket. Big kingfish turn up regularly but are hard to handle on anything but heavy tackle. Good spot to catch a feed of sea garfish.

Sussex Inlet Region

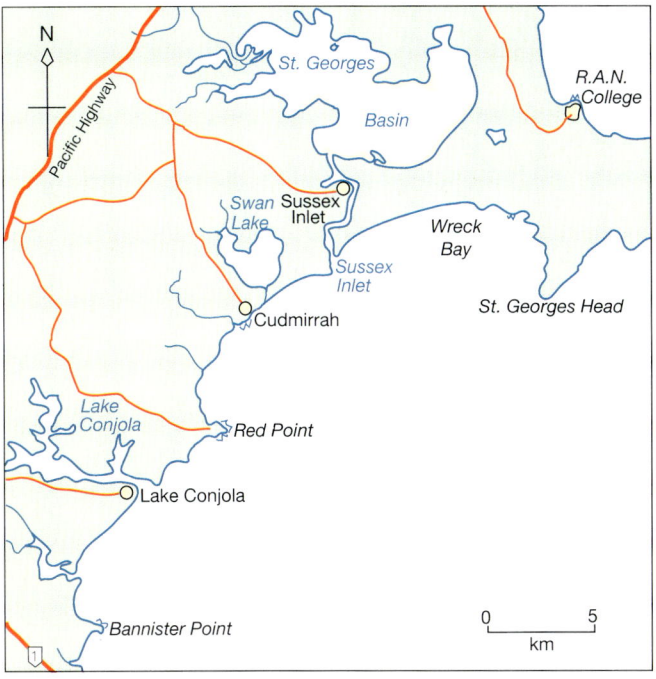

Popular holiday destinations attracting an increasing number of residents, the Sussex Inlet/St Georges Basin area and Lake Conjola are all tranquil estuaries that harbour many superb fishing spots.

Fishing the channels from a boat or the shore, good hauls of bream, flathead, whiting and luderick can be captured.

Sussex Inlet Channel fishes best on slack water at high tide for luderick, bream, and flathead. The entrance to the channel is a pulse region for bream and whiting at night, during the first hour of the run-in tide.

The sandflats of Sussex Inlet are renowned for their large prawn hauls in the summer months.

St Georges Basin is a large expanse of featureless estuary, yielding relatively few fish, but the best area is where Sussex Inlet enters the lake. Flathead, whiting and bream are all possibilities for the shore angler, while those in boats will find better catches by drifting the region.

The beaches surrounding the entrance to Sussex Inlet are prolific producers of bream, salmon, and tailor, while the ocasional mulloway is available. Beachworms and pipis are the pick of the locally available baits.

The rock platforms on the southern side of the Sussex Inlet provide rockhopping anglers with catches of luderick, tailor, salmon and bream, especially at dawn and dusk.

Offshore from Sussex Inlet there's a gravel bottom in 40 metres of water, where snapper, morwong, trevally and flathead can be taken on the drift.

Brooks Reef is further offshore and some distance to the south. This rocky bottom has several large peaks which attract kingfish, morwong, yellowfin, snapper and sharks.

There is always good trolling for game fish along the 40 metre depth in summer and autumn, and for those anglers with large seaworthy craft, the edge of the Continental Shelf is rich in tuna, marlin and sharks.

Lake Conjola, just north of Ulladulla, is a largely undiscovered estuary. The locals prefer to keep it that way, and for good reason.

The lower lake has extensive sandflats which hide many monster flathead, and fish under 4.5 kilograms barely rate a mention with the locals. Bream, flounder and garfish are other common lake inhabitants, while blue swimmer crabs and prawns are available in summer by scoop or drag nettting. The lower lake is also noted for large catches of luderick, mullet, and small leatherjacket.

The upper reaches of Lake Conjola is mainly shallow ribbon weed beds, making fishing decidedly difficult. However, as a retreat from poor weather, reasonable fishing can be discovered for bream, flathead, leatherjackets and mullet. The upper reaches can be a rewarding prawing option when the lower lake is overly busy with other prawners, or when the prawns aren't running particularly well.

The rocky coastline north and south of Sussex Inlet is good trolling water. Here the reward is a bonito.

Ulladulla to Batemans Bay

Within comfortable driving distance of Sydney, the coastline around Ulladulla attracts many holidaymakers eager to take advantage of the fishing in this area.

There are countless rocky outcrops where fishermen can catch tailor, bream, luderick and drummer, though the rocks are rugged and the water is shallower than that of Jervis Bay and other well-known spots to the north.

Warden Head, overlooking Rennies Beach, has a number of fishable rock ledges which fish best when white water is breaking over the outer reef. Bream, luderick, drummer, tailor, salmon, mulloway, snapper and trevally are regular catches.

This area can be extremely dangerous in big seas and the usual safety precautions must be taken, including suitable footwear.

Best fishing beaches are Rennies after a big southerly storm, particularly for bream and mulloway, while nearby

Racecourse Beach is a good spot for salmon and tailor. North of the town, Mollymook Beach is also known for great catches of tailor, salmon, bream and flathead.

There are a number of beaches and inlets to the south with excellent fishing.

Offshore islands which can really turn-on spectacular snapper fishing are Crampton, Stokes and Brush. Large resident kingfish can be tempted with deep-diving lures or trolled live yellowfin pike.

At Bawley Point, the rock platform drops gradually to sea, necessitating long casts to reach a clean seabed. In the right conditions this is a top spot, and anything is likely here including snapper, groper, luderick, drummer and trevally.

Murramarang Beach offers good fishing, particularly when the small lagoon empties out to sea, for salmon and tailor in winter, while whiting, bream and mulloway are caught in summer.

Merry Beach is rated as one of the top rock spots in Australia. Spinning from the northern end of the rocks for tailor and salmon can be outstanding.

Snapper Point, just to the south, is easily reached from the track at the back of the camping ground at Pretty Beach. It is one of the few deep water fishing location on this part of the coast, and has become a mecca for sportfishermen chasing big game fish by live-baiting.

The game season at Snapper Point runs until late April, depending upon ocean currents and prevailing water temperatures. Pike are caught with lures jigged off the platform and make a useful live bait for really big kingfish. Many anglers catch live yellowtail from the gulf further along the inside of the ledge, and use them to good effect on longtail tuna, mackerel tuna and yellowfin tuna, tailor and large kingfish.

Snapper Point is a consistent producer of snapper. Dawn and dusk sorties, a rising tide and octopus, tuna or red crab baits are all conducive to good catches.

South from Snapper Point is a rugged stretch of coastline where snapper are the prime angling target. O'Hara Island, Dawsons Islands and Granite Rock all provide suitable fishing reefs for boat anglers, while Clear Point and Pebbly Beach Point are land-based locations.

Pebbly Beach produces whiting in summer on locally caught beachworms, while bream, tailor and salmon are winter targets.

Depot Beach isn't good beach fishing, though the rocks running along to Point Upright are excellent for snapper, luderick, drummer, groper and bream. They are exposed to the sea, so care must be taken.

Durras township flanks the lake, which is a reasonable producer of flathead, whiting, mullet and bream. Luderick are caught around the channel markers near South Durras boatramp. Prawning can be extremely productive during summer no-moon nights on a run-out tide, but only if the lake is open to the sea.

Durras Beach is a sporadic producer, though whiting can abound in summer. Bream, tailor, salmon, mullet and sharks are caught at varying times.

South from Durras to North Head, the rocks are volcanic and rugged, though snapper, salmon, tailor, bream, trevally, luderick and drummer are caught by adventurous anglers prepared to hike in. Four-wheel drive tracks stem from the South Durras township, running to the northern headland of Batemans Bay.

Offshore anglers will find the Depot Beach, Grasshopper and Wasp Island region a mass of underwater reefs where snapper are caught close in, while drifting the 80 metre depth out wide also yields morwong and various reef fish. Yellowfin tuna, marlin and wahoo are the available game fish in summer from the 60 metre depth to the Continental Shelf, with a notable reef in 120 metres east of Point Upright.

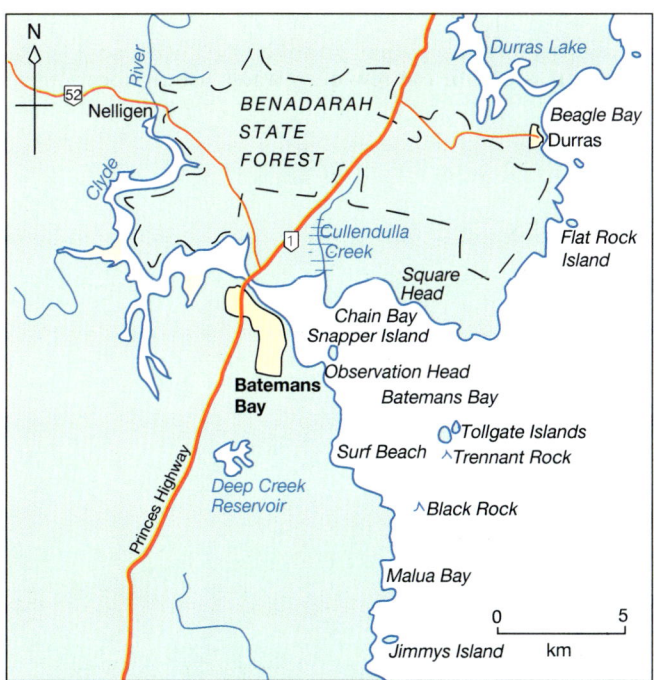

The Clyde River estuary, the wide expanse of Batemans Bay, and a number of interesting islands and reefs make this region one of the most exciting fishing spots on the south coast of New South Wales.

Big mulloway are caught in the Clyde River, and on certain outside reefs such as The Peak off Green Point.

There are ample boat-launching facilities in the Clyde River, flanking either shores of both the upstream and downstream bridges.

Batemans Bay is a large bustling town, with shopping centres, marine dealers, tackle and bait stores, and hire boats available.

For anglers who fail at catching a feed, the town has a number of seafood restaurants of high repute. The oyster barns are also well worth visiting as Clyde River oysters are undoubtedly the fattest, juiciest and tastiest in the State.

In the Clyde River, anglers working the upper reaches can catch bass on lures, while at the bridge at Nelligen there have been spectacular hauls of bream, flathead, flounder and mulloway.

Snapper Point, upstream of the town bridge, where two reefs project above the mud, is a renown spot for catching mulloway. Anywhere near the river's oyster leases is good bream country, and garfish, flounder and flathead are also available.

Clear the decks, a big Snapper's coming aboard! Specimens of this size are near average for the Batemans region.

Many mulloway have been landed by fishing the Clyde River Bridge on the ebbing tide, though bream, flathead and flounder are more common catches.

When the luderick are on, a good spot is the rock wall which runs past the marina from the old wood mill.

Contrary to its name, Snapper Island is not a snapper hotspot but is more reliable for taking bream. Between the island and Observation Head can be dangerous at low tide and boaties launching craft at Corrigan's Beach should head north and outside Snapper Island.

One of the top prawning spots in the area is Cullendulla Creek, which is also good for taking bream and flathead.

Offshore from Batemans Bay there are some outstanding opportunities for anglers chasing big kingfish, tuna, and other game fish, while bottom fishing catches feature predominantly flathead, morwong and snapper.

The Tollgate Islands, Tennant Rock and Black Rock are prominent rocky outcrops at the broad seaward entrance to Batemans Bay. Kingfish, snapper, bream, trevally, salmon, tailor, bonito and assorted reef fish reside around the region.

There are two main reefs in the area. The first runs from the southern tip of the Tollgates Island almost due east for several kilometres. The second reef commences slightly north of Black Rock and runs in a line, a few points south of east. There's also a small reef that runs between Square Head and Chain Bay, and broken reef out from Malua Bay.

One kilometre due east of the Tollgates is great snapper territory in 60 metres of water. Morwong, nannygai, leatherjacket and other reef species are also common.

Between the Tollgates and Black Rock is a general drifting ground for small snapper and flathead, dependable when the sea is running.

The reef known as The Peak, about two kilometres east of Green Point, is one of the best reefs for kingfish, snapper and mulloway.

South of Batemans Bay, Jimmies Island is an often-neglected first-class fishing spot, consistently producing snapper, morwong, kingfish and flathead.

Moruya

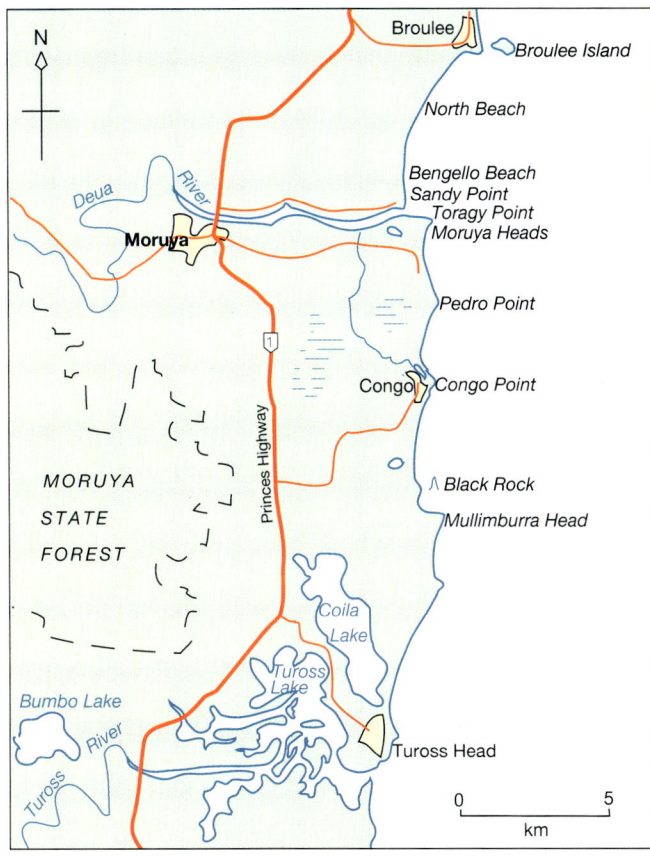

A popular holiday destination, scenic Moruya draws a considerably number of fishermen to its excellent rock, estuary and beach fishing locations.

Even if you're a handline expert, you can begin by dropping a line from the Moruya River bridge, a popular spot with kids.

The weir along North Head Road is great for flathead particularly on summer nights. Live prawns and small mullet are preferred bait.

When the prawns are running, the weir has the only outlet through which they can pass, so naturally it's a top spot using a scoop net.

Near the river mouth, the channels and sandbanks yield whiting and flathead in impressive numbers. Blue swimmer crabs are also plentiful; use old bait inside a stocking as the current is often too strong for witch's hats.

Along the rock walls on both sides of the river, bream is the main catch, with oyster leases providing a natural feeding ground for the fish. The southern wall on a run-out tide will yield luderick on green weed bait.

On the southern shore, the shallows near the heads, will yield as many yabbies as you could want, and the odd flathead will often be landed.

Along Bengello Beach, adjacent to the airport, there are superb salmon and tailor hotspots with pilchards the preferred bait,

Toragy Point is a great spot for good-sized snapper and black drummer, and the occasional kingfish. Live bait can be caught in the rocky shallows.

Offshore, the reef stretching south to Pedro Point is one of the best fishing locations in the area. Large kingfish often abound during the summer months, and snapper too, especially early morning and late afternoon.

Tuross and Coila Lakes is another holiday area a short distance to the south, well-served by motels, caravan parks, hire boats and bait suppliers.

It has been said that Coila Lake is one of the best bream spots in the State. Flathead, flounder and whiting also inhabit the lakes margins. When the lake is open to the sea, prawners delight in the runs of tasty crustaceans.

In the expansive Tuross Lake, a variety of fishing can be experienced, from upstream bass fishing to drifting the channels for bream, flathead, flounder and whiting.

Pretty Point and the Broadwater are renowned for their catches of dusky flathead, while the oyster leases off Deuamba Island are a bream angler's paradise, particularly at high tide at night.

Boat fishermen on Tuross Lake should head straight for a spot known as Four Ways. Flathead, bream, luderick, whiting, flounder and mulloway abound here. The area known as the Pipeline is a mulloway haunt, while light-tackle luderick fishing is rewarding at Sandy Point.

133

Narooma to Bermagui

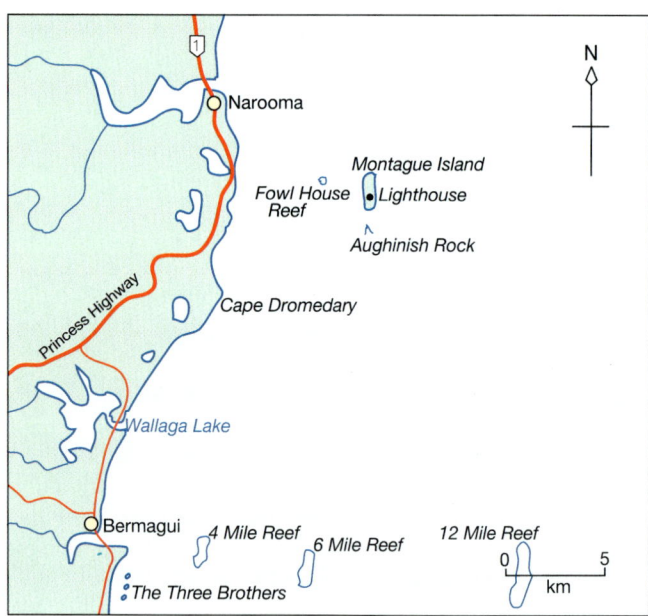

Narooma to Bermagui is the home of big game fishing in New South Wales. However, not all fishermen pursue the big predators.

Both holiday destinations provide fine fishing for the shore-based and even the handline fishermen.

The Bermagui River and Wallaga Lake yield the favoured catches of bream, flathead, whiting and luderick. Wallaga Lake is famous for big whiting and outsized flathead.

Wagonga Inlet, a blue estuary system, is rich in luderick, mullet and big whiting, bream and flathead.

The nearby beaches and rocky headlands are a much under-rated fishery. Surf fishing produces good-sized whiting and sand flathead in summer, while large salmon and tailor run in big numbers during winter. Although many of the rock ledges are dangerous during even moderate seas drummer, groper, snapper, luderick and trevally abound.

Offshore from Bermagui, Four Mile Reef to the north-east, Six Mile Reef in the south-east and the long, narrow Twelve Mile Reef due east yields yellowfin tuna, marlin and the occasional shark.

Off the southern headland and opposite the water tank is the local bait ground that yields slimy mackerel and yellowtail for offshore anglers.

Troll waters in the vicinity of the reefs with bridled tuna baits. Large trolling lures is another suitable method.

Bottom bouncers catch snapper, morwong, trumpeter, trevally and many other reef fish. Light lines and slow-sinking baits in a berley trail are the best technique for catching snapper.

The influx of visiting anglers is at its peak during March when the Narooma Sportfishing Club hosts one of the biggest angling competitions in the country.

Montague Island, 25 minutes from Narooma, is regarded as the birthplace of game fishing in Australia. Although attracting big game specialists, it is also popular with trailerboat fishermen because it offers a wide range of game species comparatively close to shore.

The island surrounds probably produces more big yellowfin tuna than any other location in Australia. Late April through to early June is the big yellowfin season. They weigh in excess of 100 kilograms. Average size of the tuna varies with seasons but is around 45 kilograms.

The best spot is off the northern end of the island. The most popular method of capture is berleying and strip baiting with fish strips or pilchards, live baiting at anchor, and trolling a bridle-rigged frigate mackerel. Frigate mackerel bait and bonito, striped tuna and kingfish can be caught by trolling around the island.

Kingfish are caught at Montague Island all year round, and they seem to be more plentiful in the south-western corner. Drifting offshore from the lighthouse, from between 200 metres and two kilometres yields good kingfish on both jigs and live baits.

The eastern side of the island is not fished as heavily and small boats can get close to the drop-off and use live baits for big kingfish, sharks and the occasional yellowfin tuna.

The north-western corner of the island is the best place for snapper, and Aughinish Rock to the south is also bountiful, though it is a dangerous region when there's a swell running.

East of Montague Island, black marlin, blue marlin and striped marlin are the glamour catch. Trolling live baits close to the island is a pulse technique, though bigger marlin are encountered further offshore.

For anglers intent on capturing sharks, makos, tigers, whaler sharks, hammerheads and white pointers lurk around Montague and the reefs running to the Continental Shelf and beyond.

The Kink, south-east of Montague Island is where the 100 fathom line runs close offshore. It's a good game fishing ground for albacore, marlin, sharks, large tuna and occasional broadbill swordfish.

The Tathra Region

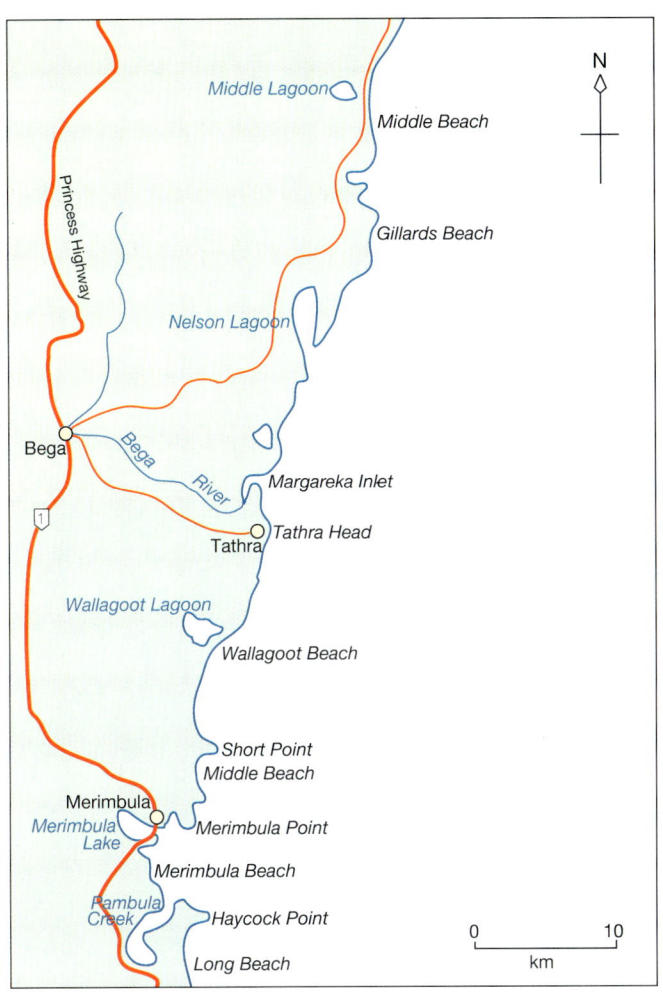

Trailerboat fishermen can catch kingfish throughout the year from the New South Wales south coast between Narooma and Eden.

Narooma Bar is one of the most dangerous on the eastern seaboard. Heavy southerly storms and strong south-easterly winds often prevent any chance of safely running to sea. But black north-easters are even more treacherous.

When a north-easter blows the bar has a nasty break across the mouth. Combined with a swell and run-out tide, the result is heavy dumping waves.

The best time to cross the bar is with a rising or full tide. There is plenty of water depth when the tide and swell run together.

Wear life-jackets and inform local coastguard by radio before crossing the entrance. Once outside, report and continue to maintain contact for notice of weather changes.

This part of the south coast of New South Wales contains excellent coastal fishing in an area that hasn't been developed. From Bega and Tathra, to Merimbula and Pambula, there are long sweeping beaches, rocky headlands, rich estuary systems and rivers.

Facilities, including all types of accommodation, tackle and bait suppliers, are available in the coastal towns. It is advisable to book on-site vans or 'weekenders' well in advance for the peak summer season.

Cowdroys, Gillards and Middle Beaches, north of Tathra, are good surf fishing locations for bream, tailor, salmon and, when Middle Lagoon opens to the sea, mulloway around the entrance during summer. Prawns are also caught here.

Baronda Head and Wajurda Point to Mogareeka Inlet is rockfishing country, with rock ledges plummeting into deep water yielding an abundance of tailor, salmon, bream and trevally during winter and autumn. Snapper are a year-round possibility. Luderick, groper and drummer live in the washes close to shore. Access is from Lake Road to Wajurda Point.

Nelson Lake, north of Bega River, with shallow, weedy water, is a productive summer flathead spinning area.

The Bega River has good stocks of flathead and bream. Whiting is a common catch during summer if you use locally pumped nippers for bait. Small tailor are plentiful in the estuary, and make a useful live bait for the mulloway, which are infrequently caught in the deep hole around Humbug Reach and Chinnook.

Luderick are found on the northern bank downstream from the road bridge, as well as along most deep, rocky shores and Chinnook Lagoon.

At the southern end of the system, Blackfellows Lagoon is good for bream and flathead. Prawns run on moonless summer nights.

Tathra Beach yields bream, flathead, whiting, tailor and salmon with mulloway around the mouth of the Bega River. Live tailor or fresh fillets are the best baits.

Tathra Head is a rockfishing region with deep water conducive to spinning for surface fish. Snapper, drummer and luderick are caught from the headland. The Pinnacle is one of the better places to try.

Luderick and drummer can be caught in Snapper bay after a southerly storm. Offshore anglers can launch boats up to 4.5 metres when outside conditions are favourable.

At Merimbula, the beach offers good opportunities for tailor, salmon, bream, and flathead in summer. Weed however, is a problem.

The headland at the northern end is a good spot in calm conditions for snapper, kingfish and tailor.

The wharf is famous for kingfish and tuna. John Dory can be caught using live yellowtail as bait. Slimy mackerel is the best bait for big kingfish and tuna.

Merimbula Lake fishes well for whiting in summer, especially off the end of the sandspit at the entrance. The entrance is also a top feeding ground for bream. Flathead and luderick frequent the area near the road bridge and the nearby stone jetty.

At the end of the channel, a moored boat allows you to fish oyster leases for big flathead, bream and luderick. The deeper parts of the lake are good for tailor and garfish.

On the northern side of the bridge there is a good launching ramp.

At Pambula, the beach fishing near the mouth of the river is productive for whiting, flathead, tailor and mullet. The shallow sandspit is also a good spinning location for tailor.

Pambula Lake has all the common estuary species, with bream being particularly prolific at night. There's good boat fishing for flathead and luderick in winter.

At Tee Tree Point, yabbies can be pumped and used for bream at night and luderick during the day.

Haycock Point is reasonably safe for rock fishing. Lure casters will catch salmon and tailor from winter to autumn and kingfish and tuna on live baits in summer. Luderick, drummer and groper can also be caught along with the occasional snapper.

Tathra Wharf is an extraordinary fishing spot. Massive sharks, big tuna and kingfish are just part of what's available.

Tathra Wharf
The wharf at Tathra is a legendary fishing spot that attracts both amateur and seasoned anglers. Large tuna, massive kingfish and sharks can be caught from the wharf.

In the mornings and evenings, yellowtail, slimy mackerel and trevally are plentiful under the wharf providing suitable live baits to catch larger game.

Salmon, tailor and barracouta can be taken year round, but January, February and March are the best months for large tuna and sharks.

Because the wharf is high off the water a sliding cliff gaff is necessary for landing large fish.

Eden

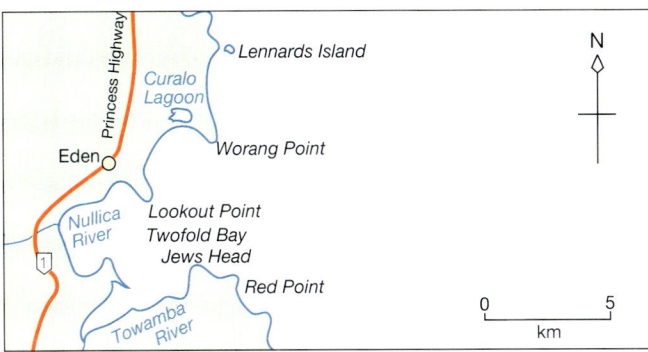

Renowned from the early days of settlement when Ben Boyd made Twofold Bay the centre of the whaling industry, Eden remains one of the busiest commercial fishing spots on the south coast of New South Wales.

Often less crowded in holiday periods than other centres it offers a variety of fish from the beaches, rocks and offshore grounds.

Nestled in Twofold Bay, Eden is protected by the surrounding rocks and beaches from the strong onshore winds and the winter southerlies from Bass Strait.

Eden wharf is a productive fishing location with trevally, yellowtail and bream the most common catches. Abalone, mullet gut, or tuna cubes are the best baits, but some salmon and tailor can be taken on live yellowtail.

In Twofold Bay, boat anglers can drift over the sandy bottomed expanses for large numbers of flathead. Fish in close for bream and whiting, or venture offshore for snapper, morwong, trumpeter and kingfish off the deep reefs. Troll for salmon, tailor and kingfish around Seahorse Shoals and Red Point, though care needs to be taken.

Jews Head, on the southern side of Twofold Bay, offers excellent shore fishing for bream, snapper, drummer, trevally, luderick, kingfish and tuna. Further east, Red Point holds large schools of barracouta, trevally, tailor, salmon and big kingfish on locally caught live yellowtail.

All rock fishing locations around Twofold Bay are potentially dangerous due to the nature of the rocks and the exposed coastline.

The Nullica and Towamba Rivers have superb estuary fishing for bream and flathead and in their upper reaches, small, fragile populations of bass.

Curalo Lake, in the north-west corner of Twofold Bay, is a small estuary that good summertime prawning and bream and flathead fishing.

Eden is a popular fishing destination with both Victorians and New South Welshmen - little wonder when kingfish of this size are available. Boat anglers are best trolling Jews Head and the Red Point area, but be alert for many dangerous breaking bomboras. Rock anglers can also encounter kingfish from these same spots, but again keep safety foremost in mind.

137

Cape Green

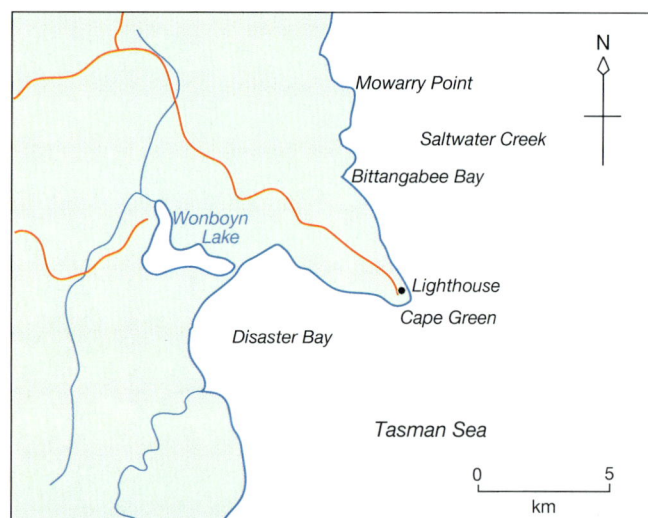

The rocky coastline north of Bittangaree Bay presents some outstanding locations for spinning for tuna, tailor and salmon. Kingfish and large yellowfin tuna are caught during the height of summer using locally caught yellowtail bait, especially at a location known as City Rock.

North to Saltwater Creek is snapper country. However, drummer and other rock species are also available. For anglers using the camping facilities at Saltwater Creek, the nearby rock spots produce tailor, salmon, and bonito.

North of the creek, there are many good rock fishing locations, though access is often difficult through the thick ti-tree scrub.

Green Cape, the prominent headland on the New South Wales far south coast, close to the Victorian border, ranks among the top land-based game fishing locations in the state.

There is excellent rock fishing for snapper, especially after a southerly, as well as drummer, luderick, sweep and tailor fishing. For those chasing big kingfish and tuna, there are many tracks leading to the tip of the headland.

Beaches north and south of the cape offer uncrowded surf fishing for tailor, bream and salmon. The beaches near the mouth of Wonboyn Lake are renowned for spectacular catches of salmon weighing over 4 kilograms. During summer, whiting and the occasional jewfish are available.

From the picnic area of Green Cape, there are good spinning spots within an easy walk. The water is deep and yields large pelagics and good-sized snapper. Yellowfin tuna in excess of 60 kilograms have been caught from the rock ledges, with the average weight 20 to 30 kilograms. Some spots are very exposed and dangerous in rough weather.

North of the lighthouse, tracks are the only way to reach a number of excellent locations. Many are snapper hot spots. To reach the water requires a difficult climb down steep tracks. The thick scrub also makes the going rough. However, once you're set up, the fishing can be sensational.

At Bittangaree Bay there is a camping area popular with local fishermen. Small boats can be launched in good weather and the fishing for bream, flathead and whiting over the flats is excellent.

Bonito venture as far south as Cape Green. They are often regarded as a nuisance by serious land-based live baiter fishermen targeting the much larger yellowfin tuna, which have been caught off The Cape weighing in excess of 60kg.

Freshwater Fishing

Every state in Australia has some trout. Only the Northern Territory has none within its borders.

Trout is an introduced fish and several species are covered under the blanket name. The family is salmonoid.

The main species are brown trout, rainbow trout and Atlantic salmon.

Highly sensitive to temperature trout need cold water. They cannot survive in warm water. This restricts them to to high altitude streams which remain cold or to more southern regions.

The New South Wales northern ranges has had trout introduced but the fishery is only average.

Catching trout is fairly easy and they respond to almost all methods of angling. For the average angler the two best methods are bait fishing and spinning or trolling with lures.

Bait anglers use worms, mudeye (dragon fly larvae), shrimp and small crayfish. These baits are fished under small bubble floats or with a light sinker. Small, light hooks get the best results.

The deeper parts of any stream and the edges of lakes are ideal bait fishing spots.

Anglers fishing with lures should use number 2 or number 3 Celtas, Pegron Tiger Minnows and small bladed spinners when fishing the rivers. On the lakes, Wonder Wobblers, Cobras, Flatfish and small minnow lures work very well.

Spinning the lakes, just slowly walk along the shoreline casting and retrieving the lure. Pick areas that project into the lakes and work the points of these areas. Look always for trees, cover or rock formations that might provide a home for a few trout.

The New England area with its higher altitudes and colder water does has good rivers for trout. The rivers east and west of Armidale are quite productive as are the Barrington Tops a little further to the south.

The mountains west of Sydney around Oberon, lithgow, Bathurst and some of the eastern flowing streams have a good stock of fish. Even the Warragamba River with the colder water coming out of the dam holds quite a fair population of trout. This flows into the Nepean River and a lot of trout are caught around the Penrith Weir in winter.

From Cowra south, the whole mountain range has trout. The dams in particular in this region hold very good populations of fish. Some of these dams also have mixed populations of native fish like catfish, yellowbelly, silver perch and Murray Cod all surviving with the trout.

Burrinjuck Dam is probably the best example of this and offers great mixed species fishing.

Canberra and the Monaro with the Snowy Mountains as the centrepiece is one of the great trout fisheries in the country. The whole area has large clean rivers and creeks and any person interested in learning about trout fishing should start here. The dams in the Snowy Mountains are prolific and glorious places to fish. The rivers in the area are also a lot of fun.

The Blue Mountains, only two hours drive west of Sydney, contains outstanding wild trout fishing. This is typical of what to expect in gorge country — a fast-flowing river, ferns, mosses and granite rock faces, all of which makes for great trout fishing in breath-taking surroundings.

Next Page
Top: Carp are a major problem in New South Wales freshwater rivers. Here, an angler gingerly leads a worm-caught specimen to the bank. Bottom: The Author fishing a Sydney suburban bass stream located only a half-hour drive from the CBD.

The Australian bass and the closely related estuary perch are two of the most sought-after freshwater sportfish along the east coast. They inhabit the freshwater reaches of estuaries, from the South Australian/Victorian border up the east coast to the Noosa River.

Bass need to migrate to salt water to spawn, a requirement that has seen bass stocks steadily decline as rivers are dammed with little though for the fish's migratory habits. The clearing of bankside cover has not helped either, as bass are a fish that rely on cover to hide and ambush their prey.

Bass are a fish that requires a degree of skill to locate and catch. They can be taken on either lures or bait depending on the angler's preference. Lure fishing is the most popular being suited to catch-and-release fishing as it is rare that a lure is swallowed as deep as a bait.

A light, single-handed rod about 2 metres long, mated to a threadline reel loaded with 3kilogram line is used with a selection of diving and surface lures. Divers, such as the Shakespeare Little S, Rebel Crawdad and Deep R, Bill Norman Deep N, Rapala Fat Rap and the Rublex Floppy are favourites with bass anglers, while the popular surface lures are the Tiny Torpedo, Hulla Popper Jitterbug and Crazy Crawler.

A small skiff or canoe makes bass fishing, where you must cast the lures at snags, overhanging bushes, willows, rock drop-offs and along the edges of weedbeds, easier than bank-side fishing.

Most of the fish are released because of the decline in fish stocks and there is a bag limit of five fish per person per day.

Bait fishing is successful on bass using worms, shrimps, crickets, grasshoppers and cicadas, fished a metre or so under a small float and drifted past areas where bass are likely to be hiding.

Bait fishing will often take bass when they are not in an aggressive luretaking mood. It also works very well when the bass are feeding on shrimps or prawns and staying close to the bottom.

Bass are also a good eating fish with a flavour not unlike bream, though angler's are encouraged to release the fish in order to preserve stocks. If you must, the smaller 0.5 to 0.75kilogram bass are likely to be males, which are more common than the larger, breeding females.

In New South Wales, dams and development have ruined many bass streams, but there are still waterways that have significant populations of this fish.

There are bass in most of the coastal systems, with good fish in the Tuross and Moruya Rivers, but the first 'significant' population is found in the Clyde River above Batemans Bay.

The Shoalhaven still has a fair population of bass above Nowra and in the Kangaroo River, however the Tallowah Dam has ruined most of the Shoalhaven fishery.

Sydney's Nepean River harbours a surprising number of bass. Anywhere upstream from Wisemans Ferry is worth a throw, but the really good fishing starts above Richmond. Around Castlereagh and at Penrith Weir yields bass. Upstream from Penrith Weir towards the junction of the Warragamba is another good area, where the occasional trout can be caught.

The Hunter River has suffered badly with siltation spoiling most bass spots. The best river in the area is the Paterson going towards Dungog.

The Manning above Wingham and its tributaries all have solid bass populations that are in a very healthy state.

The big rivers of the New South Wales north coast are the real strongholds of bass, not only in terms of numbers, but also size.

The Macleay and Nambucca Rivers are typical of what's on offer, though the massive Clarence River, where the fish have a huge territory in which to roam, is superfluous. All the tributaries inland of Grafton hold very good fishing.

The Richmond, on the other hand, is not very productive but the Tweed does have a few good fish in the upper reaches.

With the warm, afternoon sun about to set, a successful trout fisherman cleans his catch on the banks of a freshwater impoundment.

141

Victoria

Introduction

Despite fickle weather conditions, Victoria boasts a range of fish and variety of fishing styles that compare favourably with the other States. In fact, when it comes to certain facets of the fishing game, Victoria is second to none.

Australia's most sought-after fish, the snapper, abounds in the State's two big bays; Port Phillip and Westernport. With the exception of South Australia, Victoria is the only other State where large snapper are encountered regularly in an estuarine environment. It is not unusual to catch snapper in excess of 10 kilograms and when the fish are 'running', catches in excess of 100 kilograms are taken.

Flounder spearing is another angling variation unique to Victoria. Flounder are fished at night, using spotlights and pronged spears. It remains one of the best ways to catch these fine-eating flatfish.

Southern bream is fished for in Victoria using techniques that are unique to the State. It differs from other bream in that it never leaves the estuary environment.

While the array of extensive rivers and large bays spread throughout the state ensures that estuary fishing is the most-favoured option, there are offshore anglers who brave the often heavy sea conditions for rewarding catches. Southern bluefin tuna, although not overly prolific, marlin, kingfish and sharks are available for the adventurous, and most locations are serviced by adequate boat ramps and parking areas.

Rock fishing is largely overshadowed by the more popular and productive surf fishing. Big, buck salmon is one of the most avidly pursued species, although mulloway and sharks are also prize catches.

Freshwater anglers have a choice between the dusty banks of outback rivers, such as the famous Murray, where carp and native fish predominate or fishing for trout. Aside from trout streams and creeks, Victoria has many inland impoundments. Most are well-stocked with trout, some have big chinook and Atlantic salmon, while others excellent native fish.

Victoria presents a very complete angling package. It caters well for fishermen's needs, with well-established infrastructures at most locations, and it's fisheries are both scenic and productive.

Even swells do not discourage a keen angler.

Mallacoota

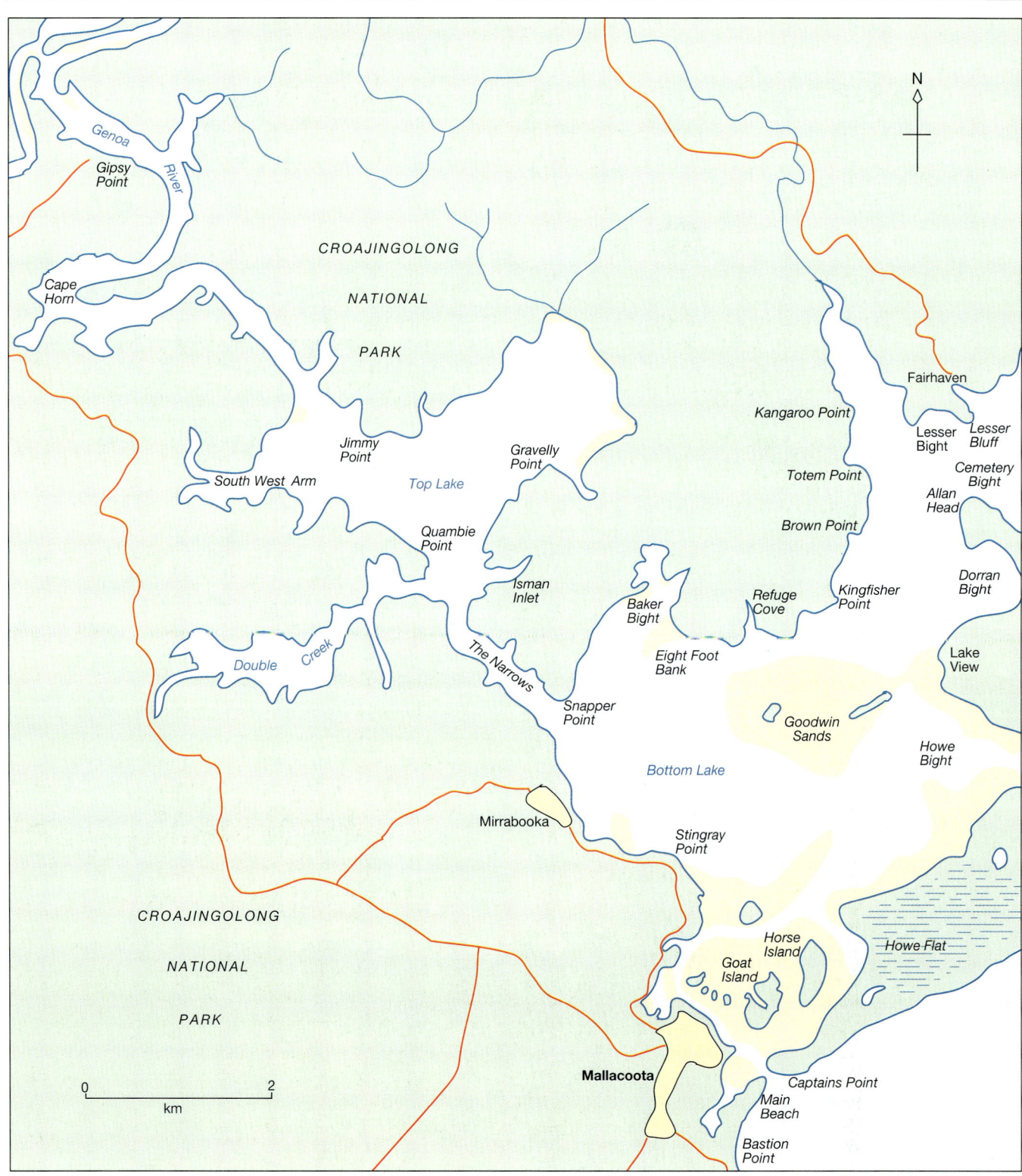

The township of Mallacoota is situated at the mouth of an extensive tidal lagoon system which serves as the combined estuary of the Genoa and Wallagaraugh Rivers. Access is from the Princes Highway at Genoa.

The system consists of two lakes, Top Lake and Bottom Lake. These are connected by a narrow but deep channel called the Narrows. There is a good boat ramp at Mallacoota which gives access to the sheltered waters of

144

Mallacoota Inlet and, if conditions at the mouth permit, productive grounds offshore.

Bottom Lake is famous for big flathead: live mullet are considered the best bait for these. Other fish taken here include tailor, luderick, salmon and occasionally a snapper. Mulloway may also be taken if you have the patience to fish for them.

There are several caravan parks, some of which have sites with lakeside frontages and mooring facilities. In addition there are a number of lakeside moorings available on a first come, first served basis. All you need is a marker with the number of your boat on it. Land-based anglers will find a number of spots to fish around the lake: favourites include Captain's Point, Bastion Point and the jetty near the entrance. Ask locally for directions.

The Narrows, the channel connecting Top and Bottom Lakes is a good spot for Mulloway fishermen. Favoured baits include small live tailor, fillets from freshly caught tailor, and octopus which are plentiful around the rocky shoreline of the lake.

Most mulloway fishermen fish from a boat at night although there is some bank access. It is a good idea to fish one rod close in to the bank and another out a bit because there is no telling where the fish will be.

The best time to fish Bottom Lake and the Narrows is from the end of summer through until the end of autumn.

Top Lake is joined by the Wallagaraugh and Genoa Rivers near Gipsy Point, about 9 kilometres from Genoa.

The facilities at Gipsy Point include a boat ramp, hotel, guest house and other forms of accommodation. A limited supply of stores can also be purchased here.

This area is particularly noted for bream although other species such as estuary perch can be taken as well. One particularly favoured spot on the Wallagaraugh is known as Bull Ring, located about 5 kilometres upstream from Gipsy Point past the Johnson Bridge.

Top Lake and associated rivers fish best from August until November when the bream move upstream to spawn. Preferred baits for bream at this time of the year include sandworm, bass yabby, prawn and crab.

Betka River estuary is along the road to the aerodrome about 3 kilometres from Mallacoota.

Estuary perch, bream and luderick are taken here in good numbers, as well as small salmon and tailor when the estuary entrance is open to the sea.

Bait can be pumped on the exposed flats down toward the mouth of the estuary especially sandworms, yabbies and soft-shelled clams. Shrimp can be netted in the shallow weedy sections.

Small boats can be launched close to the bridge. This will increase the range of the angler even more in this productive little estuary.

The surf beach adjacent to the estuary mouth produces excellent fishing for tailor and salmon during the day and gummy sharks at night.

Fishing from the rocks at Bastion Point for trevally and salmon. The occasional snapper is also caught here.

Gippsland Inlets

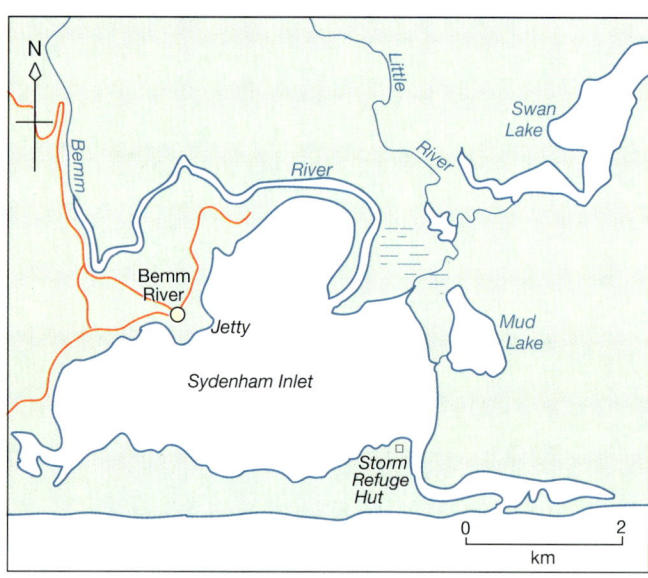

Sydenham Inlet, about 400 kilometres east of Melbourne, is the estuary of the Bemm River. This water is renowned among bream anglers but there is a bag limit of 10 fish per angler per day.

Because of the inlet's shallowness, most anglers tie their boats between poles driven into the muddy bottom. Anchoring is only appropriate in the deeper sections of the inlet.

Estuary perch can be caught on both lures and bait within the estuary and provide an alternative to bream.

The closely related bass are found further upstream in fresh water for most of the year and only congregate within the estuary from August until December to spawn. Bass also respond to the appropriate baits and lures.

Other fish caught by anglers on light tackle in Sydenham Inlet include mullet, salmon, silver trevally, flathead and garfish.

Baits recommended for bream include shrimp, worms, bass yabbies and commercially packaged baits like prawns.

Estuary perch feed voraciously from late afternoon until well into the night and will take unweighted shrimp, small live fish, and a variety of lures.

Bass have similar preferences with the addition of a number of insects including crickets. Like their cousins, bass feed most voraciously at night but will respond to repeated presentation of lure bait near a likely looking snag during the day.

Tamboon Inlet is the estuary of the Cann River. It is a tidal lagoon best reached by boat because the nearest vehicular access is at Furnell's Landing, some 22 kilometres from the township of Cann River on the Princes Highway.

When the estuary is closed to the sea, there is no problem navigating down to the inlet. However, when the entrance is open, particularly at low tide, there are rocky hazards in the river above the lagoon.

Like the other tidal lagoons on this part of the coast, it produces bream but not in the same numbers as the Bemm River or the top lake at Mallacoota. However, what is lost in quantity is made up for in size with bream over 2 kilograms regularly taken by anglers who know this water.

Other species taken from the inlet include large flathead and estuary perch. Further upstream there are bass. Eels weighing up to 10 kilograms and more are also taken upstream from the inlet on fish fillets.

When the entrance is open, there is excellent fishing for salmon and tailor, both from a boat near the entrance, and from the east shore. The rising tide is the best time to fish for these species using lures.

The beaches adjacent to Tamboon Inlet produce salmon and tailor during the evening, and good-sized gummy shark during the night.

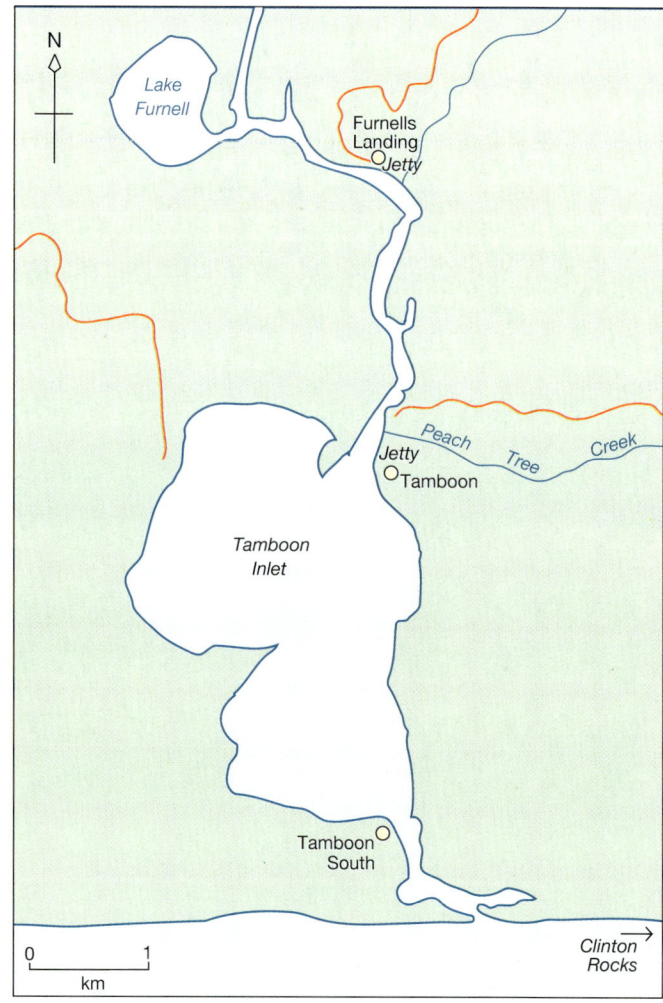

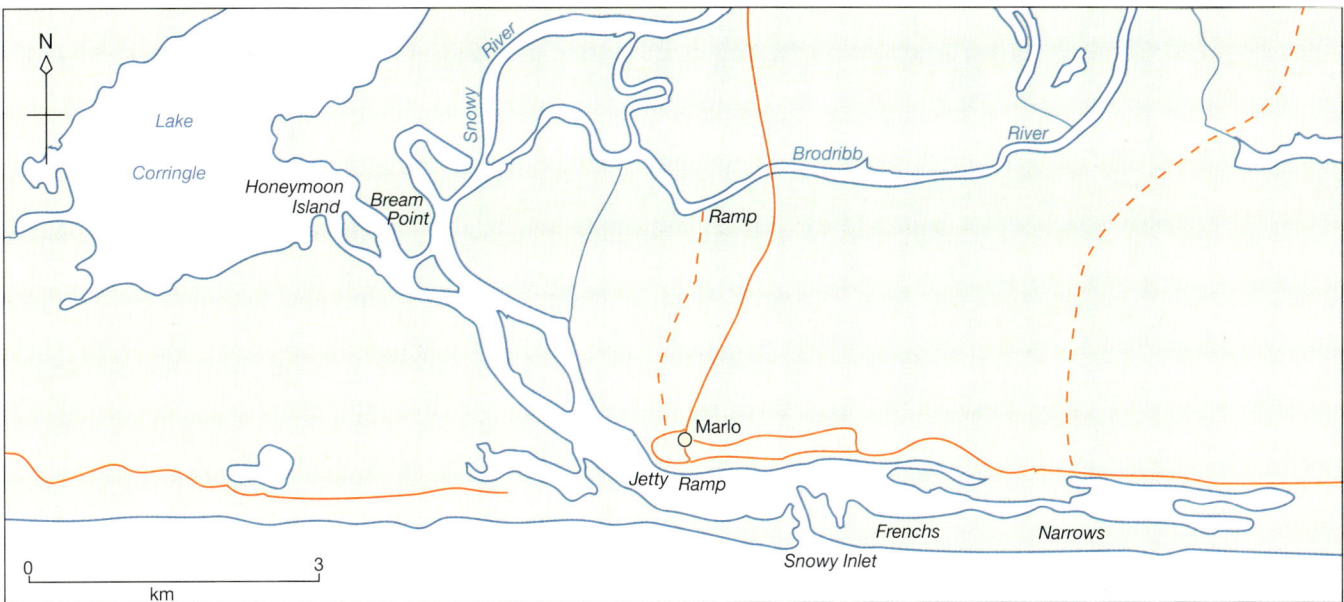

Marlo is situated on the estuary of the Snowy River some 15 kilometres from Orbost. The inlet is popular for boat angling and bank or jetty fishing.

There are two caravan parks, two boat ramps, ample car and trailer parking and a loading jetty. The Marlo ramp is suitable for launching boats to six metres. The other ramp is located on the adjacent Brodribb River.

Catches within the estuary depend on whether or not the entrance is open to the sea. If it is, then a wide variety of fish including salmon, tailor and flathead can be caught on bait and lures. Other species like mullet, garfish and salmon trout can be caught on bait using small hooks and light tackle. Luderick are also caught in good numbers at times. Good bags of bream and estuary perch are caught whether the entrance is open or closed.

Prawns can sometimes be captured within the estuary and as well as being good eating, are one of the best baits for both bream and estuary perch, the latter preferring them alive.

When the entrance is open and benign bar conditions prevail, there is access to excellent offshore fishing. About 1,500 metres offshore, a shallow bank produces excellent catches of big flathead.

Trolling close to shore, salmon and tailor can be taken on lures. Further out, tuna and barracoota are always a possibility.

Cape Conran to the east has a boat ramp that is sheltered from the prevailing south-westerly winds and swell; it gives access to the very productive waters offshore from the Cape which produce all species mentioned, plus snapper.

The beaches adjacent to the inlet produce salmon and tailor during the day and gummy sharks at night.

The beaches west of the inlet are accessible only by boat. To the east, there is access through the sand dunes alongside the Cape Conran Road.

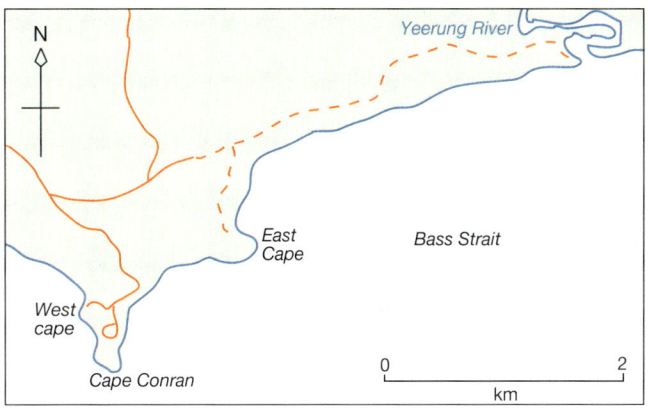

There is limited rock fishing from the Cape itself where parrot fish and the occasional snapper are taken on bait, and snook can be taken on lures.

There is an excellent beach extending from Sailors Graveyard at the Cape to the mouth of the Yerrung River. The beach produces salmon and tailor through the day and gummy sharks at night. The Yerrung River yields good catches of bream and estuary perch to the few anglers who bother to fish it.

Sydenham Inlet is an outstanding location for estuary perch.

The Gippsland Lakes

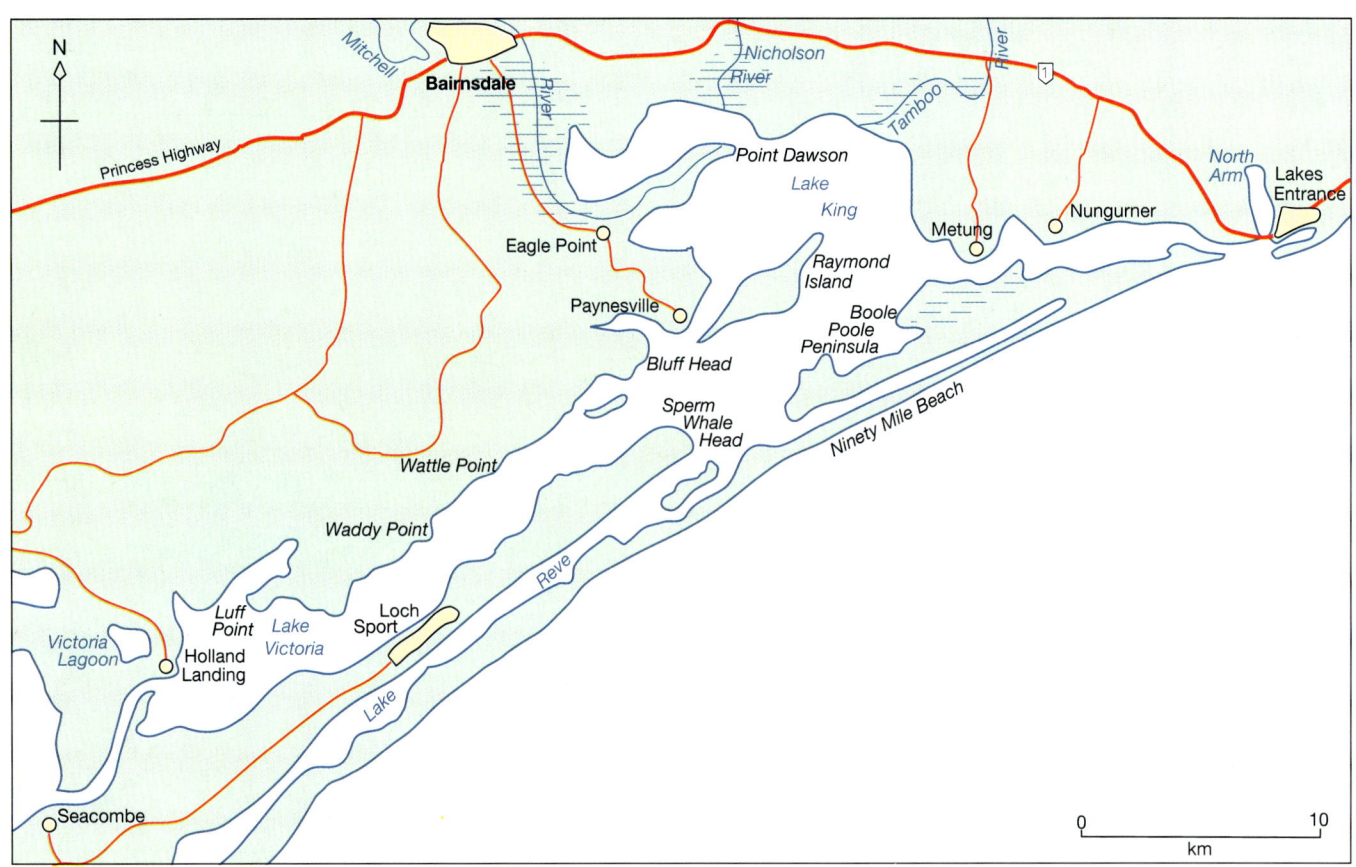

The Gippsland Lakes are a series of inter-connected tidal lagoons running to the sea through a common entrance at the township of Lakes Entrance. They cover nearly 400 square kilometres which makes the 'lakes' one of the largest estuary-tidal lagoon systems in the country.

At Lakes Entrance there is a boat launching ramp on your left as you drive in from the west. Boats to 7 metres are launched from this ramp which gives access to not only a vast expanse of sheltered water, but to good offshore fishing as well when the entrance bar allows. There are also a number of other ramps within the system.

Land-based anglers are well catered for with the number of jetties, retaining walls and beaches throughout and adjacent to the system. Beach access is via the footbridge in the township of Lakes Entrance, and via road on the east side of town; ask locally for directions.

Bullock Island, just inside the entrance is most popular with land-based anglers who take good catches of tailor and salmon on lures and a variety of other fish on bait. Access to Bullock Island is via a bridge over the narrow separating channel. You cannot fish from the bridge, but good catches of luderick are taken in the channel.

Kalimna, to the west, offers good fishing in sight of the entrance. You can fish from a boat or from the excellent jetty close to the hotel and motel at Kalimna for a wide variety of fish including bream, mullet, flathead and tailor. Snapper are taken when they enter the system, usually in summer, and mulloway are always a possibility when the water is discoloured from heavy rain.

On the shores of Lake King, Nungurner and Metung offer access to both boat and land-based anglers. Boat ramps are adequate for modest craft and there are a number of jetties and structures from which you can fish.

Metung caters well for the angler with stores and accommodation as well as hire and charter boats. Bream are the main species sought around Bancroft Bay, but a wide variety of fish can be caught at times including tailor, mullet and luderick. The deeper waters off Shaving Point at the end of town sometimes produce big mulloway.

Access to Metung by road is from the Princes Highway at Swan Reach on the Tambo River.

Paynesville is on the peninsula dividing Lake King from Lake Victoria and offers good facilities for anglers. Access is from Bairnsdale on the Princes Highway.

One of the best spots to fish at Paynesville is from the wharf at the fishermen's co-operative on McMillan Strait, the narrow channel between the mainland and Raymond Island.

Lake Victoria is a vast stretch of water, approximately 3 kilometres wide and 30 kilometres long. On its shores, the resorts of Loch Sport and Hollands Landing are popular with anglers.

Although Lake Victoria is up to 7 metres deep in places, there are many shallow banks, so navigate carefully.

McLennan Strait west of Hollands Landing is the narrow channel linking Lake Victoria to Lake Wellington and is reached by turning off the South Gippsland Highway at Longford then proceeding to Seacombe via Dutson.

Although less than 100 metres wide for most of its 9 kilometre length, the water in McLennan Strait is deep and the fishing good with access for both boat and land-based anglers.

Lake Wellington, 8 kilometres wide by 16 kilometres long, is the largest of the 'lakes'. Into it flow the Thompson, Latrobe, Avon and Macalister Rivers.

The Tambo River is navigable from the limit of tidal influence below Bruthen, all the way down to Lake King. Launching ramps are at Swan Beach and Johnsonville which are both on the Princes Highway. The concrete ramp at Johnsonville is preferred.

There is good bank access both from the road to Metung downstream, and after heavy rain, into Lake King. During long periods of dry weather they can be caught upstream as far as the 'cliffs' and the 'blue hole'.

As well as bream, there are estuary perch and mullet within the river. Favoured baits include, sandworm, prawn, shrimp, crab and bass yabbies.

The Mitchell River runs into Lake King between two banks of silt which extend into the lake for several kilometres. This is a good area to pump baits like yabbies, worms and soft-shelled clams.

This area at the mouth also attracts good populations of fish: bream predominate but mullet, flathead, tailor and luderick are all to be found here, along with the occasional mulloway.

The Mitchell is navigable all the way from Bairnsdale down to Lake King. The road to Paynesville gives land-based anglers access from Bairnsdale to the point where the river swings east toward the lake, a distance of about 8 kilometres.

During a long spell of dry weather, the best fishing is to be found well upstream, but for the most of the year the Mitchell produces good fishing.

The Nicholson River is not as popular as the Tambo and Mitchell although it has good populations of fish.

For land-based anglers, access is restricted to a limited area near the boat ramp at Nicholson, on the Princes Highway between Bairnsdale and Swan Reach.

However, the boat angler will have no problem in locating good populations of bream. There are also a number of estuary perch in the Nicholson plus a variety of other good table fish like mullet, luderick and flathead.

Both the Thomson and Latrobe Rivers are navigable all the way from Lake Wellington to Sale. One good spot to fish is at the junction of the two rivers, just downstream from Sale. Both systems have healthy populations of carp as well as various other freshwater fish including trout. The population of carp in brackish Lake Wellington probably originated from these rivers.

The Avon River lacks depth although is navigable in a shallow draught boat. Like other rivers emptying into Lake Wellington, it carries good populations of bream.

The Avon is joined by the Perry just above Lake Wellington and there is good fishing for bream in both rivers some distance above this junction all the way down to the lake.

The Gippsland Lakes are one of Victoria's most popular summer playgrounds and Lakes Entrance, shown here, one of the best fishing locations.

Wilsons Promontory/Inlets

Known just as the 'Prom' to many hikers, Wilsons Promontory National Park offers a lot to the fisherman. The scenery is absolutely stunning, beaches white and almost tropical in appearance and the distances between camp sites extremely long if you are carrying an extra 20 kilograms of fishing tackle in your pack.

It should also be noted that all persons wanting to camp

within the National Park must obtain a permit from the Park Office at Tidal River. This allows the rangers to control numbers as well as knowing roughly where everyone is in case of an emergency.

Up until a few years ago you could fish anywhere in the park, however with the declaration of the Wilsons Promontory Marine Park it has been made illegal to fish in many areas. The official reason for banning fishing from the rocks on Wilsons Promontory is to minimise damage to the rocks and to associated marine vegetation.

At Norman Bay is the closest beach to Tidal River. Access is easy and the beach is only a 5 minute walk from the large camping ground at Tidal River. In the shallow water here, surf fishing is limited to small whiting and salmon and is patchy at that. Nonetheless there are occasions when a good number of fish can be caught.

Oberon Bay Surf Beach, 4 kilometres south along a hiking track that follows the coastline out around Norman Point, is arguably the best fishing beach on the western side of Wilsons Promontory.

The beach itself is about 2 kilometres long with the better sections down towards the southern end. Here the water is also fairly shallow, but does exhibit features such as holes, gutters and rips, just the areas to look for when chasing fish. Unfortunately fishing is now illegal in Oberon Bay as it is in Waterloo Bay on the east coast.

Refuge Cove is the deepest bay on Wilsons Promontory with a little beach right in front of the hikers' camping ground. As the Cove is well protected from the ocean, there is virtually never any surf but a surge in heavy seas.

The cove is well known to yachtsmen and professionals who use it for refuge in bad weather hence the name. Salmon are not prolific off the beach, but some very large salmon, barracouta and snook can be taken spinning off the rocks at the mouth.

There are a lot of big sharks in Refuge Cove, and a line cast in off the beach at night could surprise the unsuspecting angler.

The Beach at Sealers Cove, is 15 kilometres east of the Telegraph Saddle car park. Salmon regularly frequent this area, but as the beach is shallow in places it pays to look for gutters or holes. King George whiting can put in the odd appearance.

The distances involved in hiking and fishing the Promontory are long and really should only be attempted by someone having a reasonable degree of fitness. But for those who are looking for a fishing trip that is something different, even a bit tough, then a hike around Wilsons Promontory is recommended.

Corner Inlet situated on the east side of Wilsons Promontory, is a large and shallow expanse of water connected to the ocean by the deep, fast flowing Singapore Channel which divides into 5 smaller channels.

The Franklin Channel leads to Port Franklin, the Toora Channel to Barry Beach, and the Lewis Channel to Port Welshpool. The Bennison and Milddle Channels peter out offshore from Yanakie Beach.

Although there are launching facilities at all three locations, the large rise and fall in the tide makes it

Snapper caught between Snake and Clonmel Islands, Port Albert.

important for the boat operator to know when he is able to either launch or retrieve.

Land access to all three locations is from the South Gippsland Highway. Many anglers favour Port Welshpool because of the facilities in Welshpool.

Good-sized snapper can be caught in the channels from early October until late December especially near the entrance to the Singapore Channel in the stretch known as the Singapore Deep.

Whiting of good size can also be caught at many places throughout the Inlet, but the strong tides make the use of heavy sinkers distasteful to anglers.

At Port Welshpool there is a caravan park, shops, a boat ramp and 2 piers which run out into deep water. Both of these piers produce a wide variety of fish including snapper, gummy sharks and the occasional mulloway. At the other end of the scale, good catches of mullet, flathead and silver trevally are taken with some regularity.

Port Albert situated on the east arm of Corner Inlet known as Shoal Inlet, has a caravan park, boat ramp, shops including a Fishermens' co-op, a hotel and wharf.

The tide runs strongly in the channel as it passes the wharf so a heavier sinker is needed. Nevertheless, a good variety of fish are caught here.

Snapper anglers are successful in the Port Albert Entrance between Snake and Clonmel Island, found by following the channel around either side of Sunday Island.

Good catches of whiting are sometimes taken from the shallower banks as they are elsewhere, but the strong tide makes it necessary to use heavy sinkers.

Waratah Bay

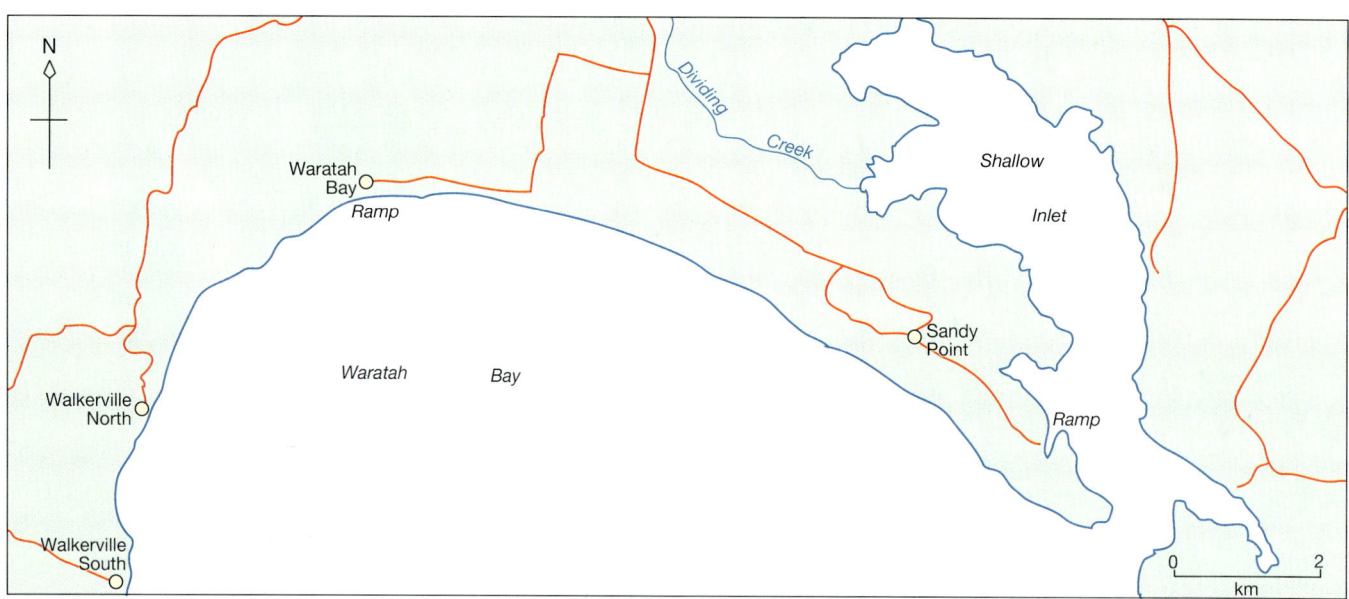

Shallow Inlet situated on the north-west side of Wilsons Promontory is about 13 kilometres from Fish Creek on the Promontory Road. There is a camping ground but no shops. A track to Sandy Point at the entrance to the inlet gives access to an excellent surf beach.

Small boats can be launched within the inlet without too much difficulty and there is a wide variety of fish to be caught.

Whiting predominate during the warmer months when some good catches are made, but other species such as silver trevally and mullet, commonly found in tidal lagoons, are also present.

When the entrance is open and deep, as it usually is, gummy sharks and mulloway add even more variety, particularly for night fishermen, while snapper make an appearance during November.

Waratah Bay is a large, crescent-shaped bay between Wilsons Promontory and Cape Liptrap. Access is either from the South Gippsland Highway via Leongatha and Fish Creek, or from Iverloch via the Lower Tarwin.

The beaches in Waratah Bay are shallow with a wide band of exposed sand when the tide is out. Mullet and salmon are taken in good numbers on the rising tide.

During summer, a low evening tide is worth trying for snapper and gummy sharks because you can walk out far enough to cast into productive water. Be ready to retreat when the tide begins rising though.

Walkerville can be reached from either Fish Creek or Inverloch. There are camping facilities here as well as shops. Although there is no boat ramp as such, you can

launch a small boat from the hard sand with little difficulty.

Although there is good boat fishing around Walkerville, the main attraction to both land-based and boat anglers is Cape Liptrap.

Cape Liptrap has a number of locations from where you can fish.

There are few good or even comfortable rock platforms, but they do give access to reasonable water where you can catch a wide variety of fish on bait and lures.

Although there is always a chance of a snapper on bait or a good-sized salmon on a lure, the species usually encountered are parrot fish and snook using the methods mentioned.

Fishing from a boat, you will certainly add barracouta to your list and occasionally kingfish.

This average size salmon was taken at Waratah Bay by spinning a metal bait-fish profile lure into a visible school of feeding fish.

Anderson's Inlet

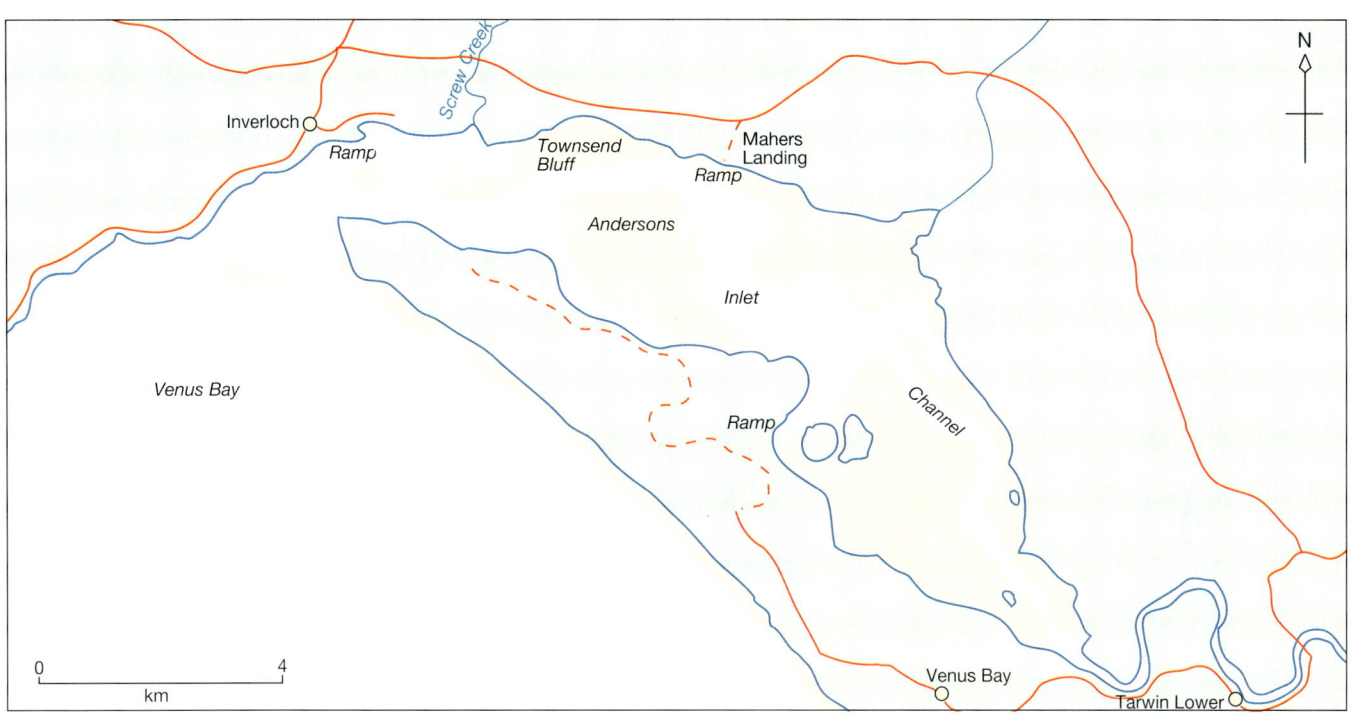

A southern bream is led carefully into the net. Anderson's Inlet holds good stocks of this very popular species.

Andersons Inlet is the tidal lagoon estuary of the Tarwin River which runs to sea through a fairly narrow channel in Venus Bay.

The township of Inverloch is at the entrance, and Tarwin Lower is on the river itself at what would very nearly be the limit of tidal influence. Both towns provide basis requirements for anglers.

The Inlet has a wide variety of fish. Estuary perch and bream are found upstream; the numerous sand banks within the lagoon sustain a healthy population of big flathead, while the deeper channels produce whiting, silver trevally, salmon, and some snapper. Good populations of mullet are found throughout.

There is a good jetty and entrance beach where land-based anglers can take a variety of fish, but it is a good idea to begin fishing on the last of either the ebb or flood tide to minimise problems with drifting week.

The boat ramp just inside the inlet from the jetty gives access to productive water, both in the sheltered inlet and offshore. Good catches of salmon are taken by boat operators trolling lures just out from the entrance.

Venus Bay, the beach south from Tarwin Lower is a place where good catches of mullet and salmon are frequently taken. The beach is fairly shallow but usually free of weed.

Cape Paterson is a rugged, rocky headland about 13 kilometres from Inverloch, providing little access for anglers except those adept at rock climbing.

Approaching the Cape from Inverloch, there are many short beaches interspersed with reefs which provide salmon and pinkies, but with the inevitable loss of tackle due to the rough bottom.

Lure fishing for snook is recommended from the few rocky access points. These bite best early in the morning and late afternoon.

The surf beach near the township of Cape Paterson is well signposted and popular, but the bottom is snaggy and much tackle has been lost here. From the lookout at the end of Stuart Street, you will see two small sandy bays which produce mullet with minimum loss of tackle.

The mouth of the Powlett River can be reached from the Bass Highway just west of Wonthaggi. While the Powlett does have its devotees who take large bream and estuary perch, the fishing is usually slow.

The beach at the entrance always seems to have plenty of interesting features and produces good bags of mullet and salmon and gummy sharks after dark.

Kilcunda is just off the Bass Highway, a short distance past the turn-off to the Powlett River heading back toward Melbourne.

Kilcunda is a productive surf beach with good vehicular and pedestrian access. One of the best places to fish is behind the cemetery, but there always seems to be people fishing there.

The San Remo turn-off from the Bass Highway is well signposted. The township offers all basic facilities for anglers including a fishermens' co-operative where you can buy a wide variety of fish if you are not successful.

For land-based anglers, the strong tide is a limiting factor but the last kick of either the ebb or flood tide will give an hour of productive fishing for a variety of fish including silver trevally.

The bottom of the tide is the easiest time to fish from the beach downstream from the bridge, because of the closer access to the channel. This is not so important from the jetty.

Point Griffith headland can be approached by turning south from the San Remo Road. Here there are some reasonable rock fishing platforms.

Turn left to San Remo then take the turn-off on your left to the rocks at Point Griffith. The rock platform most fished is called the 'Punchbowl'.

This platform can be fished in good weather with access to deep water. Here you will catch rock dwellers like rusk and parrot fish with an outside chance at a snapper.

Casting with lures you will take snook and the occasional salmon.

Western Port / Phillip Island

Koo Wee Rup

Ramp
Tooradin
Warneet | Blind
Ramp | Bight
Ramp

Ramp

Bagge Harbour
^Crawfish Rock

Western
Port

N

Middle

Spit

Hastings
Hastings
Ramp Bight

North Arm

Spit

Middle Spit Channel

Fairhaven

French

Lang
Ramp Lang

Island

Crib
Point

Balnarring

Stoney
Point
Hanns
Inlet

Tankerton

East Arm

Somers

Ramp

Grantville

Corinella

Tortoise
Head

Ramp
Point Leo
Shoreham

Western

Port

Ramp

Ramp
Flinders

Ventnor

Cowes

Rhyll
Ramp

Bass River

Cat
Bay

Kitty
Miller
Bay

Newhaven

The Nobbies

San Remo
Anderson

Seal Rock

Pyramid Rock

Woolamai
Beach

Kilcunda

Cape Woolamai

0 _____ 8
km

Western Port unlike Port Phillip Bay, is an intricate system of channels branching like the capillaries of a giant circulatory system. Port Phillip Bay is virtually a basin within the deepest area in the centre.

There are great expanses of mud and sandbanks exposed at low tide so careful navigation is essential, though the main channels are well marked and the lesser channels also have markers of sorts.

Opposite : The sandy shores lining Anderson's Inlet are very productive when fishing for bream, flathead and whiting.

There are two entrances to Bass Strait. The main entrance and channel runs around the west side of Phillip Island and is used by all shipping. The other is the east channel passing Phillip Island to the east and entering between San Remo and Newhaven where an excellent bridge gives access to Phillip Island from the mainland.

Western Port has a huge variety of fish, but the two target species are snapper and whiting. Most serious snapper anglers fish either along the main shipping channel on an alignment of beacons 9, 11, and 13 in the south, or up the head of the North Arm near Lysaght

Jetty. November is one of the best months to fish for snapper in Western Port.

At the bottom of the tide most fish are in the channels because there is very little water over the banks, but when the tide starts coming in, the whiting advance over the shallow banks in search of food, which is usually plentiful.

Popular locations for whiting are the Middle Spit, which runs right up the North Arm on the French Island side of the main channel, and all of the inlets at the head of the North Arm including Watsons Inlet to Yaringa Boat Harbour, Rutherford Inlet which runs up through the productive Quail Bank to Warneet, and the famous Tooradin channel.

Charter boats operate from Warneet and Tooradin, and good catches of whiting are almost guaranteed if you book with one of these.

The East Arm of Western Port swings to the right from the main shipping channel between Tortoise Head on French Island and Cowes on Phillip Island. It continues on through the narrows past Corinella to where it peters out into a series of shallow-tide scours between Grantville and Lang Lang.

Most good catches of fish are taken from the French Island side of the channel so a boat is a big help. The variety of fish to be caught throughout the East Arm and the lesser channels branching through the French Island Bank is truly amazing with anglers often bringing in ten or more varieties of fish in a single day.

Phillip Island can be reached from the mainland via the bridge at San Remo. Soon after crossing the bridge you will come to a sign showing the Woolamai Surf Beach which is popular with surf fishermen.

Other good fishing spots on Cape Woolamai can be reached only on foot from Newhaven. Red Rock which is about a 40 minute walk with tackle. If the tide is in, you will have to walk along the high ground which is riddled with mutton-bird holes so be careful.

Proceeding to Cowes from Woolamai Beach, the road divides and there is a sign indicating The Nobbies. After passing the quarries on the left, take the next turn left to Kitty Miller Bay, a horse shoe-shaped bay with a sandy bottom which produces whiting in the early morning and late afternoon.

To the west, some marginal rock fishing platforms produce parrot fish on bait and some big snook on lures.

The road to the Nobbies is well marked, the views are spectacular and the rocks dangerous.

Access to the best rock fishing platforms on the Nobbies is at low tide. Lure fishing is productive for salmon and snook, but watch the sea as a number of lives have been lost here.

West of the Nobbies, there are a number of safer ledges from where you can fish, but catches are not always good. Parrot fish can be taken on bait, while live baiting mostly attracts only thieving seals. Lure fishing produces some medium-sized snook.

Cowes has a boat ramp which is the only safe access to the shipping channel snapper marks to the west of Phillip Island. The treacherous Middle Bank effectively prevents boats coming across from Flinders and Balnarring in all but ideal conditions.

Anglers regularly fish from the Cowes jetty. The adjacent rocks and beaches give access to fairly deep water, but a surf rod is needed to fish there.

Rhyll on the north-east corner of Phillip Island, has an excellent boat hire service and boat ramp, plus all basic requirements for fishing. The waters of Rhyll and nearby Observation Point have prolific fish populations.

The jetty at Newhaven on the opposite side of the channel to San Remo, fishes well, although you would be advised to fish at the change of tide to avoid the strong current and drifting weed. The last hour of the ebb tide and the first hour of the incoming tide are most productive here.

As well as those mentioned, there are good boat ramps at Flinders, Stoney Point, Hastings, Warneet, Tooradin, Corinella and Newhaven, plus ramps at Blind Bight, Lang Lang and Grantville.

Gummy sharks are a trophy catch in Victoria. This one was caught in Western Port Bay, one of their favourite locations.

Port Phillip Bay

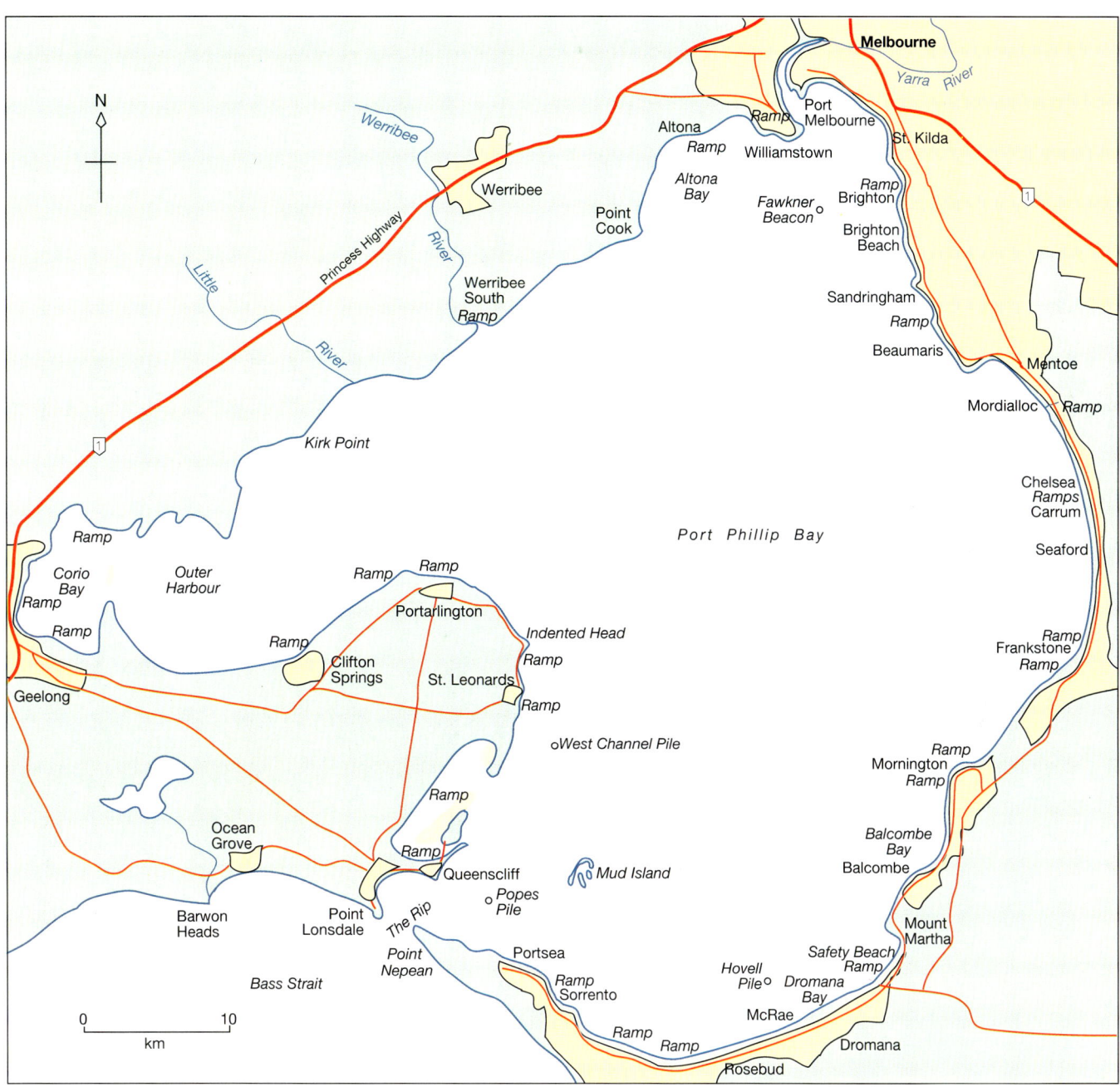

Port Phillip Bay is a tidal lagoon into which flows ten rivers and creeks. It covers approximately 2000 square kilometres with a maximum depth of around 25 metres in the centre, making it the largest tidal lagoon in Australia.

The waters of Port Phillip Bay run to sea through a narrow entrance, only 3 kilometres wide. The action of the tides has formed a large delta of sand and silt several kilometres inside the entrance, and through these there are a number of permanent tide scours. At least two of them remain deep enough to carry light to medium

shipping to the ports of Geelong and Melbourne.

Access to the tip of Point Nepean is limited to Defense Department personnel so land-based anglers cannot fish here, but boats launching from Sorrento and Queenscliff do well in the Port Phillip Heads area on a variety of fish including salmon, silver trevally, yellowtail kingfish and snapper. Whiting and garfish are also taken here in good numbers by light-tackle enthusiasts.

On the Point Lonsdale and Queenscliff side of Port Phillip Heads, anglers fish in the bight in front of Clarke's

Beacon for whiting, squid and snook, but many other varieties such as salmon are also taken.

Anglers without a boat can fish the boat harbour at Queenscliff. The Queenscliff pier, the rocks under both the Queenscliff and Point Lonsdale Lighthouses at low tide, and the popular pier at Point Lonsdale produce a good variety of fish, including sharks, to suitably equipped anglers.

On the other side of Port Phillip Heads, Nepean Bay in the shelter of Point Nepean produces whiting on bait and salmon on lures, either trolled or cast from a boat.

About 600 metres out from the end of the stone wall in Nepean Bay, anglers anchor up in the ebb tide and allow baits and lures to 'work' in the tide behind the boat in the hope of hooking a big yellowtail kingfish which are plentiful during summer and autumn.

Commercial fishermen catch yellowtail kingfish on heavy leaded handlines baited with freshly caught squid. They can often be seen over the wreck of the Eliza Ramsden between Portsea and Queenscliff or out in the Rip itself, just motoring up against the tide, rhythmically jigging their lines.

The Bellarine Peninsula on the west side of Port Phillip Heads is famous for excellent catches of whiting which are found from Swan Bay right past St. Leonards, Indented Head and Portarlington on the Prince George Bank. All of these locations have good boat ramps but the ramp at Queenscliff is the best.

Snapper are caught in all of the deeper channels off St. Leonards and from the St. Leonards pier, particularly after a strong northerly blow. The deeper mud flats wide of the banks are infested with small flathead making fishing difficult, but fish at the change of tide, particularly the high tide, and if snapper are about, the small flathead will go off the bite.

The boat ramp at Indented Head gives access to Prince George Bank, synonymous with excellent catches of good-sized whiting. Well known marks here include the Governor Reefs to the right of the ramp, and off Grassy Point further up toward Portarlington.

The first stick inside the Prince George Light is a great spot to look for sizeable whiting, particularly during the day when they are not on the bite elsewhere.

The tide scour inside the Prince George Light is popular with snapper fishermen. So too is the whole length of the drop-off into deeper water, marked by two flat-topped floating buoys out from Indented Head and visible from the boat ramp.

The Pier at Portarlington is popular with anglers, but most throw out from the pier when the most accessible quarry are the whiting and leatherjacket close in. Some good size flathead are taken from here in summer.

The Portarlington boat ramp is in the caravan park but is used by non-residents as well, but most use the somewhat better ramp at Point Richards a kilometre away.

Good-sized whiting are taken in fair numbers out near the stick on the Point Richards bank, but this area never seems to reach its full potential because of the netting pressure by commercial fishermen.

On the north side of the Point Richards channel, 3 kilometres out from the boat ramp, snapper are caught in good numbers throughout summer. The best spot to fish is behind the number 3 and number 5 beacons.

Point Richards more-or-less marks the beginning of the Geelong Arm of Port Phillip, officially known as Corio Bay, although most anglers tend to refer only to the Corio Bay inner harbour as Corio Bay.

Across on the other side of the arm, Kirk Point has an exposed boat ramp offering access to the productive waters of Long Reef, Arthur the Great and the Point Wilson Bank where the explosives pier is situated.

This area is known as the north shore of the outer harbour and is another area heavily fished by netters. Despite commercial pressure, there are still plenty of fish to be caught here with good bags of whiting possible and the occasional good catch of snapper.

The boat ramp at Clifton Springs on the south shore of the Bellarine Peninsula gives access to the excellent Curlewis bank where good catches of whiting are the rule if you know where to look for them.

A boat loaded with snapper from Corio Bay, near Geelong in Port Phillip Bay. Despite increased professional fishing pressure, snapper fishing remains very productive.

The Rip at the entrance to Port Phillip Bay is a kingfish hot spot.

Werribee River estuary boat ramp on the west side of Port Phillip gives access to the productive bream waters of the estuary and the excellent snapper and whiting grounds offshore. The entrance to the river is shallow, but if you align the two markers, on in the water, the other on the jetty in the river mouth, you will get an unobstructed passage.

For whiting, look for clusters of boats. Should you want to find your own whiting marks, by all means do so but make sure you take notice of the landmarks and any other co-ordinates that you can use to locate the spot later.

Contrary to popular belief, you don't always need to fish in deep water to find snapper. Nowhere is this more easily illustrated than off the Metropolitan Board of Works Farm back towards Kirk Point from Werribee. Using a sounder, move in until you are reading out 4 metres of water in front of the farm. As the sun goes down, be prepared for action, particularly in late October and November and again in February and March.

Wider marks are productive also, but sea lice can be bad wider out, particularly if you fish before daylight or after dark.

Point Cook/Williamstown has large expanses of broken ground in both shallow and deep water which ensures a good population of fish. Access is from boat ramps at Altona and Williamstown which have adequate parking facilities during all but the busiest times of the year.

Whiting are found close in, with particularly good areas in Altona Bay near the piles of the old jetties and at Williamstown close in behind the rifle range.

Snapper are also caught close in after an onshore blow, and you will often see boats bobbing around a few hundred metres offshore in deplorable weather.

In fair weather, look further out for snapper and be prepared to be on the water from before daylight till an hour or two after sun up, or from sunset until dark, or later.

The pier at Altona also produces quite a few snapper for anglers who are there well before first light.

At Williamstown, pier access offers anglers a wide choice, but the only good pier for snapper fishing is the Breakwater pier, and then only either during or immediately after a strong onshore blow.

The Hobsons Bay area includes the mouth of the Yarra River and the hot water canal from the Newport Power Station where good catches of bream, mullet and the occasional mulloway are taken. There is good road access to much of the Yarra and Maribyrnong River Estuaries, but the amount of shipping in the mouth of the Yarra can be a distraction.

The boat ramp at St. Kilda marina is popular and gives access to a large area of productive water for both snapper and whiting.

Land-based anglers do well from the pier, St Kilda breakwater and numerous other structures in this area.

From Elwood to Sandringham both land-based angler and anglers with boats are well catered for. The pier and breakwater at Brighton are most popular, and from October through until Christmas many anglers are rewarded with big snapper after spending long hours on the breakwater at night.

Sandringham Breakwater is also popular and a good many big snapper have been taken in the lee of the wall, not on the outside.

Serious snapper boat-anglers fish further out, and anywhere you are hooking cunjevoi from the bottom you are likely to catch a good-sized snapper, especially at dawn or dusk.

The nature of the ground south of Sandringham changes from heavy cunjevoi-covered mud to light clay with very little growth apart from patches of mussels inshore.

From Black Rock to Beaumauris Bay is one of the few natural reef areas in Port Phillip, and while there is little scope for land-based anglers along here, boats fishing close in do well. Be careful at night because navigation hazards abound here. Boats can be hired from Keafers Boat Sheds in Beaumaris Bay and there are more boat hire and launching facilities at Mordialloc.

Mordialloc jetty is very popular with anglers fishing for

garfish, particularly in calm weather. Anglers fishing the pier on dawn and dusk catch the occasional snapper as well.

Other platforms along this section of the bay include the pier at the Beaumaris Yacht Squadron and the pier at Black Rock, both popular with casual and weekend anglers.

The extensive mussel beds off Aspendale, Edithvale and Chelsea produce a lot of small to medium-sized snapper from the end of January until at least the end of March.

Good launching and marina facilities in Patterson River gives access to a vast amount of productive ground through here, including the artificial reefs in deep water off Carrum.

Seaford pier is popular for garfish morning and evening, but few big fish have been taken here because the water is not particularly deep.

Out wide from Seaford and Frankston there are extensive grounds which produce excellent bags of snapper during the warmer months of the year.

The excellent launching ramp in Kananook Creek at Frankston is 6 lanes wide and can handle quite a bit of traffic. Another ramp located nearby at the foot of Olivers hill is exposed in any sort of onshore weather.

The Frankston pier produces good size barracouta under the pier lights at night, and good catches of small salmon, mullet and whiting during the day. In good weather excellent bags of garfish are taken here, particularly in early autumn.

From Frankston to Mount Martha uniformly good snapper fishing is to be had offshore, particularly during the months of October and November when spawning fish have just entered Port Phillip Bay. Prodigious catches have been made by anglers who are in the right spot when a shoal of fish is passing.

The pier at Mornington is noted for big snapper catches during and immediately after a strong westerly or nor'westerly blow. Just south of the pier, the rocks at Nunns walk at the bottom of Stachan Avenue are also productive.

There are two boat ramps at Mornington, one in the shelter of the pier on the Schnapper Point headland and one more exposed ramp suitable only for modest craft in the lee of Point Linlet at Fishermens Beach.

Although access for land-based fishermen is limited to the rocks at Mornington and Mount Martha, excellent catches of big snapper are taken close to shore all through this area, probably because the water falls away quickly from the rocks and beaches.

There is a good rock platform at Martha Point at Mount Martha where a variety of fish can be taken including snapper. Fish at dawn and dusk for best results in good weather. After and during an onshore blow you will catch big snapper from here throughout the day while the water remains milky. Access is from Bradford Road.

The artificial reef about 500 metres out from Mount Martha is marked with a yellow buoy and produces a variety of fish including snapper. The reef also marks the location of a drop-off into deep water from which anglers take good catches of snapper from September until the end of November.

There are a number of jetties and piers along this section of the bay, most of which produce good bags of garfish, whiting and small flathead. While snapper are sometimes taken from these structures, most would be regarded as flukes.

The beaches all through this section of the bay are popular with flounder spear-fishermen who work the shallows at night with a light. Out off Rye, the deep waters of Capel Sound produce excellent snapper, but observe the anchoring restrictions in the South Channel and Hovel Pile areas.

The deep water of the Sorrento Channel runs in close to shore and anglers need not venture too far out to be in productive snapper water. One popular spot in the Sorrento Channel is off Blairgowrie and is known as the Shark Hole. It produces a quantity of snapper each year.

The whiting grounds off Blairgowrie are excellent as well, with big bags of fish common. Likewise the vast expanses of shallow water between the main channels and all the way across to the Bellarine Peninsula produce excellent bags of whiting, yet receive very little attention because good catches can be made close to shore.

The pier at Sorrento produces whiting during the day and squid at night. A good many bait fish can often be seen under the lights above the landings on the inside of the pier at night. These in turn often attract barracouta which will take an unweighted whitebait without hesitation.

The boat ramp at Sorrento is limited, both in its capacity and in parking space.

There are a number of private jetties at Portsea but fishing is not permitted from these. However, there is a good pier at Portsea where a variety of fish can be taken.

Snapper fishing is the popular small boat fishing activity on Port Phillip Bay, especially in the summer months.

Geelong and Corio Bay

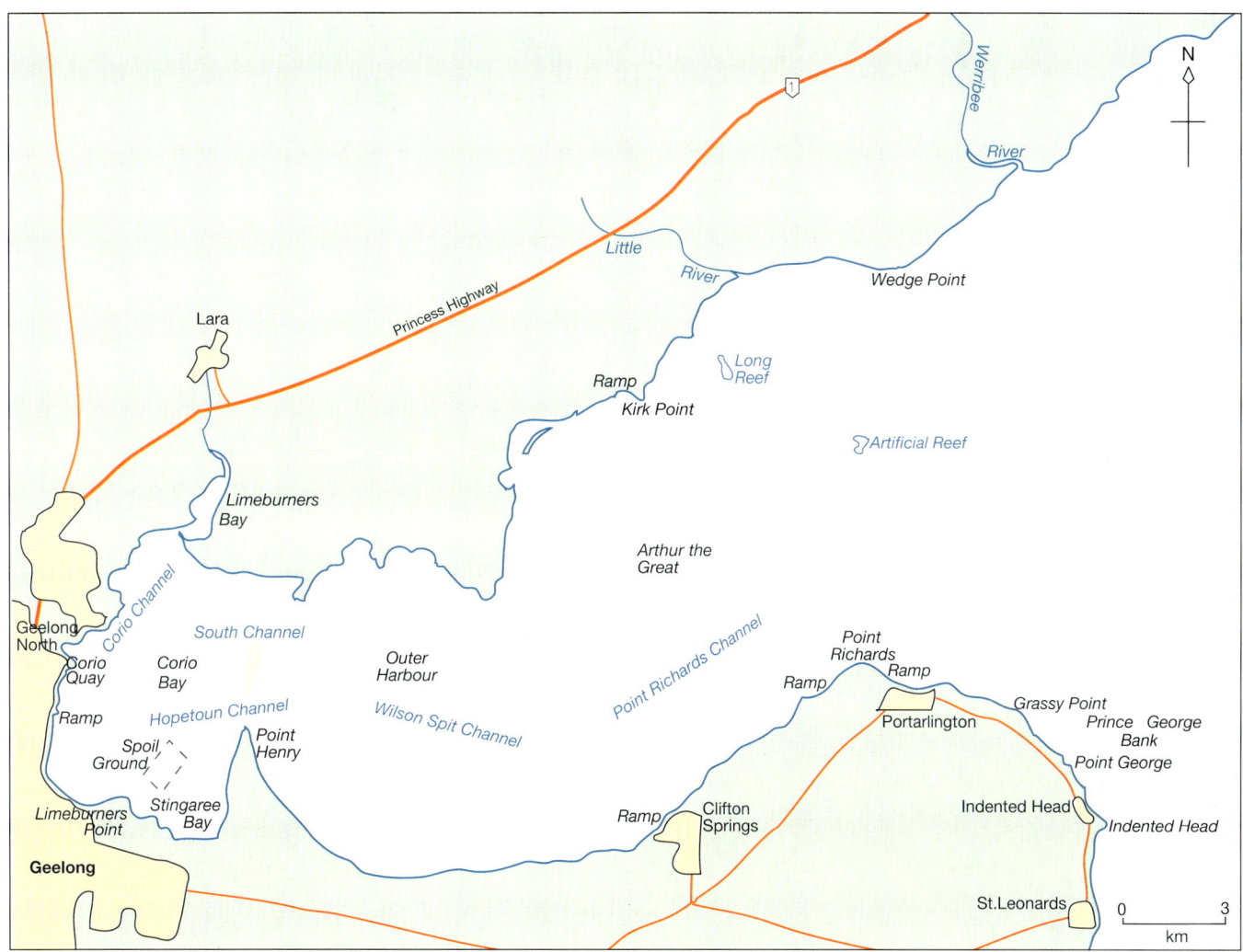

Corio Bay is divided into the inner and outer harbours by a sandbar which extends from Point Henry on the south side to Avalon on the north side. The city and port of Geelong are on the inner harbour.

The inner harbour can be fished from a number of jetties, all of which produce whiting and flathead on soft baits like pipis. These include Parkside, Rippleside and the jetty at the Geelong Grammar School Lagoon. The only pier you can fish from is Cunningham pier which produces trevally, barracouta, flathead and slimy mackerel when they are about.

There are boat ramps at St. Helens at the bottom of Swinburne Street in North Geelong, and at Limeburners Point in the Eastern Gardens near the Geelong Gun Club.

Good catches of snapper are made in Corio Bay inner harbour from late October until early December. Most anglers choose to fish along the banks of the shipping channels but the fish are spread out through the whole of the bay.

During winter, good catches of snapper are made close in along the western side of Corio Bay; in Corio Quay and in the rocks under the cliffs at North Shore. These fish remain densely shoaled in small areas.

During the warmer months of the year, the bay is alive with small flathead which are a nuisance if you are after snapper. The bigger flathead are generally caught in the shallows, particularly off Avalon. Big flathead can also be caught in the Geelong Grammar School Lagoon along with spotted ling and the occasional gummy shark. Snapper have been caught here too, but not many in recent years.

In the outer harbour, the only spot for land-based fishing is at Point Lillias, reached from the Avalon Beach road off the Princes Highway.

You will have a fifteen minute walk from your car. Using surf tackle, you can fish from the rocks for flathead, gummy shark, and the occasional snapper, in the evening.

The Avalon boat ramp is also accessed from the Avalon Beach road. Good catches of whiting can be taken straight out from here among the sticks of the old channel. The green stick nearest the ramp is a productive spot.

Be careful when navigating around to the left from the ramp or you will hit the reef surrounding Bird Rock. On no account pass Bird Rock on the shore side.

Deep water in the lee of Point Lillias holds flathead, snapper and other worthwhile varieties.

Proceeding further into this bay, you will eventually come to the South Cardinal Mark locating the wreck of the Annieura. The wreck area and surrounding ground produces good catches of snapper and whiting on dawn and dusk.

The Kirk Point boat ramp is at the bottom of Beach Road, reached after turning off either to Point Wilson on the 29 Mile Road or to Avalon Airfield from the highway.

The ramp is very exposed to weather from the south or east, but gives access to the productive Long Reef to the left of the ramp, and Arthur and the Great and Point Wilson Banks about three or four kilometres around to the right.

On the opposite side of the outer harbour, the ramp at the bottom of Jetty Road at Clifton Springs gives access to the Curlewis Bank for whiting, and the junction of the Wilson Spit and Point Richards Channels which is a great spot for snapper in late October and November.

Further out on the Peninsula the Point Richards ramp is situated at the bottom of Point Richards Road from the Portarlington Road. There is also a loading jetty and car and trailer parking.

Good whiting are caught from the Point Richards Bank; one of the best areas is marked with a stick around a kilometre to the west of the ramp.

Excellent snapper fishing is to be had a couple of hundred metres north of the number 3 and number 5 channel markers, 3 kilometres out. When there are snapper about, you will see many boats out here.

If it is too crowded here, move to the south side of the number 8 channel marker - another good spot, but not fished nearly as heavily.

The Werribee River flows into the west side of Port Phillip Bay and is a favourite among bream anglers. There is easy road access to the mouth at Werribee South where there is an excellent boat ramp.

The east or Melbourne side of the river is accessible only from K Road which runs close to the 'Willows' and the 'Barnacle Hole'. From here there is good walking access both up and down stream.

A permit is required to fish from the west or Geelong side of the river because this is all Metropolitan Board of Works Farm property. Permits are usually issued on application from the Werribee MMBW complex just off the main road into Werribee coming from Geelong.

Local blubber worms are good bait in the Werribee River along with crabs and bass yabbies. Other baits to produce fish include shrimp, soft-shelled clams and small freshwater yabbies. Packaged baits like pipis and prawns are also successful at times, but usually only on the smaller fish.

The fish move within the estuary to some extent; if you have not had a bite for a while, 50 metres can make all the difference.

Late spring is probably the best time of year to try for bream because there is a lot of spawning activity at this time. However, they will remain throughout the year provided there is no major flooding in the estuary.

Boat fishing off the coast from Port Phillip Bay to Apollo Bay can be exceptional. Snapper, salmon, whiting and flathead are some of the most sought after species.

Barwon Heads to Apollo Bay

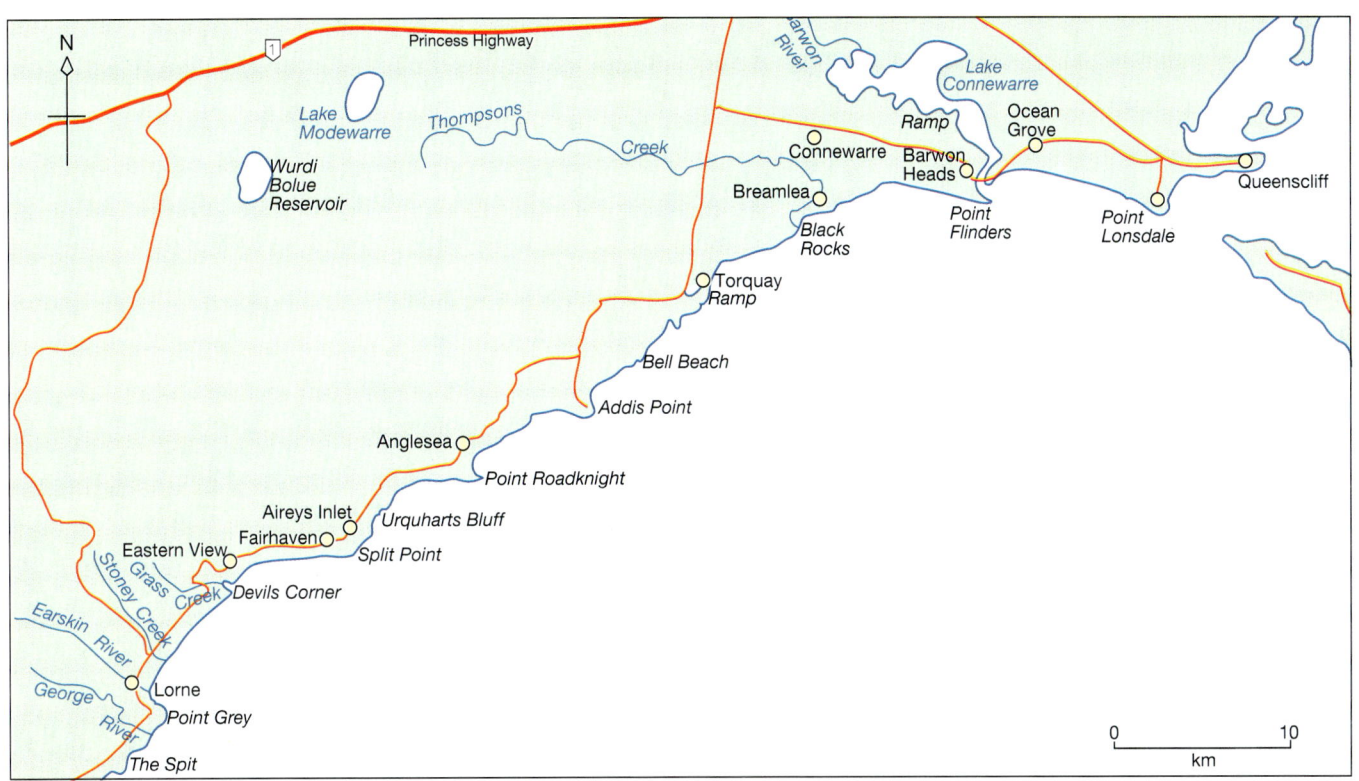

A luderick from the Barwon River. The river fishes best in autumn for all kinds of estuary species.

The estuary of the Barwon is open to the sea at all times and is fiercely tidal with a strong current on both the ebb and flood tides. The easiest time to fish the Barwon estuary from the bank is from the last hour of the ebb tide until 2 hours into the flood. Autumn is the best season to fish the Barwon.

The estuary contains small salmon, mullet, silver trevally, bream, luderick and mulloway, all of which respond to appropriate techniques.

There are boat ramps at the bottom of Guthridge Street in Ocean Grove, and Sheepwash Road at Barwon Heads. The river is shallow in many places between the ramps and the entrance so do not attempt the journey without local guidance.

The Black Rocks sewer outfall to the west, produces good catches of whiting and snapper for most of the year. The sewer line has now been extended well off shore making fishing more pleasant, but the fish are still accessible.

The Torquay boat ramp gets covered with sand from time to time, but it does give access to excellent flathead ground 4 kilometres offshore. Barracouta are available nearly all of the time, with big whiting close to the ramp from August until November.

The Fishermens Reach east of Zeally Bay caravan park

fishes best on the bottom of the tide when you can wade out far enough to cast into productive water for snapper and whiting. Late winter and early spring are good times to fish here.

The Anglesea boat ramp is for experienced operators only. Most local operators launch from the beach beside the ramp in the lee of Point Roadnight.

The Anglesea River produces a lot of small bream: most of the bigger fish are taken upstream toward the power plant.

The surf beaches fish best on evening and preferably with a low tide when the swell is down. Small snapper, whiting, salmon and the occasional mulloway are taken here. The back beach of Point Roadnight is recommended.

Grassy Creek is the most rewarding of the many spots to fish on the way to Lorne. Continue past Eastern View (which fishes well for salmon in the surf at night), and park on the left at the top of the hill immediately past Spot Creek. The rock platform is below.

Around to the west, about 24 minutes walk from the car park, over the shallow creek, is a better platform still. It has little kelp in front of it and a pool to lead fish into on the left.

Between Reedy and Stony Creek as you approach Lorne you will find some excellent rock platforms. Mullet are the main species caught from here with snapper, whiting and salmon taken at evening time.

Mullet are caught in good numbers from the Lorne pier, but garfish, silver trevally and salmon all come in from time to time. Sharks and barracouta bite at night. Big whiting and good-sized snapper are taken from here as well, particularly in the autumn. Evening is the best time for these.

The Erskine River estuary contains bream, estuary perch and mullet. The stretch between the Ocean Road Bridge and the sea is productive and upstream from the bridge, pan-size brown trout are caught in good numbers on scrubworm and shrimp.

The Point Grey reef shelters the pier. In the lee of the point, good catches of garfish can be made fishing small baits of worm or pipi under a float, and rock blackfish are also caught here from time to time. The outside of the point is too dangerous to fish on most days.

The St. George River just west of Lorne fishes well for mullet and salmon trout on the incoming tide. Deeper holes upstream from the bridge produce the occasional good-sized bream. If you are fond of walking, the upper reaches contain pan-sized brown trout.

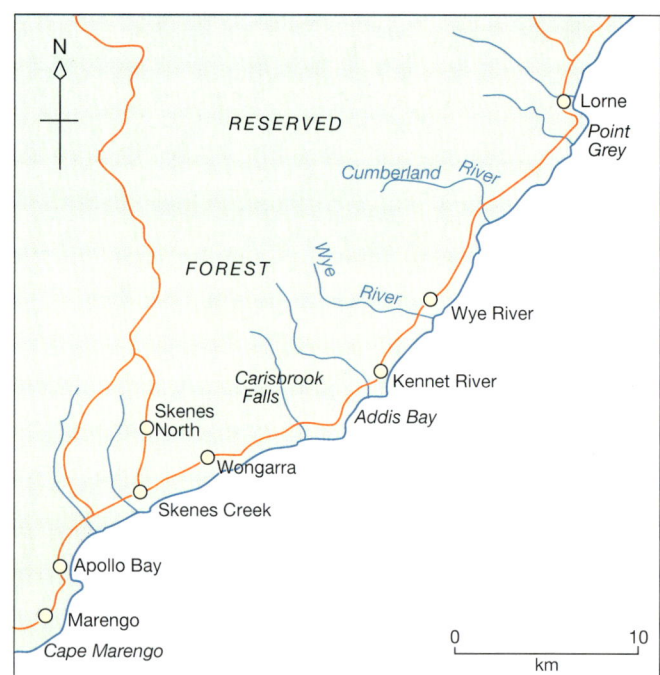

The Lorne boat ramp is right beside the pier. The ramp structure is sound but launching is dangerous with any sort of a swell running.

There is another ramp suitable for small boats only beside the main one. This ramp does not seem to suffer the same problems as the main ramp.

On the right of the pier, in the shelter of Point Grey, is a little sandy stretch between two reefs which is used for launching and retrieving boats. It is only supposed to be used in an emergency, but is used often. A four-wheel drive is recommended.

Mako sharks such as this specimen are often taken out from Apollo Bay.

The She Oak River mouth rocks on the Lorne side are pushed up sharply giving access to deep water, but the platforms are uncomfortable. Mullet are caught from here during the day and small snapper, whiting and salmon are caught in evening.

Casting into the sheltered bay at the river mouth with lures, you are likely to take a good bag of salmon, particularly on evening.

Cumberland River fishing is limited to a fairly shallow beach at the mouth which produces good catches of mullet. Rocks on the right-hand side produce parrot fish.

Upstream from the Great Ocean Road bridge, excellent catches of pan-size brown trout are taken on both bait and lures. This is a magnificent stretch with huge rock escarpments overlooking the stream.

The rocks at the base of Mount Defiance are noted for good catches of snapper during autumn but there are many more species to be caught there as well. On bait you will catch gummy sharks, whiting and occasionally a salmon. Using lures you will take salmon and barracouta. A 4 kilogram yellowtail kingfish has been taken here, too. Access is down a track from the Great Ocean Road to the left of the Howard Hitchcock lookout.

Artillery Rocks on the left after crossing Jamieson River is the most popular rock platform along the stretch between Lorne and Apollo Bay, with salmon being taken

here in good numbers. Most anglers fish from the platform directly below the track, but there are many fishing possibilities from these rocks.

Boggaley Creek rocks form an inner and outer platform with a wide gutter between. The quarry from the inner platform is garfish, but when they are about you will need to be there early to get a spot.

The Wye River is a noted resort with a hotel, shops and many options for the angler. The river produces good bags of pan-size brown trout fishing with either bait or lures. The rocks in the shelter of the point produce good catches of garfish.

The most prominent rock in the shelter of the point is known as 'Old Baldy'. It stands out a little from the rest and generally fishes well if the sea allows you to get onto it.

The Point to the right of the town is known as Radio Point because of the Telecom installation here. It is a leisurely stroll down to the rocks from where you park your car. The deep sand hole in the lee of the point is obvious and produces whiting and flathead during the day and small snapper at night.

Apollo Bay is the jewel of the Otways with excellent offshore, beach, rock and estuary fishing. The boat ramp is located in the sheltered harbour and protected from all conditions except an easterly swell.

Many anglers find the harbour meets all their fishing requirements, catching silver trevally from either the harbour walls or from a small boat within the harbour itself. Salmon and barracouta are also taken from time to time.

The estuary of the Barham River provides excellent fishing for bream both upstream and near the mouth. The best baits are scrubworm and shrimp. Estuary perch are also taken here by anglers who specialise in catching them. The Paradise Road gives access to good trout water within a couple of kilometres of the town.

Surf and rock anglers are well catered for with good rock platforms near the guest house between Carisbrook and Smythes Creek, on the eastern approach to Apollo Bay. Here you will catch garfish under a float and snapper on the bottom.

The Wild Dog beach as you enter Apollo Bay from the east, and Mounts Bay as you leave from the west, both produce good catches of salmon and some silver trevally on the evening.

The Beach at Marengo produces good catches of whiting, but you must fish the sandy patches between the patches of reef.

Left: A hefty snook and a smaller long-finned pike. These fish can be caught by trolling around Apollo Bay.

Warrnambool to Port Fairy

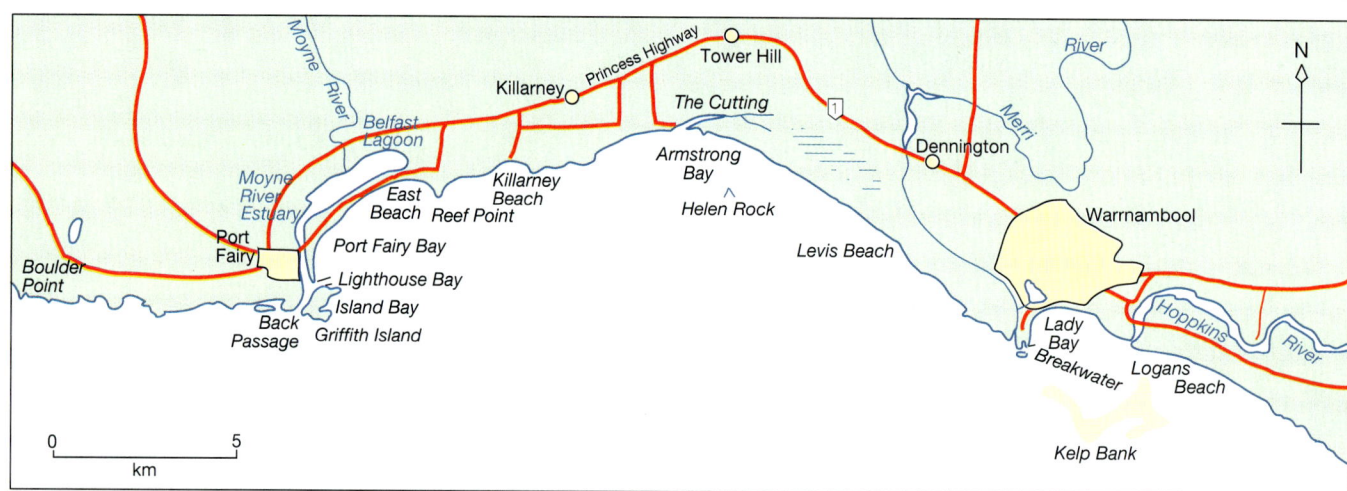

Warrnambool, located some three and a half hours to the West of Melbourne, offers an ideal base for fishermen looking for something different.

Whether an expert or novice, the scope in and around the town is enormous. The saying 'Warrnambool Has It' is quite true, good estuary fishing in the Hopkins, trout in the Merri River, salmon in the surf as well as plenty off shore fishing.

Throughout January and February there is a huge influx of tourists and vacationers into the town. This does make some of the spots a little crowded, but normally there are enough options to thin the crowds out.

There is an excellent fishing map of the area published by Southern Angler Publications - Fishing Map 3 Warrnambool. This outlines all the best spots, the rigs and baits, as well as other general fishing hints.

The Hopkins River is the most popular fishing venue in the area. Fresh bait and hire boats are available at the boat shed adjacent to the launching ramp. During the day smaller bream, mullet and occasionally estuary perch can be caught readily in all sections of the river from the launching ramps down to the mouth. Those wanting bigger specimens are better off fishing through the hours of darkness.

It is then that the bigger bream and estuary perch will be taken. Best method for the bream is a lightly weighted rig and live sandworm or bass yabbie. Estuary Perch definitely prefer the darkness and are best caught with a bait (worm) or a wet fly (Matuka) under a bubble float.

The surf has a lot to offer over Christmas with Logans, Levis and East beaches all producing good salmon during the day. Berleying helps immensely to attract and hold the salmon schools.

The Merri River has one of the best reputations in the

State for the freshwater angler. The section of the river between the weir and the river mouth holds some of the biggest brown trout.

During the summer it is best to fish up in the middle reaches of the river, around Dennington, Caramut Road to Queen Street. Lure casting as well as bait fishing are most productive for those fishing the banks of the Merri at this time of the year.

Best lures are Rapala Mini Fat Raps, Milsmaster Invincibles, Spinwell Tilos, Pegron tiger minnow and the ever-reliable celtas and ABU droppers.

By far the best times for lure casting are early morning and evening. Other areas that offer excellent trout fishing are the upper reaches of the Merri and Hopkins River. Of the upper sections of the Merri River (i.e. above the weir), there is good access and good fishing at Quinns, Brodies and McNamaras Roads at Woodford.

The upper Hopkins River waters, above the Tooram Stones, are fresh and are stocked by fisheries with trout. They also contain good stocks of estuary perch at certain times of the year.

In fact, the fishing on the Upper Hopkins River although ignored by many anglers, is one of the healthiest in the area. The best section is that below the Hopkins Falls and at the junction of the Mount Emu Creek and the Hopkins River.

The brown trout fishing between the Tooram Stones and the Hopkins Falls is the pick with plenty of fish between 1 and 2.5 kilograms. Again lure casting is the most productive way for the visiting angler to catch a brown trout. Above the Hopkins Falls there is plenty of scope right up to Ellerslie as the river consists of a succession of deep pools and runs.

One last species that should be of particular interest to the holiday fisherman at Warrnambool is the estuary perch. The estuary perch of the Hopkins river is vastly unexploited by anglers.

Fisheries reports and surveys indicate that there are more estuary perch in the Hopkins River than there are bream. The reason more are not caught is that fishermen do not fish for them correctly. As mentioned previously, night is the best time to fish and the preferred rig is a bubble float with the bait or artificial fly suspended below.

Catches of 20 to 30 in a session are not uncommon when fishing the lower section of the estuary over the spring and summer months. Best places are at the 'Danger Board', the Blue Hole, The Bridge and the cliffs. There is a closed season on estuary perch between 1 August and 30 November.

During winter the estuary perch move right up the estuary over the Tooram Stones and into the freshwater section of the river.

Overall, Warrnambool is a true angling mecca. The possibilities are endless with new species and techniques opening new ground both offshore and in the surf, estuaries and fresh water each season.

Port Fairy, to the west of Warrnambool has the distinction of being one of the more popular gamefishing ports.

The township has a long history. Many buildings classified on the National Trust back onto the scenic Moyne River that runs through the town. The launching ramp and jetty facilities located on the Moyne River provide easy, safe and protected conditions for launching.

The 'bar' - where the Moyne River enters the open waters of Port Fairy Bay is very docile. Fishing in the Bay is good and very popular over the summer months. Many fishermen anchor their boats 200 to 300 metres offshore and try for whiting. Island Bay is another good spot for whiting on calm days.

To the east towards Warrnambool the boat fishermen has the choice of the wider off-shore marks or, if it is calm, the in-shore areas off Killarney. There have been odd populations of yellowtail kingfish on the various reefs around Killarney and the Basin and even Griffith Island.

Out wide off Port Fairy there have been significant populations of southern bluefin tuna and sharks. The bluefin almost disappeared but in recent times have been making a comeback.

Lady Julia Percy Island is 20 kilometres from the entrance of Port Fairy and on calm days well worth a visit both for the scenery and the fishing.

All forms of southern gamefish inhabit the waters off Julia Percy. Trevally, sharks, including the famous white pointer and occasionally yellowtail kingfish and southern bluefin tuna. There are also stocks of bottom dwellers on the reefs in the area, including snapper and morwong.

Land based fishing around Port Fairy is also full of scope. There is excellent surf fishing along East Beach and at Killarney Beach. Salmon, whiting and snapper are all available over summer. In winter its gummy shark and salmon.

Fishing from the breakwalls to the harbour entrance can also be productive. The estuary of the Moyne River is an excellent family fishing venue. Mullet abound and in the cooler months there are good stocks of bream, salmon and trevally.

Finally there is a population of brown trout in the upper Moyne River for those interested in that sport.

Warrnambool presents a kaleidoscope of fishing options, including surf fishing for salmon as shown here.

Portland to Nelson

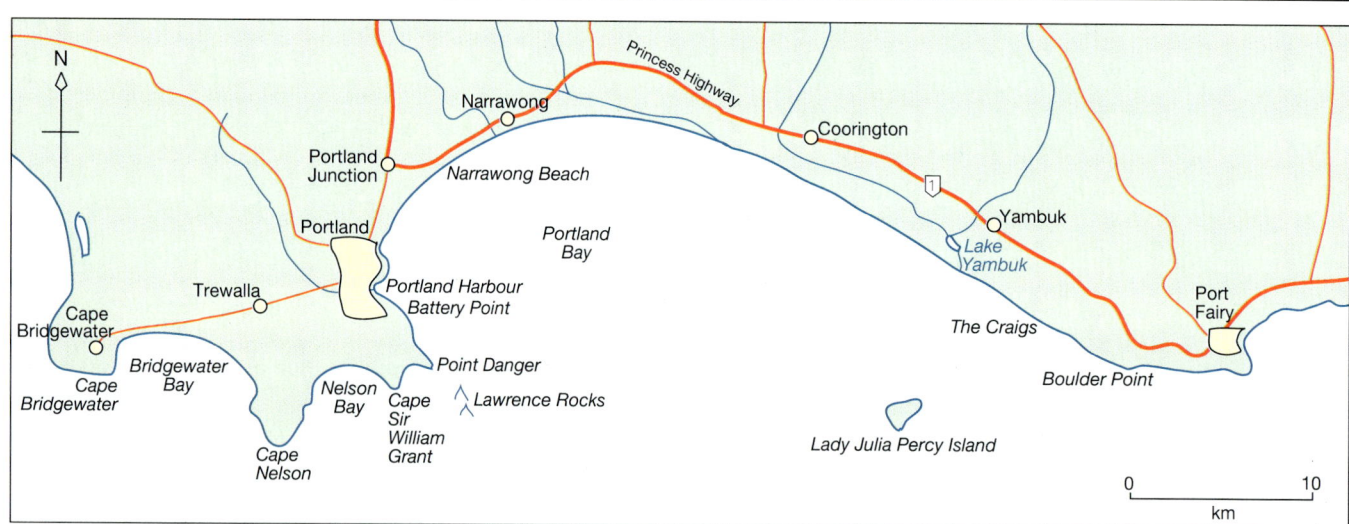

Narrawong Beach from the mouth of the Fitzroy to the mouth of the Surrey River, produces snapper, mulloway and salmon on a regular basis. Fish in excess of 3 kilograms are common in the evening and gummy sharks are taken after dark.

Access to the mouth of the Fitzroy River is clearly marked from the Princes Highway, but if you want to camp here make sure you bring everything you will need because there are no stores close by.

The Dutton Way rock wall produces good snapper both during and immediately after an onshore blow.

Anglers fishing a few hundred metres offshore regularly take good bags of whiting and the occasional snapper, particularly on evening.

There is an excellent boat ramp in the Portland Harbour, giving access to offshore grounds which produce sharks and bluefin tuna to sport and game fishermen.

Lady Julie Percy Island waters off Yambuck, back toward Port Fairy, are noted for big white pointer sharks and yellowtail kingfish. It is unwise to attempt fishing these waters with a small boat though.

Heading toward the Island from the boat ramp, you will come to the 'Cod Splat' about 4 or 5 kilometres offshore. Check your location by lining up the large white shed on the Lee breakwater with the conspicuous church spire in the background. To the west, align the triangular framed house down near the shoreline with the water tank up on the hill, and you will be correctly positioned on this fine snapper ground which produces a wide variety of other fish as well.

Portland Harbour from November until the end of March, produces snapper and whiting from virtually all of the structures within the harbour.

Popular spots are the Lee and Main breakwaters which are heavily fished through this time of year.

Yellowtail kingfish are sometimes taken from the breakwaters: the favoured technique is to fish the head of a freshly caught squid under a running bobby cork from the outside of the breakwater.

Silver trevally and warehou (sometimes incorrectly referred to as haddock or even hake, both of which are northern hemisphere fish and not present in our waters) are taken in good numbers from the structures within the harbour.

Portland represents one of the best western Victorian offshore fishing regions. Here, a big buck salmon is the catch.

The canal in the Portland harbour produces good catches of silver trevally on the incoming tide. Occasionally school mulloway have been taken here but this is not common.

Cape Nelson offers marginal access to rock fishermen for salmon, snapper, gummy shark and mulloway. Seas can be treacherous here and anglers have been drowned.

Access is from Scenic Road which follows the cliff top back toward Portland after leaving the Cape Nelson Road. Some of the tracks leading down to the sea from Scenic Road are easy to negotiate, others are dangerous.

Bridgewater Bay and Cape offer excellent fishing when sea conditions allow both from the beach and rock platforms.

Noted fish producing spots for salmon, snapper and the occasional good sized mulloway include Bishops Rock, Flat Rock and Shelly Beach.

In the lee of Cape Bridgewater and protected from prevailing winds and swells, Fishermans Cove and Fishermans Hut are reliable spots for all of the fish mentioned. It is a long walk in from the junction of Amos Road and the main road leading to the Petrified Forest.

Discovery Bay can be accessed from the Portland-Nelson Road down as far as Swan Lake where there are camping facilities and toilets. Access to the beach is via four-wheel

drive track or by foot, a distance of about 1 5 kilometres.

Good catches of salmon, snapper and mulloway are taken from the beach. Recommended baits include fresh squid and salmon fillets.

Cape Montesque is reached through the Discovery Bay Coastal Park and pine plantations after turning off the Portland Nelson Road about 1.5 kilometres past the Winnap turn off. This road leads down to Lake Monibeong where there are camping facilities (but no toilets) about 500 metres from the beach.

There is another access from the Portland-Nelson Road about 2 kilometres further along. This leads almost down to the beach just east of Nobles Rocks. Like the rest of Discovery Bay, Cape Montesque produces excellent catches of a wide variety of fish.

Nelson is a small settlement at the mouth of the Glenelg River. The estuary is well known for excellent catches of mullet, bream and mulloway, and estuary perch in the upper reaches. There are several boat ramps in the area including the main one in Nelson and another upstream from the bridge at Simpson's landing.

The majority of anglers fish between the bridge and the mouth of the river which is shallow and does not offer any access to the waters offshore.

The water becomes quite a bit deeper past Holloways drain, a minor creek flowing into the estuary, until it is about 5 metres deep at Flat Rock. After rounding McEacherns Point it becomes deeper again.

Pod worms are considered the best bream bait but if there are mullet and small salmon trout in the estuary, you will find it a problem to keep a bait on. Crabs, freshwater yabbies and soft shelled clams can be more effective under these conditions.

Anglers seeking mulloway do well by slow-trolling live mullet behind rowing boats between Flat Rock and McEacherns Point. Rowing is preferred to using a motor because the angler has more control and the motor tends to frighten the fish.

Upstream from Simpsons Landing there is good access from both sides of the river to the limit of tidal influence at Dartmoor, a distance of about 50 kilometres. The river is also navigable by boat for about the same distance.

Although not as prolific as they used to be, southern bluefin tuna are still caught by trolling off Portland.

Freshwater Fishing

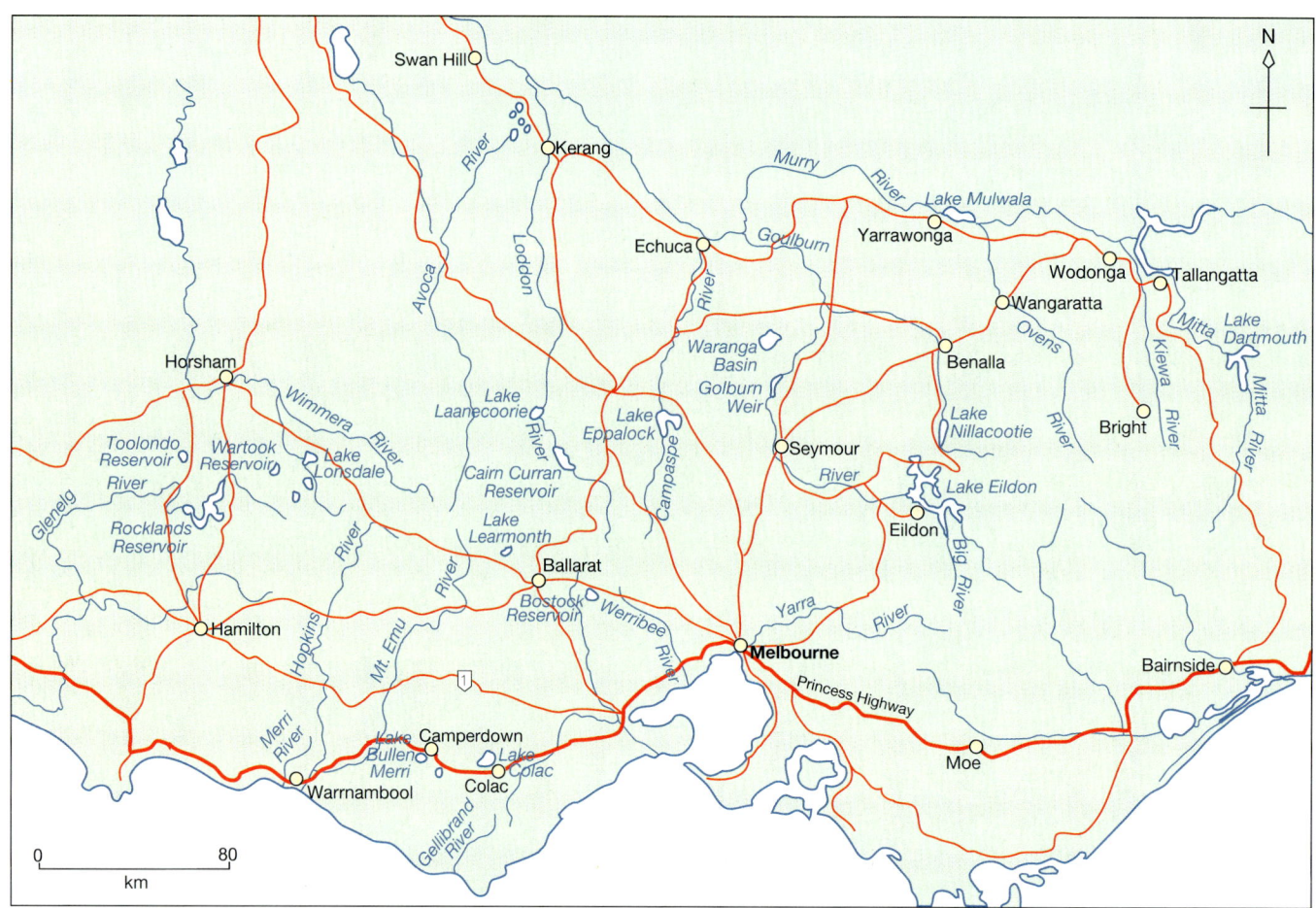

There are abundant native fishing prospects in Victoria. Lakes and rivers all over the state hold good stocks of Murray cod, trout cod, yellowbelly, Macquarie perch, silver perch and many more.

Techniques required to catch native fish in Victoria are similar to those used in other states, however, the use of bait is more popular. Nonetheless, the exciting sport of lure fishing is increasing in popularity.

The upsurge in stocks of native fish in Victorian waters has been the result of the combined effects of Fisheries stocking the waterways and the diminishing carp population.

Lake Dartmouth is the last stronghold in Australia of Macquarie perch. The fishery at Dartmouth is excellent.

To catch Macquarie perch worms or mudeyes presented well down (3-20 metres) on a sinker are required. Macquarie perch will rarely take lures. Best time is usually in spring and early summer.

Lake Eildon has stocks (both natural and introduced) of Murray cod in the Delatite Arm of the Lake. The cod

respond to deep diving cod lures and baits over the summer months.

Lake Mulwala, on the Murray River at Yarrawonga, has the best stocks of Murray cod in Victoria. They are very responsive to lures and trolled deep divers regularly produce cod between 2 - 6 kilograms. Old river beds are the best areas with the lure working right down near the bottom.

Murray River has made a come-back in recent years, especially with Murray cod and yellowbelly stocks. The best method is with bait during the early winter months of May and June when the water clears and lures are very successful.

Yarra River middle reaches offer good sport for native fish. The main species is the Macquarie Perch transplanted in the 1920's and 30's by local angling clubs.

The fishing is excellent from October to December. There are also limited stocks of Murray cod in some sections of the middle reaches.

Goulburn River below Lake Nagambie has excellent stocks and fishing for silver perch, Murray cod and yellowbelly. From Nagambie to Shepparton to Echuca, there are kilometres of river to explore.

The best fishing is over the summer months with bait fishing favoured. However, when the water clears lures come into their own.

The Wimmera area is known for its well stocked lakes and rivers. Green lake is known for Murray cod and yellowbelly; Taylors Lake for yellowbelly; Lake Charlegrark for Murray cod and the Wimmera river for yellowbelly and the occasional Murray cod.

The most productive fishing time in these areas is in October and November and through summer until April.

The Goulburn River along with its tributaries, the Acheron and Rubicon Rivers is the most popular trout river. This system is close to Melbourne and drains Lake Eildon. It is good for rainbow and brown trout all year round but is best in spring and autumn when all techniques, lure, fly and bait, produce fish.

Best areas include the Breakaway, Gilmours Bridge and the junction of the Goulburn and Rubicon Rivers.

The north-east High Country offers some challenging and spectacular fishing. The Mitta River between the township of Mitta Mitta and where it flows into the upper arm of the Hume Weir is great for big brown trout using lure casting. It is accessible from the Omeo Highway.

Other streams of the north-east that are excellent fly and lure waters include the Ovens, King and Alpine Creeks. The townships of Porpenkah and Dartmouth are excellent bases. Fishing these high country streams is excellent in late spring and summer. Fly-fishing and compact lure casting with spinner blade lures or light jigs are preferred.

The Alpine Country extends westward from these areas and on its western edge you have the rivers and streams that flow into Lake Eildon. The Big River, the Delatite, the Goulburn and the Howqua are just a few that offer excellent fishing at the right time of year.

Again, spring and summer are top times and as there is a strong run of fish out of the lake and up these rivers in winter, the prospects are good in May and June.

In the central area of the State there are a number of rivers that hold good stocks of trout and provide excellent fishing. The area around Ballarat is the starting point and the best rivers are the Mt. Emu Creek, some reaches of the Loddon, Caliban and Avoca, as well as the many small creeks in the area.

To the west, there are two famous rivers that hold the largest river run browns in the State, the Merri at Warrnambool and the Gelibrand in the Otways.

The lower reaches of the Merri runs right through the township of Warrnambool and, in stark contrast, the Gellibrand runs through the isolated rugged Otway Ranges.

Both, however, are reasonably accessible by road and both are best approached with lure casting techniques. The lower sections of each river are large enough to launch a boat and actually troll for trout.

Top: Fighting a big brown trout, a common catch in Victoria's freshwater rivers, to the bank.
Above: Success! A buck rainbow trout caught from Lake Murdeduke.

Tasmania

Introduction

Facilties in Tasmania are well established and first-class. As a recognised international fishing destination, the 'Apple Island' is well equipped to cater for fishermen, particulary in the highland trout fishing regions where the world flyfishing championships have been held. The championships attracted some of the most adept fly fishermen from around the world, and have cemented Tasmania's position high on the list of international fishing hotspots.

Tasmania has all manner of fishing; bluewater, estuary, coastal rock and pier, as well as freshwater.

Game fishermen must first battle the treacherous Tasman Ocean before reaching productive waters. Boats at least 6 metres in length are necessary, but once offshore the choice of angling targets makes the seaward journey worthwhile.

Southern bluefin tuna is the state's game fishing drawcard, having been caught to well in excess of 100 kilograms off the east coast. Mako and blue sharks are the most common catch, though albacore and striped tuna predominate throughout the game fishing season. Great white sharks, striped marlin, broadbill swordfish and kingfish are other sought-after species.

Back on the coast, Tasmania is surrounded by an abundance of bays and estuaries, each having their own unique character and charm. Fishing varies depending on population density, but remains worthwhile even in Hobart's Derwent Harbour. Flathead, whiting, southern bream, trevally, salmon, wrasse, and jack mackerel (cowanyoung) are just some of the available tablefish.

Despite the quality of Tasmania's saltwater angling, it is for its highland trout fishing that it's best known. The Great Lakes region boasts one of the healthiest and most prolific brown trout fisheries in the world. Faced with typically blustery weather, anglers are offered one of fishing's greatest challengers - to use a dry fly and tempt a big brown trout in the weedy shallows.

Experience that side of Tasmania's fishing and you're certain to return.

Tasmania is renowned for freshwater fishing. Anglers enjoy the quiet serenity of the highland lakes and streams.

Freshwater Fishing

Lakes

Lake Sorell is probably Tasmania's most productive and heavily fished lake. Every year there are trout taken from this location weighing in excess of 3 kilograms. Fishing this water is almost guaranteed a result.

The majority of trout taken are brown, although rainbows make their presence felt at times. Lake Sorell is a lure and fly-fishing area only, fishing with bait can bring a heavy fine and your tackle confiscated.

There is a launching ramp at Lake Sorell. As with most Tasmanian waters, keep an eye on the weather here because due to the lake's shallowness it can become quite rough in a very short time. Many anglers prefer to troll, covering great distances, and this method produces the heaviest bags. Each boat is allowed to troll only one rod per person.

There are a few basic lure patterns used, Cobra Wobblers being the most popular. Some brands are more successful than others but the Wigston variety are as good as any. Local makes are competitive and go by names such as Monks, Candles and Johnson. Other lures include Rapala Minnows, Nilsmasters and Pegron Spoons. One of the latest and most successful lures is the Rebel Crawdad, a small plastic freshwater crayfish imitation.

The lures previously mentioned are also used by spin fishermen. Spin fishing can be conducted anywhere in the lake except for the heavily weeded regions.

Lake Sorell offers good fly-fishing. The majority of fishing is wet fly-fishing. Fly patterns such as black and red Matuka, Mrs. Simpson, Yetti and Jumbuck are all successful.

Most anglers prefer to fish blind, covering as much area as possible. During spring, trout can be seen foraging in the shallow, vegetated areas of the lake. They can be spotted easily as their tails often protrude from the water, it is then a matter of putting the fly a foot or two in front of the fish. This will result in the take or refusal, more often the latter.

Lake Pedder is primarily trolling water Fish taken here in recent years are nowhere near the size of those taken from this water ten years ago, but nonetheless it provides good fishing. Nowadays the average sized fish weighs 1 to 2 kilograms.

The lake has good launching facilities and there is also a boat hire service.

The best time to fish is around Christmas when there is a hatch of Mudeyes (the larval stage of dragonflies), which create an interest among the fish. The best time to fish an imitation is just on dark when the fish start to move on the mudeyes.

The most popular trolling lures are any of the Minnow deep-diving range, closely followed by the Cobra Wobblers and Spoons. Trolling tackle is usually heavier because of the numbers of snags encountered. One of Lake Pedder's only drawbacks is the every-changing weather.

Great Lake is one of Tasmania's most central lakes and provides good fishing. It holds rainbow and brown trout and just recently there has been a release of Atlantic salmon in it. Its waters are very clear but this can be a disadvantage as it makes the fish very unapproachable.

Along with lure fishing, this water is also a bait fishery using wattle grubs. Although this method may not be as interesting as using a lure, it is certainly the most productive, especially after dark. Most anglers, after baiting up with their grub, cast it out and leave the rod set on the shore. Usually the line is placed on a stick or bottle and this is used as a strike indicator.

Some anglers prefer to cast and retrieve their grub slowly. Once a bit is felt, the reel is flicked out of gear and the fish allowed to run until it has had sufficient time to

Above: Brown trout from The Great Lakes area regarded as one of the great fishing areas in the world.
Next Page: Nearly every Tasmanian river and creek contains trout. This angler is upstream nymph fishing in the Elizabeth River.

swallow the bait. The reel is then put in gear and the fish is hooked. Most of the trout in this manner are rainbows, but occasionally they are outnumbered by the brown trout.

The Great Lake has good launching facilities and accommodation. Local knowledge is a big advantage as many fish congregate over hidden weedbeds. When trolling, deep-diving lures are helpful. Popular lures are 4 and 5 X Flatfish, Cobra Wobblers and Spoons.

Trolling large wet flies on unleaded line is particularly successful in weeded areas as the flies do not tend to snag the way lures do. Large fur-bodied flies and Matukaas are a good choice. Dark buck-tailed flies and Marabous are also very successful.

Great Lake also offers good fly-fishing in clear water. Working around the lakes' margins is a productive method to catch some of the lake's larger specimens, but care must be taken to keep out of sight as once a trout has noticed your presence, it will probably ignore your offerings and continue along the shore. During summer, there will be hatches of insects and good sport can be had pursuing the rising fish.

Presentation is more important than the type of fly used, and in very clear water a fine leader of tipet is necessary. Small black beetles are a good choice of fly, along with Nymphs and Woolly Worms to fall back on. Care must be taken when wading the shore because of the unevenness of the terrain. Small groups of dead trees provide good cover for the fish during the daylight hours so these places are always worth investigating.

Lagoon of Islands is primarily fly-fishing water with rainbow trout predominant. Fish average around 3 kilograms and instances of 5 or 6 kilogram fish are not uncommon.

Lake Crescent yields some of Tasmania's largest brown trout. There are ample launching facilities available and trolling and bait fishing are the two most popular methods employed.

Fly-fishing is rewarded with only marginal success because of murky water. The biggest fish in this lake are taken with small native fish called galaxius minnow, or minnow. Slightly heavier spinning tackle is required due to the snaggy area and the size of the fish. Use lures similar as those used to fish Lake Sorell

Lake Arthur, Tasmania's second most fished lake, has good launching facilities and camping area. Although the fish are generally small, they make up for this in their abundance. Bait, spinning and fly-fishing are all acceptable methods of capture.

During summer, this area offers exceptional fly-fishing, with large rises of Highland Duns.

Lake Leake has fast been growing into a very reliable fishery. Brown trout predominate over rainbows and the area offers good fly-fishing and spinning. Boat anglers have an advantage as access to some locations is difficult. The area has good launching facilities and the local anglers are happy to assist with advice.

Tackle

The most popular choice for a spinning outfit is a 2 metre spinning rod in fibreglass or graphite, on which is mounted a reasonable quality spinning reel filled with 2 - 3.5 kilogram line.

A trolling outfit consists of a more sturdy rod coupled with a slightly larger capacity reel spooled with 4 to 6 kilogram line.

Fly-fishing rods are best in the 6 - 7 kilogram line class, mounted with a medium-sized fly reel. holding at least fifty metres of dacron backing. Leader should be anywhere from 3 metres onwards, depending on the angler.

Landing nets can be fixed or folding: folding ones tend to be more popular because of their portability. For any further fishing information, contact Charlton's Sport Store in Launceston or Steve Bax at the Fishing Connection in Harrington Street, Hobart.

Tasmanian Trout Rivers and Creeks

Tasmania is blessed with many accessible freshwater rivers and creeks which contain good trout fishing. The majority of locations have stocks of fish and can be reached by a short walk from the roadside. If in any doubt about crossing property, it is best to ask permission.

Early in the season, the freshwater rivers and creeks are usually in flood, due to snow melt and excessive rainfall. Fishing the flooded backwaters can be highly successful.

The best lures for trout are the dark-bladed Celtas or Jensen Insect Spinner, although the most productive method is casting upstream with an unweighted worm. Another highly enjoyable way to capture these fish is to fly cast to them using small wet flies such as the Black Beetle, Robin and the nymph patterns. Due to the dirty water, tippet size is not critical, but presentation is, as the fish may have difficulty finding your offering in the discoloured water.

Later in the season, as the water clears, insect life becomes more prevalent, and the fish feed on the insects that are emerging and blown on to the water surface. At these times, lures only work in the faster waters, whereas the fly-fisherman comes into his own on the longer reaches and pools. Successful dry fly patterns include the Red Spinner, Highland Dunn, Black Spinner, Royal Coachman and Grey Duster.

Other species encountered in Tasmanian freshwater rivers and creeks are eels, cucumber herring, redfin perch, tench, and blackfish.

Anglers visiting during spring or early season may encounter sea-run trout, which have worked their way up from the mouth of rivers. These large fish can provide an unusual surprise in some of the smaller waterways. Methods used to take them are the same as those used for the resident trout. You are able to tell a sea-run trout by its silvery appearance, and characteristic dark-red flesh, which is highly prized on the table.

The most popular river fishing locations

In the northern half of Tasmania, small rivers and creeks predominate. Although good fishing water can be reached in the south within 30 minutes from Hobart, the choice of location is more limited than in the north.

The Tyenna and North-West Bay River (at Margate) hold large heads of small trout, which will readily accept baits and lures.

The North Esk and Huon Rivers contain fewer large fish, which are better 'educated' and exceptionally difficult to approach and hook.

Saint Patrick's River, South Esk and Brumby's Creek (at Cressy) are excellent trout fisheries.

The township of Perth, in the north of the state, is the most feasible venue for northern trout fishermen. The township lies on the South Esk River which holds large numbers of small fish from 0.5 to 1 kilogram. Any method of capture may be employed.

Hadspen picnic grounds is another popular northern trout fishery. It is a safe and productive angling location for fishermen of all ages and capabilities.

In southern Tasmania, easily accessible waters include the upper Derwent River, Huon River, Brown's River, and the Styx River.

The Derwent River is the most accessible river from Hobart. It frequently harbours large numbers of fish in its upper reaches. Derwent Bridge and Plenty are among some of the most popular locations visited during the season.

Waters Reserved for Artificial Lures
Lake Leake, Lake Sorell, Lagoon of Islands are the main ones. There are many other and this information can be gained from Inland Fisheries via their fishing codes.

Legal Minimum Sizes
Brown Trout, Rainbow Trout, Brook Trout and Tasmanian Blackfish - 220 mm.

Bag Limits
There is a bag limit on the number of trout an angler can take during the course of a day. The bag limit is 12 fish per angler per day.

For further information you can obtain pamphlets from the Inland Fisheries Commission, or The Fishing Connection in Harrington Street, Hobart. In Launceston an outlet for this information is Charletons Sports Store.

Saltwater Fishing

Rock Fishing

Rock fishing in Tasmania is undeveloped, although the potential is exceptional. Many fish inhabit the state's coastal waters from garfish to southern bluefish tuna.

The most sought-after species is Australian salmon, taken in large numbers (along with barracouta) from rocky outcrops along the coast. Flathead and cod are the other main recreational species. Whiting may be captured in the more sheltered bays and inlets. Bastard trumpeter, and sweep offer productive fishing, though they aren't caught in large numbers.

Garfish inhabit the still waters of sheltered bays and respond to bread and catfood berley. Once attracted, large numbers can be caught, as well as jack mackerel, mullet and juvenile salmon.

Luderick are found in most northern areas of the state, especially around St Helens where they may be caught with a piece of crayfish tail or green lettuce weed floated in the wash.

Land-based game fishing is unexplored in Tasmania. Pelagic fish such as skipjack tuna, albacore, kingfish and southern bluefin tuna are possibilities.

Eddy Stone Point is good rock fishing. During summer, the area has abundant supplies of salmon, kingfish, and skipjack tuna, with yellowfin tuna for those anglers prepared to live bait.

St Helens, yields tailor, yellowfin pike, trevally, and luderick in large numbers.

Because the water temperature is fairly high, prawns can be scoop or drag netted. Flathead also abound.

One of the best places to fish is the breakwall at

Offshore from the rugged southern Tasmanian coastline gamefishing for bluefin tuna, albacore and skipjack is increasingly popular.

Georges Bay. Out on St Helens Point, spinning for salmon, pike and barracouta is productive, with every chance of catching a small tuna or kingfish in summer.

Bicheno has good spots at the Gulch and the breakwaters. Numerous weed-dwelling species, such as leatherjackets, bastard trumpeter, perch or mowong and trevally, are taken from the area. Good fishing can be found anywhere in this area from the rocks, but a watchful eye must be kept on the swell. Due to the rough nature of the bottom you should lose some tackle.

Cod also frequents these areas and can be taken with a fixed bait on the bottom.

Triabunna is sheltered with good fishing from the rocky beaches or one of the built-out breakwaters.

Closer to Orford there is good flathead fishing around the Prosser River mouth. North from Point Bailey, large numbers can be taken from the rocks.

Eagle Hawk Neck has good fishing in front of the Pirates Bay car park. Large numbers of barracouta and pike are taken by spinning from the large, flat, rocky outcrops. Bottom species include cod, perch or morwong, parrot fish, leatherjackets and trumpeter.

Estuary Fishing

The Derwent River has many different species of fish. When large schools of spotted trevally move into the river huge numbers are taken from waterfront areas.

Resident species include bream, flathead, cod, whiting, perch, mullet, flounder, school sharks and salmon. The large number of launching facilities gives access to all fishing spots and there is ample water frontage available to shore-based anglers.

In Frederick Henry Bay flathead are the most sought after species, but flounder rate a close second along with cod and bastard trumpeter. There are ample launching facilities at locations such as Dodges Ferry, Cremorne, Lauderdale and Primrose Sands.

Dodges Ferry has flathead, whiting, perch, school shark, mullet and salmon. During summer oarfish can be taken in large numbers from the rocks or from a boat.

The waters in the Lewisham area are famous for large numbers of flounder. These are pursued during darkness with a light and hand spear in the sandy shallows.

The Carlton River which is always a prolific spot for salmon, either spinning in it or trolling around the river mouth or any of the rocky outcrops further down the coast. Sometimes large numbers of juvenile barracouta can be encountered, so it pays to put a short length of wire on the end of your lure.

In the bay, good-sized tiger flathead are always a possibility. These fish are excellent eating and can average a kilogram or more. They can be found all over Frederick Henry Bay but areas such as Sloping Island and Cremorne are productive.

School or snapper sharks, sometimes encountered when drifting for flathead can provide a real challenge on spinning tackle.

Sometimes when drifting you may encounter areas of rocky bottom and can expect to pick up a few perch and cod. Large leather jacket may also be caught.

Triabunna and Orford, offers a greater variety of fish with a more exposed waterway. The boating angler can expect to encounter silver trevally, pike and snotty trevally as well as the usual cod or flathead. There is good rock and beach fishing available for the shore-based angler, too.

The beach situated in front of the Orford Caravan Park is productive as is the Prosser River mouth. The Prosser River, flowing through the township of Orford, contains good bream, juvenile salmon, trevally and the occasional sea-run trout.

Anyone in search of a good catch of flathead would be well advised to try in front of the wood-chip mill.

After January, schools of striped tuna will come far enough inshore to be caught by the trailerboat angler.

Little Swanport, situated on the edge of the Swanport River, is Tasmania's bream fishing capital.

Game Fishing

Tasmania has good game-fishing potential. From January to June or July, you can encounter anything from a one kilogram salmon to a 200 kilogram broadbill swordfish. The southern bluefin tuna weighing more than 100 kilograms and in recent years yellowfin tuna have become increasingly prevalent.

At Bicheno and places further north, yellowfin tuna ranging from 10 kilograms to 100 kilograms school on the surface.

St Helens, a three-hour drive from Hobart, has adequate boat launching facilities, with a ramp outside Georges Bay for small vessels.

Aside from yellowfin tuna, large numbers of albacore and skipjack tuna abound, which attract striped marlin.

Small kingfish can be captured near the Continental Shelf by casting lures under the floating mats of kelp.

Bluefin tuna are also taken.

Maria Island which doesn't yield as many marlin at St Helens, has albacore, skipjack tuna and bluefin tuna.

On the eastern side of the island, there is a large expanse of fishable water, with many reefs and tide lines suitable for trolling. The washes on some of the larger exposed reefs provide the occasional kingfish, large trevally and barracouta on lures, making for a light-tackle paradise.

Access is by boat via Triabunna launching ramp or at the East Coaster Holiday Resort.

Eagle Hawk Neck is the center of Tasmania's bluefin tuna fishery, with a small charter boat fleet operating daily during the tuna season. Recreational anglers enjoy the vast, fishable coastline that yields more game fish than any other area in the state. It also has plenty of protected anchorages in the event of bad weather.

Anywhere from Pirates Bay to Cape Roaul, south of Port Arthur, is considered good trolling water for bluefin using large pusher-style lures, while smaller straight-runners such as feather jigs, whistlers, hexheads, pushers, and bullet heads are successful on the many skipjack, albacore and bluefin in the area.

The East Coast is a highly productive shark fishery, and any port with access to deep water is a viable location.

Mako sharks are common, with an occasional specimen taken on the troll, but many more are encountered by berleying and fishing with whole small tuna, tuna fillets, or live cowanyoung as bait. They range in size from small 1 metre specimens to 5 metre monsters.

Blue sharks, a close relative to the mako, are prolific in Tasmanian waters, and respond to the same techniques. They arrive in large numbers during spring and make interesting fishing on light tackle.

White pointers have been hooked by local game fishermen, but due to inadequate tackle the encounters have been brief. These sharks are feared by Tasmania's abalone divers who refuse to work the deeper waters off the Tasman Peninsula, where there are seal colonies.

South Australia

Introduction

South Australia is endowed with a unique fishery. While it lacks many of the glamorous game and sport fish common in more temperate waters, it is richly populated with some of the very best table varieties in the country.

Although the Southern Ocean washes the state's coastline in the south and far west, it is Spencer and St Vincent's Gulfs which hold most interest for both commercial and recreational anglers. These vast, but quite shallow inlets are home to all manner of fish, ranging from the humble tommy ruff to the majestic white pointer.

It is for enormous snapper, however, that South Australian fishing is best known. These hump-headed giants are commonly caught at ten kilograms and scarcely raise an eyebrow until they weigh better than fifteen kilograms. Located in both deep and shallow areas, reds of these proportions are tough, tenacious fighters and it is little wonder that many fishermen specialise in them.

Only slightly behind the snapper in popularity is the King George whiting. Regarded by many as the best eating fish in Australia, the whiting is prolific right across the state. It forms the backbone of a thriving industry.

Giant mulloway, many of which are taken at better than thirty kilograms each season, have also become popular with both surf and estuary fishermen. The mouth of the Murray River, in fact, is considered by knowledgeable anglers as the best mulloway spot in Australia. The fact that most of these big jew are taken on lures adds to the exciting nature of the fishery.

It is no blue water angler's paradise. Game fishing is confined to sharks, a few kingfish and the occasional bluefin tuna.

As for much of the Australian coastline, South Australia is weather affected virtually all year round. Winter northerlies give way to persistent south-westerlies in the warmer months, which whip up short, steep and generally uncomfortable seas in both gulfs. But wind is a fact of life to South Australians and there is little choice other than to grin and bear it.

South Australia's coastline with its endless kilometres of beaches provides surf fishermen with unlimited fishing. This angler spins a gutter near the mouth of the Murray River for salmon and mulloway.

Mount Gambier to Kingston

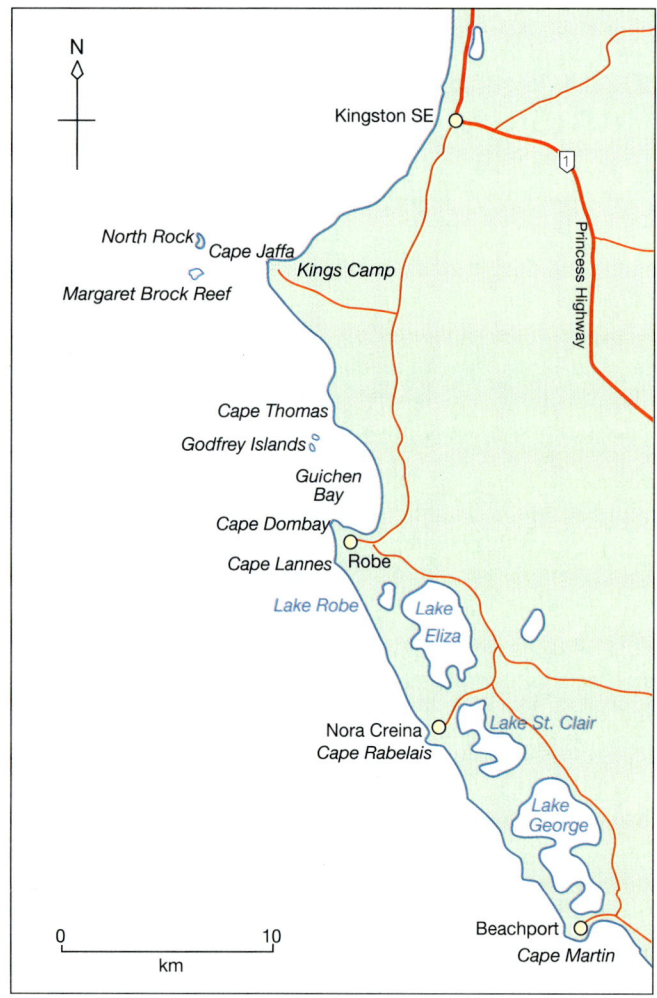

Despite being prone to long bouts of turbulent weather the south-eastern shoreline is very productive both for the land-based and offshore angler.

The picturesque Glenelg River mouth, near the township of Nelson, is popular with estuary fishers during spring and summer. Bream, salmon trout, mullet and school mulloway are the main catch, with the odd larger mulloway grabbing a bait from time to time.

Accommodation is easily located in most of the major centres in the State's south-east. Well-maintained caravan parks can be found at Robe, Kingston, Beachport, Mount Gambier and Millicent.

Port MacDonnell, a short drive south of Mt Gambier, is regarded as one of the most productive areas for light-tackle game fishing. Southern bluefin tuna and mako sharks are the most sought after species. Although school tuna have been spasmodic in recent years, a game fishing competition is still based around them each June.

The sharks, makos, blues and hammerheads are regularly encountered year-round. All that is required with them is a boat with offshore capabilities and a copious supply of berley.

Beachport and Robe, have good boat launching facilities. Robe is home to a thriving shark and rock lobster fishing fleet. Amateurs anglers can locate good hauls of snapper, morwong, garfish and King George whiting out from Robe.

Navigating into and out of Robe can be difficult for those unfamiliar with the area. Outside the breakwalls, low reef leads into both harbours making an accurate navigation chart essential for visitors.

Cape Jaffa is rapidly gaining in popularity with recreational anglers. The jetty yields good catches of tommy ruff, garfish and mullet, while there's class angling offshore.

The Margaret Brock Reef, attracts Adelaide-based anglers with big salmon, trevally, monster whiting, snapper, morwong and a host of other reef species.

The long jetty at Kingston, used primarily by the rock lobster fleet, has top fishing.

When the cray fleet is unloading its catch big mullet roam the shallows. Uncooked cray tail is one of the best baits from Kingston pier.

For those anglers equipped with heavy tackle, some of the bulkiest stingrays in the State patrol the sandy sea floor at Kingston. Youthful anglers often sit all night at the end of the jetty waiting for several hundred kilograms of stingray to swallow their baits.

Canunda Beach, is a reliable producer of school-sized jewfish, with the odd bigger specimen taken occasionally. Fish of between 5 and 9 kilograms are considered average.

Although weather plays a vital role in all forms of fishing in the State's south-east, summer provides the best fishing. These are quite windy months and seriously curtail rock and offshore angling. April through June has the most stable and predictable weather and most serious sport and game fishermen visit the area then.

Offshore from Robe, there have been a number of large broadbill swordfish taken on professional longlines at Kingston and Port MacDonnell. A handful of dedicated members from the South Australian Game Fishing Club have spent several nights drifting the depths of the Continental Shelf, using cyalume sticks and whole squid for bait, but to date only mako and blue sharks have been taken in this manner.

The Murray

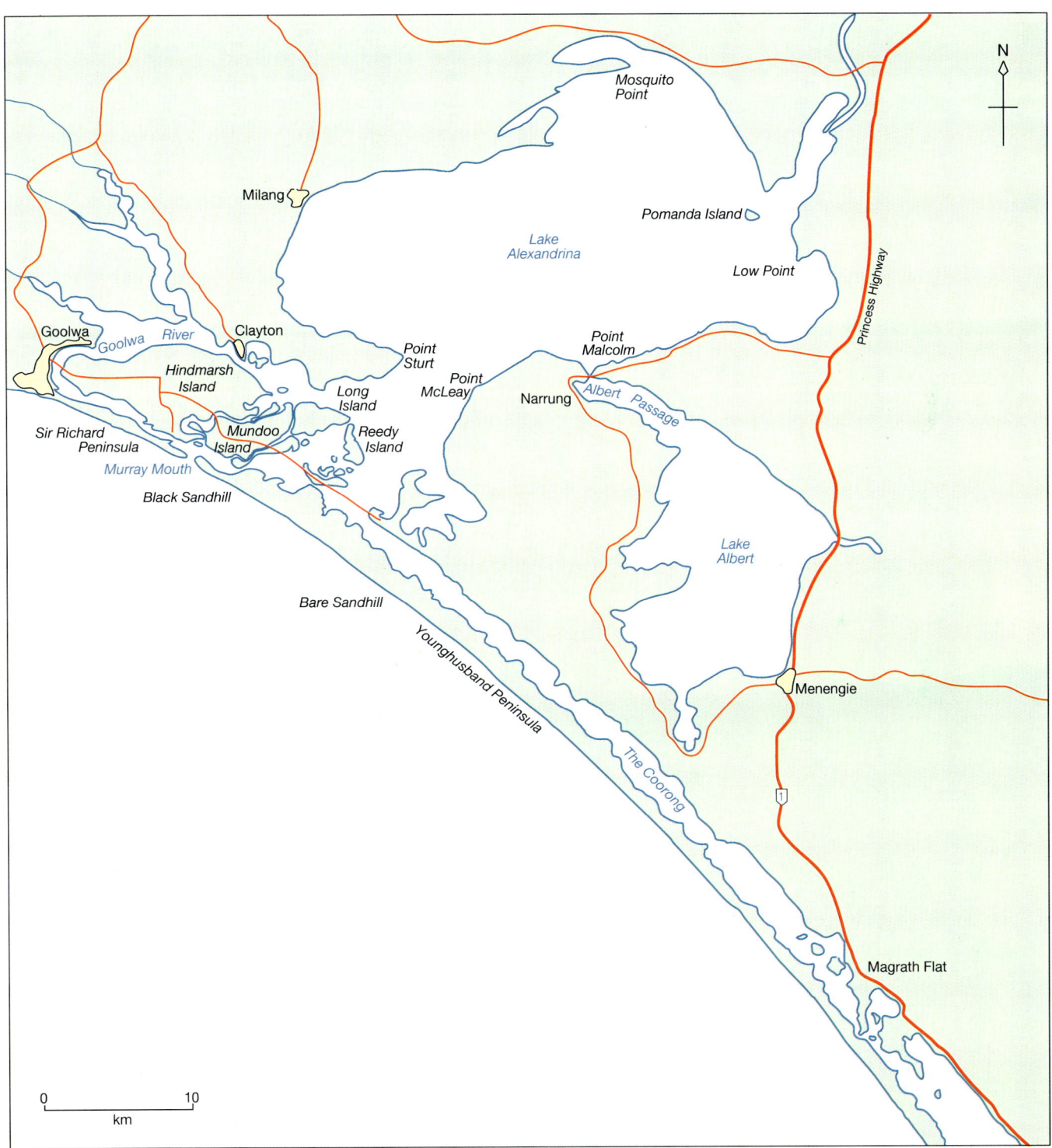

Access to the vast expanse of surf beaches and low sandhills of this area is restricted to just a few places. However, anglers with four-wheel drive vehicles can search endless miles of inshore surf for likely fishing formations.

Mulloway, salmon and a variety of shark species are found along this stretch of beach, but because it fronts the Southern Ocean, it is regularly 'churned up', and occasionally unfishable. After a southerly storm, a build-up of decaying seaweed can choke up long stretches of beach.

183

One of the most popular access points to the beach is at the 42 mile crossing, near the small settlement of Salt Creek. Drivers can leave the sealed road and cross the Coorong to the beach. The beach and sandhills are part of a slender sliver of land known as the Younghusband Peninsula.

For inspiration for an all-night session fishing the surf, visit the Salt Creek Roadhouse. A 'brag board', featuring snaps of some of the best mulloway taken in the area, keeps appetites whetted.

Remember that this is a National Park and permits are required for camping at the beaches in future without fear of having their vehicles banned.

The mouth of the Murray river has been labelled as one of the hottest surf fishing locations in the country. It is easy to catch salmon trout or mullet where the river meets the ocean. But the real lure is the monster mulloway to be caught in the area.

When the Goolwa barrages are opened to lower the river level, millions of litres of fresh water are flushed out through the mouth. Hundreds of dead or dying golden perch, redfin, carp, tukari (bony bream) and congoli attract vast schools of mulloway.

Lure casting seems the most productive angling technique. The most productive mulloway strikes are after dark, but when the bite is really a hot one, the River mouth can be an all day fishing proposition.

The Coorong Lagoon, which stretches for hundreds of square kilometres is Australia's largest true estuary system. Mulloway (usually ranging from under-sized specimens up to around 10kilograms) bream, mullet and juvenile salmon are quite common inside the Coorong. Spearing flounder after dark with the aid of a spotlight is also a popular Coorong pastime.

Because of the area's importance as a breeding and nursery area, local Department of Fisheries enforcement officers maintain a constant vigil to ensure that the Coorong's delicate ecological balance is kept well in check.

A small boat is sufficient to fish most Coorong waters. Launching ramps are located near number 19 beacon, west of the Murray mouth and also in several locations on Hindmarsh Island.

Navigation inside the Coorong, and especially in the area directly behind the Murray mouth, can be hazardous due to undetected sandbars. When the water is discoloured, these sandbars can be impossible to locate.

Caravan park accommodation is plentiful around the Coorong and its ocean beaches. There is a park on Hindmarsh Island which provides ready access to upper Coorong waters as well as the Murray mouth. Both cars and trailerboats can be taken onto the island by ferry, which operates from Signal Point, Goolwa.

The Coorong Beaches is South Australia's most productive fishing region. The mullet are plentiful as demonstrated by this catch.

Mulloway of the size shown here are not uncommon around the Murray River mouth.

Murray River Freshwater Fishing

The Murray River originates in the Snowy Mountains and flows through hundreds of kilometres of agricultural land before spilling into the Southern Ocean near Goolwa.

The fishing on the river has changed dramatically with overfishing of the native species, the introduction of several unwelcome European imports and a general decline in water quality throughout the Murray's entire length.

Salinity levels in the river is on the increase downstream and by the time the water has been used by farmers it is quite salty and perpetually turbid.

Despite all of this, it is still possible to find a few native fish in the lower reaches, but the abundance of carp will test the patience of all but the most dedicated freshwater specialist.

Between Barmera and Mannum, callop or golden perch, murray cod and the occasional silver perch are all taken. Lure fishing for natives is rarely viable because of the river's coffee colouration. Sonic lures, such as Rattling Spots, have been responsible for the odd cod and callop but it is generally more productive to soak a bait around the base of a bankside willow or prospect the margins of a flooded backwater with a bunch of worms.

The abundance of European carp has had one positive effect; at least it is now possible to take youngsters to the river and be assured of a good catch. Carp in excess of 10 kilograms are encountered regularly in some of the swamps and backwaters around Cobdogla and similar locations.

Redfin, once prolific have suffered at the hands of the carp population.

The most popular baits used in the Murray are tiger worms and live shrimps. Worms can be purchased from most tackle stores, and shrimps are easily caught in baited drop nets or in scoop nets worked through inshore reed beds.

Those who specialise in chasing big cod will usually opt for live yabbies or small carp. Both can be effective and although cod numbers are no longer large, those who stick to the task will eventually be rewarded.

Mannum is popular because of its proximity to Adelaide. There is a car and passenger ferry as well as a numerous river-side shacks. Heavy water skiing doesn't help the the fisherman, but it is still possible to catch a few carp and the odd callop from around the snags.

Other popular downstream locations include Murray Bridge, Tailem Bend, Walker's Flat, Wellington and Swan Reach.

Renmark, Barmera, Loxton and Berri are spots where cod and callop are taken at above-average sizes.

The South Australian Division of the Australian Anglers' Association hold a freshwater championship event on the river each year, which often turns up some surprising catches.

Carp are the most regular species weighed in but callop, cod, tench, silver perch and the occasional redfin are also weighed.

The South Australian Freshwater Fishing Association is also concentrating its efforts on the Murray. It has planned some 'native species only' competitions. The halcyon days of big cod, heavy bags of callop and water clear enough to fish lures are long gone.

Victor Harbour

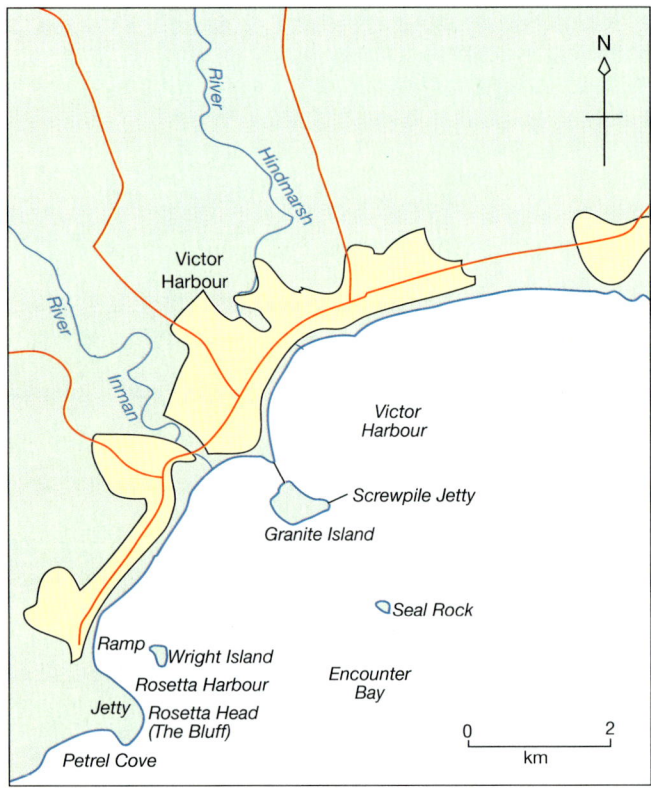

The population of Victor Harbor trebles over the Christmas break. This is the period when fishing, both on and offshore, is at its peak. Angling options range from a leisurely streamside session for bream, to game fishing excursions for mako sharks or southern bluefin tuna.

Granite Island's screwpile jetty, yields good bags of table species all year round. Tommy ruffs, garfish, mullet, salmon trout and squid can all be taken from this pier, with early morning and evening the most productive periods. Heavy-tackle anglers often look for big stingrays and whaler sharks from the jetty's seaward end plus the occasional big snapper.

Rosetta Head (The Bluff), has a small jetty renowned for large squid. Tommy ruffs and the occasional big salmon are taken here, and a few 20 to 30 kilogram mulloway grab bottom baits from time to time.

Waitpinga and Parsons Beaches are not as reliable as they were, but are still worth a try for big salmon and mulloway. Both are within an easy drive of Victor Harbour, and are conveniently reached from car parks.

As with most south coast surf beaches, Parsons and Waitpinga beaches fish best at dawn and dusk, although it is wise to plan a mulloway excursion for after dark. Both

bait and lure fishing are productive, but whole pilchards on ganged hooks is probably the best.

School mulloway, mullet, salmon and a variety of small sharks are also taken in the surf at Goolwa, Boomer, Chiton Rocks and Basham Beaches.

The Reefs wide of Victor Harbour yield good catches of snook, big snapper, blue morwong, trevally, nannygai and warehou (sea bream), along with hammerhead and mako sharks.

The two most productive reef systems lie 10 kilometres south of Rosetta Head. As Southern Ocean waters are often unpredictable, a boat of at least 4.5 metres is advisable for offshore fishing. A ground swell runs outside Encounter Bay and if there is any wind conditions can become uncomfortable in a short time.

Seal Rock, a small granite outcrop 5 minutes from the Victor Harbour ramp produces big jack salmon. These fish often as heavy as 5 kilograms make for good light-tackle sportfishing. Surface poppers and diving minnow lures are the best hardware for Seal Rock.

During the winter months, barracouta are regular visitors to the wide grounds and warehou become quite common. The warehou is a fine-fighting fish and good eating. Silver trevally weighing up to 5kg also congregate on the reefs from July until November.

While Victor Harbour has below par boat launching facilities, some improvements have been made to the Bluff ramp. Large trailerboats can be launched and retrieved with ease on all but the lowest of tide, and there is also a separate car parking area.

Accommodation is scarce in Victor Harbour during peak season. For any angler contemplating an extended visit between December and February, a prior booking for any style of accommodation is essential. There are three caravan parks, numerous motels, guest houses and privately owned shacks for rent.

Victor Harbour winters can be cold and wet. For maximum enjoyment visit between November and April.

Kangaroo Island

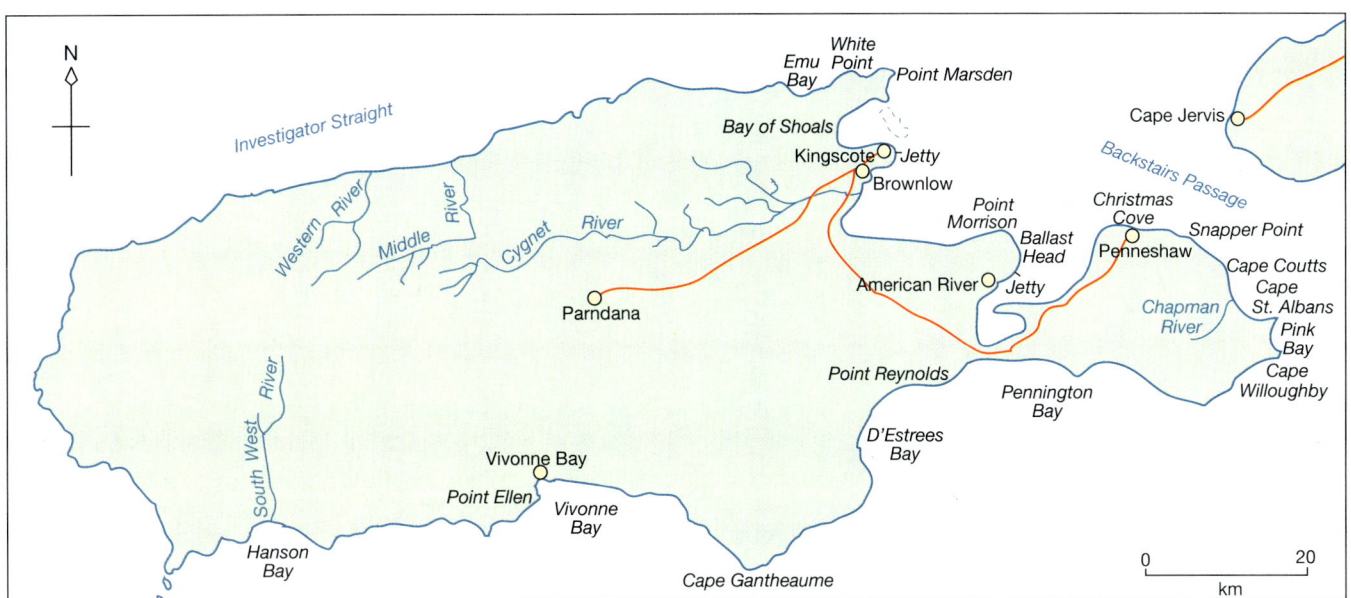

145 kilometres long and 32 kilometres wide, Kangaroo Island is one of Australia's largest islands.

Lloyd and Kendell Airlines operate regular flights from Adelaide and the Island Seaway, a large passenger and cargo ferry, runs daily between Port Adelaide and Kingscote. There is also a smaller ferry which runs across Backstairs Passage from Cape Jervis to Kingscote.

Angling options are many and varied; there are bream in the rivers, salmon in the surf, tommy ruffs and garfish from the jetties and even white pointer sharks offshore.

Several jetties provide good fishing.

The Kingscote and Vivonne Bay piers, offer top quality fish. Tommy ruff make up the bulk of the jetty catch, but there are also mullet, garfish, mackerel, snook and the occasional King George whiting. Silver trevally are a possibility in the summer months.

Nepean Bay is productive for snook, whiting and snapper. Since the bay is open to the weather from the north, forecasts should be checked before venturing too far offshore.

American River is a sheltered estuary system that attracts good-size whiting for the small-boat operator.

The Island's many rivers hold good stocks of bream. Prospects are best when the rivers silt over and become temporarily landlocked. The fish vary in size from small

'pickers' to over 2 kilograms. Solid baits, such as rock crabs and unpeeled prawns, will help avoid juvenile bream.

Offshore, game and sportfishing is plentiful around Kangaroo Island. Southern bluefin tuna, although more difficult to locate these days, are still available.

Yellowtail kings are easy to locate during the warmer months, particularly from Cape Willoughby to Cape Hart. Some of these fish weigh up to 20 kilograms. Trolled surface poppers and bibbed minnow lures appear to work well on them.

Giant white pointers are common right around the coast, particularly in areas near the sea lion colonies.

Boat launching facilities on Kangaroo Island are adequate with reasonable ramps at Kingscote, American River, Penneshaw and Emu Bay. In other areas, four-wheel drive vehicles are necessary for launching or retrieving near low tide.

For those who enjoy the occasional day offshore in a large and well-equipped vessel, there are two charter boats. Although based on the mainland, Maris Zalup's Encounter II often works the island's north-east coast, and will handle charter groups based on Kangaroo. The second company, run by Murray Borchardt out of American River, is equipped to handle any angling.

There are several well-maintained caravan parks, large guest houses and hotels to choose from on Kangaroo Island, but be sure to book well in advance to ensure accommodation.

Opposite: The Bluff boat ramp at Rosetta Head is an easy launching site in all conditions.

Cape Jervis to Noarlunga

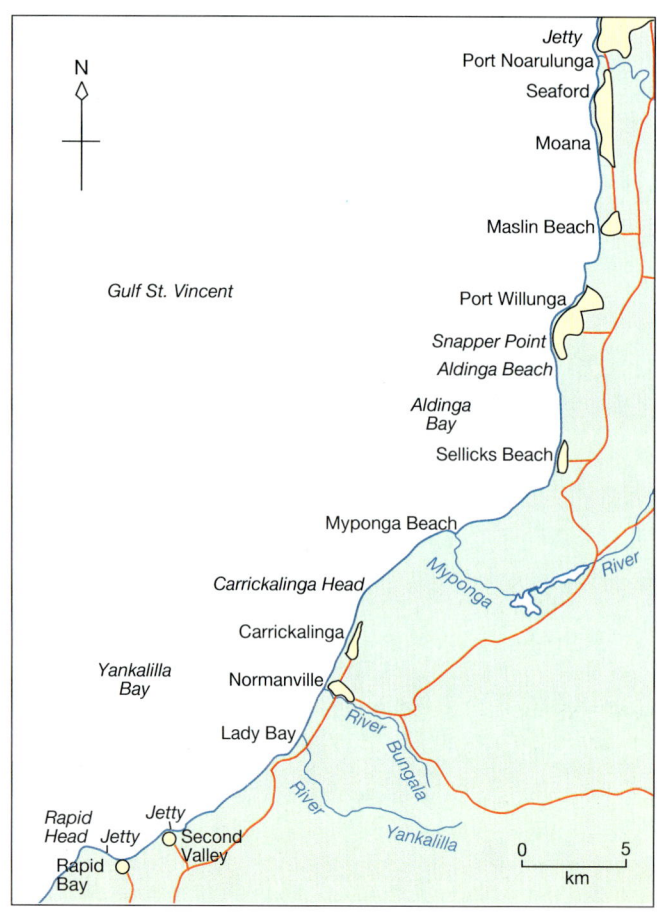

The coastline between Cape Jervis and Port Noarlunga is far removed from the rugged, cliff-strewn shores further east. Kangaroo Island blocks most of the Southern Ocean's influence, making the waters suitable for small boat operators.

Cape Jervis is one of South Australia's most famous commercial fishing areas. Backstairs Passag, in particular, the rugged corridor separating Kangaroo Island from the mainland, is the place to catch big snapper. However, the fish population has declined in recent seasons due to heavy fishing.

King George whiting, often weighing more than 1 kilogram, attracts anglers between winter and spring. Hotspots include Tunk Beach and Antechamber Bay. Big nannygai, medium snapper and school sharks are also found offshore from Tunk Beach, adding variety to the catch. Hefty salmon are easy to find in this area, as well as the occasional yellowtail king.

Rapid Bay Jetty is the most popular pier fishing venue in the state. The long jetty runs out into deep water, attracting silver trevally, mackerel, and large kingfish

during summer, though few kingfish are successfully landed. Tommy ruff are also abundant and are often found in the company of garfish. Squidding is also popular.

Normanville and Carrackalinga offer beach fishing for mullet and yellowfin whiting, and King George whiting, prime garfish and squid from the low rocks.

The gently sloping rock ledges adjacent to Myponga Beach are very popular in the summer months when there are plenty of garfish, tommies, squid and snook. These ledges are safe to fish in all but the worst weather.

North from Maslin Beach the coastline is punctuated by a series of rocky headlands. While the shore fishing is not outstanding, there are some good offshore grounds that regularly produce whiting and medium-sized snapper of between 4 and 8 kilograms. Those anglers with local knowledge catch 10 kilogram reds at certain times of the year.

Port Noarlunga jetty connects the sandy beach to an exposed reef. During winter gales, schools of salmon are washed over the reef and provide great sport for jetty fishermen. Tommy ruff, silver drummer, squid and mullet are also caught from the jetty.

Boat launching facilities on the Fleurieu Peninsula are good. The ramp at Cape Jervis handles large trailer boats at any stage of the tide. A new marina to be built at Rapid Bay will have a large public ramp.

A snapper worth smiling about caught off Cape Jervis, where Backstairs Passage is one of the better locations to catch the species.

Adelaide and St. Vincents Gulf

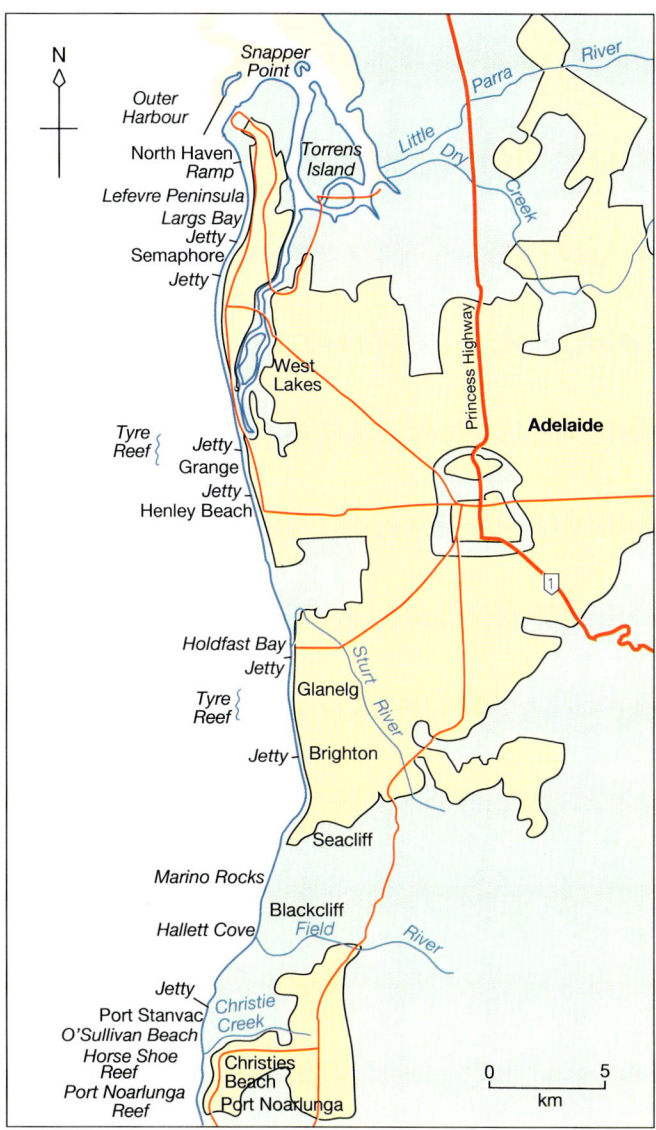

St. Vincents Gulf is unique; its maximum water depth is less than 30 metres and natural seabed features are uncommon. Although Kangaroo Island effectively blocks ocean swells from the gulf, sea conditions are still prone to rough and uncomfortable conditions.

King George whiting is the most popular fish sought by anglers in the Gulf. Although they are not as consistently large as those found along the south coast, they are reasonably easy to locate. Most specialists concentrate their efforts within 3 or 4 kilometres of the coast, where the water is less than 12 metres deep.

The popular whiting grounds of seagrass beds interspersed with sand and shale occur right along the metropolitan foreshore. Because whiting fossick through the weed for small shellfish and crustacea specialists use Goolwa cockles exclusively as bait. These meaty bivalves

can be purchased from local tackle stores, or harvested from the Goolwa surf beach. Although whiting can be found right along the Adelaide coastline, there are many favoured grounds, including the artificial reefs established in St. Vincents Gulf by the South Australian Department of Fisheries.

Grange and Glenelg Artificial Reefs, offshore from Adelaide, are top whiting areas. The Grange reef is constructed of used car tyres, in relatively deep water. It is active throughout the year, but yields its best quality fish during autumn and winter.

The Glenelg reef also made of tyres has, in addition, a sunken, derelict barge, which attracts plenty of whiting and a few big snapper. Since their establishment, these artificial reefs have been a bonus for local anglers, providing easily located grounds for those unfamiliar with more traditional whiting areas.

Yorke Peninsula, on the opposite side of St. Vincents Gulf, consists of shallow inshore waters, which are also a mecca for the small boat enthusiasts. King George whiting are the main target species and, despite heavy fishing pressure, are easy to find. Throughout the year, Edithburgh, Port Vincent, Black Point and Ardrossan produce whiting.

Garfish and tommy ruff, which are usually found together, are also popular with small boat anglers. Both species are prolific offshore from Adelaide, particularly from November until after Easter. There are no limits on the number of garfish and tommy ruff that can be taken, and 'three figure' mixed bags are common. Gents, or blowfly maggots, are the bait for garfish and tommy ruff. Live maggots are available from tackle outlets, or they can be bred easily at home.

South of Adelaide, in St. Vincents Gulf, sections of low reef at Moana, Sellicks and Noarlunga, yield snapper of varying sizes at different times of the year. Big fish are available, but only for those anglers who know the grounds well.

The northern grounds, offshore from Outer Harbour, produce snapper of a consistently large size, averaging around 10 kilograms apiece. The Outer Harbour shipping channel and adjacent silt grounds are particularly productive during spring and early summer, with dawn and dusk sorties by far the most rewarding.

The Wreck of the Zanoni, offshore from Ardrossan on the Gulf's western side, was the state's hottest big snapper ground. The wreck has now been declared an historic shipwreck site and is off limits to all fishing. A prohibited zone of 500 metres prevents anchors being dropped on the site and further damaging the wreck's structure.

Good snapper grounds occur just north of the Zanoni site and another artificial reef has been established one nautical mile to the south. Snapper are caught on this reef on occasions, but it doesn't attract and hold fish like the Zanoni.

Adelaide's fishing jetties are a blessing to anglers. There are 6 piers along the metropolitan foreshore. The water surrounding the piers is generally very shallow, but the fishing can be good.

Small to medium sized Tommy ruff is the most prominent catch from the jetty with mullet from March to April each year.

Snook, another favourite, grabs baits or lures trolled behind a boat. They are also caught under jetty lights at night. Summer is snook time around St. Vincents Gulf.

Blue swimmer crabs are popular through spring and summer in upper Gulf areas and around Adelaide. They are taken by one of two methods. The first method requires a boat and several witch's hat drop nets. The nets are baited with rabbit flesh, fish heads or stale meat and set near seagrass beds in shallow water. Catches of several dozen crabs per boat are common. The second technique involves wading the inshore sand patches, with specially designed crab 'rakes'. When a crab lie is detected, it is disturbed with the pronged rake and scooped up into a waiting tub or bucket. Areas north of Adelaide, such as Port Parham, Port Gawler, Middle Beach and Thompsons Beach are crabbing hotspots from Christmas through until early March.

The Port River estuary, north of Adelaide, is a popular recreational fishing area. Although heavy shipping traffic and associated maritime industry have caused Port River's water quality to deteriorate over the years, the fishing is still good.

Bream, mulloway, mullet, sand whiting, garfish and salmon trout are taken year round by land and boat anglers. Mulloway, the Port River's premier catch, range from school-sized specimens to 30 kilograms. Live mullet is the most productive bait for mulloway, but many are also taken on lures. A particularly rewarding location for lure tossers is the wharf fronting the Osborn power station. Fish of 25 to 30 kilograms are taken consistently here on minnow patterns each winter.

The Outer Harbour wharf, near the entrance to the Port River estuary, is an occasional mulloway hotspot. Live yellowtail make great baits but whole, fresh squid appear to be the best offering. Squid are taken from under the wharf with the aid of a light and dab net, and are most effective baits when fished at night, particularly at low tide.

The lengthy breakwater at Outer Harbour is a popular venue with rock fishermen. Mulloway, big snapper and

St. Vincents Gulf is well served with recreational jetties.

salmon are the main catch, but it is often necessary to fish an all night session to do well. Fresh pilchards are the most effective bait for breakwater anglers, although fresh squid is also superb.

Dabbing garfish at night is popular and productive activity throughout the Port River system. Garfish come to surface on still, moonless evenings and can be easily scooped up in a dab net.

Offshore from Outer Harbour, there are plenty of whaler sharks. From spring right through summer, members of the South Australian Game Fishing Club catch hefty sharks from the St. Kilda Channel and near the edges of the section bank. Small hammerheads are also prevalent when the water is warm.

Boat launching facilities around Adelaide are excellent. The North Haven complex boasts a superb multi-lane ramp, complete with boarding pontoons, wash down facilities and a large car park. There is a good ramp nearby at Outer Harbour and another on Garden Island in the Port River.

A multi-lane boat ramp operates at Glenelg, but there is a troublesome sandbar at the entrance. Once the headquarters of the South Australian Game Fishing Club, the fleet has now relocated to North Haven because of the sandbar hassles.

A little further south, the relatively new O'Sullivan Beach ramp and boat harbour attracts boaters each weekend. This facility provides ready access to most of the top southern whiting and snapper grounds.

Around the remainder of the gulf, launch ramps range from quite acceptable to rather poor. The new ramp at Ardrossan is one of the better ones, and there are other reasonable facilities at Black Point, Edithburgh, Stansbury and Marion Bay. Most of these are suspect around low water.

Accommodation is plentiful around St. Vincents Gulf, except during peak holiday periods. All coastal resorts have caravan parks, most of which are clean and reasonably priced. Hotels are also easy to find and there are a few motels and guest houses. Privately owned shacks are available for rent and are mostly handled by local real estate agents.

Above: A crowded Port River wharf indicates only one thing; the word is out that the fish are biting.
Right: Big fish are caught right in the heart of Adelaide. This 30 Kg mulloway was taken from the Outer Harbour breakwater.

Spencer Gulf

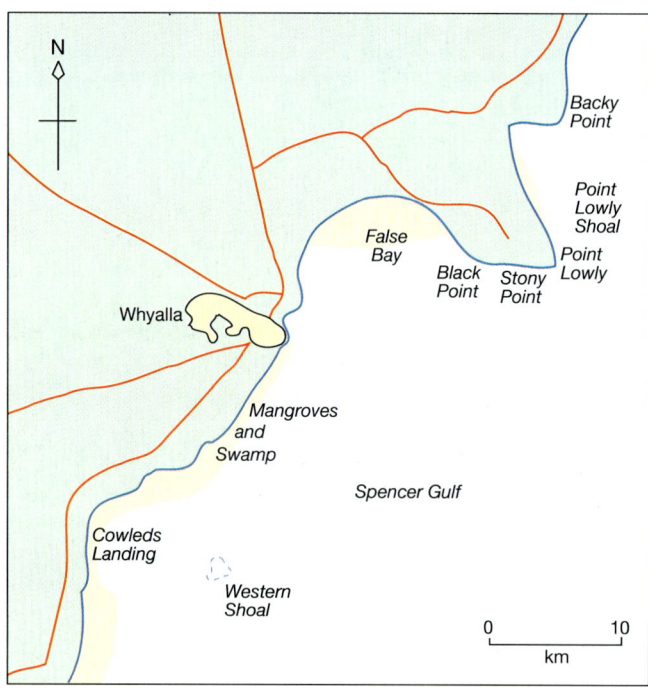

Considerably larger than the body of water on which Adelaide is situated, Spencer Gulf is one of South Australia's most bountiful fishing areas.

Whyalla, South Australia's largest provincial city, approximately 390 kilometres by road from Adelaide is the hottest big snapper location in the country. Fish weighing more than 14 kilograms are taken regularly, both on and offshore. Big whiting, snook, garfish, South Australian salmon and yellowtail kingfish also abound in the Gulf.

The shipping channels leading into the harbour are reliable snapper-producing areas during spring and summer, as is the anchorage, 4 kilometres offshore. There are also many miniature artificial reefs (snapper 'drops') , created by local anglers from old car bodies, tyres and cement blocks.

Black Point, on Point Lowly Peninsula, is the land-based snapper capital of the world. During winter, when Spencer Gulf is lashed by southerly gales, Whyalla rock fishermen break out the long rods and sidecast reels and catch hundreds of jumbo snapper.

Offshore from Whyalla, game fishermen find plenty of excitement chasing large white pointers. Whyalla is well populated by big white sharks, that will respond to plenty of berley and baits of whole, fresh snapper.

Cowell, Arno Bay and Port Neill are always reliable spots for King George whiting, snook, snapper and

tommy ruff. There is a good launching ramp at Port Neill.

Tumby Bay is a perfect jumping off point for the beautiful Sir Joseph Banks Group of islands. Huge whiting, snapper, trevally, kings and countless reef varieties are available all year round.

Port Augusta, is an underrated fishing location. Good hauls of quality snapper are taken regularly, along with whiting, garfish and blue swimmer crabs.

The Port Augusta power station pumps its exhaust cooling water into the gulf, which attracts fish. Mulloway of less than 10 kilograms are occasionally taken from the Port Augusta wharves.

At Port Pirie snapper, whiting and garfish are the big three. Port Pirie also Whyalla's first-rate action on big snapper. Unfortunately for the recreational fisherman the professional snapper netters often hit the Port Pirie area hard.

The long jetty at Port Germein is a good spot from which to set drop nets for blue crabs during summer. Although the end section of the jetty is now inaccessible, tommy ruffs and garfish can be caught from the shallow water in the bay.

Port Broughton, another popular holiday resort on Spencer Gulf, is a reliable producer of whiting and snook and a few snapper. The Broughton jetty is very popular with children for good-sized tommy ruff, garfish and squid during the summer.

At Wallaroo, the massive bulk handling jetty yields the widest variety of species from any pier in the State. Big snapper, mulloway, kings, drummer, trevally, mullet, snook, tommy ruff and several other fish can be hooked from this jetty according to season, with the 'reds' at their best during winter gales.

Offshore fishing is also excellent at Wallaroo. Big snapper begin to congregate offshore in November and usually last until the end of the school holidays. Whiting are best during winter, although they can be found in reasonable numbers all year.

Port Hughes is considered by many to be one of the best all-round fishing resorts in South Australia. The jetty produces tommy ruff, squid and garfish, while whiting, snook and snapper can be located offshore.

One of the best offshore areas accessible from Port Hughes is the steamer channel, which runs midway up the gulf to Whyalla and Port Pirie. It is about a 30 kilometres run from the Port Hughes ramp, so the weather needs to

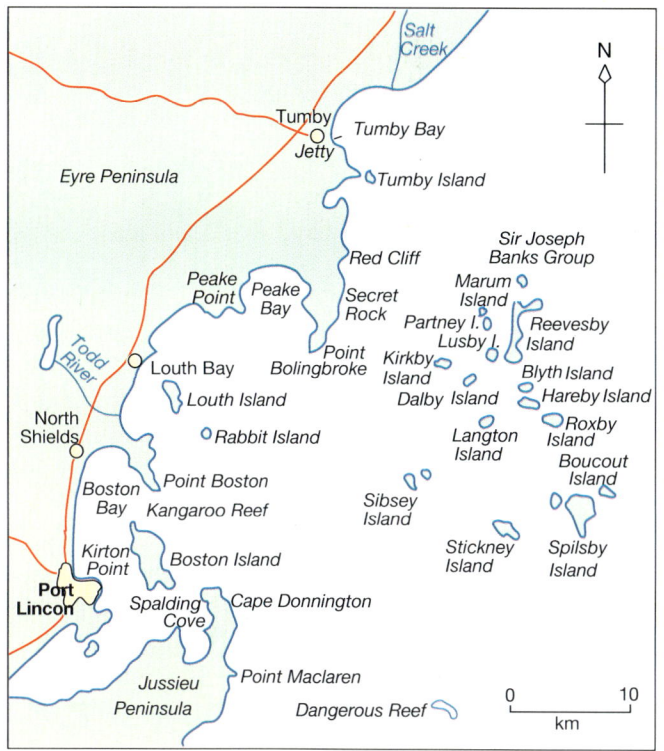

Port Neill has a first-rate, all-tide ramp, as does Tumby Bay. For visiting anglers, there can be little doubt that the waters of Spencer Gulf provide the best all-round fishing South Australia has to offer. Accommodation is very good and plentiful, but should not be relied upon during holiday seasons without prior booking.

be good before making the trip. Huge catches of big snapper have drawn boats well offshore from this resort for many years.

Wardang Island is an excellent spot for whiting, snook and snapper. The inshore weedbeds also produce plenty of squid during summer. As with most jetties around Spencer Gulf, the pier at Port Victoria always provides plenty of tommy ruff, as well as squid, snook and garfish.

Hardwicke Bay, near the foot of Yorke Peninsula, is another first-rate year-round whiting area. There are hundreds of shacks around the bay, most of which are equipped with boats.

The Point Turton jetty, typical of others around the gulf, yields tommy ruff, garfish, squid and the occasional King George whiting.

Boat launching facilities around Spencer Gulf are good. There are quality ramps at Point Turton and another at Port Victoria, an acceptable facility at Port Hughes and a good one at Wallaroo. Port Broughton and Port Pirie are both well-served, while there is a new marina and multi-lane ramp at Whyalla.

Top Right: Salmon is a common catch in South Australia. This one was taken using saltwater fly fishing tackle from the Point Lowly Rip near Whyalla.
Right: A snapper not likely to be forgotten. This one weighing in at approximately 15 Kg was caught off Whyalla.

Port Lincoln to Ceduna

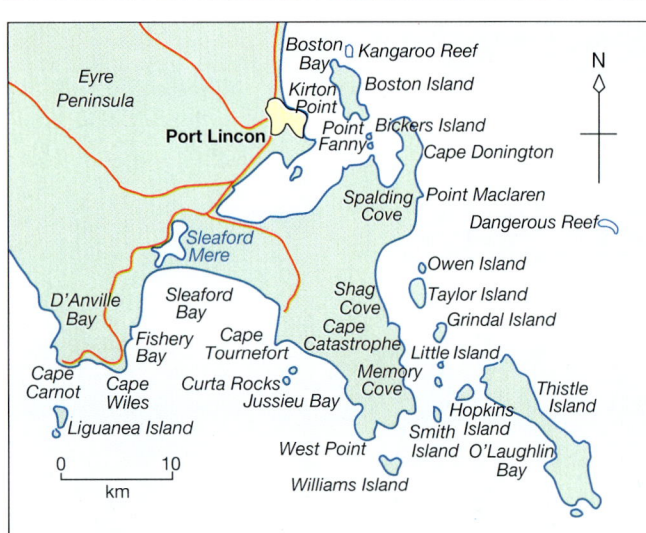

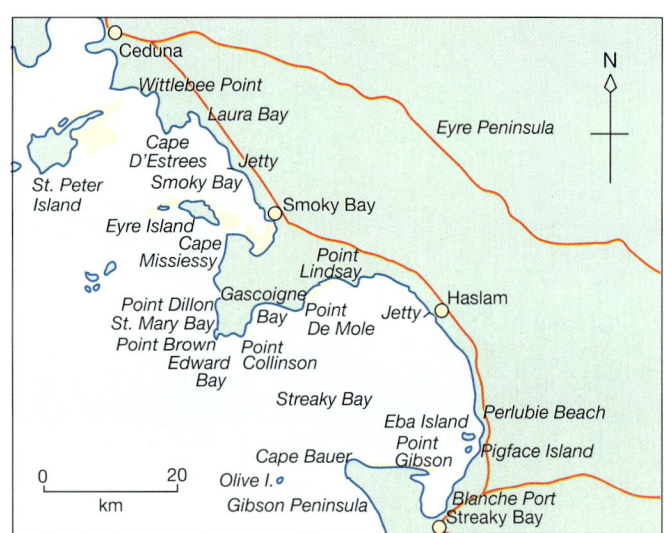

Port Lincoln, originally selected as South Australia's capital city, remains a beautiful tourist and fishing port and home to the most prosperous tuna fleet in the country.

Kirton Point Jetty yields sizeable King George whiting for persistent triers. Big tommy ruff are usually available all year round, as well as mullet in the shallows.

Boston Bay consistently yields whiting for the small-boat angler, along with salmon, garfish and an abundance of squid. Bluefin tuna and big snapper occasionally find their way inside the bay.

Port Lincoln was long recognised as the State's premier game fish centre, and indeed there are still plenty of hard-fighting varieties to be found well offshore.
Port Lincoln is well-endowed with jetties, which at times produce everything from tommy ruff to giant snapper. The longest and most productive of its jetties is the main bulk-grain-loading jetty, or Brennans Wharf as it is known locally. Big salmon, snapper weighing more than 10 kilograms, garfish, snook and squid are taken from this pier. The most hectic action occurs when the tuna fleet is unloading its catch.

The Neptune Islands to the south of Williams Island are home to the great white sharks luring several dedicated shark specialists to the area each summer.

Coffin Bay is approximately half-an-hour's drive north of Port Lincoln. Its sheltered waters are ideal for aluminium dinghies, with whiting, garfish, salmon trout, trevally and flathead readily available.

There is also good land-based fishing available at

Coffin Bay. The small jetty produces trevally, mullet, tommy ruff and salmon trout, while the Horn is a good spot to spin for snook, salmon and trevally.

Farm Beach, out near the bay's northern extremities, is renowned as one of the State's premier whiting areas.

Locks Well and Sheringa surf beaches, near Elliston, are famous producers of big salmon. Fish to 5 kilograms are regularly taken, although Locks Well is probably the more consistent of the two. Salmon are also the main catch in the surf up towards Sceales and Streaky Bays, along with the occasional tailor and mulloway.

Streaky Bay is one of the most picturesque locations on the west coast and turns on good fishing. Snook, tommy ruff, garfish and squid are taken regularly from the Streaky jetty, as well as big snapper between November and Christmas. Whiting specialists always do well offshore, and there are plenty of garfish on still summer evenings.

Smoky Bay Jetty can also be productive for tommy ruff and garfish, as can the Thevenard and Ceduna jetties a little further north. Ceduna is a great spot for snapper at certain times of the year and there are often plenty of big whiting in and around Denial Bay,

The Streaky Bay/Ceduna area is still home to the largest white pointer sharks in the world. Alf Dean's all-tackle World Record shark of 2664 pounds, (just over 1200 kilograms) taken in 1959, was hooked only a few kilometres off Thevenard.

Boat launching around the west coast is generally no problem. The public ramp at Port Lincoln is good, as is the double-lane facility at Coffin Bay. The Elliston ramp is

The Bight

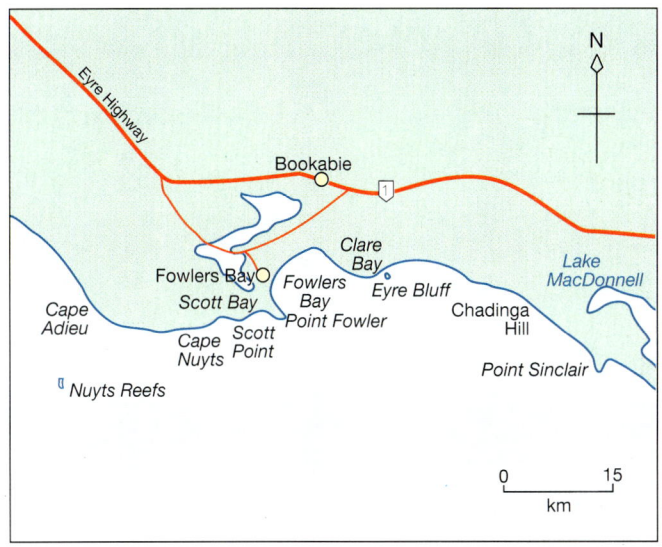

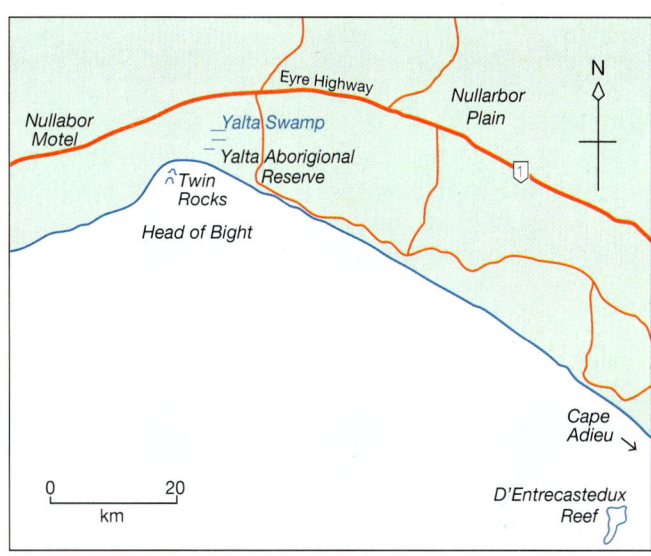

South Australia's far west coast consists almost entirely of long, well-formed beaches and rocky headlands. It is in a region of climatic extremes, with summer temperatures sometimes soaring into the mid-forties.

Fowlers Bay is considered the gateway to the far west, with a lengthy jetty which can often produce surprising catches. Yellowtail kingfish of varying sizes are regular visitors during summer, and tommy ruff are almost invariably huge. Garfish and squid are also plentiful.

Although weather can make or break boat fishing at Fowlers, a trip offshore can really prove worthwhile. The whiting in the bay regularly top 1.5 kilograms. Snapper can be easily located.

Fowlers Headland, separating the bay from Scotts Beach, is usually a safe bet for big salmon and a few nice snapper are pulled from the rocks each summer. Sweep and other rock varieties are also available from the headland.

Scotts Beach is probably the best known and most heavily and successfully fished of all the far west surf locations. At most beaches beyond Ceduna, giant mulloway are the dream of all anglers who make the long westward trek, and Scotts has produced more than its fair share of oversized jewfish each season. Specimens to 40 kilograms have been dragged onto the sand over the years.

Big whaler sharks patrol Scotts Beach both day and night and regularly scoff baits intended for mulloway. Salmon are the mainstay of the entire Bight shore surf fishing. With an average size of around 4 kilograms, they are top sport from the beach, fighting to the very end. Although fresh pilchards are probably the best salmon bait, these fish will take almost any offering when they are

in the right frame of mind. Lures are naturally effective and are sometimes preferable to bait if long casts are required to reach a school.

The further west you are prepared to travel, the better your chances become of pinning the mulloway of a lifetime. There are many beaches between Scotts and the South Australian border, some of which are inaccessible. While a four-wheel drive will put the angler within reach of most of the good fishing, a dune buggy, trail bike or balloon-tyred trike will definitely improve access.

Because of the turbulent nature of Bight waters, the far west coast surf beaches are constantly changing. A gutter which has yielded fish one week may be gone the next.

Between Cape Adieu and the head of the Bight, magnificent beaches extend as far as the eye can see, and this stretch of shoreline yields most of the west coast's truly amazing mulloway catches.

Although the best fishing is at night, it is possible to hook big mulloway from the beach during the day. Fish can often be seen, either individually or in pairs, patrolling along the back of the breakers. Casting a live salmon can sometimes prove deadly, although large salmon fillets are by far the most popular bait.

Summer is the prime time to travel to the Bight in search of mulloway, but it is often very windy at this time of year. As mentioned, the temperatures can climb unbearably between December and March, rendering daytime fishing close to impossible.

Because of the extreme remoteness of the area anglers have to take everything in with them. Abundant supplies of water are vital, as is ice if you wish to keep fish edible. Many regular visitors tow trailers equipped with generators and portable freezers.

Freshwater Fishing

Trout Fishing

Although there is little said or written about trout fishing in South Australia it is quite well endowed with fishable water and trout stocks. Rivers and creeks both north and south of Adelaide have been seeded for many years.

It has been left to the South Australian Fly Fishing Association to maintain trout populations throughout the State by breeding trout in their hatchery in the Adelaide Hills, then transporting the fry to suitable waters.

The Light, Broughton, Wakefield, Rocky and Hutt Rivers all carry nice fish. Although the climate in the State's northern areas is often harsh, many of these rivers are deep enough to enable trout to escape the summer heat. Both browns and rainbows are stocked in northern streams, which during the warmer months are still and clear, making fishing quite challenging.

The Onkaparinga, Finniss and Hindmarsh are probably the most productive southern streams, and the Onkaparinga the most popular.

South Australia has limited but productive freshwater fishing. This angler spins for trout in Bull Creek south of Adelaide.

The Onkaparinga varies along its length from a deep, still waterway to a narrow, fast-flowing torrent. It is broken roughly in two by the Mount Bold Reservoir, and carries both trout varieties plus large redfin. The State records for both rainbows and browns have come from this river.

The creeks south of the capital also support trout populations, and there are countless private farm dams liberally stocked with both browns and rainbows.

Just about all the recognised trout fishing techniques are employed on South Australian streams, including fly-fishing, lure casting, live baiting and float fishing. All can be effective, but there is little doubt that the knowledgeable fly-fisherman will consistently catch bigger trout than his counterparts with lures or bait.

As there are very few natural insect hatches on South Australian streams, most fly fishing is done with nymphs, matukas and similar wet flies. There will be an occasional rise when atmospheric conditions are suitable.

Lure fishermen take a lot of trout on bladed spinners, but quality minnow patterns seem to score most strikes. Of these, the Rapala CD5RT, the Killalure Trout Bait and the Rapala Mini Fat Rap appear to be the best. As the CD5RT closely resembles a juvenile rainbow, it will naturally attract attention in streams stocked regularly with rainbow trout fingerlings.

The Rebel Crawdad, one of the better yabby imitations on the market, is also very popular with South Australian lure tossers. Yabbies make up much of the trout's diet, so the effectiveness of a good yabbie copy is almost a foregone conclusion.

Productive baits for both north and south streams include tiger worms, shrimps, live minnows and, of course, yabbies. These can either be fished under quill floats or simply flicked out unweighted yabby tails can also be very effective set on the bottom or under the surface.

As a lot of fishable water flows through private property, access to river banks is often restricted by property owners. While many farmers don't mind angling visitors, provided they are extended the courtesy of being asked, some refuse to allow anyone onto their land except members of the Fly Fishing Association.

Scotch thistles and blackberries are the curse of the South Australian trout fisher. Almost all of the northern waters are lined with dense thistles, which invariably leave their mark on the angler after a day's fishing. Blackberries take over on the southern streams, making fishing painful in some areas and impossible in others.

Natives and Imports

The Murray River is the only South Australian inland waterway to carry native fish of any angling significance. In the past two decades, there has been a gradual decline in the State's native fish stocks.

Years ago when the Murray ran clean and clear, golden perch, cod, congolies, silver perch and the occasional tench or redfin were regular captures. The latter two varieties were the only imports, and neither proved too much of a problem.

The introduction of European carp has really turned the river's ecosystem upside down. Carp are among the most efficient and destructive feeders in the piscine world. As their numbers escalated, they quickly began to take control, endangering the native species.

For a few years it was predicted that the carp would take over altogether, wiping out the indigenous species in the Murray. Thankfully, this hasn't happened.

Golden perch, in particular, seem to be on the way back. Fishing live shrimps or small yabbies around the snags appears to pay dividends on goldens (known locally as callop), but a bunch of tiger worms will also have the desired effect if there are no carp in the vicinity. The average weight of the callop taken in South Australia would be a little better than a kilogram, although a few fish of three times that figure are taken annually.

Once abundant around Mannum, Morgan and other popular Murray ports, cod are rare these days, particularly the bigger specimens. An occasional big fellow will sometimes create excitement among regular river specialists, but the incidence of cod captures is definitely on an unfortunate decline.

Redfin perch, while no longer common in the Murray, have become established in good numbers in many of the other rivers throughout the State.

The Onkaparinga carries good redfin stocks, particularly in the section below the Clarendon Weir. Unlike some other areas well-endowed with redfin, the Onkaparinga doesn't seem to suffer from stunting, which occurs when the redfin population reproduces itself prodigiously, resulting in huge numbers of fish which never grow anywhere near their full potential.

The Wakefield River and the River Light are other rivers containing redfin. All of Adelaide's reservoirs are teeming with redfin, but most are off limits to anglers.

As redfin are well suited to stocking in dams, many farmers have seeded their waters over the years, both for sport and for the table. While rainbow trout are now more in vogue than they once were for private dams, redfin populations are well-established and are difficult to eradicate once they gain a foothold.

As mentioned, carp are now a fact of life in South Australian freshwater fishing. While they are considered a nuisance by most, some anglers scale down their tackle and actually fish for them exclusively. One thing the carp definitely has going for it is its massive growth potential. No one was really sure just how big they would grow here in the early years after their introduction, but specimens of over 10 kilograms rarely raise an eyebrow these days.

South Australian legislation stipulates that it is an offense to return carp to the water alive. Only by some quirk of nature will we see carp gone from South Australia. Meanwhile, we have no choice other than to grin and bear them.

Western Australia

Introduction

Not only is Western Australia the largest state in the country, it is a place of fishing opportunity.

For the adventurous angler, many parts wait to be discoved. The north-west coast between Steep Point and Exmouth, for example is a region, where fertile, tropical waters lap a rugged coastline and the Great Sandy and Gibson Deserts spill right to the doorstep. This is the best rock fishing in Australia. Spanish mackerel, hard-fighting trevally, and even sailfish can be caught from the cliff tops.

The tropical north-west is even more remote. If it wasn't for small townships the coast would be inaccessible to all but the most experienced off-road drivers. As it is, a four-wheel drive is still essential to safely cross the region.

On the freshwater fishing front, places such as the Ord, Drsydale, and Fitzroy Rivers contain excellent barramundi fishing, as well as an array of secondary species.

The majority of Western Australians however fish south of the tropics. The long beaches north of Perth are popular 'playgrounds' while the Swan River entertains anglers year-round, and adjaceant Fremantle has excellent beach fishing. Offshore anglers find the beautiful Rottnest Island typical of what Western Australia has to offer; everything from snapper and mulloway, to Spanish mackerel, yellowfin tuna, and marlin further offshore.

Finally, southern Western Australia, which mixes breathtaking scenery with brilliant angling of all types. Rock fishing is popular but often dangerous due to big swells. Augusta, at the mouth of the Margaret River, is another delightful fishing destination, where the Western Australian jewfish proliferates.

Freshwater fishermen can choose from numerous rivers and dams in southern Western Australia, where both rainbow and brown trout, as well as redfin are available. Marron, a prawn-like crustacean, is unique to this area, making for a succulent meal when cooked and eaten fresh.

For all interstate anglers, Western Australia really is worthy of a visit. It's a challenging region, often unforgiving on equipment; typically Australian. The fishing is, quite simply, brilliant.

The Western Australian jewfish is exclusive to this state. It ranges from the Recherche Archipelago to Shark Bay in the north. Not only are they large but also excellent eating. This specimen is a trophy catch.

Border to Esperance

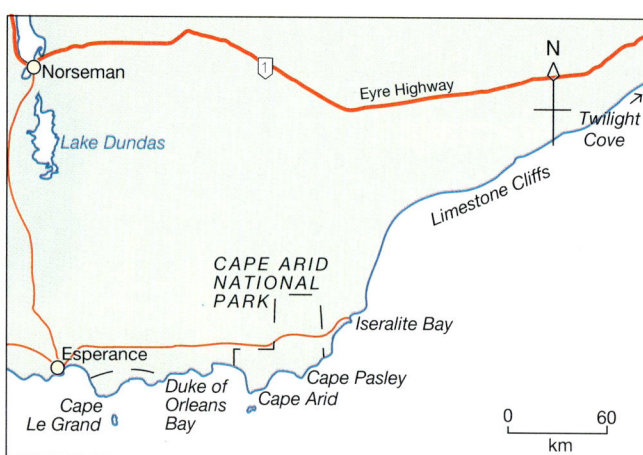

A lasting impression of a visit to Esperance and its surrounds is the clearness of the water. Couple this with an abundance of fish, especially smaller varieties, and the low number of anglers, and it paints an attractive picture.
Beach fishing is very popular, with herring abundant all year round. Salmon provide spectacular catches, while silver trevally (skippy) proliferate in April/May and remain for winter.
Flathead, tailor, snook, mulloway, whiting and sharks complete the list of angling targets.

East of Esperance, spectacular coastal scenery should delight the angler, as will the vast, firm white beaches, which can often be negotiated by four-wheel drive.
Anglers should seek a high vantage point over beaches to locate holes and gutters in which to fish.

Cape Le Grand features huge granite outcrops forming bays and inlets wash onto white sands. These headlands create good rock fishing and offer protection on their lee sides, whatever the weather.

Kennedy's Beach has outstanding shore angling, with Dunns Rock another four-wheel drive rock and beach fishing location. Boats can be launched at Wharton Beach, Lucy Bay and Alexander Bay.

Duke of Orleans, including Whartons Beach, is a large area that attracts anglers from as far away as South Australia. Tagon Beach has fabulous salmon fishing.

Israelite Bay is the last settlement on the West Australian coastline before the towering cliffs of the Bight. It owes its existence to being the last opportunity for boat launching. Beach fishing is excellent and rock fishing good. Because of difficulties in launching and retrieving, there is little

pressure on the fishery and offshore angling is outstanding.

Esperance has top-class angling available right on it's doorstep. Large town wharves and jetties provide easy access for herring, garfish, snook, mulloway, trevally, squid and others. Best weather on this part of the coast is November to February, but angling is year round.
Beaches and reefs near the town fish well for salmon, whiting, herring, trevally, salmon trout and others. Twilight Cove is very popular with its silver sands and small rocky islands. There are many other coves and bays that provide quality fishing in beautiful surroundings.
Esperance has many caravan parks, motels, hotels and guest houses and good boat-launching facilities.

The Recherche Achipelego mirrors the monster granite hills of the mainland to form a seascape of dazzling proportions, with somewhere around 100 islands. It will come as no surprise to note that the offshore fishing is outstanding.
Bottom fishing is highly productive for groper, blue morwong or queen snapper, pink snapper, nannygai (red snapper) , sweep, yellowtail kingfish, tuna, breaksea cod, samson fish, sergeant baker and others. It's a fisherman's paradise, but is treacherous.

Spectacular limestone cliffs mark the coast near the southern border.

Esperance to Albany

Scenic beauty and reliable fishing are hallmarks of this splendid stretch of Western Australia. Such are the many fine, white beaches and small reefs, safe rocks and delightful bays that the opportunities are enormous for all styles of angling. The coast is lightly fished and of such a nature that the fisherman has an excellent chance.

Many bays and headlands provide the holiday maker with a host of options. Should the weather be windy, then at places such as Bremer Bay and Cheyne Beach there is always a back beach or secluded bay to fish in safety.

Water conditions are excellent with gin clear seas giving way to deep offshore fishing locations.

Beach fishing is among the finest in the country as this section of coast plays host to the massive run of Australian salmon. The migration begins in about March, though there are resident species all year round.

Reef Beach and Fosters are surf beaches noted for outstanding shore based shark angling and a variety of small species like herring, salmon trout, skippy, silver bream, flathead, tailor, snook near weed banks, and of course many whiting. The fabled King George is also a target, especially near the reef. A four wheel drive is essential for both these beaches. Dillon Bay is popular.

Beaches west of Esperance enjoy similar conditions to those closer to Bremer, with the same sparkling clear water. All display fine white sand and some are readily accessible, like Cheynes, and Bluff Creek if you have a four wheel drive.

Hopetoun boasts outstanding beach angling and good tourist facilities in a quiet nook in the State. Protected bays can be fished with light tackle for herring and garfish.

Fitzgerald River National Park offers unparalleled wilderness and fine beaches, with rivers and inlets for variety.

The Bremer, Gairdner, Fitzgerald, Kalgan (Albany), **Pallinup** (Beaufort Inlet) and **Hamersley rivers and inlets** contain populations of black bream. Rewarding catches of squid and blue swimmer crabs are available especially in Albany.

Rock fishing is highly productive for groper, shark, samson fish of enormous size and silver bream. Herring, skippy and gardie are plentiful.

Small boats fish in safety in the many bays such as Two Peoples Bay for whiting, herring, snook, flathead, squid, skippy and others varieties. Launching is often from the beach, many of which have hard sand. Other quiet bays are Doubtful (which combines superb shore, reef, rock and deep sea fishing), Bremer, Beaufort Inlet, Starvation Bay and many more which are relatively isolated.

Deep sea anglers enjoy outstanding fishing for pink snapper, queen snapper (blue morwong), runa, trevally, flathead, nannygai, samson fish, sweetlips, snook and many others. This water can be very rough and unpredictable, and visitors should check with local anglers before venturing out. Deepsea angling is possible from Bremer, Cheyne Beach, Hopetoun, Albany and Two Peoples Bay. Launching is often from the beach.

Drifting for King George whiting at Oyster Harbour, Albany.

Albany to Cape Leeuwin

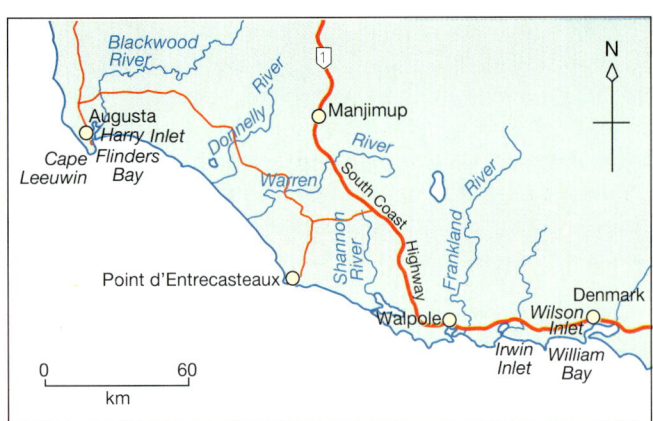

The towering cliffs and spectacular coastal scenery around Albany and Denmark give way to long wave-washed beaches interspersed with rocky headlands and fearsome cliffs, towards Augusta. Delightful estuaries add to an already outstanding fishery that offers excellent angling from beach, rock and boat.

Salmon Holes and Bornholm, west of Albany, yield Australian salmon year round. Fish numbers increase during the autumn run and on the return run from August to November. Morning and evening are the best fishing times, and there is a bag limit of 5 fish per day per angler.

Outstanding fishing exists at other beaches on this rugged coast for sharks, salmon, tommy ruff or herring, skippy or trevally, whiting, flathead and silver bream.

Herring and trevally are always available in good numbers, expecially during winter. Bigger trevally are caught around Augusta, while whiting are plentiful during summer. Flathead are usually incidental catches by anglers fishing for other species.

Torbay Inlet boasts excellent black bream fishing, while the bay contains large populations of small fish. Cosy Corner is used as a beach launching ramp, though a four-wheel drive is needed.

West Cape Howe has samson fish and yellowtail kingfish landed from the rocky headlands, mostly in winter. Snapper, West Australian jewfish, red snapper, yellowtail kingfish, trevally, blue morwong or queen snapper, and squid are all plentiful for boat anglers. Beaches such as Hortons provide shore fishing for herring and trevally.

Wilsons Inlet offers some of the best King George whiting fishing in the State, albeit small fish. Bay or small pink snapper are caught in winter, while flathead, along with river prawns, are prolific in early summer. Ocean Beach provides fine surf angling.

Irwin Inlet, like Wilsons, has good estuary, beach, and quiet bay angling at places like Peaceful and William Bay. The beaches neighbouring the inlet are great for herring and trevally, as are the surrounding rocky headlands.

Walpole and Nornalup Estuaries are highly regarded as a variety of fish can be caught from their placid waters. Silver and black bream abound, particularly in the two rivers which drain into the twin estuaries. Herring, King George whiting, tailor, trevally, flathead, flounder, and bay snapper will respond to small baits and lures. Dinghy fishing is especially productive in these waters, while shore access is difficult because of heavy bush.

Broke Inlet is more isolated and therefore lightly fished. Caravan parks around Walpole and Nornalup allow angling parties to camp on the estuaries' banks, with small boat launching well catered for.

River fishing is an added attraction on this south west corner of the State. Brackish waters harbour scores of black bream, and where fresh water exists there is some fine trout fishing. The Warren River is one such place, providing excellent trout fishing down near the mouth. Succulent freshwater crayfish or marron also inhabit freshwater rivers and impoundments in southern Western Australia.

Warren River beaches have angling of the highest quality. Tailor, salmon, sharks, herring, trevally, samson fish, groper, flathead and silver bream are some of the many species available. Yeagarup is an excellent location, though a four-wheel drive is essential for access. Black Point is notable for general angling. There is no special season other than for the salmon run.

Windy Harbour has a caravan park and limited launching facilities requiring a four-wheel drive. However, the offshore angling is of a high standard, complementing the beach and rock fishing which also rates favourably. Beaches along this entire stretch of coastline are virginal, begging to be fished by those adventurous souls who don't mind contending with massive sand dunes.

Augusta is situated on the Hardy Inlet. Whiting fishing, especially from a dinghy, is very good, and at times herring and trevally are caught in the inlet. Black bream travel down as far as Molloy Island in winter, but as the freshwater flow diminishes in summer you may need to head upstream as far as the Alexander Bridge, where marron are trapped in the freshwater reaches.

Offshore fishing is excellent but limited by a very dangerous bar.

Cape Leeuwin to Perth

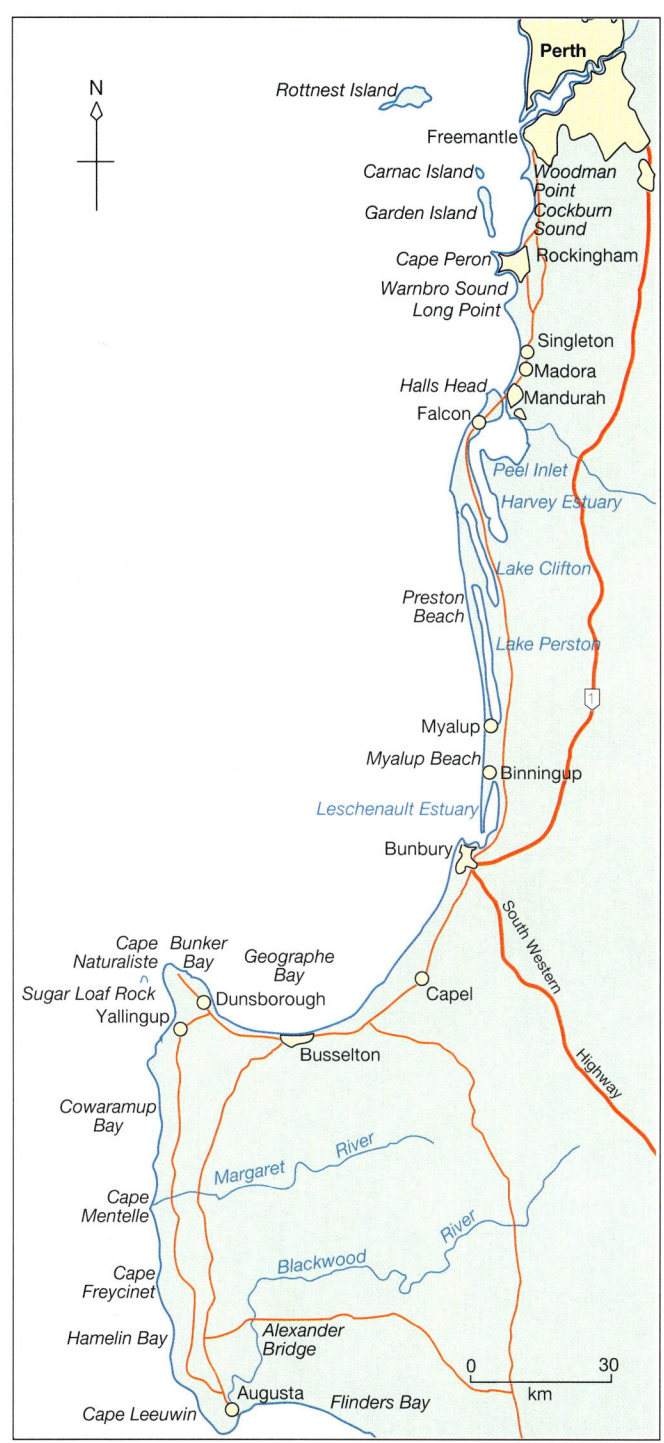

abound over soft bottomed areas in the region, while there is exciting angling for sharks, pink snapper, queen snapper or morwong, trevally and other species. Amateur crayfishing is outstanding.

The area is well populated with many caravan parks and chalets, though ramps for boat launching are limited.

Hamelin Bay has good fishing for whiting, herring or tommy ruff, and salmon in autumn. Trevally or skippy, silver bream and good deep-sea species are available year round. Western Australian jewfish and King George whiting are premier catches in Hamelin Bay where there is a reasonable boat ramp.

Eagle Bay has excellent rock fishing, though it's a low and dangerous area.

Conto's beach rock angling is profitable at times, adding mulloway to the list of available species, while the Margaret River and Cowaramup Bay have magnificent fishing from rocks for herring, especially around April when scores of these tasty little fish gather en masse. Garfish are prevalent year round.

At Eagle Bay, protected waters allow small boat and rock fishing for salmon, tailor and herring. Schools of garfish frequent the area, as does the blue swimmer crab which is also a prolific inhabitant of Geographe Bay where squid are a secondary possibility.

Yallingup Canal, Sugarloaf Rocks, Injidup and Wyadap are all dangerous in big seas, though they boast good rock fishing. Species which are likely to be encountered are herring, salmon, skippy or trevally, snook, groper (a limit of one per day), tailor, mulloway, black drummer, and buffalo bream.

Bunburry has a variety of fishing. There's deep sea angling for jewfish and snapper, and in the shipping channels, mulloway, shark and on occasions many bonito. Late summer, autumn and winter are best.

Bunbury, and the beaches near Peppermint Grove provide surf fishing for tailor and herring, while in the harbour small blue mackerel are common. Leschenault Estuary is famous for its crabs, river prawns when in season, and for large numbers of King George whiting. Bream and mulloway are commonly caught in the Collie River.

Bunbury has many caravan parks and motels, and the launching facilities are excellent.

Myalup to Mandurah is a beach fishing stretch with many species, but tailor predominates from summer through to autumn. Morning and evening fishing is most

Cape Leeuwin to Cape Naturaliste coastline has big seas and granite headlands. Large waves pose a danger for shore-based anglers.

Offshore, jewfish are prevalent around the deep reefs. They follow the crayfish run towards shore and move closer in winter. King George whiting of excellent size

productive. When whitebait schools move up the coast, many other fish follow them, including trevally, herring, mulloway, whiting and small sharks.

Unfortunately this stretch of coastline has no launching ramps. Near Mandurah, tailor is a prime summer catch on the reefs. Winter species include skippy, whiting, herring, salmon and silver bream. Halls Head is easy to fish for chopper tailor, herring and bream. Cobbler or eel-tailed catfish, and mulloway can be found at times.

Offshore fishing at Mandurah is good for jewfish, snapper and skippy on the reefs.

Peel/Harvey Estuary one of Western Australia's finest waterways, features blue swimmer crabs almost year round, and the massive king prawn run in autumn. Bridges are top locations for smaller estuary fish and occasional mulloway.

Madora, Silver Sands, San Remo, and Singleton are summer hotspots for tailor, with early morning and evening the best fishing time.

Warnbro Sound fishes well for tailor from the shore at Long Point, while squid and whiting are there year round.

Many boat anglers venture out from the good ramps at Rockingham to fish the Five Fathom Bank for snapper, whiting, skippy, salmon, snook, bonito, tailor, jewfish and queen snapper.

THE SWAN RIVER AND PERTH

Few Australian capital cities share the diversity and quantity of popular angling species caught in the Swan River. Some of the most productive fishing spots are no more than a long cast from city skyscrapers! Surf fishing along the adjacent coastline is excellent, with the beaches easily accessible and, except in the best of tailor runs, uncrowded.

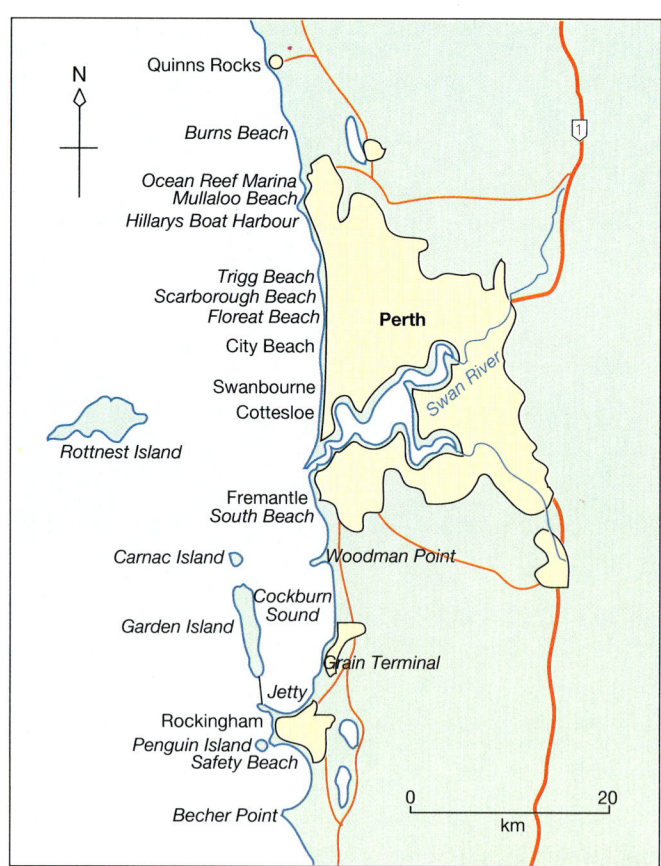

City fishing at Perth is excellent and attracts crowds of anglers like this one gathered on Floreat Beach fishing for tailor and herring.

River fishing is at its best in spring and summer, although tailor can be caught year round. Bream and mulloway are at their best in spring, while flathead and flounder most prolific in summer. These five species form the basis for Swan River fishing although cobbler (catfish), trumpeter, crabs and prawns are also popular, and incidental catches of trout, giant herring, baby amberjacks, samson fish, trevally and even tuna add variety. Sharks are uncommon in the Swan River.

In the Swan and Canning River, the best fishing reaches are downstream from the Mt Henry Bridge over the Canning, and the Causeway over the Swan River. Mulloway will travel a little further upstream. They are commonly caught behind the Maylands Police Academy. Bream also moves well up from the estuary.

Shore fishermen often find bream and mulloway in the same places. Some of the best, proven locations are Maylands, Belmont, the Causeway, the Narrows, Canning and Mt Henry bridges, the old brewery site on Mounts Bay Road, jetties in the Claremont/Mosman area, and Fremantle Harbour. Boat fishermen favour Mosman Bay and Blackwall Reach for mulloway, but will fare better for bream only a short cast from the bridges or jetties.

Flathead and flounder are found together, and will take the same offerings. Whitebait is the universal bait as it is prolific in the river, although small leadhead jigs work well.

The flatfish are concentrated in the lower estuary. Shore fishermen will find them easiest to catch from the jetties

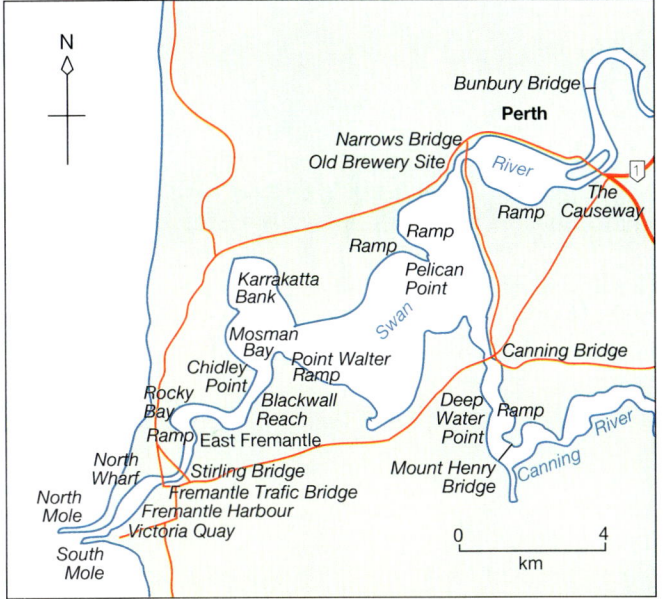

around east Fremantle, or by wading the shallows and casting jigs into deeper water. Boat anglers frequent Rocky Bay, Mosman Bay, Point Walter and Karrakatta Bank.

Tailor of good size and quantity are caught in the Swan River. Trolling from dinghies accounts for most of the catch, although casting lightly weighted whitebait from jetties, particularly in the Claremont/Mosman area, can be successful in the evenings. Tailor are caught over the same area as flathead and flounder and all through the day; birds diving on whitebait are a good sign.

The metropolitan coastline has two staple species for the beach and rock angler: tailor, small in summer and bigger fish in mid-year; and herring, which are known as tommies, tommy ruff, rough or ruffies.

Herring are the far more prolific of the two. The peak catches occur during May when the spawning run brings enormous numbers of the fat, 25 centimetre fish to the metropolitan area. Anzac Day is the traditional 'start' of the herring season but the fish are available year-round.

There is nowhere along the city coastline where you won't catch herring. Famed hotspots include Grant Street at Cotteslow, the rock groynes at Cottesloe, City Beach and Floreat, and Mullaloo Beach.

Berley is significant and every herring rig incorporates a berley 'blob'. The berley is considered more important than the bait; herring will take prawns, maggots, or a baitchaser rigs consisting of luminous green tubing or a plastic drinking straw cut into 25 millimetre lengths.

Tailor bite best in November, December and January. The fish are small, but school in great quantities. Beaches south of Fremantle experience the first runs, beginning with the stretch between Mandurah and Fremantle, then Long Point (Becher Point, south of Safety Bay). Swanbourne and Floreat beaches, are reliable spots, and Cottesloe and City Beach have the best rock groynes.

Bigger tailor are caught mid-year, using big baits

around reefs such as Swanbvourne, Cottesloe and Leighton. The hours just before dawn and after dusk are usually best.

Other important species include garfish, 'pilch' and whiting. The whiting are too small to be worth pursuing on their own, but they frequent the same locations as small herring. All three species demand smaller hooks than the usual herring size, and light tackle.

Surprisingly, mulloway are a rare catch from metropolitan beaches. The Swan River is a much better bet. When they are caught they will most likely weigh under 3 kilograms, whereas the river fish average 10 kilograms.

Cockburn Sound, Palm Beach jetty and the ASI groyne are famous for regularly producing snapper in excess of 10 kilograms for shore-based anglers, while those with boats will find the same fish on gravel out from the ASI groyne, or around the grain terminal.

The same locations in Cockburn Sound are also amongst the best places during a bonito run, when kilogram-plus tuna will chase lures in preference to baits, and offer a sprightly battle on sporting tackle. They appear in early summer and stay until April.

Rottnest's West End and the back of Garden Island produce salmon from March to summer.

Leighton, Swanbourne and Trigg are excellent tarwhine and skipjack trevally grounds where the reef meets the sand. They are a year-round catch but are at their best in autumn and winter.

The Moles

If one location around the metropolitan area deserves special mention, it is the Fremantle moles. The north and south moles form the entry to Fremantle harbour, and almost every species mentioned can be caught from them.

The north mole is the most likely place for shore-based fisherman to catch salmon, perhaps while spinning for bonito! Even a few shark mackerel have been caught from here. Fishing from the south-west tip into the teeth of a winter storm may be uncomfortable, but it has produced impressive catches of big mulloway and snapper. Cast a mulie (pilchard) with a big star sinker hard into a north-west gale as a cold front builds, and you may join the many who have encountered enormous skippy (trevally) and 4.5 kilogram-plus tailor from these rocks.

The south mole with a south-westerly blowing into an outgoing tide, is a certainty for chopper tailor around dusk. Both moles produce garfish, herring, blue mackerel, skippy and 'pilch' in calmer weather.

Perth Offshore

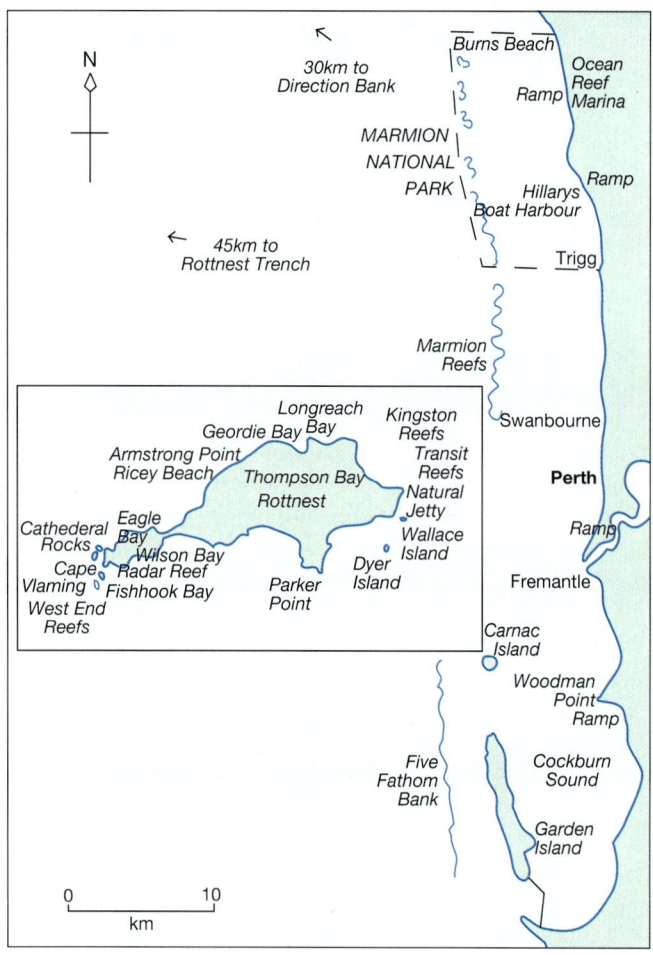

Salmon and herring hug the reefs, particularly Eagle Bay, Cathedral Rocks, Fishhook Bay and Radar Reef.

Direction Bank and the Five Fathom Bank both hold concentrations of fine-eating bottom fish, notably the prized Western Australian jewfish. The locations are usually pinpointed with an echo sounder, then fished by drifting with heavily weighted lines and an assortment of baits. A sea anchor is essential.

The Marmion Reefs, also known as the Three-Mile, form a broken line of small sub-surface and visible reefs for many kilometres. They are popular with small-boat anglers chasing herring, garfish and trevally. There are also incidental catches of tailor, samson fish, jewfish, snapper, salmon and mackerel. The visible reefs directly out from Trigg, Marmion, Burns and Quinns are the most popular. The clean sand also produces plenty of school whiting from a drifting boat.

Launching ramps are plentiful with facilities at Two Rocks and Ocean Reef, a popular departure point for fishing Direction Bank, Burns and Quinns. Hillarys Boat Harbour, headquarters for the Marmion Marine Park, has 4 ramps with more planned. The Swan River has the Leeuwin launching ramps at East Fremantle, while Woodman Point, in Cockburn Sound, has the major ramps south of the river.

Rottnest Island, offshore from Perth, is a holiday mecca with a staggering array of fish for both shore and boat anglers.

Boat fishing weather is best during autumn, although there is no period during the year when the fishing is totally 'shut down'. Winter and spring mean storms and big swells, but there are plenty of intermittent fine days. Summer days are often victim to Western Australia's unique combination of a strong offshore breeze in the morning, followed quickly by an equally strong sea breeze in the afternoon.

Rottnest Island is a focal point for many boat fishermen. Its famous West End is a haven for herring and salmon from March to July, Spanish mackerel and yellowfin tuna from January to May and samson fish, jewfish, breaksea cod and skipjack trevally year round.

The game fish are usually caught trolling from a few hundred metres to within 3 kilometres of West End or along the south side to Parker Point. The bottom fish favour the south-west side and Duffield Ridge.

Samson fish are one of the most difficult to catch offshore from Perth which makes this 37 Kg catch on a 8 Kg line a real achievement.

Fremantle to Geraldton

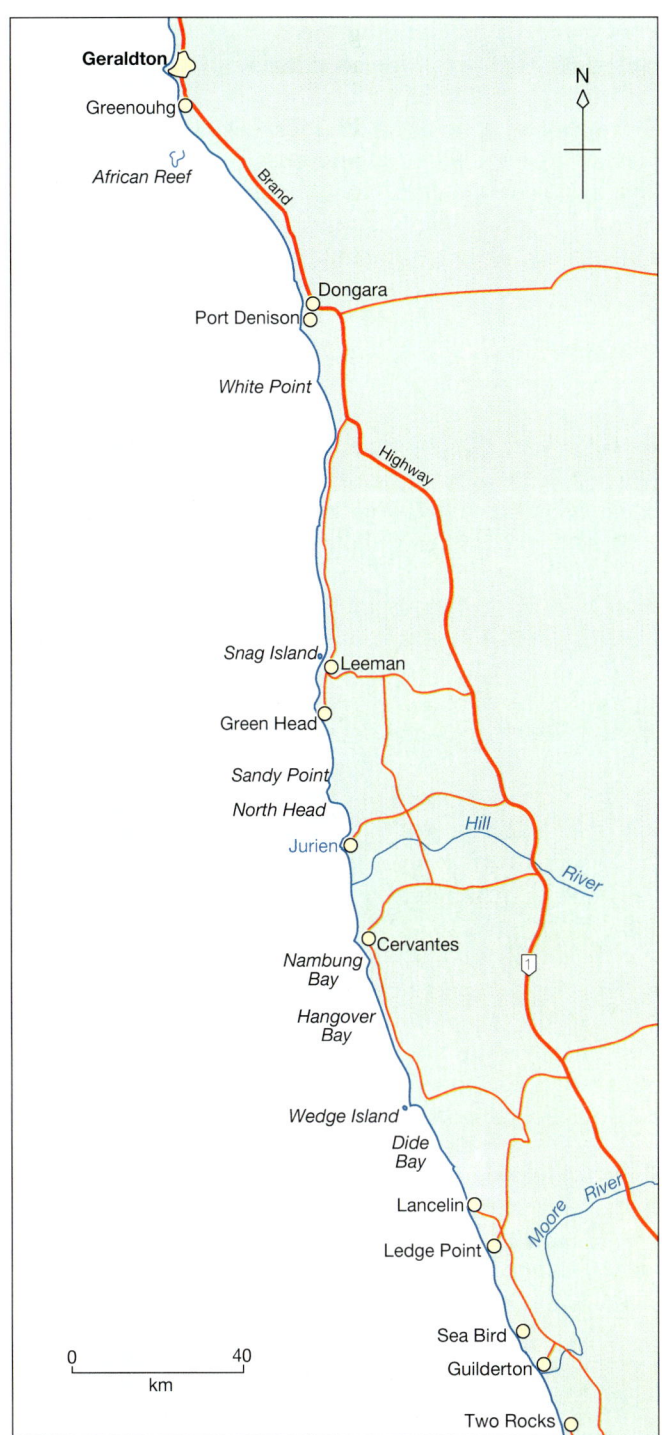

Geraldton
Greenouhg
African Reef
Brand
Dongara
Port Denison
White Point
Highway
Snag Island
Leeman
Green Head
Sandy Point
North Head
Hill
Jurien
River
Cervantes
Nambung
Bay
Hangover
Bay
Wedge Island
Dide
Bay
Lancelin
Ledge Point
Moore River
Sea Bird
Guilderton
Two Rocks

0   40
km

The coast from Fremantle to Geraldton contains superb shore-based fishing for tailor and mulloway. Boat anglers will revel in the bottom fishing for Western Australian jewfish only a few hundred metres offshore, while pelagic sportfish are prolific when warm currents prevail.

Fishing is good year round, though the afternoon south-westers prohibit offshore expeditions and make shore fishing a challenge. April, May and June have the calmest weather.

The Moore River yields black bream, and in late spring excellent tailor and mulloway, from the reef north of Guiderton. To reach the best shore fishing regions requires a 3 kilometre walk or a reliable four-wheel drive.

Lancelin, the last stop before the dirt tracks heading north to Wedge Island, sports tailor and mulloway. Boat anglers will find adequate beach launching off the hard, fine-grain sand, and herring, trevally and garfish abound in the area.

Wedge Island has no sealed-road access, but the fishing makes the trip over the corrugated tracks by four-wheel drive worthwhile. Boats launch hard-packed sand of the beach. Beach fishing anywhere between Lancelin and Cervantes yields tailor, mulloway and herring.

Cervantes is popular for boat fishing due to easy launching. The back beach produces tailor in the evenings. Shore-based anglers will find Hangover Bay or Hill River worth a visit.

Jurien Bay has a modern marina, ample facilities, and all-weather launching for boats of all sizes. Once renown for its beach fishing for tailor, mulloway, samson fish, herring and trevally, Jurien is now the lower west's headquarters for offshore bottom fishing and light-tackle game fishing.

Catches of jewfish and baldchin groper come from broken ground 3 kilometres offshore or, when weather permits, from the Second Bank out 20 kilometres. Samson fish are always prolific, and Spanish and shark mackerel appear through summer and autumn.

Leeman, just north of Jurien, fishes similarly.

Port Denison has excellent offshore fishing, but has a reputation for big fish being landed from the reef entrance and boat harbour walls. Further north, the S-Bend Caravan Park marks a shore fishing region for tailor, mulloway, jewfish and samson fish from the nearby reefs. The mouth of the Greenough River is a good spot for tailor.

Geraldton isn't recreational boat fishing territory due to commercial fishing pressure and a flat, featureless bottom for many kilometres. Mackerel can be caught offshore during summer.

Geraldton to Kalbarri

Port Gregory has a clean beach protected by offshore reef, a jetty and a river mouth (Hutt River) to act as a focal point for passing schools of tailor and mulloway. Bottom fishing offshore is excellent, with great mulloway and snapper no more than 6 kilometres out.

Lucky Bay and Wagoe Beach, accessible by four-wheel drive only, have seen some of the best tailor and mulloway fishing imaginable, and also consistently produce snapper, shark, big trevally and samson fish. An occasional mackerel is caught. Beach and reef fishing is often closed out by strong southerlies or big swells.

Kalbarri is the mid-west's premier recreational fishing location. The Murchison River has easy launching for trailerboats, although traversing the mouth requires caution in a big swell. Offshore fishermen will find trolling for mackerel and yellowfin tuna productive within a few kilometres of the mouth, and bottom fishermen will find plenty of jewfish, baldchin and associated species.

The shore fishing locations around Kalbarri are too numerous to mention. Keep in mind that there are massive tailor and mulloway caught here, so it pays to use top-quality big mulies (pilchards), garfish or mullet strips for bait. Lures, particularly poppers, are also successful from the shore. Call into the local tackle shop for up-to-the-minute information on where they are biting.

The Murchison estuary, right in front of town, is a nursery area for whiting and baby tailor. The sandspit near the launching ramp is very popular with anglers at dusk.

The coastline up to Shark Bay is largely inaccessible, except for a couple of kilometres of good territory within walking distance north of Kalbarri. The tracks leading into the most remote rock fishing spots are hard going and require intimate local knowledge.

The Abrolhos Islands, lie scattered 50 kilometres offshore between Geraldton and Gregory, and support a major professional fishery that may one day be important to the tourism industry.

Unfortunately, at the time of writing, only some crayfishermen are allowed to camp on the islands, meaning recreational fishing and diving is virtually confined to boats large enough to make the half-day crossing from Geraldton and sleep the anglers on board.

Charters are available with some professional 'wetline' boats, either at the wharf or through the Geraldton Tourist Bureau. All manner of game fish frequent these islands, although the professional fishermen only concentrate on coral trout, emperor and jewfish.

The coastline between Geraldton and Shark Bay is without doubt some of the best fishing country that Australia has to offer, though much of it is inaccessible due to rugged coastline and vast distances.

Although there is approximately 350 kilometres of coast between Geraldton and the entrance to Shark Bay, Horrocks and Kalbarri are the only two locations accessible by bitumen.

One other point of interest, Port Gregory, is reached by a gravel road from Northampton.

Horrocks is a lovely hideaway holiday spot, 70 kilometres north of Geraldton. It has reasonable boat launching with the beach protected from swell by a reef. A small jetty caters for youngsters with handlines, and beach and rock fishermen will find plenty of variety. The mouth of the Bowes River (4 kilometres south) is famous for tailor and mulloway.

Shark Bay

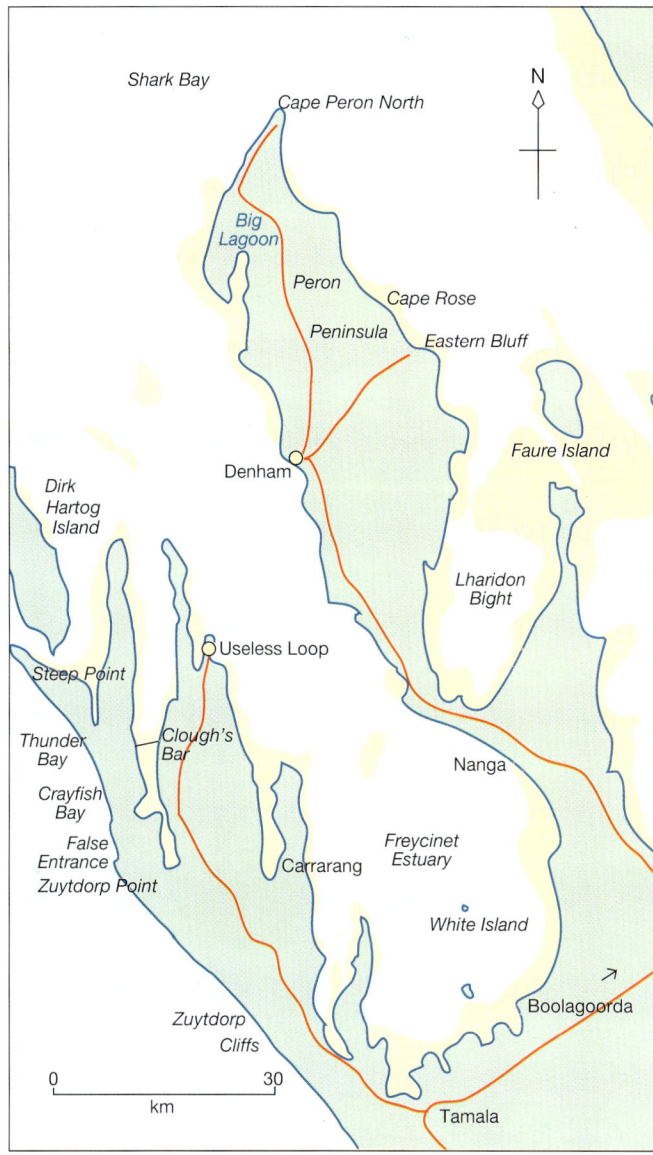

The huge expanse of Shark Bay in the North of Western Australia is the role model for the perfect fishing location. Anglers cast baits and lures from small boats to connect with pink snapper (for which the area is famous), shark, tailor of monumental size, north-west snapper, mulloway averaging 20 kilograms, Spanish mackerel, spotted mackerel, shark mackerel, and massive cod.

Small baits often account for whiting, flathead and flounder. Blue swimmer crabs and squid add to a rich smorgasbord.

Key fishing locations are the channels and coral outcrops. Night is the best time to catch large predators. Even the shallow unproductive waters during the day will surprise at night. Pink snapper in particular become active and many fine specimens are caught.

There is a bag limit of 10 pink snapper per day per angler; the minimum legal length is 41 centimetres.

Mulloway also become active at night, and it's not uncommon to encounter really large specimens.

Best time of the year to visit Shark Bay is from March to August. Strong southerly winds begin in October and blow increasingly during summer, abating from January onwards.

Denham is the only town on the twin bay. It has shops, caravan parks, chalets, a hotel/motel and proposed resort development. Boat launching is excellent.

The small jetty is regularly fished and shore fishing is carried out at accessible locations south of the town, with evening the best fishing time. Many boat anglers fish the deep channels within a couple of kilometres of town, while Dirk Hartog Island shoreline is outstanding for access to fish-rich waters.

Cape Peron Station offers camping for a fee on the quiet beaches at the tip of Cape Peron, where you can fish from shore at night and have both sides of the peninsula within easy reach. Snapper, mulloway, tailor and cod are the favoured species.

Small boats are launched from the beach and a four-wheel drive is essential, though some boats run from Denham to the coral outcrops at the tip of Cape Peron.

Monkey Mia is home of the magnificent dolphins, and a top fishing location. The bay is productive for whiting and blue swimmer crabs, with some huge mulloway at night.

Cape Rose, about 5 kilometres north, is outstanding for evening fishing (watch the strength of the sea breeze). Deep holes and channels near Faure Island allow good bottom fishing and channels next to sandflats offer good angling for bluebone groper. Many spotted mackerel patrol drop-offs near weed.

Nanga has a caravan park, small shop and boat ramp, with good day angling around White Island's coral outcrops. Night fishing is excellent along the bay foreshores even a small boat is a huge advantage.

Rocks just north of Nanga, such as Eagle Bluff are used by snapper anglers, particularly at night.

Some islands in the southern end of Hamelin Bay are very lightly fished, offering fabulous angling.

Towards White Island day fishing is good over coral, while at night you need only travel a small distance offshore to find snapper, shark, tailor and mulloway.

Steep Point to Exmouth

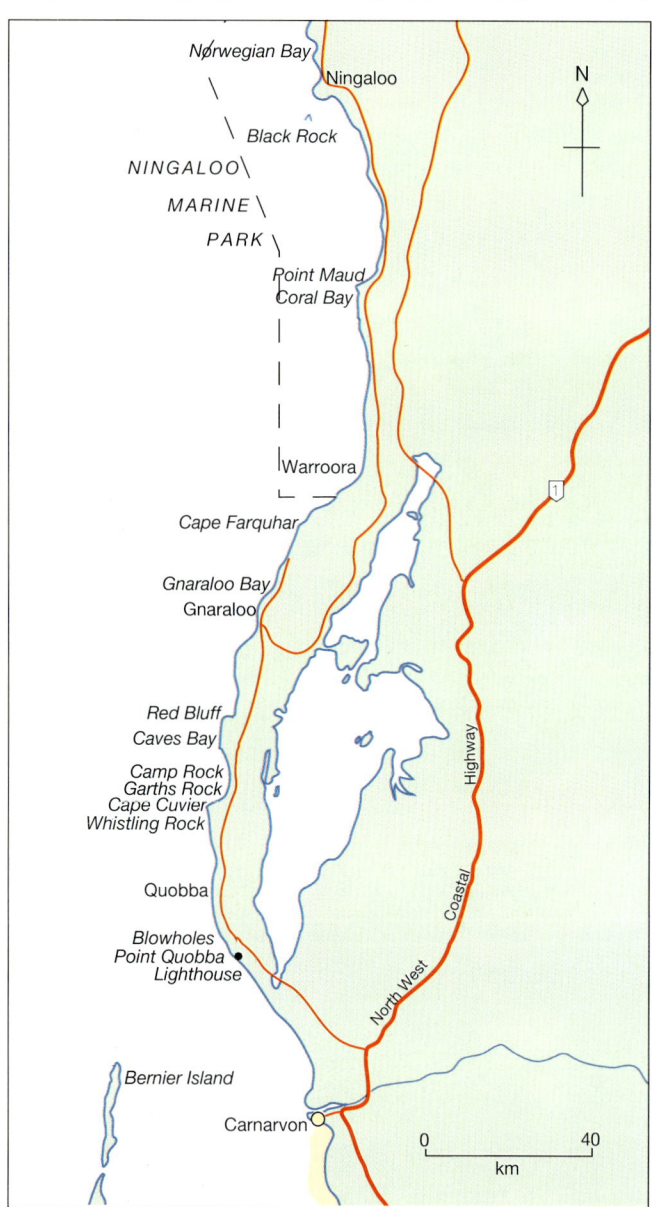

The first of the acknowledged west coast rockhopping locations is Zuytdorp Point, better known as False Entrance. It is typical of many locations; nothing more than a landmark on a map, high off the water, difficult to fish, sometimes dangerous in a big swell, but the scene of some superlative game fish captures from the rocks.

Crayfish Bay and Thunder Bay, like False Entrance, are accessible only by four-wheel drive. They have rarely seen an amateur boat, due to the unforgiving coast and the distance from Shark Bay launching ground. Although they produce good game fish, they are best known for their bottom fishing, especially for pink snapper.

Steep Point is the most westerly point of mainland Australia and one of the greatest land-based game platforms in the country. It has probably seen more captures of sailfish and Spanish mackerel than any other rock fishing location. Wahoo and dolphin fish have been hooked from the rocks here, and Steep was the site of Western Australia's first marlin capture from the shore. Enormous sharks are an everyday occurrence, and tuna, giant tailor, cobia, yellowtail kingfish, amberjacks, samson fish, shark mackerel and snapper are common.

A full-time ranger collects camping fees and rubbish, and helps to keep the four-wheel drive track in good order. No facilities are available. Access for all of these locations is from the same track off the Useless Loop road, and tyres should be run on reduced pressure immediately after crossing the 3 kilometre-long Clough's Bar, a man-made causeway.

Carnarvon, past Shark Bay, has a long jetty which is the centre of activity during tailor and mulloway runs. Sharks, trevally and mackerel are common from the jetty, and queenfish can be expected in the warmest months.

At the Blowholes, great rock fishing is available. It's a popular camping area south of the famous Quobba Station.

Along the next 100 kilometres of coastline, many isolated yet worthwhile fishing locations abound. Blows 1 and 2, the Boundary (the southern border of Quobba Station), High Rock, the 2-Mile Whistling Rock, Garth's Rock and the Ledges, Camp Rock, The Caves and Red Bluff all have their own fishing 'fan clubs'.

Access is by conventional car except, at times, to the Caves. The track back up from Camp Rock and the one into Red Bluff can be hard on vehicles.

Basic accommodation is available, but camping on Quobba is only allowed at the homestead or at Red Bluff. Like Steep Point, most anglers visit Quobba and the Blowholes for the superb land-based game fishing.

Ballooning with big baits for Spanish mackerel is popular, and quite a few specimens over 40 kilograms have been landed. Spinning with bibless or deep-running minnow lures, or leadhead jigs is practiced while others favour casting mulies (pilchards). Many of the platforms are ideal for saltwater fly fishing.

Due to the height off the water at most of these locations, an adequate gaff is essential. Fixed gaffs are usually composed of several sections, and should measure at least 6 metres when assembled. Rope gaffs which clip onto the angler's line and slide down directly onto the fish's head, are just as popular.

The peak season at Quobba is May to August inclusive, but as with Steep Point, the fishing is year round. Early spring is the quietest time of the year - depending on the currents! Ballooning weather is definitely at its best in winter for Quobba, as easterly winds are reliable.

Gnarloo is the next station north and has good accommodation at the homestead. Shore fishing for snapper and emperor is best, as there is little deep water in close.

Access is via the Quobba road, and there is excellent over-the-beach launching for any size trailerboat into a protected bay. The outside fishing is outstanding for game and bottom fish.

Warroora Station cannot be reached from Naraloo, but is accessed by a track from the Exmouth road. It features shallow, protected waters, and is popular with campers fishing for emperor from the shore or small boats.

Coral Bay is the next stop, but vastly different from Warroora. The town has all manner of accommodation for the throngs of winter sunseekers. Shore fishing is delightful, but not outstanding, with dart, queenfish, trevally and emperor making up the bulk of light-tackle catches.

Boat fishing is the feature of Coral Bay. Launching is good across the beach and boats can be safely moored in the protected bay. The Ningaloo Reef forms a barrier between scattered coral lumps and the deep-blue offshore waters.

Ningaloo is another station with similar fishing to Warroora, except that the 100 fathom line is close to the mainland - as close as 3 kilometres offshore. With reasonable weather, even dinghies can be trolling in big marlin country! The main track leads straight in from the Exmouth road. Larger boats reach this area by water on day trips either from Coral Bay or Exmouth. For more detail on fishing Ningaloo Reef, see the Exmouth section.

Carnarvon and Quobba do not attract as much amateur boat fishing as Shark Bay or Exmouth. In Carnarvon's case, this is because of mundane fishing close in. For Quobba, difficulty in launching and lack of facilities can be held responsible.

Quobba can be fished by boats launched either from the Blowholes or Red Bluff. Red Bluff will allow nothing larger than a 4 metre dinghy to be launched, and even that can be tricky. However, if you can access offshore you can bottom and game fish within a few hundred metres of the coast.

Many Carnarvon locals trailer larger boats up to the Blowholes. This is four-wheel drive only launching, across a soft beach ramp. Boats can be moored close to shore either side of the ramp. An erratic 'bar' must be traversed out of the bay, which is safe except in a large swell.

There is no need to travel more than a few hundred metres offshore for fish, although mackerel fishermen usually head 12 kilometres north to The Patch, which is often carpeted with mackerel mid-year.

Professional mackerel fishermen catch marlin here, but those targeting billfish will do better about 5 kilometres offshore where there are also plenty of wahoo.

Care must be taken when re-entering the Blowholes bay. There is no specific safe route, and afternoon sea breezes create a large swell.

Steep Point is a rock fisherman's paradise. From the high cliffs all kinds of fish are hooked but landing them requires a cliff gaff. These anglers are using a gaff to haul up this large spanish mackerel.

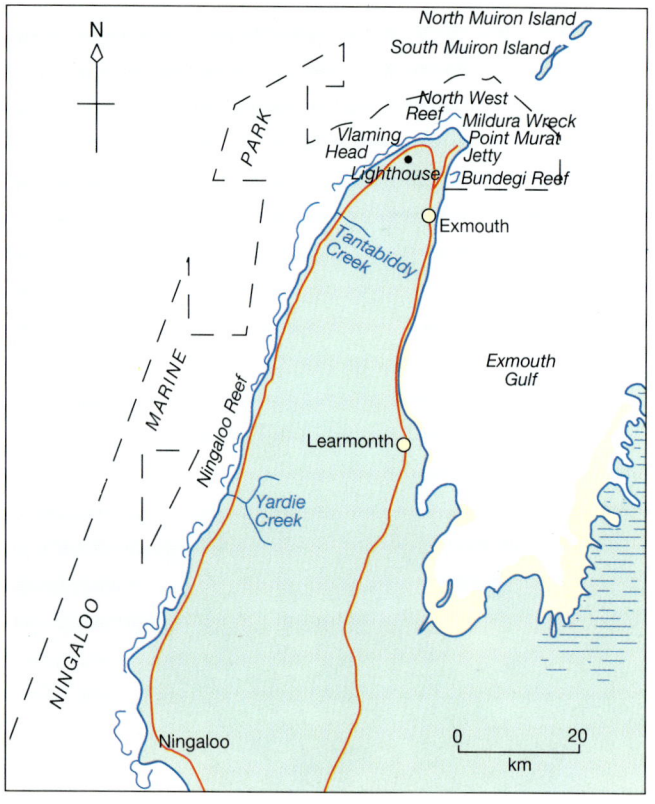

Exmouth is a favourite destination for those escaping the southern winter chill. Accommodation is well catered for, with numerous caravan parks, hotels and chalets, as well as the Cape Range National Park for self-contained camping. Several charter boats operate year-round, both for game fishing and bottom fishing. May and June are the only months with any worthy rainfall, but even then they average only a quarter as much as Perth at the same time.

Short-term holidaymakers usually trailer boats which can be launched from Exmouth, Bundegi Beach or Tantabiddy Creek. The Muiron Islands, 20 kilometres offshore from the tip of North West Cape, are an exceptional location with the full gamut of game and bottom fish on tap. Queenfish are particularly prevalent in the sandy bays. Boats in excess of 6 metres are recommended, as the intervening ocean is notably unpredictable.

Ningaloo Reef, which reaches from the tip of the Cape down the west coast to Gnaraloo, is the basis of the Ningaloo Marine Park. Fishing is permitted, with the exception of a couple of well-publicised closed areas. For most of its length, Ningaloo Reef is only a couple of kilometres offshore. Tantabiddy Creek is the usual departure point for boats, and trolling for mackerel, sailfish, marlin and tuna is productive the moment the reef passage is reached. Dinghy fishing inside the reef is great for emperor and golden trevally, with the odd shark and cobia turning up.

Two tournaments are held every year: Gamex, in October, is at the best time of year for weather and variety

of fish, while the Capricorn Cup in January is aimed at marlin and sailfish. The Cup has shown that trolling lures is more effective on billfish at Exmouth than bait, and has also proven that worthwhile quantities of billfish are available in summer.

Game fishermen mostly stay within a kilometre of the back of the reef, unless marlin and dolphin fish are specifically sought. Deep-water bottom fishermen will find plenty of red emperor, cod and coral trout. Enormous giant trevally, mackerel and cod are regularly encountered using poppers cast to the back of reefs.

Land-based anglers in Exmouth are not left out. Most long-term tourists fish the shallow rubble flats adjoining the Cape Range National Park, on the west side of the cape, for emperor, queenfish, bluebone and golden trevally. The beaches and jetties on the Learmouth side are good for whiting, tarwhine, mullet, small trevally and school mackerel.

The Oysters, just to the right of the Mildura wreck on the tip of the cape, can be fished just after high tide with lures for queenfish, tuna, mackerel, trevally and barracuda. Giant trevally weighing more than 20 kilograms can be caught on poppers at night.

Yardie Creek is the southern limit of the two-wheel drive track through the National Park. Shore fishing into the ocean is excellent, although most people visit the Creek to run a dinghy up into the spectacular gorge. Small cod and mangrove jack can be caught on lures.

The US Navy jetty at Point Murat can only be fished in the company of an employee of the communications base, but if that can be arranged try leadhead jigs or deep-running minnows at dusk and at night for trevally.

The lower Exmouth Gulf is interesting country for mangrove jacks, small trevally and queenfish, but access by land is very difficult. Dinghies reach the area from Learmonth.

Queenfish taken in the lower Exmouth Gulf is unhooked for release.

Dampier to Broome

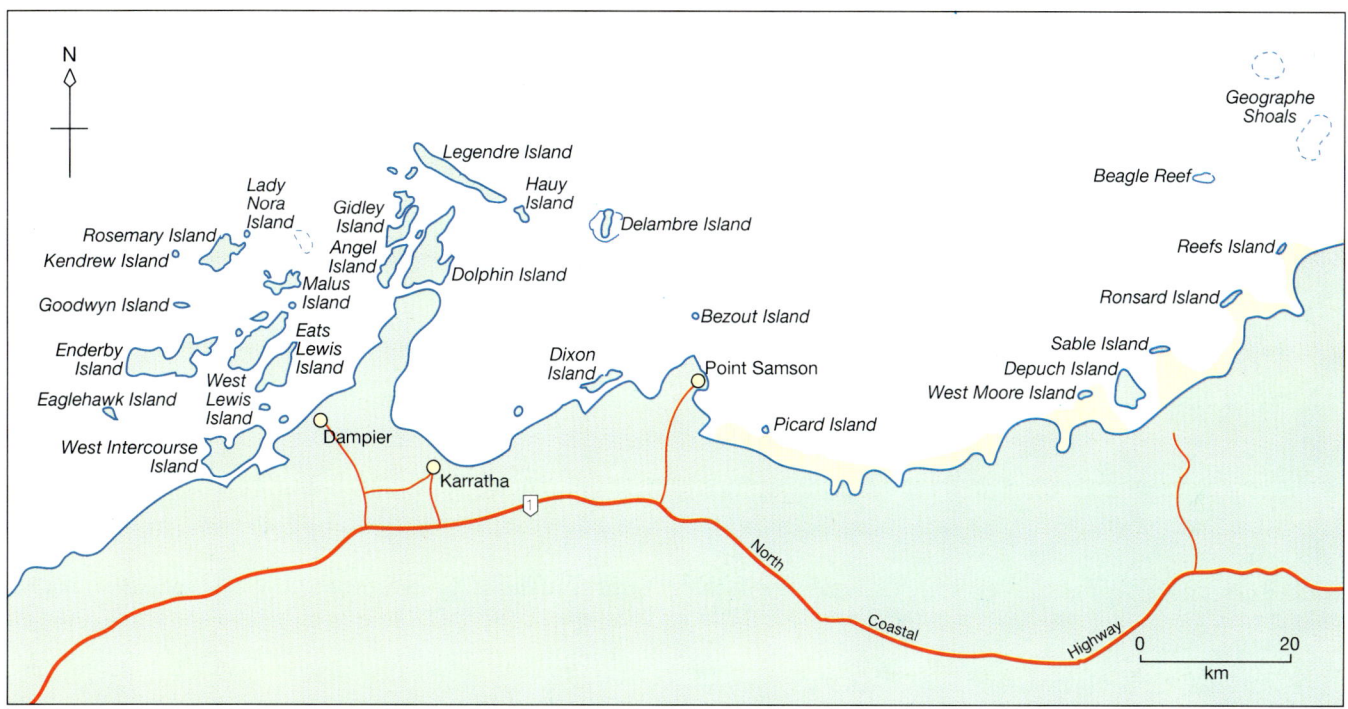

Dampier, on the Burrup Peninsular, overlooks the Dampier Archipelago. Because of the many islands, there is always a place to fish irrespective of the weather conditions. Most of the holiday shacks have been restricted to the East and West Lewis islands and the Malus and Rosemary Islands. Rosemary Island is the base for the North West Game fishing Club.

Fuel and tackle are available at Dampier, and boat ramps are located at the Hampton Harbour Sailing Club, Foul Point and near Tidepole Island. Mean high water spring and neap tides range from 4.4 to 0.9 metres. Care needs to taken on the spring low tides due to shallow water.

Dampier is best known for its sailfish between June and September. The King Bay Game Fishing Club runs the Dampier Classic in early August each year. Sailfish can be located several kilometres west of Bare Rock, and between Bare Rock and South West Reefs, Roly Rock, behind Kendrew Island, The Patches off Rosemary Island and Madelaine Shoals.

Other game fish caught at Bare Rock and Roly Rock include Spanish mackerel, cobia, giant trevally and barracuda. Large schools of shark and spotted mackerel frequent the area close to Roly Rock, while the Kendrew, Goodwyn, Lady Nora and Brigadier Islands and Miller and Nelson Rocks are good trevally fishing grounds.

The Madelaine Shoals is a good area for Spanish mackerel, tuna, trevally, sharks and black marlin.

Flying Foam Passage is reliable for tiger sharks, spotted mackerel, and around the shallow waters and sandbars for queenfish.

In the Depuch Island area, a dirt track opposite the Whim Creek Hotel winds over 20 kilometres to Balla Balla Creek, the jumping off point to Depuch and Forestier Islands. Launching off the earthen bank requires care at low tide due to soft ground, and also on spring high tides when flooded water turns the adjoining saltpan into 'slush'.

The estuary itself is a good producer of threadfin salmon, mud crabs and black jewfish in the deep holes. There are many other unnamed estuaries along the coast to the south-west and north-east which are productive for mangrove jacks, threadfin and mud crabs

Depuch and Forestier Islands offer good fishing for trevally and queenfish around the wrecks of the Depuch anchorage Black jewfish can also be prolific in the deeper parts of the anchorage.

Port Headland has good launching facilities. The main ramp in town is fairly steep and has a hump at the bottom to prevent car and trailer plummeting into the deep water. There is a good double ramp at the sailing club but the channel suffers from siltation. There is a smaller ramp located at Finucane Island to service small boats wishing to fish the estuaries for salmon, mangrove jacks, and cod.

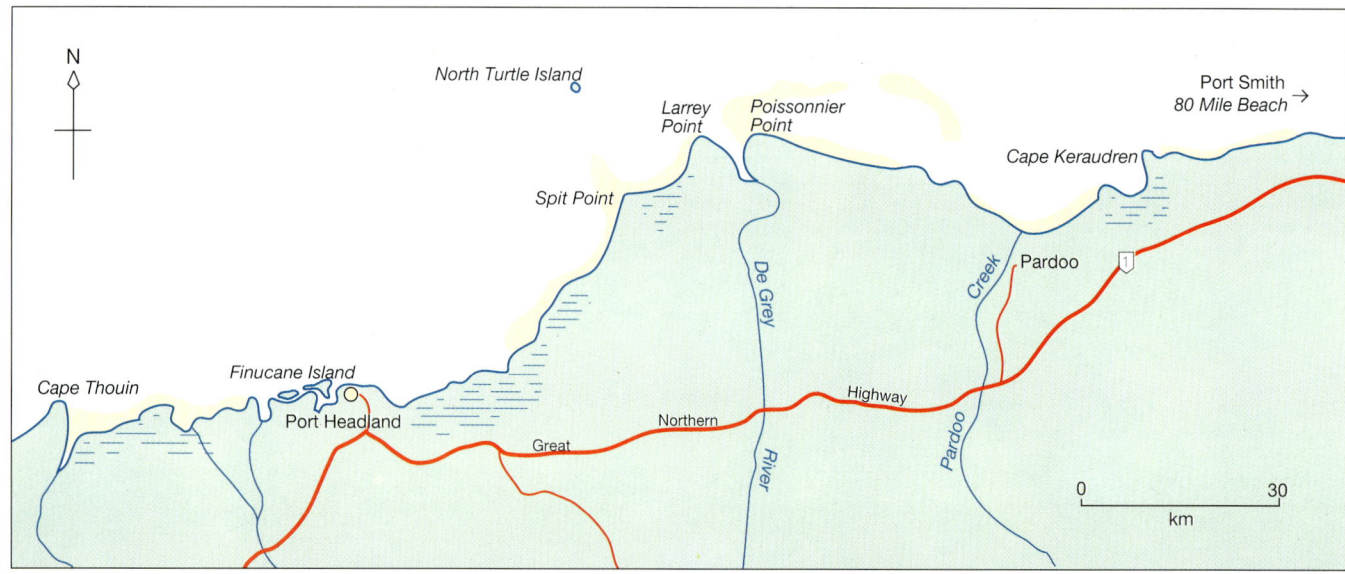

It is not recommended for larger trailerboats.

Reasonable fishing can be had in the creeks near Port Headland for most of the species mentioned above. The odd barramundi is taken from November to April. Care needs to be exercised in the estuaries due to the large tidal range, which can leave dinghy fishermen stranded until the following high tide.

Port Headland has an excellent channel-marker system to enable the large iron ore ships to navigate across the relatively shallow water and into port. The various channels are dredged. Most boat fishermen anchor next to the buoys and bottom fish for reef species or attempt to catch trevally, queenfish, mackerel and cobia. The buoys extend almost to Cornelisse Shoal, which is a top area for mackerel, trevally and sailfish.

Good reef fishing for blue bone, coral trout, and spangled emperor can be had around Minilya Bank, Coxon Shoals and the Turtle Island groups.

Cape Keraudren contains superb fishing. Pardoo Roadhouse is 160 kilometres north of Port Headland, and situated 14 kilometres opposite along a good dirt road is Cape Keraudren. A small concrete ramp facing the estuary is available for launching at high tide. However, low tide launching is possible off the gravel beach below the ramp, with no chance of becoming bogged.

This whole area fishes well for salmon and mangrove jack in the estuary, queenfish and trevally from the numerous reefs and headlands, and superb bottom and game species offshore. The reef fishing is virtually untouched and has huge numbers of red emperor, coral trout, and so on. This location is well worth visiting and camping, with fresh supplies available at Pardoo roadhouse.

80 Mile Beach yields threadfin salmon, shark, queenfish and black jewfish, and north of Port Headland some 231

kilometres is Sandfire Roadhouse offering fuel, food and accommodation. Just south and 10 kilometres off the highway is the 80 mile beach caravan park.

Port Smith is approximately 170 kilometres south of Broome by road (70 kilometres by water), the last 23 kilometres over a graded dirt road to where Port Smith caravan park is situated.

Port Smith was once a pearl shell operation, but is now used as an access point for pearling farms located just outside the bay. Launching is off the sand and the estuary offers good fishing for mangrove jack, threadfin salmon in the Dry season, and queenfish and trevally.

Just offshore there are various reefs which are virtually untouched. They swarm with coral trout, various emperors, cod, bluebone, spanish flag, golden trevally and others. Anglers experience problems of coral trout stealing live baits intended for mackerel around the reef.

Spanish mackerel are prolific along the northwest coast.

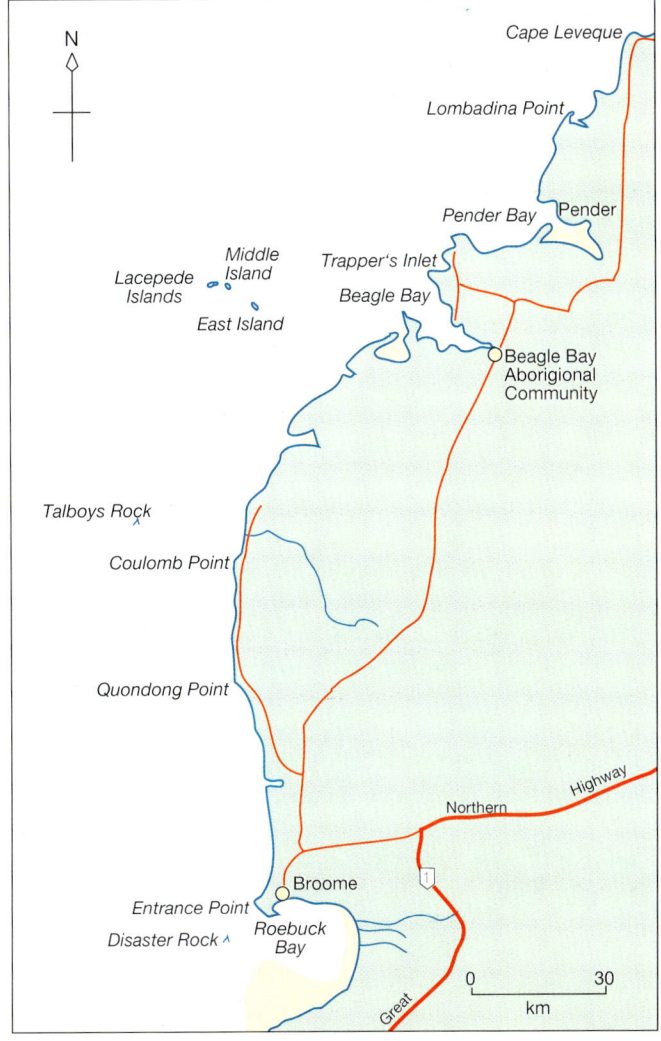

is located 150 to 200 metres from the main boat ramp, next to the channel light. The hole covers an area the size of a football field, with the average depth varying between 30 and 45 metres.

Another hole to the west of Entrance Point is part of the eastern ledge of the Roebuck Deeps, the major channel entering Roebuck Bay. While the depth can be as great as 100 metres, to get at the jewfish it is necessary to anchor in the 35 to 60 metre range and fish the sloping edge of the channel.

Due to extensive tidal variation at Broome (up to 10 metres) the jewfish holes can only be fished effectively on the neap tides.

Broome's creeks are best known for threadfin salmon, especially when the easterly winds of the Dry season prevail.

Areas such as Dampier, Crab, Willies and Barred Creeks along with the Thangoo system are good producers of salmon. Mangrove jack, finngermark, small trevally, queenfish and mud crabs can also be found. Due to extensive tide variations it is easy to get stranded if you don't keep a check on water levels.

Disaster Rock, 13 kilometres south-west offshore from Broome, is a series of reefs which hold large schools of trevally, barracuda and mackerel in season. Fishing is best when the tidal flow is strongest; either on a flood or ebbing tide. Once the tidal flow slows, change to bottom fishing for coral trout and fingermark.

Further offshore to the north-west are the 16 to 26 kilometre areas, a series of reefs running north/south at 23 kilometre intervals. Bottom fish are prolific.

North of Broome the fishing is superb all the way along the protected coastline to Cape Leveque.

Quandong Point is a good location for blue bone, Spanish flag, maori sea perch, snapper and cod. Prawns are a good bait for most species. Good numbers of Spanish mackerel, barracuda, trevally, tuna and sailfish can be found around the reefs.

Talboys Rock, about 70 kilometres north of Broome, is difficult to locate, but large numbers of mackerel, trevally and reef fish are to be found there.

The Lacepede Islands, a series of low-lying sand cays surrounded by numerous reefs, sandbars and shallow water, are excellent fishing for most species, although sharks are a nuisance.

Beagle Bay, Pender Bay, Tappers Bay and Lombadina are all top locations for both pelagic and bottom fishing, as well as baramundi and mangrove jacks in the creeks. Access is along the Cape Leveque Road. Permission needs to be obtained to enter the Aboriginal missions of Beagle Bay, Lombadine and One Arm Point.

The best time to visit Broome and the Kimberley region is during the Dry season from April to November. Offshore easterly winds flatten the seas, and the breeze normally drops around midday.

Broome's anglers are well catered for with fuel, food and fishing tackle. However, the boat ramps are inadequate.

The one at Entrance Point is dual lane, though the concrete only extends down to the 6 metre high tide line. If the tide is less than 6 metres, and that is most of the time, you will need to launch off the beach at the bottom of the ramp. The sand is hard to the 2 metre line, after which it becomes soft and bogging is inevitable.

The second boat ramp, at Town Beach next to the Roebuck Bay Caravan Park, is single lane and suffers badly from siltation.

At Broome, the jetty is a popular fishing spot for cod, blue bone, queenfish and golden trevally. Barramundi are available at night from under the lights at the end of the jetty during the Wet season.

No other place in Australia can match Broome for easily accessible black jewfishing. The most popular hole

Freshwater Fishing

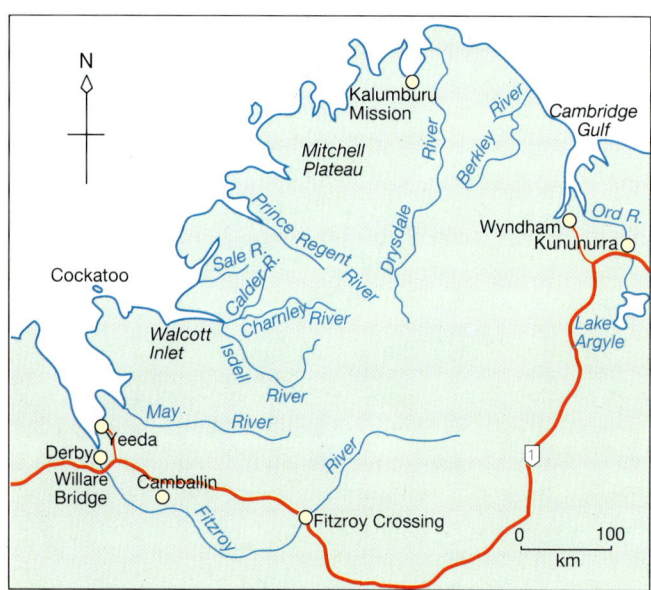

Tropical Freshwater

In tropical Western Australia, the Pilbara and Kimberley regions have little permanent freshwater fishing. There are several lagoons that hold barramundi year round, but even the mightiest of rivers can dry only a couple of months after the Wet season rains.

There are few species that can tolerate this changing environment. Sooty grunter, tarpon, long tom, archer fish and catfish survive in the fresh water, while barramundi and mangrove jack move with tidal influence in the lower reaches of the rivers.

The Kimberleys contain the largest body of fresh water in Australia, the man-made Lake Argyle which holds commercial quantities of huge catfish, and some sooty grunter and long tom.

Ivanhow Crossing or the Diversion Dam gates, a short trip from Wyndham, are hotspots for barramundi in the Wet season.

Further down the Ord River are the Dry season locations, although a quarantine area encompassing the tidal reaches restricts access. Charter operations out of Kununurra have special permission to enter the area. Carlton Crossing and Sandy Beach are in the freshwater stretch, and can be reached by four-wheel drive.

There are also helicopter and floatplane charters which reach the otherwise virtually inaccessible rivers and Wet season coastal creeks across the top end of Western Australia.

Wyndham has little freshwater fishing close to town, as it is situated amongst tidal mudflats. The Penetecost River

crossing, which is influenced by the ocean tides, is a good location for barramundi. Other river locations are accessible by four-wheel drive.

From Wyndham and Cambridge Gulf to Derby, access is a major problem. Cruising yachts and adventurous off-roaders are at an advantage, as there is no way for an average tourist to reach the Mitchell, Prince Regent or Sale Rivers, or Walcott Inlet with its feeder rivers, Calder, Charnley and Isdell. This entire area is an unscathed natural sanctuary for barramundi.

Derby, although also situated among tidal mudflats, has the distinction of being built at the mouth of the Fitzroy River. Willare Bridge, Yeeda and Langi Crossing are not far from town and offer good barramundi fishing, while upstream pools also offer tarpon and catfish. The river is dammed at Camballin. The larger sooty grunter and catfish are upstream from the dam, while the barramundi reach hundreds of kilometres inland to Geikie Gorge.

May River is a small river also accessible from town via the Bigg River road. It is a good barramundi spot, with threadfin salmon also available.

Live pop-eye mullet, caught with a cast net , are the best bait for barramundi throughout the Kimberleys.

Although barramundi and tarpon are caught as far south as Onslow, there are few freshwater creeks south of Fitzroy that hold fish all year.

Temperate Freshwater

The far south-west corner of the State has a wealth of streams, rivers and impoundments. Rivers meander through huge jarrah and karri forests, leaving a succession of deep pools to attract both the fly fisherman and the spinman.

Rainbow and brown trout are introduced species and constant restocking has to take place because of limited natural breeding. The voracious redfin perch, also an introduced species, have run riot by eating the fry of other more valuable freshwater inhabitants, including the splendid freshwater crayfish or marron.

Redfin do offer the freshwater angler the opportunity of a large catch. Small lures, such as the Rapala Mini Fat Rap, 8 gram Nilsmaster, and small Halco Laser work on both trout and redfin. Many of the south-west's rivers are heavily overgrown and limited opportunities exist for fly fisherman, other than in impoundments.

Warren River and Lefroy Brook are the best natural waterways to catch quantities of large rainbow and brown trout. Autumn and spring are favoured times. The Warren

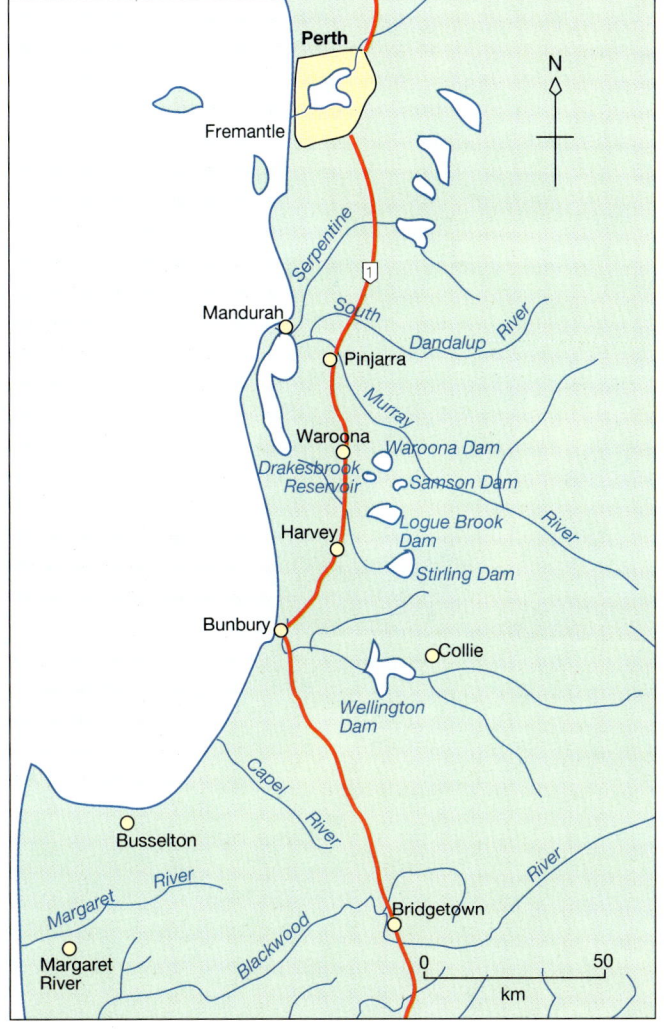

favoured sports with visitors to this superb, thickly forested countryside.

Samson Dam, Logue Brook, the Upper Blackwood River, and Waroona Dam are other top fly waters, although redfin have diminished trout numbers in the latter. An excellent caravan park is situated at Waroona Dam, which is also a marron or crayfish lurk.

Blackwood River holds many marron in its upper reaches and also some large trout, sometimes caught in farm waters open to the public.

As in all Western Australian freshwater fishing, summer temperatures cause the fish to seek deep cooler waters. Rivers like the Blackwood and Warren have only a trickle of water then and fish seek refuge in perennial pools among the karri forests around Pemberton.

Around Perth there is little freshwater action as water supply dams are off limits to anglers. Lake Leschenaultia has a limited season on introduced stock, and a farm at Lesmurdie a private hatchery.

The Murray River is superb, especially for redfin, with fine trout in lesser fished water. Near Dwellingup is best, and many fine rocky pools exist near the Baden Powell waterspout. Right down near Pinjarra big fish have come from some surprising water quite close to the estuary.

Drakesbrook Reservoir, below Waroona Dam, has a large population of redfin, and quiet stretches of river can house big marron. A strictly controlled season exists on the vulnerable marron stock.

At Harvey Weir, trout are best pursued in spring to early summer, while many Harvey locals use baits and lures year round for redfin.

In Stirling Dam, lures are suited to the expansive, easily accessible waters. Marron are keenly pursued.

Wellington Dam fishes well for redfin, and is a very popular for catching marron.

River drains the wettest part of the State and trout are taken right at the mouth, where it reaches the sea.

Lefroy Brook has excellent lure and fly-fishing water, and some reasonably accessible bank, unlike the inhospitable Warren which can only be fished from a few deep, long pools.

Bedelup Park has been developed as a tourist complex near Beedelup Dam. Trout and marron chasing are

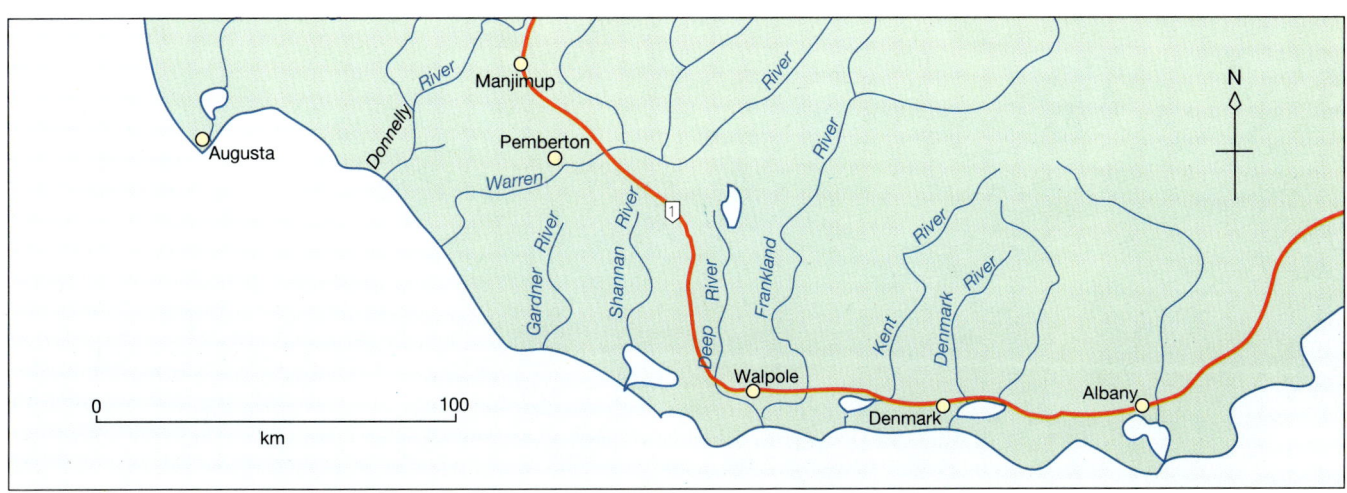

Northern Territory

Introduction

The Northern Territory has some of the most prolific fishing in Australia. With vast, unique wetlands with their numerous freshwater rivers and billabongs, it is the perfect environment for barramundi.

The Territory is the undisputed barramundi capital of Australia with wetlands such as the Kakadu National Park providing stunning fishing opportunities.

Despite the quality and quantity of freshwater angling, the Northern Territory also has world class saltwater fishing in the many mangrove-lined creeks, tidal rivers, bays, offshore islands and reef complexes.

The list of fish available from these regions is seemingly endless. Barracuda, black jewfish, cod, coral trout, emperor, fingermark, mackerel, queenfish, sailfish, sharks, sweetlip, tuna, and so the list goes on.

However, access is often limited by the Wet Season rains, poor or flooded roads and crossings or by large Aboriginal reserves as in Arnhem Land. A properly equipped four-wheel drive vehicle is a basic necessity if you are planning to make for use of the Territory's fishing opportunities.

There is no better place to fish than the Northern Territory. It is largely undeveloped, pristine and one of the last great wilderness areas in the world. The fishing is exciting and the scenery and wildlife a colourful experience.

Fishing in the mangrove creeks of the Northern Territory is excellent for barramundi. But while lures are the most popular technique, live bait produces better results if you are looking for trophy-sized specimens.

West Coast to Darwin

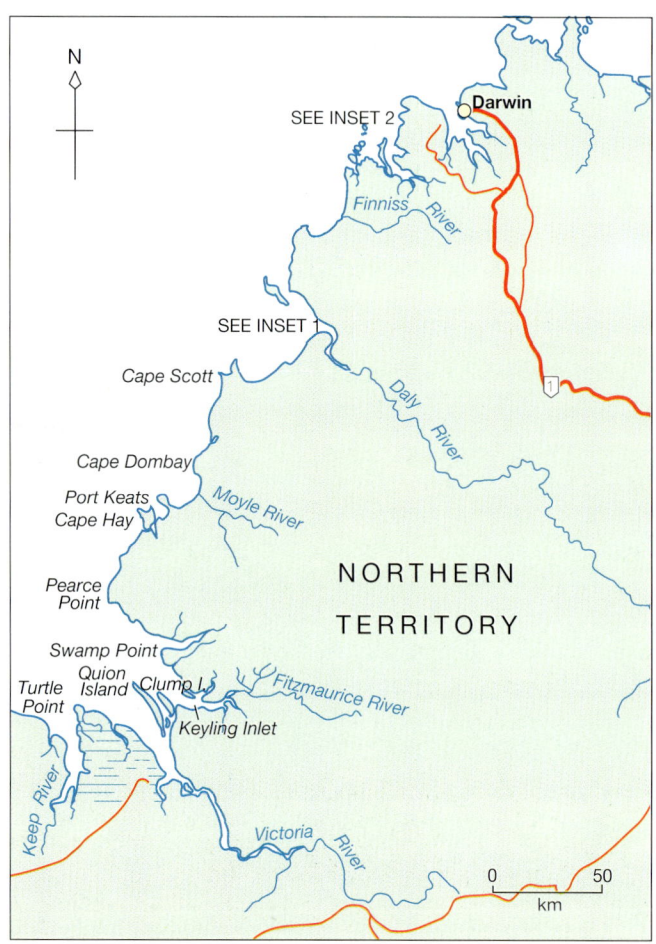

A virgin fishing area access is difficult except by boat from Darwin. Much of the land south of the Daly River is Aboriginal reserve or remote cattle stations in rugged terrain. What access there is consists of rough four-wheel drive tracks, impassible in the Wet season.

Sufficient fuel and provisions and complete self-sufficiency must be achieved if intending to fish these areas.

The land offers protection from easterly winds. Seas rarely exceed 1 to 1.5 metres, with little or no swell during the Dry season.

The area is a maze of mud, sandbars and reefs making navigation hazardous. There are no warning signs which adds to the problem. A close eye must be kept on marine charts and tide tables. Spring tides can vary up to 8 metres.

The Keep River is reached from Kununurra, through Legune Station in the Northern Territory. It is necessary to obtain permission from Legune before entering the saltwater reaches of the river. In the tidal areas, the river is murky brown limiting the effectiveness of lures.

The main fish species are barramundi, threadfin salmon and catfish. Live mullet is the most effective bait. Fish the run-offs, creek junctions and around snags.

The Victoria and Fitzmaurice rivers are difficult to get to at the lower reaches. Most boat launching is near Timber and Big Horse Creeks from the river banks. The seaward reaches of the Victoria and Fitzmaurice are rarely fished due to lack of access points and the long run downstream from the Timber Creek region.

The mouth of each river is very wide and studded with numerous sandbars. The waters are hazardous, especially on spring tides where swirling eddies work against prevailing winds, creating short, sharp chop. The area known as the Entrance, where the waters funnel through a narrow gap in the river, is particularly dangerous.

Here the water is discoloured, resulting in better fishing upstream around Bullo River, Angalari, Sandy Island and Timber Creek. Lures are very effective when water clarity permits, while live mullet and cherabin is the best all-round fish taker.

The Fitzmaurice is one of the most inaccessible rivers in the Northern Territory with access overland in the freshwater reaches but not to the salt water because of rock bars and waterfalls. The saltwater reaches can only be negotiated by boat from the seaward end.

This 7.75 Kg queenfish was taken at Point Blaze by lure casting.

There is excellent fishing for barramundi and mangrove jack upstream; closer to the mouth are large threadfin salmon and big barramundi. In clear water live and dead baits are the most productive.

Port Keats to Cape Ford is Aboriginal land, necessitating a permit from the Northern Land Council to enter. The alternative is to travel by sea from Darwin. There is excellent barramundi, threadfin salmon, mangrove jack and queenfish, and the water is much clearer compared to areas further south.

Top barramundi spots are Moyle, Little Moyle and Cape Dombey around the snags, tidal gutters and oyster-encrusted rocks.

Queenfish prefer the points inside the small bays and along the beaches by the mouths of estuary systems.

The whole area has good offshore reef fishing for golden and north-west snapper, Spanish flag, cod, coral trout and emperor. Spanish mackerel abound from April to November. Emu Reefs, located offshore, is a productive spot for mackerel, barracuda and trevally.

Cape Ford and Scott offers superb reef and pelagic fishing at the bottom of the tide. The area is studded with rocky headlands and offshore pinnacles.

The Perons Islands are located nearly 130 kilometres by sea from Darwin, although overland access can be achieved through La Belle Station to Channel Point. The Perons consist of two islands, at their closest point only 3.5 kilometres from the mainland.

There is a deep hole between Channel Point and the islands which produces large numbers of black jewfish on the change of tide. The northern end of North Peron has a large reef system which produces queenfish, golden and giant trevally. To the west are extensive reef systems producing excellent catches of reef fish, including the fabled golden snapper (fingermark) and red emperor.

About 8 kilometres to the south-west of North Peron is Bateman Shoal, a productive area for reef fish, large numbers of mackerel, trevally, tuna and sailfish. Offshore from the Peron Islands is often alive with pelagic fish.

A sandspit off the western side is a productive queenfish location. The oyster-encrusted rocks between the two islands and the rocky areas towards the bottom end of South Peron are prime locations for big saltwater barramundi and large giant trevally.

Point Blaze and Point Jenny are top reef fishing locations, particularly within 500 metres of shore. A little bay to the south-west of Point Jenny is one of the hottest locations for big queenfish, particularly on a making tide.

Blaze Reef, to the north, produces good bags of reef fish, and pelagic species during the Dry season.

Fog Bay and the Finniss River is a commercial prawning ground, with a relatively featureless bottom. Access to the Finniss River by sea is hampered by extensive mud flats, although there is land access through Finniss River Station. The saltwater reaches of the Finniss are featureless and not often fished by recreational anglers, despite its proximity to Darwin.

Further to the north, around Native Point, are rocky areas just offshore which produce big saltwater barramundi using lures, particularly on larger tides during the build-up to and just after the Wet season.

Dum In Mirrie Island to Quail Island, approximately 50 to 60 kilometres from Darwin, consists of six islands surrounded by extensive sandbars and reefs.

Sandbars offshore from Grose Island, at the southern and northern ends of Bare Sand Island, and a reefy area on the eastern side of Quail Island, are prime locations for queenfish. Poppers, deep-diving minnows and spoons are very effective.

Bass and Roche Reef, Loee Patches and Jones Bank produce good numbers of mackerel and trevally, along with top reef fish. Using a depth sounder, many uncharted reefs can be located. A close watch on the tide tables is needed to avoid running aground.

Lorna Shoals to the north produce large numbers of bottom fish, trevally, mackerel, tuna and occasional sailfish. Live baiting with small reef fish is deadly on mackerel, cobia and sharks.

The Angalari river flows into the Victoria River and is typical of a turbid Territory river. Just the right environment for barramundi.

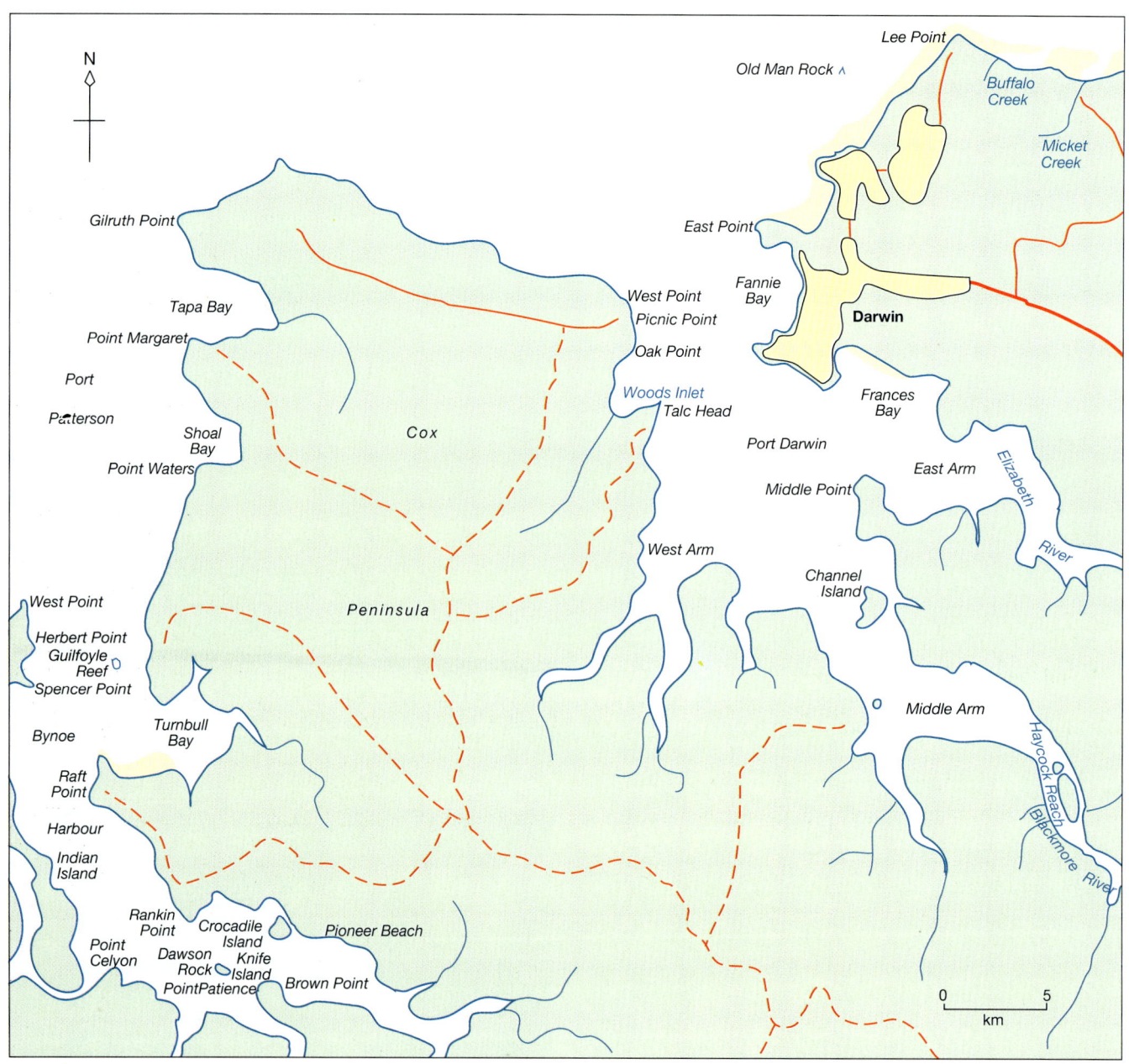

The waters close to Darwin offer excellent saltwater fishing from the neap to the springs tides. On large spring tides, the water may become discoloured, especially if coinciding with strong easterly winds. Peak fishing season is from April to November.

Darwin is well-serviced with all types of accommodation, boat ramps and marine facilities, and the harbour flanking the city is a good fishing region.

Bynoe Harbour is located an hour's drive over good roads from Darwin. Anglers can launch boats off Pioneer Beach, Rankin Point or Raft Point.

There is excellent barramundi fishing in the harbours, creeks, and off rocky points on the north-eastern tip of Indian Island by casting to small gutters, or trolling along the edges of the mud banks on the last two hours of the run-out or first hour of the making tide.

Fingermark bream abound in most estuary systems near rock bars, shaley areas and snags caused by mangroves falling into the water.

Queenfish can be located close to the beaches along Raft and Rankin Point and around Crocodile, Indian and Knife Islands. A reef that runs to the west of Knife Island produces trevally, barracuda and small mackerel in season. The deep hole between Raft Point and Indian Island is good for black jewfish and fingermark bream.

Charles Point is located about 20 kilometres west of Darwin and is signposted by the turbulent water caused when both Darwin and Bynoe Harbours' tidal currents converge over shallow ground.

Between Gilruth Point and Charles Point is an extensive reef system which produces queenfish and wolf herring, particularly on a rising tide. There is also a small creek for good barramundi and mangrove jacks on live bait from October to December, while off Charles Point are numerous reefs and pinnacles which produce good numbers of black jewfish, fingermark and assorted reef fish, especially from October and February.

Along Cox Peninsula, small creeks yield the odd barramundi, fingermark, queenfish and threadfin salmon.

Darwin Harbour is a tremendous fishing region, despite the city's proximity.

At Mandorah is the wreck of the Mandorah Queen. It's a prime location on neap tides for black jewfish and fingermark.

The beaches from West Point to Oak Point, and Talc Head are all prime haunts for good-size queenfish.
Between Talc Head and the Port of Darwin are several artificial reefs formed by the sinking of vessels, which produce black jewfish, fingermark, cod and reef fish.

Darwin Harbour then enters west, middle and east arms, all of which produce barramundi, threadfin salmon, javelin fish, fingermark and cod. Most barramundi are taken by casting to small run-offs from the mud banks or trolling the upper reaches of the creeks. Many javelin fish and fingermark are taken on cut fish bait at Haycock Reach and the top end of middle arm.

The Shell Islands, just off the East Arm boat ramp, yield large giant trevally, small queenfish and big spanish mackerel in season, along with reef fish on the bottom.

Darwin's jetties produce good size queenfish, particularly on live herring, along with barramundi under the lights. Milkfish can be caught at Frances Bay, the Navy Base and East Point, provided the water is berleyed with plenty of bread and cubes of crusty bread are fished near the surface on small hooks. Note that it is illegal to fish at Doctor's Gully where milkfish are hand fed.

From April to October, large Spanish mackerel, barracuda, longtail tuna and giant trevally can be found around East Point, Old Man Rock and Lee Point. Mackerel are taken by trolling deep-diving minnow lures, berleying at anchor using pilchard baits, or live baiting with small reef fish.

Shoal Bay Peninsula, north-west of Darwin, is a haunt for large saltwater barramundi. Access is by boat, which can be launched from the excellent concrete ramp at Buffalo Creek or off the river bank at Micket, King or Howard Rivers. As it is all real 'tiger country', we recommend you obtain a 'mud map' from the local fishing tackle stores before heading off.

Caution must be exercised when launching off the river banks on spring tides as the mud causes bogging.
The upper reaches of Micket and Howard Rivers form into pools separated by shallow water. If the water depth exceeds around a metre, the holes often contain good numbers of barramundi waiting for the incoming tide. December is the best month.

Located just off Tree Point is a large oyster-encrusted rock about 100 metres long where big barramundi from 8 to 20 kilograms gather. Anglers fish this area from September onwards, casting large minnow lures into the eddies surrounding the rock on an outgoing tide or the first hour of the incoming tide.

Fenton Patches is located about 25 kilometres north-north-west of Darwin, and is a series of sand and reef ridges on an otherwise featureless bottom.
An artificial reef and FAD (Fish Aggregation Device) have been placed in the area, which should attract and hold schools of travelling fish.

Good numbers of sailfish and some black marlin have come from Fenton Patches, mainly on trolled garfish or mullet. The area also produces good numbers of Spanish and spotted mackerel, which can be caught right through the Wet season.

Large schools of golden and giant trevally haunt bait schools at Fenton Patches, creating a feeding frenzy on the surface. Boats can approach the schools, and anglers casting lures will encounter exciting action, although the area can go quiet on the top and bottom of the tides.

Shoal Bay, an excellent barramundi ground, isn't very far from Darwin. This 4 Kg fish was taken on a live bait of mullet fished from the mangroves.

Bathurst and Melville Islands

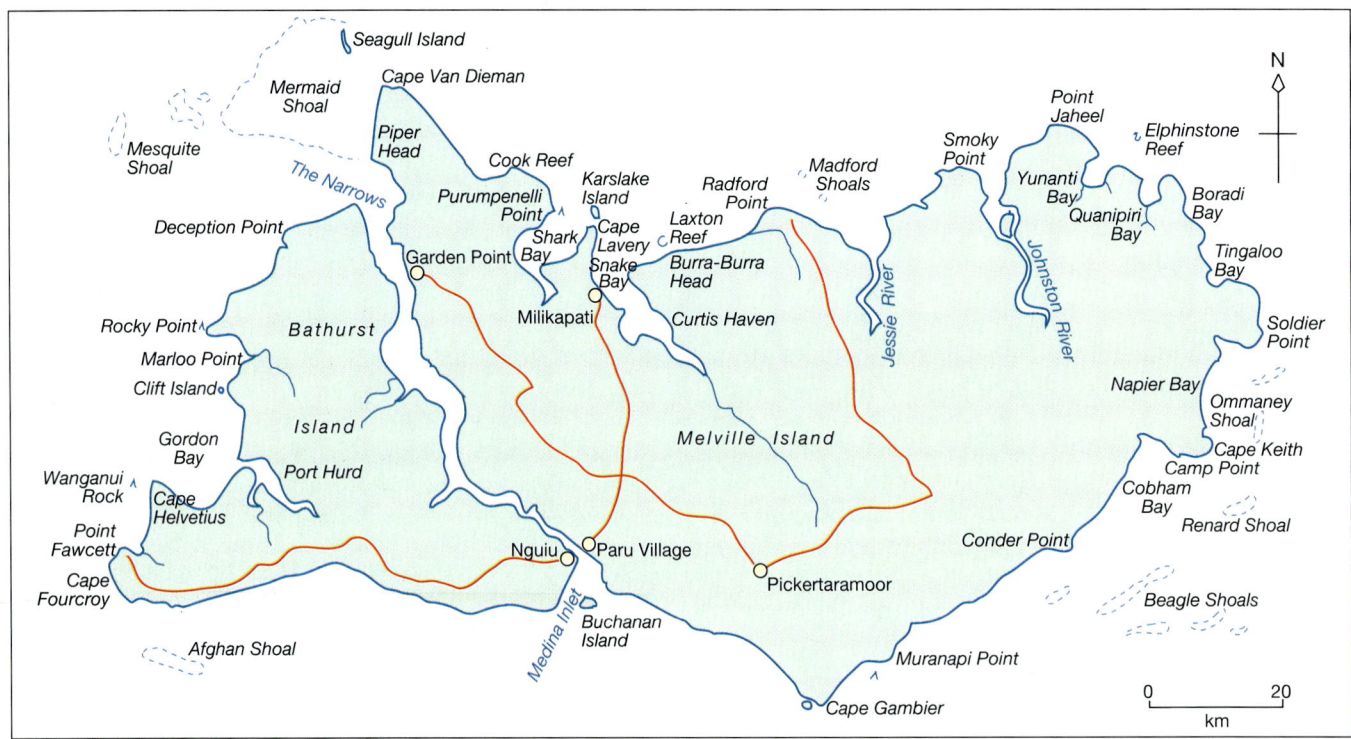

To fish on Bathurst and Melville Islands requires a permit from the Tiwi Aboriginal Land Council. Anglers can fish the waters adjacent to the islands without a permit, although an application is before the courts for a 2 kilometre sea closure around the islands.

Barra Base lodge, on the southern entrance to Port Hurd, offers comfortable air conditioned accommodation, cooked meals, bar and spa. Guides accompany parties of two anglers on estuary fishing expeditions in customised dinghies, although larger craft are available to pursue pelagics further around the numerous headlands and reefs. An airstrip grants access from Darwin in 30 minutes.

Port Hurd is a large estuary system with three arms that divide into numerous creeks. Large saltwater barramundi are caught, particularly following the Wet season in April and May. Deep holes harbour large numbers of the fabled black jewfish on the neap tides.

Beach fishing from the southern entrance in front of the lodge produces large tiger sharks at night, groper (which are released), threadfin salmon, queenfish and bream.

Second Creek, from the mouth on the southern side, is the best for big saltwater barramundi and threadfin salmon averaging 8 kilograms. Trolling or casting to any of the snags, particularly towards the bottom of the tide, will produce resident barramundi, fingermark or mangrove jack. Casting lures to snags in the upstream reaches produces barramundi, mangrove jack, fingermark, javelin fish, queenfish, archer fish, trevally, cod and sharks.

At the southern end of Gordon Bay, a series of tidal creeks cut off on spring low tides, draining a large freshwater swamp that produces numbers of big saltwater barramundi around the numerous snags.

Cape Fourcroy is a meeting place of currents, and the seas can be large and confused. Boat fishermen are advised to travel about 8 kilometres out to sea to avoid the worst of it. There are numerous reefs and headlands around the Cape which produce big mackerel, trevally, queenfish, and good bottom fish.

Tangarapu Creek has a large resident population of queenfish and barracuda close into the red cliffs at the mouth. The estuary mainly produces mangrove jack.

Afghan Shoal, located about 7 kilometres south-east of Cape Fourcroy, produces large numbers of mackerel and trevally.

Offshore from Cape Helvetius are numerous reefs including Wanganui Rock (breaks), which produces Spanish, broodbar and spotted mackerel, queenfish and giant trevally, billfish and superb bottom fish.

About 20 kilometres to the west is the Bathurst Trench where the bottom rises to 220 metres to 20 metres further to the west. This is the main area for billfish, tuna and mackerel.

Clift Island, in shallow water towards the northern end of Gordon Bay, is studded with reefs. The water at the eastern end is shallow and unnavigable on low tide. Good barramundi are to be found amongst the oyster-encrusted rocks on the south-western side.

The water drops away at the western end and is a prime area for queenfish, big trevally and Spanish mackerel in the Dry season.

Gullala Creek, at the top end of Gordon Bay, is very productive for baramundi and threadfin at the northern entrance, at the bottom of the tide and on first of the rising tide.

On the southern side, after passing a major arm to the south, the terrain changes to oyster rocks which produce trevally, queenfish, cod and mangrove jack.

Rocky Point must be fished with caution as dangerous reefs are scattered for 5 kilometres offshore. These reefs are the hunting grounds for mackerel, trevally, queenfish and big barracuda and large fingermark.

Caution and Deception Points have a series of rocks protruding out to sea which produce trevally, queenfish and barracuda. Care needs to be exercised with the bomboras off Deception Point as they are difficult to see through the murky water.

Aspley Strait contains hazardous rock bars, though it produces good fingermark and black jewfish, especially in a hole 40 metres off Garden Point Mission at the northern end of the strait. Due to currents, the area can be successfully fished only on the neap tides.

Cape Van Dieman to Snake Bay is excellent fishing, especially along the headlands.

Offshore, the sandbars and reefs punctuated by Seagull Island are best fished on a rising tide to avoid the numerous natural hazards. The most prevalent fish are giant trevally, queenfish, barracuda and mackerel. Cook Reef, Purumpenelli Point and Karslake Island produce pelagic fish. Using a depth sounder numerous reefs which have fingermark bream, coral trout, emperor, and cod can be located within a short distance of the mainland.

Goose creek contains quantities of barramundi. Due to the shallow water, access should only be attempted from the sea at half tide or higher. While there are good numbers of saltwater barramundi the area is more famous for its freshwater barramundi, located well upstream where the water flows in from swamps and natural springs. Saratoga are also located in the upper reaches.

The Jessie and Johnson Rivers are prolific producers of most species available on the islands. The entrance to these rivers is studded with fringing reefs.

Brenton Bay is a good location for barramundi. There are numerous uncharted reefs offshore which produce huge numbers of fish as the waters are virtually untouched. Prevailing north-easterly afternoon sea breezes during the Dry season can make conditions offshore uncomfortable.

Soldier Point and Cape Keith at the end of Melville Island are severely affected by south-east trade winds in the Dry season. They are best fished during the build-up to the Wet season when westerlies prevail.

Offshore there are numerous shoals from Hinkler Patches to Beagle Shoals in the south. These areas produce large numbers of pelagic and bottom fish, although sharks can be a problem.

There are numerous estuaries along the south-eastern side of the island, with some rock bars at the entrances. Again most of the fish described will be located as the area is not often fished.

Threadfin salmon although considered only second to barramundi are equally spectacular fighters and are as good to eat. Bathurst Island's Port Hurd is one of the country's leading threadfin locations.

Darwin to East Alligator River

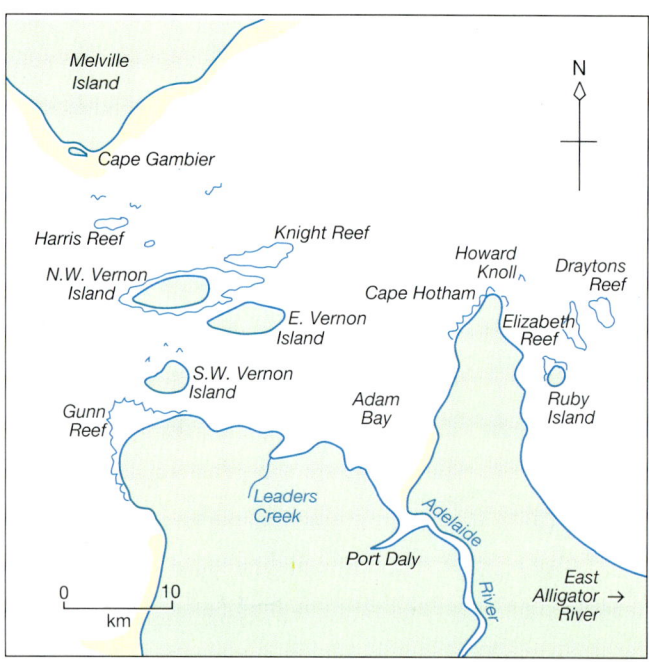

The Vernon Islands are three mangrove-covered atolls between Gunn Point on the mainland and Cape Gambier on Melville Island. The area features deep channels, dangerous reefs and fast flowing currents. Marine charts are needed to avoid running aground. The islands are always visible on high tide.

Access by boat launched from the concrete ramp in the upper reaches of Leaders Creek. Fishing in Leaders Creek can be productive for barramundi, threadfin salmon, fingermark and the odd jewfish and mud crab.

The numerous creeks on the islands can only be entered on the top half of the tide. Many unsuspecting fishermen become trapped in these creeks on a falling tide.

The most prevalent fish in the creeks are mangrove jack. On spring tides they move back into the mangrove roots, making them difficult to locate. On neap tides, however, it is only necessary to keep trying various clumps of roots in the shade. Mixed in with the mangrove jack are some big cod. If trolling or casting in the creeks the main species are giant trevally, queenfish and barracuda.

The deep holes located inside the atolls can be fished if you're prepared to wait to leave on the next rising tide. On bait, snapper, emperor, Spanish flag, moon fish, cod and mangrove jacks can be caught.

The edges of the atolls are productive trolling grounds for trevally, queenfish, barracuda and Spanish mackerel when the water is draining back into the channels. Henry Ellis Reefs yield large numbers of giant trevally, and to a lesser extent mackerel and barracuda. Bottom fishing is excellent on the neap tides.

The Adelaide River can be reached by launching at Leaders Creek or off the beach at Point Stephens. The beach at Point Stephens is not recommended as the water is shallow and suffers afternoon north-east winds. There is launching for dinghies closer to the Adelaide River from a steep bank at Saltwater Arm. Care must taken as it is innundated by tides in excess of 7 metres.

The Adelaide River is excellent for fingermark, bream, salmon, cod and mud crabs.Near the mouth of the river it narrows and there is a series of submerged rock bars and deep holes known as the Narrows. Fishing on the neap tides in this area is superb for large black jewfish, fingermark and cod.

Cape Hotham has numerous offshore reefs and rocks. Besides the usual reef fish, the area is well known for its trevally, queenfish, mackerel and tuna. The cape can become quite rough when the prevailing south-easterlies blow during the Dry season.

Care must be taken when fishing the large reefs and Ruby Island, on the eastern side of the cape. The reefs are submerged at high tide, and the seas can become quite rough when a north-easterly is blowing.

Reef and pelagic fish are taken from this area. Some barramundi and estuary species are available in the small creeks on the eastern Cape.

The Mary River reached by travelling along the Arnhem Highway then north to Shady Camp. It is about an hour's boat run from Shady Camp to the mouth of the river.

Fish the low tide for barramundi at the mouth of the river by casting lures, or live baiting to the numerous run-offs and smaller creeks entering the main river. At high tide fish the snags with bait for fingermark, threadfin salmon, and cod.

The Wildman, West Alligator, South Alligator and East Alligator Rivers can be accessed by four-wheel drive off the Arnhem Highway. The track is not suited to larger trailerboats, which can be launched from a concrete ramp on the Arnhem Highway, to the north of the bridge. It is about a 3 hour run to the mouths of the rivers.

Other than the usual estuary species, there is excellent reef fishing close to shore off the Wildman and South Alligator rivers. Large numbers of fingermark and jewfish are taken from small boats over reefs in only 3 to 4 metres of water. There is excellent fishing for bottom species in the vicinity of Field Island at the mouth of the South Alligator, although care needs to be exercised when navigating due to reefs and sandbars.

There are good launching ramps at Cahills crossing on the East Alligator.

Arnhem Land

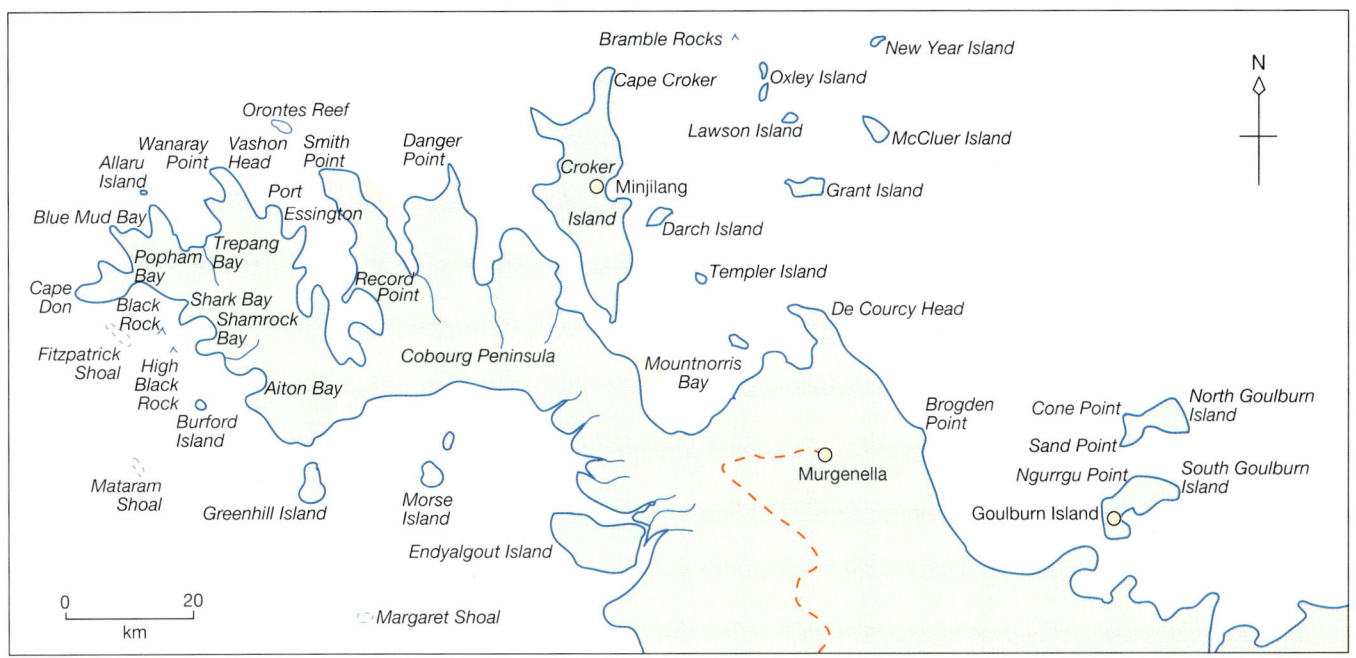

The entirety of Arnhem Land is Aboriginal owned, and visitors are required to obtain entry permits from the Northern Land Council based in Darwin. Access can be gained by sea, providing you don't set foot on land but whether entering the various creeks constitutes a breach of the Aboriginal Land Rights is disputable. In any event, unless you have very good reason to enter Arnhem Land and fishing is not regarded as a sufficient reason permits are likely to be denied.

There are exceptions. Coburg Peninsula is a conservation area (Gung Park) administered by the Aboriginals and the Northern Territory Conservation Commission. Overland access is allowed to a set limit of vehicles (permits can be obtained from the Conservation Commission in Darwin) to travel via the Arnhem Highway and north through the western Arnhem Land region to Port Essington. There are even a series of cabins erected by the Commission at Black Point that are available for hire through Wimray Pty Ltd.

Due to bauxite and manganese mining at Gove and Groote Eylandt, access can readily be obtained.

In the Cobourg Peninsular area, Cape Don at the western extremity of the peninsula, about 150 kilometres by sea from Darwin, is infamous for its turbulent water and strong currents. The water from Van Diemens Gulf

exits through Dundas Strait, dividing Cape Don from Melville Island.

Shark, Shamrock, Silvio and Aiton Bays, to the south-east, are protected by the land from prevailing Dry season south-easterly winds. Most bays have fringing reef and small estuaries in which the creeks are prolific producers of mangrove jack and fingermark bream. The fringing reef harbours queenfish and trevally.

Right: Queenfish are not good eating but they are entertaining performers on light tackle, jumping repeatedly once hooked.

North-east from Cape Don are rocky peninsulas, broad bays, numerous coral reefs and bomboras, so extreme care should be exercised when travelling by boat. It is wise to consult the AUS 308 marine chart.

Allaru Island, to the north of Blue Mud Bay, is renown for its trevally and mackerel. Vashion Head has a number of reefs extending out to sea.

Cranks Reef, to the north of Port Essington, is a prime location for mackerel, trevally and a whole host of reef fish.

Port Essington itself has numerous queenfish and trevally, whilst the small creeks contain primarily mangrove jack and some barramundi. Record Point is a sandbar and a hotspot for queenfish and giant trevally.

At the head of Port Bremer, further to the east, is Sandy Island Number 1 and Number 2. They both produce trevally, queenfish, mackerel, various snapper and emperor, Spanish flag, coral trout and cod.

Somerville Bay, on Croker Island, is protected in the Dry season, but the numerous reefs offshore produce large numbers of bottom fish. The creek is home to mangrove jack, barracuda, queenfish and the odd barramundi.

Cape Croker's waters can be dangerous, although it is a great ground for pelagic fish. If weather permits, Bintomart Shoal is worth the visit.

On Oxley Island, a small estuary on the north-western side is plagued with mangrove jack. At the entrance to the creek are rocks encrusted with big blacklip oysters.

The area to the north west of Oxley, known as Bramble Rocks, is not only good for bottom fishing, but has huge numbers of Spanish mackerel from April to December.

McCluer Island has excellent bottom fishing. At night, the reefs on the western side produce red emperor.

New Year Island has pelagic and reef species. At times the area is alive with milkfish feeding on dead plankton.

Hogmancy Shoal, at the eastern extremity of the group, is the best location for Spanish mackerel. Troll from the deep water to the shallow shoals using lures or rigged baits. Sharks can become a pest at times.

Grant and Lawson Islands, and the reefs between them, are prolific fish producers. Sailfish are regularly reported throughout this entire region.

North and South Goulburn Islands are about 60 kilometres to the south-east of Grant Island. There is an Aboriginal mission situated on South Goulburn Island. Main fish from this area are trevally, queenfish, mackerel, mangrove jack and barramundi in the estuaries, and various reef fish offshore.

The area to the east is rarely fished other than by Aboriginals, due to the remoteness of the region. The King, Clyde, Blyther, and Liverpool River systems produce the normal array of estuary species, and have rarely seen a lure before.

The Wessel Islands, towards the eastern side of Arnhem Land, are the most northerly island in the area. This area is better approached from the port of Gove.

The main island of the group is Marchinbar. The western side is made up of a series of small bays and beaches; the eastern side has a cliff face along its entire length. Both regions produce large numbers of fish.

The Racon beacon off Cape Wessel and very deep water to the north-east are prolific with mackerel, trevally, barracuda and billfish.

Barracuda are regarded as poisonous to eat but savagely attack trolled baits and lures and fight strongly once hooked.

Gove to Goote Eylandt

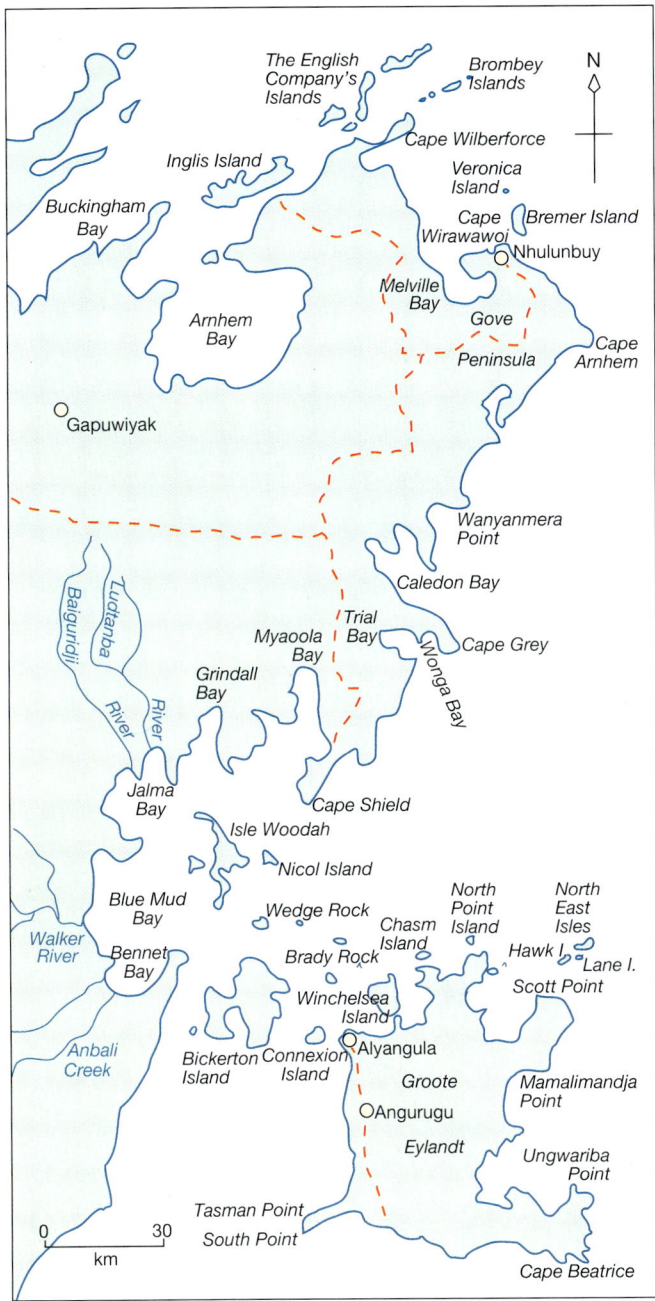

Gove and the township of Nhulunbuy on the north-eastern extremity of Arnhem Land have a population of approximately 3000, well-serviced wharf facilities and launching ramps in Gove Harbour.

Access to the area is restricted to jet aircraft, although there is a four-wheel drive track via the Roper River in the Dry season (a permit is necessary). The road is rough with numerous creek crossings, and not suitable for towing even a small boat. Perkin's barge service will freight boats to the town from Darwin.

Groote Eylandt is south of Gove and situated in the Gulf of Carpentaria, approximately 40 kilometres from the mainland. Perkin's barge also services Groote Eylandt.

The eastern side of Arnhem land is subject to strong easterly winds and swells. Groote is more fortunate than Gove with the main township of Alyangula on the western side of the island being protected from the easterly winds. The many lees of the islands scattered throughout the area offer good protection from the wind.

Truant Island is best known for it's black marlin and sailfish. Marlin are found in the deeper waters north of Truant Island. The sailfish are located near the many shoals in the area, and off the island itself.

Truant Bank, comprising Buccaneer Rock, Pugh and Barbette Shoals, produces large quantities of Spanish mackerel, barracuda, various species of trevally and reef species such as emperor, coral trout and Spanish flag. Trolling almost anything, lures or bait, will catch pelagics. Anchoring, berleying and casting lures back into the berley stream is also effective.

Barricade Shoal and Attack Shoal produce pelagics and reef species, including mackerel, tuna and barracuda.

Bromby and English Company Islands produce large quantities of mackerel, trevally and barracuda. The Bromby Islands are a popular fishing and camping location for Gove anglers.

There are numerous islands, reefs and rocky headlands in this area with most having prime fishing locations.

Bonner Rocks, halfway between Cape Wilberforce and Gove, is a small series of reefs running off Mt Bonner. Besides reef fish, cobia, mackerel, barracuda, trevally and tuna are available.

It is very difficult to troll a lures through this area and not catch fish.

At Gove, the harbour has two concrete launching ramps located at the yacht club, near the general cargo wharf. Tides are less than half that of Darwin, with the mean high water springs averaging 2.9 metres and low averaging 0.7 metres.

Gove Harbour's mangrove creeks produce queenfish, tuna, mangrove jack and the odd barramundi. Around the wharves are giant trevally and black jewfish.

West Woody and East Woody Islands, outside Gove Habour, produce queenfish, giant and golden trevally, barracuda and mackerel in season.

North-east of Gove are the Bremer Islets, which include Bremer, East Bremer, North-East Bremer, Bremer Rock, Forlsche Rock, Veronica and Higginson Islets, and Sykes Shoal.

This area produces some enormous mackerel and cobia, particularly in the Higginson and Bremer Rock areas. There is also the usual array of longtail tuna, barracuda, trevallies and reef fish. At times the ocean is alive with huge schools of pelagics.

Dalywoi Bay, further south, produces queenfish around the sandbars and headlands, and mangrove jacks further up the estuary system. Located just out from the mouth is Arnhem Shoal and to the south Arnhem Rock. Besides the pelagic species, these reefs produce large numbers of fingermark bream, red emperor and other reef species.

South to Groote Eylandt, there are numerous bays and headlands between Gove and Groote. Safe anchorages for small craft can be found in Caledon and Trial Bays. This whole area is virtually untouched.

Blue Mud Bay has various river systems feeding it, of which the Walker River is the largest. The bay is very shallow and strict adherence to the tides is necessary to obtain access to the estuaries.

The Walker River is a large system navigable by boat to the first major rock bar, approximately 40 minutes run upstream. The river is littered with snags and has numerous small queenfish and barracuda plus mangrove jack and barramundi.

There are also several creeks feeding the main river, the junctions being prime hotspots for sedentary barramundi. Other worthy creeks in the area include those in Jalma Bay and Bennot Bay and to the south, Anguruki Creek.

Between Arnhem Land and Groote Eylandt are numerous islands including Bickerton, Woody and Connection Islands. Although Woody Island is situated in shallow water it produces abundant queenfish, giant and golden trevally and barracuda.

On the south-east corner of Bickerton Island, and facing Warwick Channel, is a series of small islands and reefs known locally as 'Skinny City', referring to the number of queenfish located nearby. When the tide is running in this area, the place is alive with vast schools of them.

Located to the north of Groote are small islands including Bustard, Hawkenest, Wedge and Brady Rocks. These are prime locations for large barracuda and giant trevally along with numerous reef fish on the shoals.

Alyangula, the main town on Groote Eylandt, has two concrete ramps, of which only one is really suitable for launching. Alongside the jetty is the main ramp, although care is needed when launching in the shallow water on low tide. The town beach ramp suffers severe siltation problems, making it virtually useless.

To the north-east of Groote is some beautiful country. Chasm Island and the shoal just offshore are productive, as is Pinnacle Rock, located off Jagged Head.

In the last few years game fishermen have been travelling as far east as North East Islet and fishing not only the islands but also Moresby Rock. Marlin and sailfish have been taken from this area along with huge numbers of pelagics.

South of Alyangula, at the south-west corner of the island, are Tasman and South Points, which during June to September produce enormous numbers of Spanish mackerel.

The area to the south-east towards Cape Beatrice is virtually untouched. There are numerous bays and islands and uncharted reefs. Those fishermen lucky enough to get there have reported unbelievable fishing for coral trout, red emperor and cod.

Most of Groote Eylandt, particularly away from Alyangula, has not received much fishing pressure. There are large numbers of unknown and uncharted shoals, which have never seen a baited hook.

The areas around both Groote and Gove are some of the best light-tackle game fishing and bottom fishing grounds in Australia. There is still a whole lot more exploring to be done in these areas.

A barramundi worth a lifetime of fishing. Although fish of this size are not common, the rivers , billabongs and creeks are the places to

Freshwater Fishing

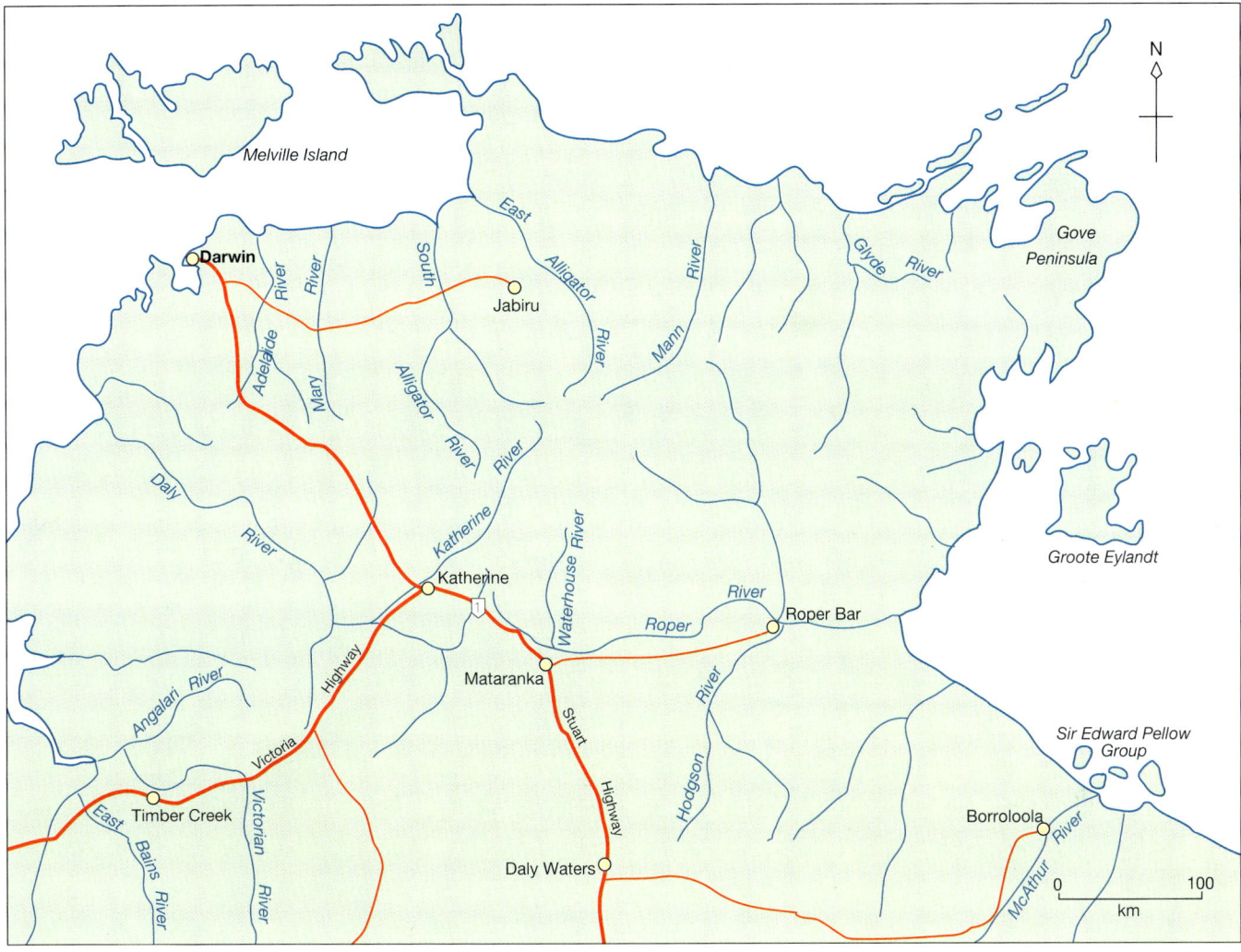

The Northern Teritory contains some of the country's finest fishing for idigenous freshwater species. Wetland regions such as those in the Kakadu National Park, river systems including the Roper, Alligator and Daly, plus a myriad of intermittent billabongs, creeks and river ensure that the freshwater fishing enthuasiast is never short of a place to cast a line.

Heading the list of popular angling targets is the barramundi, which proliferates in Northern Territory freshwater fisheries, although saratoga, sooty grunter, tarpon, archer fish and the forktail catfish are also common.

Techniques used for catching these species range from the more popular lure casting to live baiting.

A four-wheel drive is a basic requirement for finding the more isolated freshwater fisheries. One of the prime times to fish for barramundi is during the build-up to the Wet Season, making an off-road vehicle essential as unpredictable rains affect conventional vehicular access. A small, portable cartopper, punt or canoe mated to an outboard is useful for waterway travelling.

Finally, the potential dangers associated with crocodiles demand the upmost respect when fishing Northern Territory fresh water, while swarms of mosquitoes and sandflies, the uncomfortable tropical climate, and remoteness of many fisheries present their own particular problems.

The McArthur River is reached from the Barkly Highway, and the Tabelands Highway to the township of Borroloola. In the upper tabelands fish for sooty grunter and for barramundi and mangrove jacks in the lower fresh and saltwater stretches.

The Roper River is reached by four-wheel drive from the overland track from Borroloola running across the Cox and Hodgson Rivers, or turning off the Stuart Highway just before Mataranka. This leads to the Roper River Bar, with fresh water upstream and salt below.

Upstream from the bar the Waterhouse River has superb barramundi, saratoga, archer fish and sooty grunter.

The Hodgson River flows into the Roper River's tidal reaches. It yields barramundi and saratoga, while sooty grunter proliferate in the upstream extremities.

The Katherine River is regarded as one of the Territory's finest freshwater fisheries, producing good numbers of barramundi in breathtaking surroundings. Some of the best fishing territory falls within the Katherine Gorge National Park.

At Pine Creek, the Kakadu Highway leads to the bountiful Kakadu National Park, where incredibly productive fishing is on offer for everything from barramundi to tarpon.

Further on, the East, South and West Alligator Rivers, the Wildman River, and billabongs systems of Nourlangie, Jim Jim, Magela, Alligator and Wildman are accessible.

However, on the road from Pine Creek, even a four-wheel drive may have difficulties if the South Alligator Crossing is running high.

Kakadu National Park is a region of vast wetland flood plains and monsoonal forests bisected by the East, South and West Alligator Rivers, and the Wildman. The barramundi fishing attracts many tourists. Tarpon, saratoga, catfish and sooty grunter are also caught in the region.

The South Alligator River contains good stocks of barramundi, saratoga, sooty grunter and archer fish, although often drying out during the Dry Season. The Seven Mile Hole is one of the better locations.

The well-known Yellow Lagoon at Cooinda is a superlative barramundi fishery within easy reach.

Nourlangie and Jim Jim Creeks and their billabongs are regarded as some of the best freshwater fishing creeks in Kakadu National Park.

The East Alligator's upstream reaches are bordered by sandstone cliffs and mountains and is a superb freshwater barramundi fishing area, with saratoga and tarpon also prevalent. A boat is a great asset for fishing this river, although the crossing over Magela to Oenpelli is one of only a few productive land-based barramundi spots in the Territory.

The West Alligator River has tidal influence 38 kilometres upriver, and is reached from the Arnhem Highway. Fishing is productive for barramundi and other freshwater species.

The Wildman River and productive Two Mile and Four Mile Billabongs are well visited by anglers targeting barramundi, with saratoga, tarpon, catfish and archer fish common.

The Mary and Adelaide Rivers are reached by turning west after leaving Kakadu on the Arnhem Highway. Shady Camp and Corroboree Billabongs on the Mary River and the river itself are all worthwhile fishing locations.

A 40 minute drive further past the Mary brings you to the Adelaide River, which is another popular fishery. Both rivers harbour barramundi, saratoga, sooty grunter and tarpon.

The Daly River is only a short distance from the Adelaide River, and attracts the lion's share of freshwater fishing interest in the region. It is a renown producer of big barramundi.

The Victoria River Sytem, west from Katherine Gorge on the Victoria Highway, has good access to its freshwater fishing reaches, as does the neighbouring Baines, Wickham and Bullo River tributaries. Barramundi, saratoga, sooty grunter, archer fish and tarpon are caught in both systems.

A mangrovejack common to Northern Territory creeks.